THE
UNVANQUISHED

Also by Patrick K. O'Donnell

The Indispensables:
The Diverse Soldier-Mariners Who Shaped the Country,
Formed the Navy, and Rowed Washington across the Delaware

The Unknowns:
The Untold Story of America's Unknown Solider and
WWI's Most Decorated Heroes Who Brought Him Home

Washington's Immortals:
The Untold Story of an Elite Regiment Who
Changed the Course of the Revolution

First SEALs:
The Untold Story of the Forging of America's Most Elite Unit

Dog Company:
The Boys of Pointe Du Hoc—the Rangers Who Landed at D-Day
and Fought across Europe

Give Me Tomorrow:
The Korean War's Greatest Untold Story—the Epic Stand
of the Marines of George Company

They Dared Return:
The True Story of Jewish Spies behind the Line in Nazi Germany

The Brenner Assignment:
The Untold Story of the Daring Spy Mission of World War II

We Were One:
Shoulder to Shoulder with the Marines Who Took Fallujah

Operatives, Spies, and Saboteurs:
The Unknown Story of the Men and Women of World War II's OSS

Into the Rising Sun:
In Their Own Words, World War II's Pacific Veterans Reveal
the Heart of Combat

Beyond Valor:
World War II's Ranger and Airborne Veterans Reveal the Heart of Combat

THE UNVANQUISHED

The Untold Story of Lincoln's Special Forces, the Manhunt for Mosby's Rangers, and the Shadow War That Forged America's Special Operations

Patrick K. O'Donnell

Atlantic Monthly Press
New York

FIRST EDITION

Published simultaneously in Canada
Printed in the United States of America

First Grove Atlantic hardcover edition: May 2024

Library of Congress Cataloging-in-Publication data is available for this title.

ISBN 978-0-8021-6286-1
eISBN 978-0-8021-6287-8

Atlantic Monthly Press
an imprint of Grove Atlantic
154 West 14th Street
New York, NY 10011

Distributed by Publishers Group West

groveatlantic.com

24 25 26 27   10 9 8 7 6 5 4 3 2 1

To Union Jessie Scouts Sergeant Joseph Frith, Major Henry Young,
and all of America's Shadow Warriors who gave the last
full measure of their devotion to the United States and
have never been brought home.

CONTENTS

Contents

Part III: Sheridan's Scouts and "Come Retribution"

PREFACE

"[America needs] guerrilla bands of bold and daring men organized . . . to sow the dragon's teeth . . . [behind the lines] . . . men calculatingly reckless with disciplined daring, who were trained for aggressive action . . . it will mean a return to our old tradition of the Scouts, the Raiders, and the Rangers."[1] In the midst of a raging World War, Colonel "Wild Bill" Donovan warned President Franklin Roosevelt of the United States' dire need for special operations forces and introduced his bold plans to draw inspiration from irregular or unconventional Civil War units to forge those forces.

During the fall of 1941, Germany appeared on the verge of winning World War II. Enemy special operations played a crucial role in the conquering Axis tide. Of the major powers of World War II, America was the furthest behind, lacking special operations forces entirely. With America on the brink of war, Donovan desperately prepared his organization for the conflict. The brilliant and daring, yet soft-spoken, visionary took risks and embodied the spirit of the new organization he led: the Office of the Coordinator of Information. Within a year, it would emerge as the Office of Strategic Services (OSS).[2]

Facing an existential threat, Donovan understood the urgency of creating these units expeditiously. From the three-story granite building atop Navy Hill in Southwest Washington, DC, Donovan would gather his senior staff in his office, Room 109. Donovan despised red tape and bureaucracy, and his door was open to members of any rank or station for innovative suggestions. The flat and nimble organization was an idea factory that teemed with extraordinary Americans from all walks of life, including President Roosevelt's son Jimmy.[3]

The hands-on World War I Medal of Honor recipient's mind whirled with ideas—most brilliant, some fantastical. Crumpled notebook paper often littered Room 109, the nerve center of the former trial lawyer's organization, as Donovan's operatives sifted through ideas for the agency. In a race against time, American amateurs were up against German professionals. William J. Donovan knew America must "play a bush-league game, stealing the ball and killing the umpire."[4] Likely Donovan's idea, the OSS would mine America's rich history of irregular warfare and would draw inspiration from the Civil War. For months, Donovan had been fighting an uphill battle against America's aversion to shadow warfare and ossified bureaucrats who believed elite units bled away manpower from conventional forces. In the fall of 1941, the OSS forged the Special Activities Branch.[5] OSS commandos and frogmen operating behind the lines during World War II are the stuff of legend. Their derring-do was decades ahead of their time, much like today's special operations forces, and OSS utilized and enhanced important tenets developed by their Civil War predecessors. Many tactics and principles remain the same to this day. What is old is new. They extensively researched the actions of the Jessie Scouts, Rangers, and Confederate Secret Service during the Civil War.

PROLOGUE

I have spent much of my life researching and dissecting America's elite special operations units—capturing thousands of their oral histories, unearthing their stories in the archives, attending their reunions, and walking their battlefields. Many OSS veterans mentioned the OSS connection to the Civil War. All thirteen books I have written focus on American elite and special operations units. Four books focus on the OSS, and I am a director and historian of the OSS Society. These extraordinary individuals were my friends. My daughter called many of these exceptional Americans "Uncle." Every day, I wear Uncle Frank Monteleone's wartime scapula. He wore the same scapula as super spy Moe Berg's radio operator when the two OSS men hunted for Nazi nuclear technology behind the lines. Frank gifted the priceless artifact to me weeks before I left for Iraq and the Battle of Fallujah. He fatefully told me, "Where you are going, you will need this now."

Two lonely roadside signs stand today along winding Virginia country byways. One marks the site of a hanging tree where Union Jessie Scout Jack Sterry spoke his last words. Through his cunning, he tried to lead the Confederate Army down the wrong road, away from where it was crucially needed. The other placard, pitted with flaked silver paint, memorializes where John Singleton Mosby's Rangers deployed a mountain howitzer to destroy a Federal supply train on May 30, 1863. During that action, a shell from the artillery piece pierced the train's boiler, causing a massive explosion of steam and metal. At Grapewood Farm, the Confederates made a desperate stand with the howitzer that nearly killed their leader and some of his finest Rangers. I serendipitously stumbled upon the placards, inspiring me to ask questions and make connections. Another book found me. Both markers proved to be portals into this epic untold story about the same units the OSS analyzed to forge American special operations in World War II.

xiv *Prologue*

Kabletown, West Virginia, November 18, 1864

Lead balls whizzed past the Jessie Scout's head as he made the ride of his life. Confederate riders bore down on Private Henry Pancake, firing volleys from their pistols and barely missing the Federal Scout. Glancing back to his rear, the Union rider watched another group of Mosby's Rangers murder a wounded Union officer. "I had to beat them in that horse race or die, and as there were forty horses on the track after me it looked every minute like dying."[1] The Jessie Scout knew that if he were captured, he would be executed as a spy for wearing the Confederate uniform in disguise. The swarm of Mosby's Rangers edged closer. As Pancake sped west toward the tiny hamlet of Rippon, he recognized a rider in Union blue, his captain, Richard Blazer.

Digging his spurs into his horse, he galloped toward the officer.

"Where's the boys?" Blazer stammered.

"All I know is just one behind, and I guess they've got him by this time,"[2] yelled Pancake.

Another storm of lead flew by. The Rangers closed within thirty yards, their revolvers peppering away at the two. From the throng of Confederates, four men broke out to pursue Blazer and Pancake. They were "the best soldiers in Mosby's command":[3] Sam Alexander, Syd Ferguson, Cab Maddux, and Lewis "Terrible" Powell. Riding "one of the fastest and fleetest and hardiest animals in the battalion," Ferguson gained on Blazer and Pancake. "I am going to get out of this,"[4] muttered Pancake as he spurred his horse and bolted forward.

The hunters had become the hunted—one of the countless engagements involving irregulars in a largely unknown shadow war that raged behind the scenes of the great battles of the Civil War.

The Civil War irregulars on both sides who raided trains, sabotaged supply lines, captured generals, and gathered critical intelligence were the most eclectic, motley crew imaginable. Patriots and traitors, soldiers of fortune, rascals, heroes, and visionaries, they innovated and expanded on a unique form of American warfare.

On the Union side, the Jessie Scouts, and another little-known Federal group, Richard Blazer's Independent Scouts, disguised themselves as Confederates to gather intelligence and perform hazardous, special missions behind enemy lines. For their valor, they earned seven[5] Medals of Honor, including one awarded to a former Confederate who switched sides to fight for the North. Many would not survive the conflict to receive recognition or medals, and as a result, their story has been overlooked.

The two groups of Federal Scouts borrowed tradecraft from each other, worked together, and eventually moved closer until they merged. Through their irregular tactics, they changed the course of the war. They were also, arguably, the US Army's first modern* special operators and counterinsurgency forces. *The Unvanquished* follows this core group of Union Scouts throughout the war; they underwent various name changes but are referred to here by their original title: Jessie Scouts.

The Scouts sought to counter many of the South's most dangerous men, including Mosby's Rangers. Led by John Singleton Mosby, with just hundreds of disciplined men, they tied down tens of thousands of Federal troops, cut Union supply lines, captured generals, and pioneered a form of warfare that, had the South adopted it on a larger scale, would have prolonged the Civil War and perhaps resulted in a different outcome. Meeting like rivals in a Western, the groups engaged in encounters that escalated into fights to the death on horseback.

This book intertwines the Union and Confederate stories, telling both in their entirety for the first time, emphasizing the Jessie Scouts. Their story is the narrative through line that connects the groups. This narrative uncovers a much larger story, which touches on many inflection points of the Civil War and provides a new perspective on the conflict. In the latter portion of the war, the South leaned on irregular forces, led by the Confederate Secret Service, to extend its survival and change the course

---

* The Civil War is arguably the first modern war in the industrial age, and these Jessie Scouts, Rangers, and Confederate Secret Service operatives were born in that cauldron. America has a long history of unconventional warfare from before the American Revolutionary War up to the Civil War, but this book links the origins of modern special operations to this Civil War period. The scope of *The Unvanquished* is to unearth and tell the stories of the Civil War units the OSS examined for inspiration during World War II when they formed special operations units in the various branches of the organization. What the OSS did to forge these specialized units in 1941 and throughout the war is a complex story, as are the decades after the war that led to the enhancement of modern American special operations. This period of development is a separate story that demands its own book.

of the war. In bold, novel operations, they employed political warfare to influence a population and the presidential election of 1864 in the hope of securing the South's independence. Southern operatives attempted to execute massive jailbreaks to free prisoners of war and assassination. Initially gatherers of crucial tactical intelligence that led to the severing of Southern railways, the North's Scouts later deployed to combat irregulars and Mosby's Rangers. In a previously untold story, these commandos played a vital role in winning key battles that directly influenced the election, and, later, the intelligence they gathered led to the defeat of Robert E. Lee's Army of Northern Virginia. Jessie Scouts also helped foil the South's more extensive plans for guerrilla warfare. Ultimately, they roved beyond the southern border to conduct one of America's first proxy wars, with a major European power in Mexico bristling with tens of thousands of troops.

Despite the Jessie Scouts', Rangers', and Confederate Secret Services' different backgrounds and points of view, they had one thing in common: they all started from scratch, creating tactics and organizations, often on the fly, that laid the basic framework for modern American special operations and unconventional warfare.[6]

The book's narrative, told by those at the tip of the spear, thrusts the reader into the boots of the participants. Ingrained with true grit, these visionaries and pioneers were often in the right place at the right time, and their individual and collective actions changed history. Events and actions affected by the Jessie Scouts that occurred nearly 160 years ago, often at tremendous personal cost, secured Americans' freedom. Their legacy remains imbued in the fabric of today's modern operators.

THE
UNVANQUISHED

I

THE JESSIE SCOUTS
AND MOSBY'S RANGERS

Virginia and West Virginia, 1862–1863

1. THE JESSIE SCOUTS

"This way, General Hood," said the Confederate guide as he "gracefully saluted and pointed northward." Mounted and clad in the butternut of a cavalry trooper, the guide sat astride the fork in the road at the tiny hamlet of The Plains, Virginia.

General John Bell Hood "halted his column and closely questioned the guide, feeling certain that he was in error. And yet it would seem that the guide must be right. He was intelligent, confident, definite, certain of his instructions, and prompt and clear in his replies."

That morning, August 28, 1862, at 10 a.m., Hood's Confederate troops marched up the road toward Thoroughfare Gap to Manassas. As the Second Battle of Bull Run raged, Hood needed to reinforce General Stonewall Jackson immediately or Jackson's troops might be overwhelmed by the Federals. "The situation was critical; no exigency of war could be more so. It was not merely the issue of a battle, but the fate of a campaign that hung in the balance,"[1] recalled John Cussons, head of General Hood's scouts, who was present at that moment.

The guide convincingly urged Hood to take the road north away from the battlefield, where he claimed General Jackson was retreating.

"Did General Jackson himself give you these instructions?" asked Hood.

"Yes, General."

"Stonewall Jackson's trains, General. He is pushing them toward Aldie, where I supposed you would join him," responded the guide.

"I have heard nothing of all this!" exclaimed an astounded Hood.

"Then I'll tell you what it is, General Hood; those devilish Jessie Scouts are at it again!—cutting off Stuart's couriers! Jackson has heard nothing from Longstreet since yesterday morning, and he's afraid you'll follow the old order and try to join him by Thoroughfare Gap."

"How did you learn all these things?" asked General Hood, "and there was a note of severity in his voice." The guide furnished Hood with a somewhat plausible answer, but Hood grew suspicious.

"Who and what are you?" demanded General Hood. As Cussons recalled, the general "was perplexed and anxious, yet scarcely suspicious of treachery—the guide was so bland and free and unconstrained."

"I am Frank Lamar, of Athens, Georgia, enrolled with the cavalry of Hampton's Legion, but now detailed on courier service at the headquarters of Stonewall Jackson."

"Where's your saber?"

"I captured a handsome pistol from a Yankee officer at Port Republic and have discarded my saber."

"Let me see your pistol."

The weapon was a fine, silver-mounted Colt revolver with one chamber empty.

"When did you fire that shot?"

"Yesterday morning, General Hood, I shot at a turkey buzzard sitting on the fence."

Hood handed the pistol to Captain Cussons, who scrutinized it and determined the weapon had been recently fired. According to Cussons' recollection, "The guide interposed, saying that he had reloaded after yesterday's practice, and had fired the shot in question at another buzzard just before the column came in sight, but that he didn't suppose General Hood would be interested in such a matter." Cussons observed, "The guide was mistaken. General Hood was decidedly interested in the matter."

The Hampton Legion marched with Hood, and a message went down the line requesting that the colonel commanding the legion immediately report to the crossroads. With that order, "the guide suddenly remembered that he had never really belonged to Hampton's Legion; that the story grew out of a little romance of his and had grown out of a love affair. In the Shenandoah Valley, he explained, there was a beautiful maiden who had caught his fancy, but the girl was romantic and did not care for plodding foot-soldiers. All her dreams were of knights and heroes and cavaliers on prancing steeds, so he had deserted from the infantry and captured a horse, and his real name was Harry Brooks."

"Search that man!" exclaimed General Hood, impatiently; for the general was baffled and still uncertain. As Cussons noted, "All his life had been passed in active service, yet this was a new experience to him."

The next discovery raised eyebrows. In the lining of the man's vest was found the insignia of a Confederate captain—three gold bars.

"What is the meaning of that?" asked General Hood, sternly.

"Really, General Hood," he said, "you ask me such embarrassing questions. But I will tell you. It was just this way. Our girls, God bless them, are as devoted and as patriotic as can be, but you couldn't imagine the difference they make between a commissioned officer and a private soldier. In short, I soon saw it was all up with Harry unless he could get a promotion."

With panache and confidence, the guide smoothly answered Hood that Southern women were starstruck over officers instead of lowly grunts. He put forth "an air of boyish diffidence and a touch of reproach in [his] reply. Its demure humor was half playful, yet modest and natural, and its effect on the spectators was mainly ingratiating," remembered Cussons. "General Hood missed all of this. He was standing apart, talking earnestly with two of his commanders, Colonel Wofford and Colonel J. B. Robertson. . . . General Hood felt the responsibility of his position, felt it keenly, painfully. . . . Communicative as the guide was, the general could not read him. He might be an honest youth whose callow loquacity sprung from no worse a source than that of inexperience and undisciplined zeal, or he might be one of the most daring and dangerous spies that ever hid supernal subtlety beneath the mask of guilelessness."

Cussons recalled, "Meantime, the precious moments were slipping by!—fateful moments!—moments on which hung the tide of war; the fate of a great campaign; the doom perhaps of a newborn nation.

"And there at the parting of the ways sat our boyish guide—frank, communicative, well-informed—leaning on the pommel of his saddle, with the negligent grace of youth and replying with perfect good humor to all our questioning."

As soon as Hood felt suspicious of the guide's story, he sent out men to verify his statements. Reconnaissance was made down each road, all of which were infested with Yankee cavalry. But, as Cussons observed, "priceless moments were thus lost, and altho' we felt that Stonewall must be sore beset, yet we could not guess which road would take us to his battle or lead us away from it."

"Meantime diligent questioning went on by staff officers and couriers, the benefit of every doubt being freely accorded, for many of us believed, almost to the last, that the guide was a true man." As the men continued to interrogate him, Hood's soldiers brought a mortally wounded Confederate scout they had found left for dead and hidden in the bushes. With his dying words, the scout conveyed that he had been "shot by one of our own men!" and his dispatches stolen. All eyes immediately turned to "the guide." Unshaken, he boldly declared:

"Stop! I have three more words for you. I am neither Frank Lamar, of Georgia nor Harry Brooks, of Virginia. I am Jack Sterry, of the Jessie Scouts. I did not kill that rebel, but I was with those who did. His dispatches by this time are safe enough! I should like my friends to know that I palavered with your army for a good half hour while General Pope was battering down your precious old Stonewall. Now men, I am ready!—and in parting, I will simply ask you to say, if you should ever speak of this, that Jack Sterry, when the rebels got him, died as a Jessie Scout should!"

A handful of men selected a large tree* and hurled a rope over a heavy limb, then snuggly affixed a noose around Sterry's neck as he remained mounted on his horse. General Hood gave the order for the men to march.

"The writhing figure swung for a little while in the soft morning air, and was still, and there had gone forth to God who gave it as dauntless a spirit as ever throbbed in mortal clay," recalled Cussons.

Jack Sterry sat astride the crossroads of history; at the right time and right place, he tried to shape the course of events by his actions. Sterry was part of an extraordinary group of men. Often referred to as Jessie Scouts, they were named after the wife of Major General John Charles Frémont,

* A historical Civil War roadside marker located in The Plains, Virginia, titled "Death of a 'Jessie Scout'" provides an epilogue to the incident: "Nearly 75 years later, highway workers unearthed the remains of two soldiers, thought to be the spy and his victim when widening Route 55." I spent many days writing my books *The Unknowns* and *The Indispensables* at the Front Porch restaurant. This marker sits next to a favorite writing nook on the literal front porch of the establishment. The location where Hood's men hanged Jack Sterry and the location of the incident are only yards away.

an explorer and a politician who was a US Senator from California and the first presidential candidate for the Republican Party in 1856. At the start of the Civil War, Frémont was a general officer in command of the Department of the West. Known as "the Pathfinder" for his pioneering missions that explored and mapped the West while fending off hostile Native Americans, Frémont organized the specialized group of operators at the beginning of the war in St. Louis and employed them in Missouri, which was embroiled in guerrilla fighting.

His wife, Jessie Ann Benton Frémont, was the daughter of a US senator. The flaxen-haired beauty grew up at her father's side, rubbing elbows with politicians and sharing his political views, including becoming an outspoken advocate against slavery. Brilliant, powerful, charismatic, and a tremendous advocate for her husband, one admiring journalist of the time dubbed Jessie not only a "historic woman but the greatest woman in America." In many circles, it was known Jessie "was the better man of the two." Reportedly, she first advised her husband's Scouts to wear their enemies' uniforms. "Jessie, who had been with her husband until lately, frequently saw these men and became very popular with them. Hence their present attachment to her. They swear by her and wear her initials on their coats, inserted in a very modest but coarse style."[2] In addition to embroidering her initials, they also adopted Jessie as their namesake.

When John Charles Frémont moved east in the spring of 1862 to take command of the Mountain Department, located in southwest Virginia and what would become West Virginia, he brought men who understood rugged terrain and an enemy skilled in guerrilla fighting. The taming of the American West and conflict with Native Americans, including the adaptation of some of their fighting tactics, would have a profound impact on the foundations of American special operations and unconventional warfare. One contemporary stated that the Pathfinder "proceeded to follow his notion derived from experience in the Western frontier. He knew that the safety and efficiency of his army in a wild, wooded, and rugged region depended on the accuracy with which he received information of the plans and movements of the enemy. He at once called around him a set of Western frontiersmen, who had served all through the campaign in Missouri. Some had been in the border wars of Kansas; some served long years on the Plains, hunting the buffalo and the Indian; men accustomed to every form of hardship, thoroughly skilled, not only in the use of the rifle, but drilled in all cunning ways and devices to discover the intentions, position, and strength of a foe. The best of these men were selected and placed in a small organization called the Jessie Scouts."[3]

One of the Jessie Scouts' mentors, and an original member, was "Old Clayton, who had come with General Frémont from the West." Old Clayton developed his survival skills while exploring the American West with Frémont and contending with hostile Native Americans. As chief scout and trainer of raw recruits, "he conceived a great fancy for 'the boys' and gave them a deal of advice and instruction."[4]

Commonly known in camp as Clarence Clayton, but also Chatfield Hardaway, Old Clayton could not only give advice to colleagues but also serve up tactical acumen to their opponents. One such incident occurred in the fall of 1862. When scouting in a Confederate uniform in advance of a large Union cavalry force, he saw a lighted house on the side of the road. When he approached the dwelling, a Confederate picket challenged him. Clayton coolly responded that he was a friend.

When Clayton bantered with the picket, the soldier revealed he was with a Confederate cavalry unit. Suddenly, nine men, including a Rebel officer, darted out of the house onto their saddles and confronted Clayton with their cocked revolvers. The Confederate officer demanded to know his identity. The wily scout informed the Confederate officer that he was a scout of Captain Duval's Confederate Cavalry,[5] and they were riding to reinforce a certain Confederate cavalry colonel. The Jessie Scout was told that the very officer he was going to reinforce was standing before him.

"Captain Duval will be overjoyed to meet [you]," Clayton convincingly responded.

According to a contemporary account, "At that moment the cavalry came down the road, and while the Colonel and his men were covering the scout," Clayton called for the captain to come over and calmly introduced him to the Confederate colonel. The Union captain and his men surrounded the Southerners and "very coolly asked them for their arms." Old Clayton then "apologized for practicing the ruse to save his life." The Rebel colonel reportedly then "asked for a knothole to crawl into, remarking that he had been sold too cheap."[6]

Members of the US Army, civilians, and later even a turncoat former Confederate cavalry trooper,[7] the Scouts morphed into the enemy, taking on their uniforms, accents, and mannerisms: "He seems a Tennessean, a Georgian, an Irishman, a German—anything indeed but what he really is," recalled one contemporary.[8] To pass off as Confederates, the Jessie Scouts developed false backgrounds for men they impersonated and learned convincing cover stories to pass themselves off as the enemy. They began wearing white scarves knotted around their necks in a particular way in order to identify each other behind the lines. Jessie Scouts also developed a stilted coded conversation to identify friend from foe.

> SCOUT ONE: "Good morning."
> SCOUT TWO: "These are perilous times."
> SCOUT ONE: "Yes, but we are looking for better."
> SCOUT TWO: "To what shall we look?"
> SCOUT ONE: "To the red and white cord."[9]

They developed the exchange deliberately so that it could not be guessed.

By the summer of 1862, the group numbered roughly two dozen men, including three Scouts recently captured and executed by Confederate troops. Considered spies for wearing the enemy's uniform, they faced death if they fell into enemy hands.[10]

Their first commander, Captain Charles Carpenter, was initially a fitting leader for this handpicked group: "He was by no means a figure to be passed by. Fancy a poacher who is half brigand and wholly daredevil, and you catch a glimpse of his air. His high-topped velvet boots are drawn up over his wide velvet trousers. No vest is worn, and the expanse of a broad chest affords a fine field for the once snowy shirt-bosom of Parisian pretensions and fine material."[11] Dark haired, blue eyed, five feet six, and "sinewy and ready for a fight, fun, or frolic, [Carpenter] mingled his dash and boldness with remarkable prudence and caution." Armed with a Colt and a breechloading rifle for distance shooting, Carpenter bragged he was a crack shot at more than a quarter of a mile.[12] Trappings and appearance aside, at his core, Carpenter ardently hated slavery and told one reporter a tall tale that he was a member of John Brown's party that attacked the Harpers Ferry arsenal in 1859 "by crawling through a long culvert, or covered drain, which led from the famous engine-house to the river. The Captain does not love the slave lords,"[13] the journalist wrote after interviewing Carpenter.

When not adorned in velvet and gold chains, daredevil and glory-hound Carpenter had sneaked into Confederate Fort Donelson* in Tennessee in early February 1862 wearing a Confederate uniform, masquerading as an enemy officer: "I went into Fort Henry two days before the attack on it and brought General Grant an accurate account of the position and number of the Rebel forces and defenses," he later recalled to a journalist. "I have General Grant's letter certifying to that. Also, I went into Fort Donelson, while our troops lay at Fort Henry. I went in there in Confederate uniform; and I have General McClernand's letter to show that I brought him information that proved to be accurate. On my way out a cavalry force passed me, while I lay by the roadside; and its commander told one of his men to leave a fine flag, which he feared would be torn on the way. The flag† was stuck into the road, that a returning rebel picket might carry it in. But I got it, wrapped it around my body, and rode into Fort Henry with it."[14]

Carpenter's information gleaned while posing as a Confederate no doubt had a role in the battle for Fort Donelson waged between February 11 and 16, 1862. The capture of the fort opened the Cumberland River as a route of invasion into the South. Brigadier General Ulysses S. Grant forced General Simon Bolivar Buckner to accept terms of unconditional surrender, earning Grant the immortal nickname "Unconditional Surrender" Grant.

A master of disguise, Carpenter once wore a woman's dress to execute a clandestine mission: "Once [I] Rode down to the Rebel pickets at Wilson Creek, dressed as a woman to deliver a letter . . . and this trip was made because 'the General' wanted to know precisely the position of part of the Rebel lines." Not so lucky, other members of Carpenter's command were sometimes captured by Union forces. One Jessie Scout was initially arrested for being an enemy spy, "James Alexander, who was arrested in the uniform of a [Confederate] Captain of Cavalry, was released yesterday. Finding him to be one of the Jessie Scouts, as he reported."[15]

Ingenuity was a hallmark of the Scouts, who often had to perilously improvise on the job. They were selected for their aplomb, audacity, valor,

* I found Carpenter's original crudely drawn map of Fort Donelson in a dusty box located in the National Archives.

† A portion of Carpenter's captured flag still exists and is on display at Wilson's Creek National Battlefield.

and intelligence, "special faculties born in some few men,"[16] wrote one contemporary author.

In the fall of 1862, Company K of the 1st West Virginia Cavalry was drawn up into formation. Mostly teenagers who had nonetheless experienced the fire and test of combat, they listened to their commander, who sternly called for volunteers for "extra dangerous duty."[17]

Seeking excitement, seventeen-year-old, dark-haired, blue-eyed Archibald Hamilton Rowand Jr., from Allegheny City, Pennsylvania, glanced at his best friend.[18] They "discovered they were of one mind." Nicknamed "Barefoot," the strapping five-foot-nine cavalryman recalled, "I looked at Ike Harris and Ike looked at me, and then we both stepped forward."[19]

The two young soldiers had volunteered without realizing the seriousness of their decision.

"[We were] directed to exchange our blue uniforms for suits of Confederate gray taken from the prisoners."[20] The shock that they would be impersonating enemy scouts and operating behind Confederate lines fell full upon them. "We wished we had not come."[21] Although gifted with a powerful intellect, Rowand did not yet fully comprehend the gravity of hazardous duty. "We were boys—wanted to know what was the 'extra dangerous duty' and when we found out hadn't the face to back down."[22] Asked after the war if men still existed who would do what he had done, he responded, "Yes, if they begin as young as I began, and have no better sense."[23] Fortunately for Rowand, his youthful upbringing in South Carolina granted him a mastery of the Southern dialect that, combined with his quick wit, saved him from many close encounters. Ike Harris, his brother James, and many of Rowand's fellow Jessie Scouts would meet death, either at the ends of Confederate ropes, like Jack Sterry, or while attempting to shoot their way out of an ambush.

Reluctant twenty-two-year-old James White was forced to join the Jessie Scouts. Having lost his mother at an early age and then his father after they moved to Lewis County, Virginia (now West Virginia), the native Rhode Island orphan apprenticed as a cabinetmaker before joining the 1st West Virginia Cavalry, where he acted as a guide and courier. A natural escape artist, White broke free from Confederate captivity behind enemy lines multiple times before and after joining the Jessie Scouts. White initially wanted no part of the motley crew and requested to return to his old unit. "So notorious were they for acts of lawlessness, and so little were they acquainted with the country that [I] resolved to not become recognized with that body."[24] But White had immediately proved too valuable as a Scout, and he was denied permission to go back to his old cavalry unit.

Shortly after Frémont moved his unit east, Carpenter's shadier exploits, exemplifying White's impression of the unit, caught up with him. A contemporary newspaper called Carpenter "as consummate a rogue as can be found outside any state prison in the country." A con man and a thief, he would take anything that wasn't nailed down. "Coming upon a deserted mill [in Union Missouri] and finding nothing else of value that could be stolen, [he] carried off the cylinder head of a steam engine and sold it for old iron."[25] He stooped so low as to promise old women and children a concert on a steamboat and, after collecting their money, disappeared with it. After being arrested by Federal authorities for one of his countless infractions, Carpenter warranted these words from a judge advocate: "I have no doubt about Carpenter being a bad man, one in whom no confidence could be placed, and a man who would do almost *anything* for money."[26] Carpenter had mixed motives, rabid antislavery blending with a desire for personal gain, and he was drummed out of the service.

In the wake of the scandals and Frémont's refusal to serve under Major General John Pope in the newly formed Union Army of Virginia, which culminated in his eventual resignation from the US Army, the Jessie Scouts were largely disbanded. But a small remnant, including Rowand, White, and others, remained in General Robert H. Milroy's command, and they would courageously repair the unit's reputation. *The Unvanquished* follows this core group and other men who would join their ranks through the war. The term "Jessie Scout" would also be universally adopted by both sides to refer to Federal Scouts who wore Confederate uniforms. Despite his fall from grace, Carpenter offered an evocative description of his unit that captured its unique quality: "A scout is a man who finds out how far the enemy's pickets extend, the position and strength of the enemy, and also ascertains such general facts as may be useful in the conduct of war. There are no rules for the operations of scouts: they are generally independent and have little if any organization; they are in fact, spies. You cannot call 'us fellows' anything less than spies, but scout is a more

respectable name. Scouts are armed, and either fight or surrender, according to the chances. I have often been asked what was the business of the
scout; and the best answer I ever gave was, that it is his business to find
out other men's business."[27]

The line between scout and spy blurred. Scouts led armies in the
field, advancing far ahead of their commands to conduct reconnaissance
and gain intelligence on enemy forces. "In all advance movements . . . of
the commands, I served under, the scouts were sent in advance," Rowand
recalled. "[We] would capture a Confederate, would ride up to a Southern
citizen, man or woman, get all the information out of them, and being
dressed in Confederate uniform the Southerners would naturally think
we were their own men and tell us everything they knew."[28]

One source at the time described the Scouts as "men whose hearts
were zeal for the Union and of hatred for the slave aristocracy and their
rebellion. Such men, when they have also the activity, and presence of mind,
ingenuity, and courage needed for this office, are the best that can be got."[29]

2. Three Winters and the Rise of the Irregulars

By 1863, the Civil War that immersed Archibald Rowand, James White, and the other Jessie Scouts had entered its third winter. The hope for a short war envisioned at the beginning of 1861 seemed nowhere in sight, and the massive modern conflict had mushroomed into a constant clash of hundreds of thousands of troops on multiple fronts stretched across well over a thousand miles. Through scores of battles, the South proved remarkably resilient and, recently, once again, victorious at Fredericksburg.

The butcher's bill of battles through the early months of 1863 had been immense, and the days of a flood tide of volunteer enlistments in the North were gone. Flagging support for the war forced the North first to pay bounties to encourage soldiers to enlist, and when that failed to secure adequate numbers of bodies to fill the ranks, the Federals would soon be forced to resort to a draft.

On the first day of 1863, Abraham Lincoln issued the Emancipation Proclamation, "that all persons held as slaves" within the rebellious states "are, and henceforward shall be free."[1] The proclamation fundamentally transformed the nature and tone of the war and its ideals, even though it was limited to enslaved individuals in the Confederacy and did not include Union border states where slavery remained legal. It would also enable hundreds of thousands of Black Americans to enlist in the Union Army and Navy.

The previous year, 1862, had brought bloody fighting and larger armies. In massive battles such as in Shiloh, Tennessee, the Confederacy had an opportunity to annihilate a western Federal army under the command of Ulysses S. Grant but failed. In the east, General George Brinton

McClellan assumed command of the Union Army of the Potomac and became known as the great organizer as he whipped the Federal force into fighting shape. McClellan attempted to seize the Confederate capitol at Richmond during the Peninsula Campaign from March through July. Initial hopes that the campaign would capture Richmond and end the war led Union secretary of war Edwin M. Stanton to make one of the war's great blunders. In April 1862, he suspended Federal recruiting efforts and sent volunteers and recruits who were about to enter the North's armies home. About two months later, after bodies had piled up from the bloody battles, he reversed the bungled policy.

Major General George McClellan's failure of the Peninsula Campaign led to the emergence of General Robert E. Lee as the leading Southern commander. At the Second Battle of Manassas, a Federal army nearly met its end and its retreat to Washington, DC, opened up a gateway in the Shenandoah Valley for an invasion of the North. Through a stroke of good fortune, the North captured a document wrapped around three cigars that outlined Lee's invasion plans. Based on the document, McClellan molded his defensive plans and repulsed Lee's army on September 17, 1862, at Antietam, Maryland, the bloodiest day in American history, when over 23,000 soldiers were killed or wounded, or went missing, during the course of the twelve-hour battle. Despite the horrific losses, because of McClellan's lackluster pursuit, Lee successfully retreated across the Potomac.

During the fall of 1862, Lincoln authorized an unprecedented crackdown on civil liberties. He suspended habeas corpus and military trials for civilians who were accused of interfering in the war. Any US citizen could be thrown in prison for an accusation of disloyalty. The order read, "To arrest and imprison any person or persons who may be engaged by act, speech, or writing, in discouraging volunteer enlistments, or in any way giving aid and comfort to the enemy, or in any other disloyal practice against the United States."[2] The crackdown, combined with the military failures and horrendous loss of life and limb, bred growing dissatisfaction with the war and unrest in midwestern states. The midterm elections of 1862 were a rout for Republicans in key states: New York, Pennsylvania, Illinois, Ohio, and Indiana, all of whose electoral votes Lincoln won in the presidential election of 1860. Republicans held the Senate but saw their margins in the House drastically reduced.

After the midterm elections of 1862, Lincoln sacked McClellan. A variety of factors led to his dismissal. Weeks earlier, McClellan had brazenly outlined his vision of how the war should be conducted. In what would be dubbed the Harrison Landing Letter, McClellan emphasized the need for a limited war without abolishing slavery and for the appointment of a general-in-chief. Republican politicians saw a parallel to the Northern Democrats' "Address to Democracy of the United States." In their manifesto, they stated they "were opposed to waging war against any of the states or people of the Union for any purpose of conquest or subjugation or interfering with the rights of established institutions of any state."[3] "Established institutions" was the Democrats' euphemism for slavery. McClellan pleaded with one powerful lawyer, "Help me dodge the n***er—we want nothing to do with him."[4] The general had contempt for the commander in chief, often calling Lincoln a "baboon" and "gorilla," and was also partisan, unwisely stating to several Republican senators, "[I am] fighting for my country and the Union, not for abolition and the Republican Party."[5] For his insubordination, Stanton wanted Lincoln to fire McClellan immediately. Lincoln sensed that his dismissal before the midterms could cause a firestorm and shrewdly waited until after the elections.

The battlefield disasters continued for the North as Lee repulsed a Union offensive on Richmond at Fredericksburg in mid-December 1862. On Fredericksburg's Marye's Heights, Federal frontal assaults against an entrenched Confederate enemy behind stone walls proved futile and demonstrated the obsolescence of infantry assault tactics against a fixed position with rifled muskets and dug-in troops. Failure begat failure for the North's armies. After the debacle at Fredericksburg, many Republicans blamed the disaster on Lincoln, and some demanded he resign. Reelection in 1864 seemed increasingly unlikely for the war's most persistent advocate. Support for the conflict in the North waned to a new low—a stark contrast to the first year of the war.

A short war, over in weeks, was what both sides had envisioned in 1861. The battle of Bull Run at Manassas, Virginia, which led to the flight of the Union Army and threatened Washington, DC, quickly shattered any thoughts of a quick victory over the South. Over a month before the Confederate victory, some of the war's first battles were fought in western Virginia, where McClellan repulsed and routed Confederate forces at Philippi, not far from Grafton and the vital Baltimore and Ohio Railroad. The victory kept most of the northwestern portion of Virginia in Union hands. Other Union victories followed, setting up the conditions by which the new state of West Virginia would be admitted into the Union in June 1863. The Confederacy would contest the western portion of the state through conventional forces and raids on Union lines of communication. The South used the area as a buffer zone to protect their lines of communication and minerals such as salt and lead, vital to the Confederate war effort. In addition, a Southern-leaning population in the western part of Virginia made it fertile ground for guerrilla warfare.

Local Southerners ambushed Union forces in hit-and-run attacks. Channeling the American Revolution and Native American–style warfare, many mountain men aimed to protect their homes and attack the enemy, but in the guise of military combat, they often used violence to settle old scores. The irregular tactics proved successful in tying up large numbers of Union troops and keeping the western portion of Virginia contested. The Union presence in western Virginia would lead to the Partisan Ranger Act, authored by Colonel John Scott in March 1862 and passed by the Confederate Congress on April 21, in an attempt to rein in the guerrillas. The act allowed for the formation of companies, battalions, and regiments of partisan rangers for unconventional warfare. Partisan rangers would be subject to the same pay and regulations as regular soldiers but would operate independently, albeit with some oversight by the regular Confederate Army. These irregulars could also sell captured arms and munitions to Confederate quartermasters and receive full value. A grisly provision in the original act assigned a bounty for killing Union soldiers, but this politically toxic provision was dropped in the final bill.

A recruitment advertisement in the *Richmond Examiner* explained the nature of the warfare and the type of men wanted for service: to "wage thermoactive [*sic*] warfare against our brutal invaders and their domestic allies; to hang about their camp and shoot down every sentinel, picket, courier and wagon driver we can find; to watch opportunities for attacking convoys and forage trains, and thus rendering the country so unsafe that they will not dare to move except in large bodies. Our own Virginia traitors—men of the Pierpoint and Carlisle Stamp—will receive our special regards. . . . It is only men I want—men who will pull the trigger on a Yankee with as much alacrity as they would on a mad dog."[6]

Discipline and leadership were keys to effective partisan units. But discipline proved elusive, and the Confederate partisans harmed civilians loyal to both sides. Lee expressed his frustration that "they have become an injury instead of benefit to the service, and even where this is accomplished, the system gives license to many deserters and marauders, who assume to belong to these authorized companies and commit depredations on friend and foe alike."[7] A debate between advocates of conventional and unconventional warfare raged for much of the war. Some Confederates considered irregular warfare ungentlemanly and a drain on manpower from conventional units—an argument that would surface for the next hundred years of American history. But discipline, leadership, and skill would evolve in ranger and irregular Southern units. Ultimately, covert, special operations would be used strategically in an attempt to alter the course of the war.

The Federal Jessie Scouts focused on tactical battlefield reconnaissance—scouting in front of the armies and gathering intelligence. They also concentrated on routing out Southern partisans. Learning and evolving as events unfolded, both North and South laid the groundwork for modern special operations forces.

One of the most innovative and pioneering of those units would be known as Mosby's Rangers.

3. "I AM MOSBY"

March 9, 1863, the road to Fairfax, Virginia

The horses' hooves made little noise in the melting snow as the twenty-nine riders rode through the drizzling rain. "Inky darkness and their black rain ponchos made it impossible to "tell from our appearance to which side we belonged, although all of us were dressed in Confederate gray,"[1] recalled one rider. The Rangers thought they were simply going on another of their midnight forays, ambushing enemy troops and frustrating Union forces. Mosby had not communicated the nature of the mission to any of the men except the recent arrival Sergeant James F. "Big Yankee" Ames, who only weeks earlier had been a member of the Union Army. Mosby would place his entire trust in this deserter and rely on him to get his men through Union checkpoints. They were attempting to pass through a gap in the pickets into enemy territory guarded so heavily that "no one dreamed of the possibility of an enemy approaching them,"[2] with the intention of capturing Colonel Percy Wyndham.

A flamboyant English adventurer and soldier of fortune with experience in many European wars, Wyndham sported an overwhelming ten-inch pointed mustache and beard. The Englishman called Mosby a horse thief and clumsily sent his men after the Rangers but failed to apprehend the elusive Confederates. Violating the code of war, Wyndham remarkably threatened to torch the entire town of Middleburg, Virginia, claiming its residents provided sanctuary for the Rangers. Middleburg's elders then pleaded with Mosby to stop his raids, but at the behest of General J. E. B. Stuart, Mosby's superior officer, the partisan leader remained in the area and penned an elegant retort to the town leaders.

Mosby wrote, "Not being yet prepared for any such degrading compromise with the Yankees, I unhesitatingly refuse to comply. My attacks on scouts, patrols, and pickets, which have provoked this threat, are sanctioned both by the custom of war and the practice of the enemy; and you are at liberty to inform them that no such clamor shall deter me from employing whatever legitimate weapons I can most efficiently use for their annoyance." Mosby closed the letter with, "As my men have never occupied your town, I cannot see what possible complicity there can be between my acts and you."[3]

Frustrated by Mosby's raids, "along with his own unsuccessful attempts at reprisal," Wyndham "had sent me many insulting messages," Mosby later wrote. "I thought I would put a stop to his talk by gobbling him up in bed and sending him off to Richmond." Once the shocking revelation of their destination had been revealed, one Ranger pointed out "the difficulties and dangers that surrounded us." Mosby responded, "I told him our safety was in the audacity of the enterprise." He continued, "I had only twenty-nine men—we were surrounded by hostile thousands." Leading them through the pickets was "Big Yankee" Ames, "who knew to what point he was piloting us. . . . Without being able to give any satisfactory reason for it, I felt an instinctive trust in his fidelity, which he never betrayed."[4] They were heading into the belly of the beast: approximately 2,500 Union cavalry were encamped at Germantown. Working through back trails, Mosby's men skirted the camp.

The raid had a narrow window for success. The Rangers would have to enter Fairfax Court House while the Union troopers slept and leave enough time to once again pass by the thousands of cavalry sleeping at Germantown and an infantry brigade at Centreville. They rode in from the south on Chain Bridge Road, which was friendly Union territory—making it appear that the Rangers were just another returning Federal unit.

The Rangers reached the unsuspecting sleeping town of Fairfax Court House around 2:00 a.m., two hours after they intended, leaving them only a few hours to achieve their goal and make their retreat before daylight. "Nothing of the kind had ever been attempted before the war, and no preparations had been made to guard against it. It is only practicable to guard against what is probable, and in war, as everything else, a great deal must be left to chance," recalled Mosby.[5]

A single sentinel halted the cavalcade and asked for identification. Ames boldly responded, "5th New York Cavalry."

With raincoats concealing the Confederate uniforms and Ames dressed in Union blue leading the column, the troops appeared to be a returning Yankee patrol and passed unmolested. Then, in keeping with the Rangers' practice of capturing anyone who saw them, "of course we took the sentinel with us."[6]

Once inside the town, Mosby ordered Ames and a few men to enter Wyndham's headquarters. To their dismay, they discovered that the colonel had left the camp earlier that day and was bound for Washington by train. "The irony of fortune made Ames the captor of his own captain"[7] as he took Captain Augustus Barker, 5th New York Cavalry, who was acting as assistant adjutant general, into custody.

Deprived of the insulting Wyndham, Mosby then went after General Edwin H. Stoughton, whose location in the town he learned from a captured guard. At twenty-five years of age, the foppish Stoughton was one of the youngest officers appointed by Lincoln as a brigadier general. The audacious Confederate captain strode up to the white-columned porch of the colonial red-brick house owned by Doctor Gunnell, where the Union general was staying, and knocked loudly on the front door. When a head popped out of a second-story window inquiring who was there, Mosby answered boldly, "5th New York Cavalry with a dispatch for General Stoughton." He heard the footsteps "tripping downstairs, and the door opened," revealing a lieutenant dressed in his nightshirt. Mosby grabbed the man by his collar, whispered who he was, and demanded to be taken to the general's room.[8]

Upstairs they found the general lying on a bed, "buried in deep sleep" and surrounded by uncorked champagne bottles and other telltale signs of there "having been revelry in the house that night," as Stoughton "had been entertaining a number of ladies from Washington." After throwing off his blankets and trying unsuccessfully to wake the sleeping officer, Mosby finally "pulled up his shirt and gave him a spank." In response to the general's indignant inquiry into the meaning of the "rude intrusion," Mosby leaned over and asked, "General, did you ever hear of Mosby?"

"Yes. Have you caught him?" the general asked eagerly.

"No. I am Mosby—he has caught you."[9]

As Stoughton dressed, the Confederate officer pulled a piece of coal from the fireplace and scrawled on the wall in large letters, MOSBY, as an act of psychological warfare to imbue intimidation and fear in his operations.

As remarkable and daring as their mission had been so far, a still greater feat remained before them: to make their retreat back through the enemy camp with Stoughton and scores of men and horses in tow without being apprehended and before the daylight revealed their small number to their captured prisoners.

"Captain, you have done a bold thing; but you are sure to be caught," Stoughton warned the daring Mosby as they rode side by side in the darkness.[10]

The Rangers apprehended anyone who stood in their way: "Instantly there was a clutch at my throat. I felt the cold muzzle of a Navy-six pressed firmly against my temple and in language that made mine seem a poor phantom of 'cuss' words. I found the intruders were two ferocious-looking Confederate cavalrymen. They told me they were Mosby men. . . . I was taken out and mounted on a horse without saddle or bridle,"[11] remembered one Yankee prisoner.

As they were retreating through town, another officer in his nightshirt called from an upper-story window, asking what cavalry they were. Mosby's men laughed at the ridiculous situation and sent two riders up to search the house for Lieutenant Colonel Robert Johnstone, from the 5th New York Cavalry, the very unit the Rangers were impersonating, who was staying there with his wife and children. Upon hearing their laughter, the colonel fled the house and hid "in a place, it is not necessary to describe"—the outhouse—while his wife battled the two Rangers "like a lioness in the hall and obstructed them all she could in order to give time for her husband to make his escape." The poor colonel "lay there concealed and shivering with cold and fear until after daybreak . . . as naked as when he was born and smelling a great deal worse," revealed Mosby.[12]

To throw off any potential pursuers, Mosby rode first toward Fairfax Station before changing directions. The Confederate recognized the difficulty of the retreat. "It was as difficult a problem to solve as steering between Scylla and Charybdis. Yet I was cheered by the knowledge that if I succeeded, an adventure so full of romance would strike a deeper impression on the imagination of men than a battle."[13] In complete darkness, they attempted to thread the needle between the campfire of the Union troops in Centreville and the camps on either side of it.

A man of action and always willing to put himself in harm's way to protect his men, Mosby often lagged behind to listen for pursuers or, at one point, rode forward alone to reconnoiter a Union watch fire a hundred yards ahead, only to find the post deserted as daybreak was nearing.

Luckily Mosby had the services of an excellent scout, John Underwood, a true outdoorsman, a forester "who knew every rabbit path in the county."[14] "His person was short and thick-set, and he had a shock of white hair, which stood erect in unrestrained independence. His whole appearance was that of a wild man, but his eyes, ever in motion, indicated watchfulness and an intelligent mind," remembered one Ranger. "He is distinguished, above all other men whom I have known, by a wonderful faculty which enables him to thread with unerring certainty, in the darkest night the intricate forests and tangled brushwood of the country in which he lives."[15] Underwood was familiar with the section of the country like the back of his hand. Mosby admitted, "I was largely indebted to [Underwood's] skill and intelligence for whatever success I had at the beginning of my partisan life, for he was equally at home threading his way through the pines or leading a charge."[16]

Mosby's twenty-nine Rangers and their prisoners moved through the thick forests dangerously fast, losing a few captives and horses along the way but racing against the rising sun. As one Union trooper recalled, "away we went on the wildest devil's ride that ever human beings took."[17]

Finally, the Rangers reached Cub Run, within view of the enemy camps and their menacing cannons in Centreville. This usually tranquil stream now was a raging river from the spring rains and melting snow. "I did not deliberate a moment but plunged into the torrent and swam to the other shore. The current was strong, but so was my horse," wrote Mosby. He also recalled that a shivering Stoughton emerged next to him, saying, "Well, Captain, this is the first outrage I have to complain of." Mosby claimed, "It was a miracle that not a man or horse was drowned although many were swept down the stream."[18]

Once they emerged on the opposite shore, the Rangers were safe, knowing that no Union cavalry would attempt the treacherous crossing. Their prisoners knew it as well. As Mosby recorded, the optimistic, ambitious young Stoughton "saw the Union camp . . . on the heights around Centreville, [and] he lost all hope of being recaptured."[19]

After the raid, Lincoln allegedly quipped of Stoughton, who was never popular with his troops, that he "did not much mind the loss of a brigadier general, he could make another in five minutes. But those horses cost $125 apiece!" Conversely, Mosby's historic special operation would earn him the immortal name: the Gray Ghost.[20]

"Youngbloods of the South. . . . War suits them, and the rascals are brave; fine riders, bold to rashness, and dangerous subjects in every sense . . . the most dangerous set of men which this war has turned loose upon the world,"[21] wrote General William Tecumseh Sherman about Mosby's Rangers. Native Virginian John Singleton Mosby was one of the most unlikely and reluctant young bloods of the war. The slight-of-build, five-feet-seven, 128-pound, clean-shaven, sandy-haired twenty-seven-year-old admitted he was the "frailest and most delicate man in the company" when he joined the Confederate Army as a private in 1861 and "so depressed at parting with my wife and children that I scarcely spoke a word."[22] The thoughtful, bookish lawyer had studied Latin and Greek at the University of Virginia before marrying a congressman's daughter and settling down in Bristol, Virginia.

While at the University of Virginia, Mosby stood up to a bully—a man who had earlier knifed a student and nearly killed another with a rock. After the assailant threatened and lunged at the nineteen-year-old Mosby, he shot the bully square in the mouth using a pepperbox pistol, which remarkably only slightly injured him. After a five-day trial, a jury found Mosby guilty of unlawful shooting and innocent of malicious shooting and sentenced him to a year in jail and a $500 fine. Mosby was pardoned after serving seven months and the fine was rescinded; the event propelled him to study law.

Despite his slight build, Mosby had an iron constitution and, over the course of the war, would survive numerous skirmishes and battles and several separate life-threatening gunshot wounds. Although the son of slaveholders, he was not an advocate of slavery, an institution he abhorred later in life; however, after the war, Mosby warned against revisionist history: "Now while I think as badly of slavery as Horace Greeley did, I am not ashamed that my family were slaveowners. It was our inheritance— Neither am I that my ancestors were pirates or cattle thieves. People must be judged by the standard of their age."[23] Mosby initially opposed the secession of the Southern states from the Union, but his beliefs changed when Virginia seceded; he remarked to a friend, "When I talked that way, Virginia had not passed the ordinance of secession. She is out of the Union now. Virginia is my mother, God Bless her! I can't fight against my mother, can I?"[24] Like many Southerners, Mosby fought for his home, family, state, and country, exclaiming, "I am not ashamed of having fought on the side of slavery—a soldier fights for his country—right or wrong—he is not responsible for the political merits of the course he fights in. . . . The South was my country."[25]*

Mosby would emerge not only as a guerrilla leader who pioneered a new form of warfare but also as a master spy with ties to the Confederate Secret Service. He understood the importance of actionable and strategic intelligence and knew how to keep a secret; he would remain an enigma who would take many of the great mysteries of the Confederacy to his grave.

But during the opening years of the Civil War, there were some early hints of the immense capabilities behind his reticence. While at first glance his slight, stooped figure, unkempt hair, lack of swagger, and soft voice did not inspire confidence, his piercing blue eyes held "the secret of the power over his men." One of his Rangers, teenager John Munson, remembered, "When he spoke, they flashed the punctuations of his sentences."[26]

On the wintry night of December 30, 1862, in a mansion known as Oakham near Middleburg, Virginia, Mosby approached General J. E. B Stuart, asking if he could borrow a few men to conduct guerrilla operations in the Union Army's rear area. This bold request would change history. Just ten months older than Mosby, James Ewell Brown "Jeb" Stuart earned a reputation as "the eyes and ears" of the Army of Northern Virginia. As cavalry commander, Stuart led many successful reconnaissance missions

---

* Mosby would later denounce those who promulgated what would become known by some as the Lost Cause myth. After the war, he switched parties to become a Republican and befriended and campaigned for Ulysses S. Grant, which garnered the hatred of some of the men he led during the war. Mosby stood by his convictions, enduring threats to his life and being shot at. Unflinching, he would quip after the war, "Hell is being a Republican in Virginia." John S. Mosby, *Take Sides with the Truth: The Postwar Letters of John Singleton Mosby to Samuel F. Chapman*, ed. Peter Brown (Lexington: University Press of Kentucky, 2007), 46–47.

and raids. Behind blue eyes, a ruddy complexion, and a reddish beard was a man of "dash, great strength of will, and indomitable energy,"[27] Mosby remembered.

Thanks to his courage, skill, and keen intellect, Mosby rose through the ranks from private to lieutenant. The daring officer participated in some of Stuart's most significant operations out front as a scout. Following a scouting assignment, he devised and led Stuart's celebrated hundred-mile-plus ride around General George McClellan's Army of the Potomac in June 1862 to gain intelligence on the Union commander's intentions. Mosby recalled,

> We penetrated McClellan's line and discovered that several miles of his right flank had only cavalry pickets to guard his line of communication with his depot at White House on the Pamunkey. Here it seemed to me was an opportunity to strike a blow. . . . On discovery of the conditions, I hastened back to Stuart and found him sitting in the front yard. It was a hot day—I was tired and lay down on the grass to tell him what I learned. A martinet would have ordered me to stand in his presence. He listened to my story, and when I finished, told me to go to the adjutant's office and write it down. At the same time, he ordered a courier to go with him to General Lee's headquarters. I did as he requested and brought him a sheet of paper with what I had written. After reading it, Stuart called my attention to it not being signed. I signed it, although I thought he only wanted a memorandum of what I said—General Lee had never heard of me. Stuart took the paper and went off with a courier at a gallop. As soon as he returned, orders were issued to the cavalry to be ready.[28]

Stuart's ride was incredibly successful, and newspapers across the South raved that he diverted the Union commander's attention, attacked McClellan's lines of communication, and captured more than 165 prisoners, nearly 300 horses and mules, and a bounty of supplies.

On another scouting mission, operating behind the lines with only nine men, Mosby surprised a Union regiment posted by Bull Run Bridge. Boldly, Mosby and his men "charged them with a yell"[29] and fired into the Federals while Mosby shouted orders to imaginary units. Assuming a brigade of Stuart's cavalry was about to engulf them, the Federals turned tail and ran.

That December evening at Oakham, Mosby confidently proposed, "by incessant attacks, [to] compel the enemy either greatly to contract his lines or to reinforce them."[30] Stuart listened and granted the request of an independent command. He loaned the Virginian a mere six men.[31]

Six poorly equipped men would eventually morph into nearly a thousand who would tie up ten times their number. But at the time, Mosby knew he had his work cut out to prove his worth as an independent commander. "The means supplied me were hardly adequate to the end I proposed, but I thought that zeal and speed of movement would go far to compensate for the deficiency of my numbers. There was a great stake to be won, and I resolved to play a bold game to win it."[32] Mosby believed the enemy's rear and supply lines were points of vulnerability. "A small force moving with celerity and threatening many points on a line can neutralize a hundred times its own number." He would add, "The military value of a partisan's work is not measured by the amount of property destroyed, or the number of men killed or captured, but by the number [of the enemy] he keeps watching [him]. Every soldier withdrawn from the front to guard the rear of an army is so much taken from its fighting strength."[33]

Mosby had iron faith in his abilities. But other than Stuart and Fountain Beattie, Mosby's best friend and "most trusted lieutenant," few thought the "quixotic enterprise"[34] would amount to much. Mosby's earlier attempt at partisan warfare had led to his recent capture. On that occasion in July 1862, Stuart had given him one man: a club-footed convalescent exempt from military service. With a letter in hand from Stuart authorizing the enterprise and describing Mosby as "bold, daring, intelligent and discreet,"[35] the two men set out for General Stonewall Jackson's command, where they hoped to borrow a few more men to grow a guerrilla force. Mosby did not get far. A roving Union cavalry unit captured the would-be guerrilla chief while he was attempting to catch a train from Beaver Dam to Gordonsville, Virginia. The troopers sent Mosby to Old Capitol Prison in Washington, DC. Donning the flamboyant dress of Stuart's cavalry, Mosby stood out: "His gray plush hat is surmounted by a waving plume, which he tosses, as he speaks, in real Prussian style. . . . By his sprightly appearance and conversation, he attracted considerable attention,"[36] wrote his captors.

But Mosby turned a personal disaster into an opportunity. The Federals sent Mosby, one of the first Confederate prisoners to be exchanged in the summer of 1862, on a steamer to Hampton Roads. The boat loaded with Mosby and Confederate prisoners lingered for several days waiting for clearance to move up the James River to Richmond. Nearby, a fleet of Union transports lay in at anchor, and Mosby immediately wondered where the Union vessels were heading. "As a prisoner, I kept up my habits as a scout."[37] Mosby became friendly with the steamer's captain, whom Mosby quickly sized up as a Southern sympathizer. "I asked him to find out where the transports were going. When he returned, he whispered to me that Aquia Creek on the Potomac was the point. That settled it—McClellan's army would not advance in the [Peninsula Campaign] but would follow the transports northward."[38] This meant the reinforcements were headed toward Union general John Pope, who would be conducting a new offensive from around Fredericksburg.

The Confederate scout rushed to convey the priceless intelligence to General Robert E. Lee. After docking near Richmond, he painfully hiked several miles on a hot summer day, sucking on an occasional lemon he purchased at Fort Monroe, until a fellow trooper loaned him a horse and he continued on his way to Lee's headquarters. Lee's gatekeepers immediately accosted the lowly lieutenant. "I dismounted and told a staff officer, who was standing on the porch, that I had important information for General Lee and wished to see him. As I was roughly dressed and unkempt, no doubt the officer thought I was presumptuous to ask the privilege. In the imperious tone customary with staff officers, he said that I could not see the General. I protested that I must, but he would accept no explanation."[39] Mosby turned to leave, but another officer overheard his impassioned pleas and escorted him into Lee's headquarters. "I found myself in, what was then to me, the awful presence of the Commander-in-chief."[40] Poring over maps, Lee exhibited a "benevolent manner" that put the young scout at ease. The Union's intended target for their next offensive had befuddled Lee for days. He had written Stonewall Jackson earlier, "Some of [the Union] gunboats have moved up to Malvern Hill and have taken position as if to sweep the ground preparatory to its occupation by a land force. In a day or two their object may be disclosed."[41] Like manna from heaven, Mosby reported to Lee his assessment of the Union troop movements, answering the very question that vexed the Confederate commander. But Lee hesitated;

"he did not know what confidence he could put in my report," remembered Mosby. He then told Lee his name and that he was the scout for Stuart's ride around McClellan. "Oh," Lee remarked. "I remember." Lee asked a few more questions and ordered a courier to send Mosby's report to Jackson immediately. On his way out of the room, Mosby opened his haversack and put a dozen lemons on the table. Lee responded, "Give them to the sick and wounded." Mosby left them on the table with "little expectation of ever seeing him again."[42] But Lee took a keen interest in the scout.

Armed with Mosby's intelligence, undoubtedly confirmed through Lee's other sources, Lee ordered Jackson to strike Union general John Pope before the Union reinforcements Mosby spotted on the steamer arrived. When the Battle of Cedar Mountain unfolded, and Mosby stood at a nearby outpost, he heard booming artillery from Jackson's guns, turned to his close friend Fount Beattie, and exclaimed, "I brought on that battle."[43]

On that cold night at Oakham, as he later related, Mosby explained his area of operations to Stuart: "My idea was to make the Piedmont region of the country lying between the Rappahannock and Potomac Rivers the base of my operations. This embraces the upper portion of the counties of Fauquier and Loudoun. It is the rich pastoral country, which afforded subsistence for my command, while the Blue Ridge [Mountains] was a safe point to retreat if hard pressed by superior numbers that could be sent against us. It was inhabited by a highly refined and cultivated population, who were thoroughly devoted to the Southern cause."[44] A portion of this area controlled by the Rangers would come to be known as "Mosby's Confederacy" and would remain unconquered during the war.* In the southern portion of the area lie the sprawling Bull Run Mountains, pierced by the Thoroughfare Gap. A stretch of roadway connects the towns of the Plains, Salem (now Marshall), Rectortown, and Piedmont, passing through the Manassas Gap to Front Royal, Virginia. East to west along the Little River Turnpike (currently Route 50 and portions renamed John S. Mosby Highway) lie the towns of Aldie, Middleburg, Rector's Crossroads (now Atoka), Upperville, and Paris. The turnpike ambles through Ashby's Gap,

---

* I have spent years visiting safehouses, sites of skirmishes, and remote mountain trails in the area.

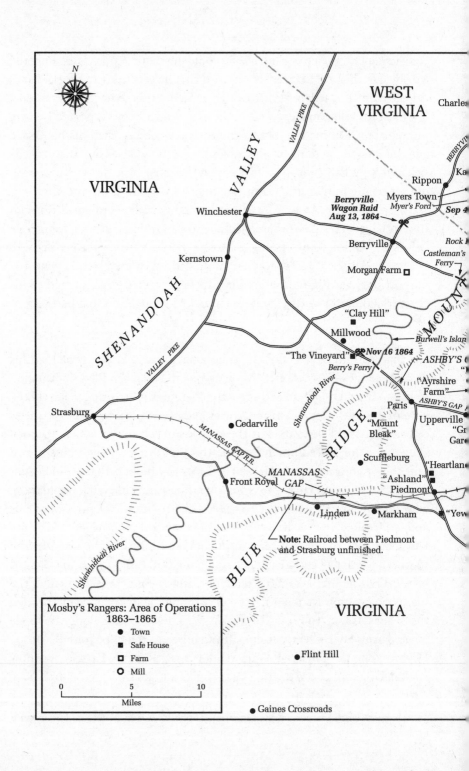

N

WEST
VIRGINIA

Charles[

VIRGINIA

VALLEY

VALLEY PIKE

Rippon

Myers Town
Myer's Ford

*Berryville
Wagon Raid
Aug 13, 1864*

Sep 4

Winchester

Berryville

Rock

Kernstown

Morgan Farm

*Castleman's
Ferry*

SHENANDOAH

"Clay Hill"

Millwood

Burwell's Island

VALLEY PIKE

"The Vineyard"

Nov 16 1864

ASHBY'S

Berry's Ferry

Shenandoah River

"Ayrshire
Farm"

MOUN[

ASHBY'S GAP

Strasburg

Paris

Upperville

"Gr
Gar

Cedarville

MANASSAS GAP R.R.

"Mount
Bleak"

RIDGE

Scuffleburg

"Heartlan

*MANASSAS
GAP*

Front Royal

"Ashland"
Piedmont

Linden

Markham

"Yew

Shenandoah River

BLUE

Note: Railroad between Piedmont
and Strasburg unfinished.

VIRGINIA

Mosby's Rangers: Area of Operations
1863–1865

● Town
■ Safe House
□ Farm
○ Mill

0   5   10

Miles

● Flint Hill

● Gaines Crossroads

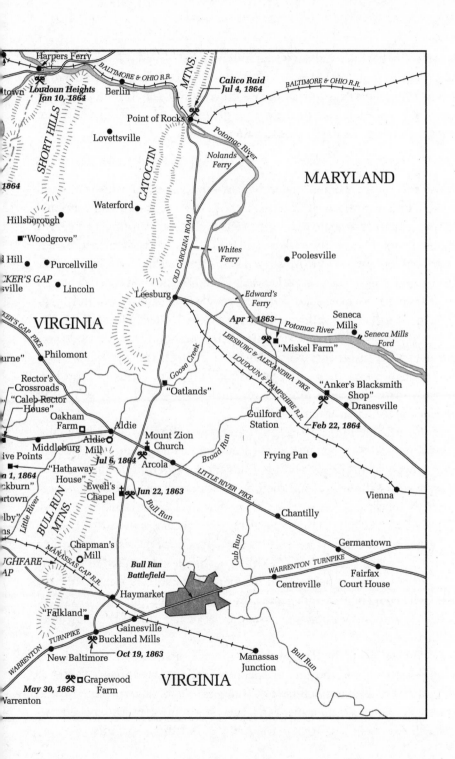

Harpers Ferry

BALTIMORE & OHIO R.R.

CATOCTIN MTNS.

Calico Raid
Jul 4, 1864

BALTIMORE & OHIO R.R.

town

Loudoun Heights
Jan 10, 1864

Berlin

Point of Rocks

Potomac River

Lovettsville

Nolands
Ferry

MARYLAND

1864

SHORT HILLS

Waterford

OLD CAROLINA ROAD

Hillsborough

"Woodgrove"

l Hill

Whites
Ferry

Poolesville

Purcellville

KER'S GAP
sville

Lincoln

Leesburg

Edward's
Ferry

Seneca
Mills

VIRGINIA

Apr 1, 1863

Potomac River

Seneca Mills
Ford

R'S GAP PIKE

urne"

Philomont

LEESBURG & ALEXANDRIA PIKE

"Miskel Farm"

Goose Creek

LOUDOUN & HAMPSHIRE R.R.

"Anker's Blacksmith
Shop"

Rector's
Crossroads

"Caleb Rector
House"

"Oatlands"

Guilford
Station

Dranesville

Oakham
Farm

Aldie

Feb 22, 1864

ive Points

Aldie
Mill

Mount Zion
Church

Broad Run

Frying Pan

Middleburg

Jul 6, 1864

Arcola

LITTLE RIVER PIKE

Vienna

1, 1864
ckburn"

"Hathaway
House"

rtown"

Ewell's
Chapel

Jun 22, 1863

Bull Run

Chantilly

lby"
as

BULL RUN MTNS.

Little River

Chapman's
Mill

Cub Run

Germantown

GHFARE
AP

MANASSAS GAP R.R.

Bull Run
Battlefield

WARRENTON TURNPIKE

Fairfax
Court House

"Falkland"

Haymarket

Centreville

WARRENTON TURNPIKE

Gainesville

Buckland Mills

Oct 19, 1863

New Baltimore

Manassas
Junction

Bull Run

May 30, 1863

Grapewood
Farm

VIRGINIA

Warrenton

spanned by the Shenandoah River at Berry's Ferry, and rolls into the city of Winchester and the Shenandoah Valley. Snickersville, a tiny village in Loudoun County, sits astride the entrance of Snickers Gap and another entry to the Shenandoah. As the war progressed, Mosby positioned his men near these crucial entry points to gain an advantage over his opponents.

Mosby's Rangers operated under the Partisan Ranger Act, which endorsed the use of unconventional warfare methods in areas that the conventional Confederate Army could not reach, such as northern Virginia or Mosby's Confederacy. The partisan leader and his men would master their unconventional style of warfare (Mosby called it irregular warfare), which grew in size and scale as the war progressed. Had these methods been deployed on a greater basis by the Confederacy, they would have significantly prolonged a war that, in itself, nearly destroyed the United States of America. To gain independence, the primary thing the South needed to do was survive. Most insurgencies are difficult to control, and the North never had enough troops to occupy the entire South. A cessation of hostilities in what many deemed a forever unwinnable war would have resulted in independence for the South.

Eventually, only a few irregular units were officially sanctioned, since the Confederates found undisciplined partisans could be more trouble than they were worth. Mosby and his Rangers, however, honed and crafted unconventional warfare, and their activities continued to be sanctioned. Mosby's collection of men grew within a few weeks. The numbers swelled, "receiving accessions to [his] command from various sources."[45]

Under the act, men were entitled to a portion of the spoils of war they secured. Uniquely and unselfishly, the guerrilla leader refused to take any of the booty. Mosby handpicked his men, all volunteers—extraordinary men who could operate independently, be self-reliant, and work as a team. These highly disciplined men would emerge as some of the most elite soldiers of the war.

He stationed the Rangers to live in safe houses with Confederate families throughout the area of operation and expected them to meet at designated rendezvous points. The Rangers' operations were intense and incessant. The partisan leader ran a tight ship. Any man who missed two roll calls would be sent back to the Army of Northern Virginia.

Fountain "Fount" Beattie was one of Mosby's original six men. The two Virginia natives met in 1861 while both served in Company D of the 1st Virginia Cavalry. Although seven years Mosby's junior, Beattie became Mosby's "most intimate companion and friend, for they had enlisted together when the war broke out and were never separated," wrote Ranger John Munson.[46]

Mosby had no trouble finding volunteers. "It has always been a wonder with people how I manage to collect my men after dispersing them. The true secret was that it was a fascinating life and its attractions far more than counterbalanced its hardships and dangers," he later recalled. "They had no camp duty to do, which, however necessary, is disgusting to soldiers of high spirit. To put them to such routine work is pretty much like hitching a race-horse to a plow."[47] Unable to furnish horses for its men, the Confederate government instead gave them forty cents a day to compensate them for the use of their own horses. They were given a furlough to find another if they lost their horse. "A great many of this class of men came to me, to whom I would furnish captured horses in consideration of their going with me on a few raids,"[48] wrote Mosby. The Rangers procured most of their mounts and equipment from the Union raids they conducted.

One of Mosby's earliest Rangers was a local volunteer, "Major" William Hibbs, a disheveled, gray-haired, middle-aged blacksmith with small, black eyes. "His hat, a faded felt riddled by sparks from the forge, rested sideways on his head, above a matting of gray hair that hung low over his forehead like a fetlock. . . . The only part of his raiment that represented the army was an old gray military coat, held together by a strange array of buttons, only two of which bore the initials of the Confederacy."[49]

Horses ran on forage. As an expert scrounger, Hibbs had the inglorious but vital role of quartermaster and became known as the "chief of the corn detail." Where there was corn and grain, there was "infrequently a distillery included in the itinerary," as one Ranger fondly recalled.[50] While Mosby was largely a teetotaler who ordered stills destroyed since they sucked up priceless grain for the horses, Hibbs had a fondness for libations. After locating a still, he would drink all he wanted first and then, and only then, tell Mosby about the still's location.[51] But Hibbs was not a noncombatant: "No braver man followed Mosby. Many years past military age, he rode side by side with his own two sons in the foremost ranks, and his scarred body attested to his familiarity with hot battles."[52]

However, Mosby's most infamous Ranger had first betrayed his command and his country: Union sergeant James Foster Ames. The muscular Ames, who later earned the nickname "Big Yankee," was a thirty-year-old sailor from Bangor, Maine, with dark hair and piercing blue eyes. In February 1863, Ames somehow found Mosby and his men at Blackwell Farm, located near Upperville, after deserting the 5th New York. He evinced a passionate hatred for the Union government as well as the officers in his command and would later reveal his disdain for Lincoln and the Emancipation Proclamation, stating, "The war had become a war for the Negro instead of a war for the Union."[53] An excellent judge of character, Mosby believed Ames' story but still needed to verify his fealty. The Union deserter did not have a mount, so Ames' first test was to go back to his old command, unarmed, and steal a horse. Still dressed in Union blue, Ames and another young man in "full Confederate uniform" who also wanted to join the Rangers covertly "entered the camp of the 5th New York Cavalry at night on foot and [rode] out on two of the finest horses they could find in the stables."[54] The other men still harbored suspicions, but Ames eventually won them over through ruthless conduct. While on one mission, he ran into a Union trooper from his command who, unaware that Ames had deserted, greeted him: "How are you, Sergeant Ames?"

"Well," Ames responded, then shot the man dead.[55] Mosby later wrote of the Yankee deserter, "He seemed to burn with an implacable feeling of revenge toward his old companions in arms. I never had a truer or more devoted follower."[56]

As Mosby's band of guerrillas grew in number, his operations to target Federal troops and their supply lines grew bolder.

4. MISKEL FARM

The gray gloom of winter hung over the landscape and white snow still caked the ground on the last days of March 1863. Over sixty of Mosby's men gathered at a favorite rendezvous point, Rector's Crossroads, mounted and armed to the teeth. Most of the men did not know each other, Mosby remembered as he referenced Shakespeare, observing, "[They were] almost as motley a crowd as Falstaff's regiment."[1] The crew included several infantrymen recovering from their wounds who tied makeshift wooden crutches to the saddles of their horses. "The shaking up of the kaleidoscope does not produce more variegated colors than appeared among them."[2] This group of men held the crew together and would form the Rangers' leadership core as it expanded. "The cohesion of this strange band was love of adventure and confidence in their leader,"[3] one Ranger remembered.

Riding most of the day en route to their next raid, the Rangers dismounted and spent the night at Miskel Farm, which was owned by a sympathetic Southern farmer and located near the Potomac between the Broad Run and Difficult Run Rivers. The estate had forage for the horses and seemed to offer a welcome respite from the cold wintery weather of the previous day. Still, its location made a cul-de-sac with rivers to the back and flanks. There was only one way in and out—through the main gate of the homestead, a lane that led to the turnpike.

Making themselves at home, the men ate a little dinner, drank hard cider, and settled in for the night, mostly billeted in the barn and outbuildings. Several Rangers, including Mosby, stayed in the main house and slept next to a roaring fire. Shortly after dawn the following day, a piercing voice shouted, "Mount your horses! The Yankees are coming!" "Mount up, boys!"[4] screamed Ranger Dick Moran, who waved his hat and rode his horse at breakneck speed through back trails into the encampment that frigid morning. Cold wind bit into the forty-nine-year-old father of ten's face as he approached the farm.

Moran had been visiting a friend on the road to Dranesville on the night between March 31 and April 1. There are indications that before joining Mosby, Moran conducted "his own personal war" on the Yankees. Moran "delighted in shooting down the poor pickets after finding out their whereabouts in the daytime,"[5] one correspondent later wrote. The Ranger spotted scores of Federal troopers riding toward Miskel. A Union citizen had alerted the 1st Vermont Cavalry of Mosby's presence in the neighborhood. Six companies, or about 150 men, led by Captain Henry Flint, set out to hunt and destroy Mosby. They barreled down the lane that led to the entrance of the farm. When Flint reached Miskel, he ordered troopers to bar the gate near the turnpike. He then split his men and ordered fifty troopers to circle behind the farm and attack from the rear while the bulk of his force made a headlong charge into Mosby's camp.

Pandemonium unfolded in the fenced barnyard. Yelling and cursing, Rangers ran to their horses and tried to bridle and saddle their animals in the face of the Union assault. "It looked as though the light and life of the Guerrilla must be swept from the face of the earth. Never before or after had the Federal troops had such a chance to secure Mosby and wipe out his men,"[6] recalled one Ranger.

On foot, Mosby rallied his men: "Charge 'em; charge 'em and go through 'em!" He motioned with his hand to emphasize the order.[7] The Rangers often acted on a distorted version of the Golden Rule: "Do unto the other fellow as he would do unto you—and do it first."[8] Everything depended on "getting the bulge on them," what Rangers referred to as seizing the initiative by gaining an advantage with a violent and powerful attack that often stunned their opponents. One Ranger summed it up as "the boldest front oftenest wins the fight."[9] The Rangers responded to Mosby's admonition with "a demonic yell which . . . once heard [one would] never forget . . . as reapers descend on the harvest of death."[10] Pistols blazing, the Rangers charged into the Yankees. Mosby held two smoking Colts that he fired into Flint's oncoming men. In the scuffle, Harry Hatcher, nicknamed "Deadly," whose family owned a mill near Middleburg, handed Mosby the bridle of his horse; the partisan leader mounted it and rushed into the melee. Hatcher soon vaulted onto a captured horse and joined the fight.

On the attack, the Rangers "seemed to bewilder" Flint's men. Some of the Yankees charged with sabers, but most employed their Remington pistols, which in some cases misfired. In one such instance involving Ranger William H. Chapman, who, with his brother, Sam, rode with Mosby, both antagonists' weapons were a foot apart when they discharged. "The Yankee pistol snapped, but Chapman did the deadly work. He fired six shots and emptied five saddles."[11]

The effectiveness of the Rangers' Colt Navy and Army six-shot revolvers, coupled with their shooters' deadly proficiency, became evident. An Army chambered a .44-caliber bullet, while the Navy shot a .36. Either ball tore gaping holes in a target's body. Rangers later boasted "they could shoot a squirrel's eye out at thirty yards." Each of Mosby's men wielded several Colts in battle, which proved deadly at thirty feet. From Miskel Farm forward, Rangers relied on their Colts as their principal weapons, eschewing the sword for close-quarters battle.

One Union officer recalled, "It was a hot place. The enemy, using pistols, had more shots than us. We were in close proximity, separated not by more than [100 to 130 feet] from each other."[12]

Flint split his command and ordered some of his men to flank the farm and attack from the rear to tear a hole in the fence and "get at them with the saber."[13]

"Come on!"[14] Flint yelled. Five bullets felled the valiant Yankee. Leaderless, the Vermonters became "panic-stricken and fled precipitously" down the lane. The Rangers attacked the cavalry's flank and rear as they rushed toward the closed gate, a deadly choke point. Here the men "got wedged together, and a fearful state of confusion followed."[15]

Sam Chapman, a former divinity student, swung into action. After emptying both barrels of his pistols, he drew his saber and rode to the front of the Confederate ranks, "standing straight up in his stirrups, dealing [saber slashes to the] right and left with all the theological fervor of Burly of Balfour,"[16] wrote Mosby. Wearing the scarlet uniform of a British officer, Captain Bradford Smith Hoskins joined Chapman and also slashed and hacked the Federals with his saber. Hoskins had joined Mosby's command as a volunteer in March. He cut an impressive figure with his gleaming steel saber and his fine steed. The British officer was an anachronism and a throwback to the Crimea, where he had fought and where actions such as the famous doomed Charge of the Light Brigade unfolded. A soldier of fortune, Captain Hoskins had first appeared in Canada in 1861 and traveled to the United States in 1862. In Baltimore, he appeared to be destitute, selling his watch and clothing to support himself. He finally made his way to Richmond, where he received a letter from Stuart instructing him to report to Captain Mosby. Unlike Mosby, he wasn't a teetotaler, spending St. Patrick's Day downing "whiskey, punch, and sentiment. He missed the train in the morning in consequence."[17]

With the weight of many of their horses pushing against it, the Vermont troopers broke through the gate and fled down the Leesburg and Alexandria Turnpike.* Mosby's men galloped off in pursuit and hunted them down. First Lieutenant Charles A. Woodbury attempted to rally his routed men until "Big Yankee" Ames fired his pistol and put a bullet in Woodbury's head. Sam Chapman, riding next to Ames, then bolted between two Union troopers and told them to surrender. Instead of capitulating, one of them turned and slashed at the preacher turned Ranger. Chapman's life might have ended there had not another Ranger galloped up at high speed and body-checked the cavalryman, knocking him off his horse.

Chapman, Ames, and the other Rangers pursued the fleeing remnants of Flint's command down the pike for several miles before they returned to the farm.

During the melee, Mosby lost several men wounded, and one later died. The Rangers captured scores of prisoners and about a hundred Union horses, as well as weapons and equipage—enough gear to outfit the many new men who swelled into Mosby's ranks.

The incident brought a promotion: the Confederate Congress elevated Mosby to the rank of major. Conversely, the North viewed Mosby as a dangerous threat, and they strengthened their efforts to destroy those who continued to emerge as the South's most dangerous men as they enhanced, expanded, and pioneered a unique form of warfare.

At Miskel Farm, Mosby had pulled off a remarkable victory: outnumbered two to one, he had captured eighty-two men, wounding or killing twenty-five others. One of the seriously wounded Union troopers was Lieutenant Josiah Grout. Mosby considered the wound mortal and provided

---

* The Leesburg Turnpike is now Route 7. Miskel Farm still exists and is a private residence located in Sterling, Virginia. A marker memorializing the skirmish is at the intersection of Dairy and Bobwhite Lanes.

the officer comfort—the Rangers did not execute prisoners. Decades later, Sam Chapman, Mosby, and Grout were reunited—Grout then the governor of Vermont—at the Arlington Hotel in Washington, DC. The men spoke freely of the war they had survived. The two Rangers were introduced to the governor's wife. "After looking around and without a trace of ill-nature," she turned to Chapman and Mosby and observed, "Why, you do not look like dangerous men." Chapman asked when she first became acquainted with the governor. She responded that she had first heard of him from the newspaper article and his severe wounding at Miskel. Chapman thoughtfully replied, "How time does smooth the wrinkled front of war."[18]

5. THE GRAPEWOOD FARM ENGAGEMENT

In the final week of May 1863, forty Rangers mounted their horses outside Middleburg at Patterson's Farm. "The weather was superb. Every tree and bush was in full leaf of flower. The potency of nature infectious; the temperature of our spirits infectious,"[1] remembered Sam Chapman as the posse set out toward Catlett Station. Two horses towed Mosby's "little gun,"[2] creating a plume of dust in their wake. "A bit too large to carry in a holster, but not big enough to be called a cannon,"[3] the mountain howitzer hurled a deadly twelve-pound shell—ideal for the next mission. Mosby planned to use his latest weapon to disrupt their first train and interdict the Federal supply lines.

With his gleaming steel saber, former British officer Bradford Hoskins rode next to Mosby, a contrast to Mosby's other men, who deemed the sword obsolete and embraced six-shooter Colts. The partisan leader flatly stated, "The tradition of chivalry inherited from the ancient knights of using the sword in single combat still asserted its dominion over him, but my other men had no more use for that antiquated weapon than a coat of mail."[4]

After scouting out the heavily defended Union position at Catlett Station off the Orange and Alexandria Railroad, Mosby knew his men were embarked on a nearly suicidal mission. "The enterprise on which I was going, when judged, by common standards of prudence, appeared not only hazardous but foolhardy." The rails remained a strategic lifeline. Union soldiers and cavalry camps blanketed the roads in intervals of every mile, and trains bristled with infantry guards. "Retreat [was] difficult, if not impossible,"[5] remembered Mosby.

The forty Rangers threaded through the Federal positions to a wooded area near Catlett Station, where they hid and bedded down for the night. The next morning, Union trumpets from nearby camps blasted reveille, awakening the sleeping Rangers. Working through a narrow lane in the woods, they approached the railroad. Heavy Union patrols guarded the supply line, "mov[ing] up and down so constantly, the track was hard to get to,"[6] recalled Sam Chapman. Here the Rangers snipped telegraph wires, tied them to the tracks, and unfastened one of the long iron rails. Affixing the telegraph wire to the loose rail, one of Mosby's men concealed himself behind a tree and waited for the train.

A Ranger gave the signal when he heard the sound of an engine chugging along, belching grayish soot and steam. Sam Chapman loaded the howitzer, and "all awaited the event with breathless interest."[7] The unsuspecting train barreled along at full speed and approached the ambush. A Ranger yanked the wire and threw the steel rail off the track as the locomotive tried to halt but careened off.[8] As Chapman was about to pull the lanyard and fire the gun, Private Richard Paul Montjoy, a swarthy and handsome Mississippian, previously with the famed Louisiana Tigers before joining Mosby's command, screamed, "Goodness! You will all be scalded to death. Move back seventy-five yards."[9] Terrified of the deadly steaming water from the engine, the Rangers wisely fell back.

Chapman's gun barked, and a twelve-pound shell slammed into the wooden cars. "We moved back and put a shot through the dome, and such a noise and such a spray of steam never enveloped us before."[10] The Confederate fire scattered the infantry guard riding on the train as they ran for their lives, blindly firing a few shots into the woods. Another round from the howitzer penetrated the engine's boiler, resulting in a horrific explosion of steam and metal.

The Rangers surged forward, plundered the train, and "were well laden with spoil,"[11] grabbing oranges, lemons, shad, and mailbags. Before torching a dozen cars and scattering, the Rangers helped a newsboy off the wrecked train who had broken his leg in the ambush.

Sounds of cannon fire and shots from the melee alerted the nearby troops. Bugles sounded "to horse,"[12] and the 5th New York Cavalry mounted and rode toward the firing. The 1st Vermont and other units followed. Sergeant Herman Richards, an immigrant from Germany, and fellow troopers from the 5th New York Cavalry bore down on the Rangers about a mile from the ambuscade, attempting to block their escape. The Union Army's ranks consisted of a massive number of immigrants such as Richards who had arrived in the United States only a short time before the war. A clerk who enrolled the German into the regiment could not "understand him"[13] and changed his name from Rusch to Richards.

Mosby ordered a halt, and Chapman unlimbered the cannon and fired a shot into the Union cavalry. The shell burst, "creating a stampede, and they scattered."[14] The Rangers galloped through the opening made by Chapman's shell and thundered down the road back toward the tiny hamlet of Greenwich. With Yankees on all sides, Mosby wanted to keep the gun as "a point of honor" instead of scattering his men and directing them to flee in different directions, so he ordered Chapman to limber the howitzer and ride off down Burnwell Road.[15] With the howitzer and the bulk of the men, Mosby and several of his Rangers boldly set up a rear guard to slow their hunters. Lieutenant Elmer Barker led Mosby's pursuers that day descended on Mosby, Captain Hoskins, and the other Rangers. "Soon a hand-to-hand conflict began with the advance-guard, consisting of about fifteen, whom we succeeded in driving back, but we lost in the encounter the gallant Captain Hoskins, who fell from the horse mortally wounded,"[16] chronicled a contemporary historian.

Barker found himself "alone for probably one or two minutes (it seemed like hours). I fired all the shots in my revolver, and then drew my saber, they [were] trying to shoot me, crying 'Surrender Yank!' and I trying to kill them."[17] Eventually, one of Barker's men rode up and saved the Union officer as Mosby rode off.

The Confederate rear guard bought precious time for Sam Chapman to set up the gun on a hill near Grapewood Farm, owned by Warren Fitzhugh.[18] A narrow country lane about a hundred yards from the Fitzhugh house flanked with fences funneled the Union cavalry into a kill zone. As Mosby rode up to Chapman, Montjoy, and Beattie, who were operating the gun, he noticed "their faces beamed with what the Romans called the *gaudia certaminis*,* and they had never looked so happy in their lives."[19]

---

* Latin for "the joys of battle," an expression reportedly employed by Attila when addressing his troops before the 451 CE Battle of Châlons.

Led by Barker, the 5th New York charged up the narrow rocky lane "where three horses could scarcely walk abreast."[20]

As the 5th attacked, Chapman ignited a round from the howitzer's barrel. The shell exploded in the New Yorkers' ranks. Unwavering, Barker yelled, "I think we can get that gun before they fire again. Let's go!"[21]

Another one of Chapman's grapeshot shells exploded among the groups of Union riders in the narrow lane. The piece hurled metal balls, similar to a giant shotgun, penetrating the flesh of horse and man, killing three and wounding several, including Barker, who took two balls of grape to the thigh. The New Yorkers charged several times as Rangers countercharged from the sides of the road and blasted away with their Colts, driving the Yankees back to a bend in the road. From there, the surviving New Yorkers joined the 1st Vermont Cavalry.

The New Yorkers, bolstered by the Vermonters, now one hundred strong, charged up the country road again. At point-blank range, about fifty yards, the cannon belched more of its deadly iron, slaying and wounding more men. As the Federals reeled, Mosby ordered a charge, and the Rangers drove the Yankees down to the base of the hill. Mosby later recalled, a Union cavalryman "struck me a blow with his saber on the shoulder that nearly knocked me from my seat. At the same instant, my pistol flashed, and he reeled in the saddle."[22]

The Yankees finally broke through, and the ground around Chapman's cannon deteriorated into a fierce hand-to-hand struggle where "many of the enemy were made to bite the dust."[23] The Rangers also lost many men. Fighting preacher Sam Chapman manned his howitzer and seemed invincible. "Sam Chapman had passed through so many fights unscathed that the men had a superstition that he was as invulnerable as the son of Thetis,"[24] recalled Mosby.

Montjoy and Beattie, surrounded by a wall of blue, surrendered. Chapman stood by his gun until he exhausted his ammunition and was critically wounded by a bullet. When he finally succumbed, his Union captor threatened,

"I'm going to finish you."

"Why? I am your prisoner now," Chapman responded.

"Yes; but you shot me here in the shoulder."

"Well, I suppose I had a right to, as we had not ceased firing then,"[25] argued Chapman.

Members of the 5th New York made the trooper desist. Remarkably, hours later, the Union soldier felt guilty for attempting to execute Chapman in cold blood and begged the fighting preacher's pardon—which the Confederate granted. "Humanity will assert itself, in war as well as in peace," Chapman reflected decades after the war. Losing a great deal of blood and passing out, "I fainted while in their hands. It was the only experience of the kind I have ever had. The sensation was rather pleasant as consciousness was leaving me. I have wondered often since if I shall die as easy as that."[26] The troopers carried Chapman and Captain Hoskins to Grapewood[27] and later to The Lawn, a mansion owned by a fellow Englishman, Charles Green, in Greenwich. Green considered his home not only his castle but even a part of Great Britain, and he liked to fly the Union Jack over the grounds of the estate. At The Lawn, Hoskins, in great pain from his wounds, called on Chapman, and the two men "tried to cheer each other up."[28] The next day, the British officer died before Chapman's eyes, and Green buried his body in the nearby church cemetery.

Mosby barely avoided capture. As he and his men scattered, he and his horse ran into a tree.[29] Within days, however, and despite another close brush with death, Mosby was back reconnoitering Union positions and plotting new missions. He often ventured out alone or with another. Fatigued from the Grapewood Farm engagement and other operations, a few days later he lay down under the cool shade of some chestnut trees and fell asleep. Two Federal soldiers discovered Mosby and, with pistols drawn, demanded his surrender. One Ranger recalled Mosby's catlike reflexes: "Never losing his presence of mind or expressing, in the least degree, excitement under the trying circumstances, he suddenly jumped up, and with one arm, knocked away the pistols pointed at his breast, with the other hand he shot one of his would-be capturers, and the other ran away."[30]

Days later, while patrolling with Ames, Mosby was surprised by seven Federal troopers. "Three Yankees were killed, and both parties having exhausted the loads in their pistols, Mosby's adversaries drew their sabre and attacked him. He was as skillful in warding off their thrusts with the pistol as an experienced swordsman, although he had never had a sabre in his hand before the war." Upon hearing the firing, Ames arrived on the scene and saved Mosby's life. "Being skilled in the use of the sabre, [he] made two of the enemy bite the dust with his sabre, while the other two fled for their lives," wrote one Ranger.[31]

6. BACK IN THE SADDLE

After recovering from the Grapewood Farm debacle, Mosby rode to James Hathaway's house—one of his many safehouses—and the waiting arms of his wife, Pauline. After raids, the Rangers would often have downtime. Sometimes called "featherbed soldiers," since the partisans did not endure the same camp life and outdoors as regular soldiers, the men often boarded in mansions and plantations in Fauquier and Loudoun Counties, where many of them had family. But for Mosby on the night of June 8, 1863, the respite was short. A detachment of the 1st New York Cavalry attacked Hathaway's stately red-brick home and stormed into the bedroom to find an indignant and tight-lipped Mrs. Mosby under the bedsheets. The wily guerrilla leader had slipped out the second-story bedroom window onto the large branches of a black walnut tree. Hugging the tree, he hid from the patrol, which looked everywhere but up the tree.* Carting off Hathaway, the Yankees left the area—one of the countless close calls the partisan leader survived unscathed. After the Federals left, Mosby slithered back into the bedroom into Mrs. Mosby's arms.

Rangers knew the egress points of a safe house, but often carpentry played a vital role in keeping them out of sight of a Federal search party. Concealed compartments beneath trap doors in the floorboards and rooms behind false walls hid Rangers when there was not enough time or the means to escape.

June 10, 1863, marked the time when the Rangers finally reached more than sixty in number, at least on paper—enough to form a company. Mosby explained, "I had about that number on my muster roll; but at least a third of them were in prison, having been captured at various times by

* The home and the 250-year-old tree still stand on the historic site.

raiding parties of the enemy." Confederate military law allowed men to
elect their own officers. However, while Mosby granted his men latitude
to perform on the battlefield, he ran a tight ship and was hands-on down
to the most minor details of his command. In a farmhouse at Rector's
Crossroads that is still standing, Mosby selected the officers, a tradition he
continued through the war. He explained, "I had to go through the form
of an election. But I really appointed the officers and told the men to vote
for them. This was my rule as long as I had a command."[1] Company A
would be the first of many companies that would together form a battalion
of Rangers, the 43rd Virginia Cavalry.

As the war progressed, the South had further plans to duplicate Mosby's model of guerrilla warfare on an even more extensive basis. However,
many traditional officers such as Lee and Joseph Johnston frowned on
irregular or unconventional warfare, believing it bled off some of the best
troops from regular army commands. This criticism of special operations
and unconventional warfare would continue for decades in American history, leading up to and including World War II.

After the Confederate victory at Chancellorsville in early May 1863, Lee
planned his second invasion of the North to allow room for his army to
maneuver and relieve pressure on Virginia. An invasion of the North could
also further demoralize the war-weary Union and embolden the growing
peace movement. Lee also hoped for a crushing military victory that might
end the war outright.

To divert Federal forces from Lee's thrust north, Mosby crossed the
Potomac and raided Seneca, Maryland. Mosby and his men then moved
down the Little River Turnpike on their way back into Virginia.

Riding along trails in the woods, the Rangers stealthily approached
Union general Joseph Hooker's headquarters outside Fairfax. "My command was now inside of Hooker's lines and environed on all sides by the
camps of his different corps. Along the pike, a continuous stream of troops,
with all their impediments of war poured along." Surrounded by tens of
thousands of troops, Mosby probed for a Federal weakness. After discov-
ering three horses at a house along the pike, in the darkness, Mosby and
several of his men rode up to the orderly holding the horses and asked to
whom they belonged. He answered that they were the property of two

captains who had just left headquarters. Mosby leaned down to the man and whispered, "You are my prisoner. My name is Mosby." The orderly, an Irishman, misheard the partisan leader and barked, "You are a d—d liar. I am as good a Union man as you are." The gleam of starlight revealed Mosby's Colt revolver, "and [he] had nothing further to say." Next, Mosby snared the officers and scooped up dispatches containing "just such information as General Lee wanted, and were the 'open sesame' to Hooker's army."[2] Mosby got the priceless intelligence to Jeb Stuart, who had moved up into the Middleburg–Aldie area. Stuart deployed his cavalry as a screen to keep the Union cavalry's probing eyes from seeing Lee's Army of Northern Virginia as it moved up the Shenandoah, terminating in what would be the Battle of Gettysburg. Mosby, who reported to Stuart, furnished tactical intelligence of Union troop movements. What unfolded was one of the largest cavalry engagements of the war as Stuart's men battled Union general Alfred Pleasonton at the Battle of Upperville on June 21, 1863.

Mosby recalled, "On the afternoon when Pleasonton followed the Confederate cavalry through Upperville to the mountain . . . I determined again to strike at his rear." Mosby gathered his command. Moving through a narrow path on Bull Run Mountain in the dead of night, one of his men dropped his hat and stopped to pick it up. The front of the column moved forward while the back stopped. "This cut my column in two; and half of it wandered all night in the woods, but never found me,"[3] wrote Mosby.

The column with Mosby slept through a downpour on the side of the mountain. As they slept, according to Mosby, an African American "carried the news of our being on the mountain to General [George] Meade." The Union general gathered cavalry and infantry and prepared a nasty surprise for Mosby at Ewell's Chapel in Haymarket. The Rangers halted near the church and saw a body of thirty cavalry drawn up about one hundred yards in front of them. "I instantly ordered a charge; and, just as we got upon them, they ran away." The trap had been sprung. A company of infantry hiding in the church emerged and started firing on the Rangers. Mosby barely escaped with his life: "I was not ten steps from the infantry when they fired the volley."[4]

Federal lead struck many of the Rangers; one man lost a leg, and Mississippian Richard Montjoy had a finger shot off his hand as they performed a maneuver they called the "skedaddle" and fled toward the mountain. One Ranger stated, "I never heard the command given. The Rangers seemed to know instinctively when that movement was appropriate, and never waited for the word."[5]

Despite the losses, the men were soon back in the saddle and, days later, hit a poorly defended twenty-wagon train. The Rangers delivered the booty of weapons, horses, and equipment to Stuart's quartermaster. Here with Stuart, Mosby would play an important role in a battle he did not fight: Gettysburg.

Stuart had received communication from Lee requesting several cavalry brigades to continue to screen the Army of Northern Virginia from Union observation as it traveled north and crossed the Potomac. "I think the sooner you cross into Maryland . . . , the better," wrote Lee, but he left the specifics to the major general's discretion. "You will, however be able to judge whether you can pass around [Hooker's] army without hindrance."[6]

Having just arrived from Yankee-occupied territory, Mosby gave Stuart his best intelligence that the Union troops were not moving and that his forces should be able to pass easily through a gap in the Federals' lines. The plans fell apart in Haymarket when, on June 25, instead of a clear path, the thousands of Confederate troops ran into rear elements of Major General Winfield Scott Hancock's II Corps on the move north toward Leesburg, Virginia. Both groups occupied the same route of egress, the Old Carolina Road. Stuart planned to advance down the road and screen Lee's advancing army. Stuart assaulted the slow-moving Federal wagon train, unleashing volleys from six cannon. Then, after II Corps formed a line of battle, Stuart was forced to retreat toward the small nearby village of Buckland Mills and circle around the Northern troops to the south and east, adding sixty miles and taking him "out of communication with Lee for eight critical days."*[7] The engagement and location of II Corps and additional delays and decisions on Stuart's part cost precious time and robbed Lee of one of his essential eyes and ears at perhaps his greatest hour of need in the Battle of Gettysburg. For years, Mosby would defend his friend against blame for the critical Confederate loss on the Pennsylvania battlefield.

After the departure of Stuart's cavalry, Mosby mounted up a portion of the Rangers to join Lee. They entered the Shenandoah Valley at

---

* I often serendipitously uncover history in plain sight. Road signs, like the one quoted here, have been the inspiration for several of my books.

Snickers Gap and crossed the Potomac at Hancock, Maryland, west of the Army of Northern Virginia. Riding in Mosby's group north was Ranger James Joseph Williamson. Fueled by tales of Mosby's daring exploits that he had heard while held in the Old Capitol Prison, after his release, the young Rebel took a train to Gordonsville, Virginia, and then walked on foot through the Virginia countryside to Mosby's Confederacy to join the partisan leader's band. Riding beside Williamson was "Big Yankee" Ames. As they rode north, Ames divulged to Williamson, "Well, I am going with you, but I will not fire a shot," said Ames. "When the Emancipation Proclamation was issued and I saw the war was for the negro and not for the Union, I joined the South, and am willing to fight to repel the invasion of her soil and am willing to give my life in her defense, but I will not fight on Northern soil."[8]

Mosby intended to scout for the Army of Northern Virginia and the planned rendezvous with Lee at Mercersburg, Pennsylvania. When they arrived at the town, they were informed the army had passed through. On unfamiliar ground and with a small band, Mosby decided to ride back to Virginia. Along the route home, they captured some two hundred cattle. As the men crossed back over the state line, an old woman expressed her "earnest prayer" that they would not be able to get across the river with the cattle. Ames asked if she had ever heard of Mosby and then informed her these were Mosby's men. "The old lady's faith in the efficacy of prayer seemed somewhat shaken at this announcement, for she abruptly turned away, saying: 'Oh, then you'll get off safe enough, I'll be bound!'"[9]

The battle began on July 1 when Confederate troops clashed with Union cavalry. Both sides quickly reinforced the area. The Union Army occupied a fish-hook-shaped defensive position on Cemetery Hill, Culp's Hill, and Little Round Top. On July 2, Lee launched several attacks to break the Union line, including a nearly successful attack on Little Round Top, but was repulsed. On July 3, Lee launched a massive frontal assault across an open field on the center of the Union lines, resulting in a horrendous number of casualties. The Union line held. After three days of fighting, Lee retreated from the battlefield, ending his plans for invasion of the North. In addition to what unfolded on the battlefield in Pennsylvania, unrest continued in the North. Thousands of troops had to be pulled out of the Gettysburg campaign to quell unrest as mobs turned more than fifty buildings in lower Manhattan into smoldering ruins. To fill their depleted ranks, the Federals resorted to a draft in the summer of 1863, resulting in riots in New York City for four days. Scores of Black people were lynched and beaten to death, and hundreds of people died during the rampage. Rankling the poor and immigrants, affluent Northerners could buy their way out of service by paying $300.

The twin Confederate defeats at Gettysburg, Pennsylvania, and Vicksburg, Mississippi, in the first week of July 1863 cast a pall over the Rangers. The loss of Vicksburg, and some 29,000 Confederate soldiers who surrendered there, ensured Union control of the Mississippi River and cleaved the Confederacy in two. The Rangers also found Mosby's Confederacy swarming with General Meade's troops, who had pursued Lee's retreating army. Ranger James Joseph Williamson recalled, "There was now no time for rest, in the midst of Meade's army on those hot July days—the sun glaring down with intense fierceness, the air filled with the dust raised by the steady tramp of the thousands of cavalry and infantry, and the long trains of wagons and batteries of artillery that lumbered along the roads. Our little band was darting in here and out there—at one time making a dash into a wagon train before the guards were aware of our presence, and before they could recover from their surprise, dashing off under cover of the woods; at another time gobbling up some luckless sutler and refreshing ourselves from his stores."[10] Williamson painted a vivid picture: "Men were covered with dust, through which the perspiration trickled down their faces, making them look more like painted or tattooed savage warriors than civilized beings."[11]

Some of the men in the thick of the action were "Major" William Hibbs and his sons. Hibbs was on point and saw a force of infantry in the woods. "And wheeling his horse, [Hibbs] called to our men to come back, but a volley was fired before they had time to obey. A young man named Flynn was shot and fell from his horse which came out with us sprinkled with his master's blood; and William Hibbs, Jr. had his horse killed. One of the prisoners, who was within range, was killed, and another fell off his horse and broke his neck as we were moving off."[12]

The Rangers intensified their raids on Union supply lines by targeting wagon trains. On one of those numerous operations in late August, Mosby and a portion of the command rode to Annandale, Virginia. Mosby eyed several unguarded bridges for destruction, but a patrol of forty Union cavalry troopers escorting scores of horses passed by the Rangers. Mosby decided to delay burning the bridges and trailed the Union party. Near Billy Gooding's tavern, the Gray Ghost ordered a charge.[13] The sudden attack scattered the Federals, but Mosby was shot during the melee, wounded in leg and side. He placed one of his lieutenants in command of the Rangers and convalesced at his parents' home near Lynchburg. In less than a month, Mosby was back in the saddle.

He was then joined by his eighteen-year-old brother, Willie. Within a week, he conducted another daring raid into the heart of Federal-occupied northern Virginia, in Alexandria. Mosby hoped to bag the provisional governor of the Restored Government of Virginia, Francis H. Pierpont, but the governor traveled to Washington that night, to Mosby's dismay. So instead, Mosby and his men rode down Telegraph Road for four miles to Rose Hill Plantation. Colonel Daniel F. Dulany made the mistake of opening the front door.

Mosby asked in a polite tone, "Is this Colonel Dulany?"

Assuming the Confederates were Jessie Scouts (Scouts often wore Confederate uniforms), Dulany responded, "Walk in, gentlemen, and be seated."

As the party entered the room, Mosby announced, "My name is Mosby."[14]

While the stunned Dulany stood silent, absorbing the gravity of the event, he recognized his son, French Dulany, a member of Mosby's Rangers. The war had pitted thousands of families against each other. Upon seeing his father, French exclaimed:

"How do Pa—I'm very glad to see you."

"Well, sir, I'm d—d sorry to see you."[15]

After promising he would not escape, the colonel prepared his things for travel and confinement in Libby Prison, and the group rode through Federal pickets. On the ride back to Mosby's Confederacy, the Rangers doused turpentine on the railroad trestle at Cameron Run under the unsuspecting eyes of two Union forts. The boldness of Mosby's raid, so deep into Union-occupied Alexandria, allowed them to easily set the unguarded bridge on fire.

Despite the losses at Gettysburg and Vicksburg, the South's fortunes appeared to have stabilized. On September 18–20, a detached corps from

Lee's Army of Northern Virginia under the command of General James Longstreet, led by General Braxton Bragg, won a decisive victory at Chickamauga in northwestern Georgia. In the aftermath of the battle, the rail hub of Chattanooga had been surrounded and placed under siege by the Confederates, neutralizing a route of Northern invasion to Atlanta. The South halted many Union advances on the Confederacy, and the war continued to drag on. War-weariness in the North grew as it faced a seemingly forever war with no end in sight and not much to show for it but tens of thousands of new Federal casualties. Hundreds of miles to the northwest of Tennessee, the South's irregulars contributed to the Northern despair. The exploits of Mosby's Rangers would be magnified in the Northern and Southern press. In the backwater front of the new state of West Virginia, the mountains teemed with the South's irregulars, who gradually took their toll on Union forces and stalled Union momentum on that front.

To neutralize them, one discrete unit of Jessie Scouts was formed to combat Southern irregulars and eventually capture or kill Mosby.

7. THE LEGION OF HONOR: BLAZER'S SCOUTS

"Make sure your piece is in condition for use"—the command went down the line in a hushed tone. The disciplined lieutenant halted his men to ensure they were ready for action. The Scouts woke before dawn and "were again threading the mountain by-paths in silence—no word above a whisper dared any man to speak." Most of the men trod on strange ground, acting as guerrillas and applying the unconventional skills of the very men they hunted. Deep behind Southern lines in the crags of West Virginia's Appalachia, Lieutenant Richard Blazer and his Scouts approached the enemy. The thirty-four-year-old Blazer would emerge as one of the war's most unlikely heroes. The Ohioan had no martial bearing, with "a faraway look in one eye, and a nearby sleepy look in the other," recalled one of his men. He sported a disheveled look: his vest improperly buttoned, coat collar out of whack, boots scuffed. Lacking spit and polish, Blazer flopped on the parade ground, often issued the wrong commands, marched out of sync, and "messed with the men or not, just as he felt disposed, and straps apart, would not have seemed more fit to command than any of his fellows."[1]

His appearance matched his temperament, which alternated from "silent to even morose, jolly and sometimes cross." A few years earlier, the citizen soldier from Gallipolis, Ohio, piloted a boat up and down the muddy waters of the Ohio River and later served as a teamster transporting coal. In 1862, Blazer joined Company B of the 91st Ohio Volunteer Infantry Regiment as a first lieutenant.[2] Despite his quirks, he cared deeply about his men.[3]

Independent in thought, the Federal officer tackled problems with steely silence. He despised red tape and was described as "indifferent to both its color and its texture." Blazer was a man of action who led from the front and hurled himself into the heart of combat, "one [on] whom dependence could be placed in an emergency."[4]

That emergency manifested itself in the form of Southern irregulars, Thurmond's Rangers, a band of Confederate "cutthroats" who had "long been feared and for good reason."[5] They were ravaging the Union Army of West Virginia, conducting a guerrilla war, raiding outposts, and picking off Union patrols near the New River Gorge. Fighting in the region centered on three objectives: control of the new state of West Virginia, established in June 1863 as a slave state committed to the gradual emancipation of enslaved people; defense of vital railroads and supply lines; and access to natural resources. By September 1863, the Union controlled much of the new state. However, a thousand-plus-strong Confederate army and the presence of roving bands of partisans such as Thurmond's rendered swaths of the western part of the state contested.

Colonel Carr B. White, commanding officer of the 2nd Brigade, 3rd Division, established the unit with Order 49. The elite group of commandos was tasked with rooting out Thurmond's Rangers and, as the war progressed, would continue to hunt the South's most dangerous men. A close friend of Ulysses S. Grant and a physician, White oozed masculinity. One Union officer observed, "You feel his manhood. Although he is plain and unpretending in his manners, wholly free from ostentation or display, and talked as if he had known you always."[6]

White penned Order 49 on September 5, 1863, authorizing three lieutenants, eight sergeants, eight corporals, and one hundred privates— all volunteers—to form the independent company. "None but experienced woodsmen and good shots will be accepted."[7] White directed each unit in his command to report the names of the most qualified and suitable men for the Scouts. These handpicked volunteers from the 12th, 23rd, and 91st Ohio Infantry Regiments would form the nucleus of this burgeoning elite unit. Some of the men had been Jessie Scouts in General Milroy's command. The order further stipulated that at least half the company would be expected to scout in the field. Later the commandos expanded recruitment to other units, including the cavalry. Along with being picked men, the unit also acquired a moniker. While the name's origins are unknown and it may have even originated with their Confederate adversaries after the war, the Scouts gained the lofty title of Legion of Honor. Later, the Army referred to the men as Blazer's Independent Scouts.

The soldiers volunteering as Scouts knew they were signing up for extremely hazardous duty. Ignoring the danger, plenty of men volunteered. With no training and three days' worth of rations, over 120 volunteers plunged into the mountains of West Virginia on foot in early September, hunting for an elusive foe that seemed to melt away and suddenly reappear "everywhere,"[8] an all-too-familiar aspect of guerrilla warfare.

On their first mission, Blazer commanded at least half the company* but remained silent on his intentions. One volunteer recalled those early days: "It seemed to be taken for granted that some way they would find [Thurmond] so away we went. The boys respected his silence."[9]

Blazer effectively employed a bedrock element of counterinsurgency tactics: intelligence. He operated with kind words and a smile, which loosened tongues. The Ohio officer "questioned every woman and child he saw."[10] Eliciting the smallest nuggets of information, he assembled and fitted the intelligence into a mosaic that resided exclusively in his mind. Blazer established a rapport with civilians, many of whom hated the Scouts for obvious reasons—their boys either were fighting for the Confederacy or were part of Thurmond's Rangers. Others sat on the fence. Few were loyal to the Union. But over time, Blazer's approach bore fruit.

The Scouts' earliest days in the Appalachian Mountains in September 1863 proved uneventful as they plodded along narrow, remote mountain trails interrupted by spectacular vistas that would not have been out of place in Switzerland. They traversed deep gorges and whitewater rivers and climbed steep cliffs and rocky summits, cutting through thick undergrowth in the forested rocky terrain around the New River Gorge, where the New and Gauley Rivers meet and merge into the Great Kanawha River.

One Scout remembered that after an exhausting day of marching, while camped for the night, "the boys discussed their commander in whispers, as absolute silence had been enjoined from the very start, not only enjoined but enforced, and the man of little camp drill and less tactics as

* Captain John White Spencer officially commanded the Independent Scouts, but actual command in the field fell on either Lieutenant Richard Blazer or Lieutenant Harrison Gray Otis. Spencer quickly faded from the scene, and the two lieutenants took a leading role in commanding the Scouts.

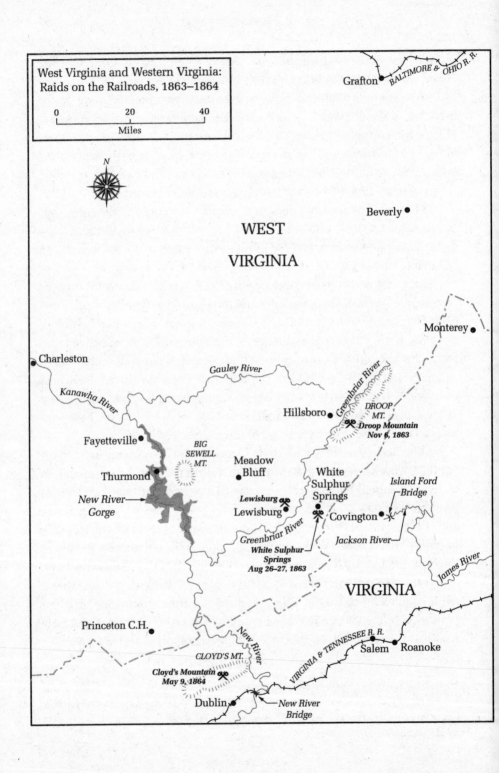

West Virginia and Western Virginia:
Raids on the Railroads, 1863–1864

0   20   40
Miles

N

Grafton   BALTIMORE & OHIO R. R.

Beverly

WEST

VIRGINIA

Monterey

Charleston

Gauley River

Kanawha River

Greenbriar River

Hillsboro

DROOP
MT.
Droop Mountain
Nov 6, 1863

Fayetteville

BIG
SEWELL
MT.

Meadow
Bluff

White
Sulphur
Springs

Island Ford
Bridge

Thurmond

New River
Gorge

Lewisburg

Lewisburg

Covington

Greenbriar River

Jackson River

White Sulphur
Springs
Aug 26–27, 1863

VIRGINIA

James River

Princeton C.H.

New River

CLOYD'S MT.

VIRGINIA & TENNESSEE R. R.

Salem   Roanoke

Cloyd's Mountain
May 9, 1864

Dublin

New River
Bridge

per books, had already proven himself an excellent disciplinarian."[11] Blazer was a leader whom the men immediately respected.

Sharing command with Blazer was Lieutenant Harrison Gray Otis from the 12th Ohio Infantry, a printer who volunteered to escape "the lethargy of garrison life but had a free play to indulge [his] penchant for doing audacious things in war." Starting at age fourteen, Otis learned the print trade as an apprentice working as a composer with the *Louisville Journal*. The Ohioan had a smattering of formal education but a way with words, eventually leading him to found the *Los Angeles Times* in 1881. In Louisville, Otis married Eliza Ann Wetherby and was elected a delegate from Kentucky for the new Republican Party that in May 1860 had nominated Abraham Lincoln for president. An ardent abolitionist, his family home doubled as a safe house and a way station on the Underground Railroad.

Blazer and his men conducted the tedious and deliberate shoe-leather detective work of collecting and piecing together seemingly disparate details from civilians and literal tracks to divine the whereabouts of their everelusive quarry. After "another uneventful day passed," undaunted, Blazer advanced yet again. "The boys were surprised when they were ordered to prepare torches of pine. . . . With a lighted torch in hand, [Blazer] led off over the mountain path unknown to all of them, the command following in single file through the tangled way, with a lighted torch here and there along the line."[12]

At about midnight the hunters halted and made camp. While his men slept, Blazer kept guard. Leading by example, he willingly endured the same hardships as his men and, "possessed with a hardy constitution and all his life inured to hardships, kept watch with the sentinel until morning was close at hand."[13] Blazer broke camp before dawn and resumed the manhunt. After an hour of moving down winding mountain trails, Thurmond's bivouac came into view—a sleeping, unsuspecting Confederate camp. Blazer fired a volley, yelled, and charged into the center, snaring over a dozen prisoners and horses and a small herd of beef cattle before the enemy was even fully awake. After a brief firefight, remnants of Thurmond's gang fled, disappearing into the mountains. Blazer had just dealt his enemy a shocking blow—and his stock with his men soared, as one recalled, "[We] invest[ed] Blazer with a character hitherto unsuspected."[14]

8. Deliverance:
The Thurmonds

Richard Blazer and Harrison Gray Otis had their hands full hunting Thurmond's Rangers and battling nature. Not only forbidding as a setting in which to conduct conventional military operations, the western part of Virginia, a cauldron of political unrest, proved problematic for both the North and South, but would prove well suited for irregular forces. The politically torn area comprised both the overwhelmingly Union area near the Ohio River in the north and the largely pro-Confederate southern and eastern portions of the state, with their smattering of Union sympathizers. The two camps battled for the center and eastern portions of the state. It was a brother-against-brother contest: about 20,000 West Virginians fought for the Union and an equal number for the Confederacy.[1] Southern victories in early 1862 eclipsed early Union victories in 1861 and kept the portions of the state politically contested. Allegiances for those on the fence swayed with the tide of battle. A Northern victory at the Battle of Antietam in September 1862 pushed that tide toward the Union.

When West Virginia became the thirty-fifth state in the summer of 1863, allowing slavery, some 18,000[2] enslaved people lived there, held by roughly 3,600 slave owners—a tiny portion of the population. Most West Virginians did not own slaves, yet the small but powerful minority of slave owners controlled the state's initial destiny.

Key lines of communication ran through central and lower West Virginia: several turnpikes (current Route 50) ran from Winchester through Grafton and the James River, and Kanawha Turnpike traversed from Charleston and Gauley Bridge through Lewisburg into Virginia. The Federals focused their attention on defending the area around the B&O

Railroad, one of the Union's most important supply lines, which ran across the northern portion of West Virginia, connecting Washington, DC, with the Midwest. Penetrating and holding the rugged and mountainous spine of the southwest portion of the state would prove a formidable challenge. The South used the area as a buffer zone to protect their vital lines of communication (especially to the western portion of the Confederacy) and guard resources crucial to the war. It was here that the Thurmond brothers called home.

The Thurmonds ardently supported the Confederate cause and also owned enslaved peoples. Brothers Phillip and William Thurmond founded Thurmond's Rangers, two companies of partisans from local clans in the area. Forty-two-year-old William would never surrender or take the oath of allegiance even after the war ended. In West Virginia, chaos and lawlessness reigned, and the Thurmonds thrived. Phillip organized the first company on May 2, 1862, followed by his brother several months later. In the heart of Appalachia, where feuds among clans such as the Hatfields and McCoys were woven into the culture, the bonds of blood and friendship ran deep and reinforced their allegiance to the Confederate cause.

Composed of many outlaws and deserters, paramilitary groups such as the Thurmonds', often derisively referred to as "Bushwhackers" by the Union, terrorized or protected the civilians around them depending on their loyalties. "They were knights of the ravines and caves . . . terror to the country. Noted for deeds of daring behind rocks, lying behind logs like other venomous reptiles, only more certain death when they drew a bead on a man. Besides blocking the roads in every possible way, annoying the advance guard and prisoners, they would lurk along the rear of a column and shoot footsore, sick, exhausted and helpless soldiers, who fell easy prey to these fiendish, barbarous bushwhackers,"[3] one Union officer recalled.

A principal area of operations, Greenbriar County, would change hands several times throughout the war. Thurmond's Rangers would protect families friendly to the South and intimidate those with Northern loyalties. Repercussions were often dire. Reverend C. S. Donnelly, a firebrand Confederate preacher, recalled the wrath of the Thurmonds: "If a man and his family in the area were known to be Union sympathizers and that knowledge was available to the Rangers, why, then, God pity those Union sympathizers! The Rangers rode herd on such people and were busy at it both night and day. Enemies and others opposed to the tactics of Thurmond's Rangers often called them Bushwhackers . . . which meant they were not averse to lowering the boom on Union people, shooting from the bushes or woods along the side of the road. In turn, Union soldiers made life miserable for the families of the Rangers."[4]

Before the arrival of Blazer's Scouts, the Federals employed something akin to a scorched-earth policy to combat the bushwhackers. One Union officer described laying the torch to the homes of suspected Rangers: "I was furnished with a list of names of ten or more suspected men. About six miles from camp, I came to the first suspect. He of course, had taken to the bush, but his wife and children were at home. I told her my orders and why the house must be burned. I gave directions to my men to put her furniture on the lawn. Of course, tears flowed like water, and her large flock of children wailed aloud. I continued stony-hearted. The furniture was now out of the house, the supply of meat in the smokehouse was also out and safe from fire when, well!—I marched on and left them weeping. But I had told her if any more bush-whacking took place we would lay the whole country waste."[5]

Instead of winning hearts and minds (which may have been unwinnable since so many men fought for the South), the Union policies steeled resolve, hatred, and a cycle of violence. Within this cauldron, Thurmond's Rangers conducted guerrilla warfare by hiding in safe houses and rallying at a designated point to conduct raids on Federal outposts and units, after which they would melt back into the civilian population to engage in farming and other domestic activities. Intelligence played a vital role. The Thurmond brothers established a series of spies and couriers who would relay Union movements so they could pounce on Federal weak points. One Union officer described the Rangers' tactics: "A little squad from a neighborhood would station themselves on a hill near the roadway where our supply trains would have to pass, the trains always being guarded by a few troops. These rascals would fire on the train, frequently killing or wounding the mules, occasionally hitting a driver. If the troops pursued after them, they could easily elude the troops and perhaps appear again on a hill farther on, on the route."[6]

In addition to raids on supply trains, the irregular unit acted as cavalry in the Confederate Army as the war progressed, often serving under General John Echols, and later were designated the 44th Virginia Cavalry Battalion. Six-foot-four Echols towered over most of his men in both stature and education. A Virginia Military Institute—and Harvard-educated lawyer and member of the House of Delegates before offering his military service to his home state of Virginia, Echols had extensive battle experience before his assignment in Appalachia. The Virginian deployed the Rangers in various activities, such as scouting, conducting reconnaissance, and warning the Confederates of Federal attacks in the area.

"The rules of war do not apply to [Thurmond's Rangers because they were guerrillas] and no mercy was shown them if captured, but the trouble was to capture them,"[7] lamented one officer in the 23rd Ohio. The Scouts were formed for just that purpose.

Forty-three-year-old grizzled veteran Asbe Montgomery joined Blazer's Scouts from Company A of the 9th West Virginia Infantry as a noncommissioned officer in the position of orderly sergeant. The gray-haired six-foot-two veteran commanded respect from his men. He recounted a tense moment one evening in the fall of 1863 at Boyer's Ferry, located on the winding New River. As the Scouts lay resting from an arduous march, a young woman emerged from the woods bounding toward them, yelling that Thurmond and his guerrillas were at her house and had ambushed the Scouts' pickets, killing one and capturing another, and "were coming down on us 'like a thousand of brick' [and] were going to use us up like salt." Not prepared to engage so large a force, Lieutenant Otis ordered Montgomery to move the men down the New River. "I did it double-quick, thinking something was not just right."[8] When they reached a ford, an advance group of ten men crossed and marched up a hill to hold the road until Otis came with the rest of the troops in canoes.*

"We advanced without a word to break the silence, each one once in a while looking at his comrades, showing determination to stand by each other." The newly appointed orderly sergeant encouraged his men, "Now, my brave boys, perhaps we may soon hear a shot from that cruel wretch, and I don't want a man to flinch. Just stand to me, and I will take you through or die with you."[9]

---

* The Scouts, a predecessor to their modern counterparts, were a special operations force, deploying highly maneuverable small boats or canoes to traverse the various rivers in the area.

The men reached their destination, always anticipating an ambush or firefight to commence. Instead, the tension lasted throughout the night as the Scouts continued "to reconnoiter . . . but found no one." Thurmond's Rangers proved elusive. The following day after breakfast, the Scouts returned to camp and searched for their wounded comrade, "as we were rather dubious of going to him in the dark, the night before." They marched to the house and had set half their company on the road "for fear of a surprise" when "suddenly we heard the fun commence," recalled Montgomery.

Like a swarm of locusts, "about 600 Rebs" descended on the Scouts' advanced outpost. As the Union men fell back, Montgomery's men returned fire. Despite the overwhelming odds, the Scouts remained remarkably unscathed as they retreated toward the New River. "But poured the shots into [the Confederates] so hotly that they gave away, so we all got outside of their line; and such skedaddling as we did was not pleasant—over logs, rocks, and through briers,"[10] wrote Montgomery.

These surges of pure terror and adrenaline broke up the monotony of often uneventful stretches in this cat-and-mouse game. Montgomery noted the "wolfish" nature of the Scouts and boasted, "Camp life did not suit these brave and hardy yeomen . . . determined to stand by and fight for in every emergency. I believe some of them would travel and undergo any hardships to get a crack at a Johnny."[11]

By traveling lightly and swiftly, the American commandos effectively morphed into the role of guerrillas to hunt the Thurmonds. The Scouts quickly adapted to their environment, mastering it. They marched night and day, hoping to "pounce upon [Thurmond] 'like a cat on a rabbit,'"[12] remembered Montgomery.

Montgomery and the Scouts lived life on a razor's edge, as he eloquently expressed in a book he later wrote: "In fact, my reader, you who have never been in the habit of scouting cannot form an idea how daring a company becomes after being blessed with success for a time; and feeling that your all is at stake, your country, life, and dearest friends, one will rush forward to battle, with gun in hand, and firm nerves, not dreading even death, though staring you in the face oftentimes. I have seen our brave boys, when in pursuit of the enemy, in full stretch, straining every nerve to see who would get the first shot at a Johnny."[13] Crack shots utilizing a variety of rifles and carbines, Blazer's Scouts dealt death from a distance, "so sure was their aim that they could knock a squirrel out of any tree, every pop, and I have often watched them holding on a Reb, at long range, as steadily as a marksman at a target, and seldom failed to bring him down."[14]

As Blazer and his Scouts continued to pioneer tactics to combat Southern irregulars in West Virginia, Mosby's Rangers continued to expand and gain strength in Virginia.

9. LEWIS POWELL

More men continued to flock to Mosby. In the tiny remote village of
Scuffleburg nestled in a hollow of the Blue Ridge Mountains, difficult to
access but perfect for partisan activities, Mosby formed Company B and
selected officers and its commander, Captain William R. "Billy" Smith.
He "was no ordinary man." A veteran of the Black Horse cavalry, Smith
was an ardent Rebel whose father was a wealthy and powerful plantation
owner in Fauquier County. Smith's men "idolized him." He was charismatic
and convivial, and "his conversation was of that frank and generous nature
which captivated everyone who met him,"[1] remembered one Ranger.

On an autumn day in October 1863, a tall, well-built, dashing young
private with striking blue eyes joined Company B. Lewis Thornton Powell,[2] a nineteen-year-old Floridian, had been wounded at Gettysburg and
admitted to a Union field hospital with a gunshot wound in his right wrist
and a broken arm. Using his charm and presence, the wounded prisoner of
war managed to wangle a position as an orderly. His outward appearance
belied an inner "ferocity of character."[3] It is suspected that after befriend-
ing and likely seducing a sympathetic secessionist nurse, Powell acquired a
Yankee uniform and escaped once he was transferred to West's Buildings
Hospital in Baltimore.

The nurse Powell developed a relationship with was Margaret "Mag-
gie" Branson. Branson's father was an operative for the Confederate Secret
Service.[4] Their boarding house doubled as a safe house for the clandestine
service, the shadowy organization that specialized in spy craft, election
interference, communications, sabotage, and other forms of unconventional
warfare. Very little is known about Powell's involvement with the group at
this time, but within days, the masquerading Union soldier made his way
to Scuffleburg and Mosby. Powell had a flair for escape and kept his cool

during dicey situations. Once when the house he was boarding in as one of Mosby's Rangers was surrounded by Union cavalry, Powell "blacked his faced with lampblack and walked out of the house."[5] A complex soul, Powell also had a softer side; he was generous and liked children and animals. But his ruthlessness and effectiveness allegedly earned Powell the moniker "Lewis the Terrible."

The Rangers continued to expand, and by the end of the fall, Mosby added an additional company, Company C, commanded by William H. Chapman. As his numbers grew and his raids expanded, so did Union determination to stop Mosby.

10. "Lurk like Wild Creatures in the Darkness"

Everything war related in contested West Virginia during the fall of 1863 revolved around railroads, supply lines, and minerals. One of the costliest railroads to construct at the time, the Virginia and Tennessee, stretched over 200 miles from Lynchburg northwest to Bristol and included a branch to Saltville, Virginia. Five tunnels, over 230 bridges, and nineteen depots lined the route. The South depended on this vital artery to move troops and crucial supplies such as salt, lead, and saltpeter, which flowed from Confederate factories and mines in western Virginia.

Although established in the 1820s, American railroads came into their own during the Civil War, and their use in transporting troops and supplies from one front to another was part of what made this conflict the first modern war. While the South had much less to work with, having only about a third of the rail lines of the North and limited manufacturing capacity, its leaders realized the potential of trains to move troops and supplies sooner than their Union counterparts. The Confederates worked miracles with what they had, starting with the first major contest of the Civil War, the Battle of Bull Run in July 1861, where they used rail lines to move their limited number of troops quickly from unthreatened areas in Virginia. The North soon recognized the crucial nature of the rail lines. Consequently, ripping up track or restoring destroyed lines became a top priority, and, here, Jessie Scouts would play a crucial role.

Severing the vital Virginia and Tennessee rail line proved more difficult than initially thought. It took the Union three separate attempts to reach the railroad. General William Woods Averell led the first raid in August 1863, which targeted the track along with a rather unusual objective:

a library brimming with law books located in Lewisburg, West Virginia. Averell's superiors deemed that the tomes could be of use to the judiciary of the new state.

Renowned for his skills on horseback and as an experienced Indian fighter, Averell also held various patents after the war, including one that pioneered asphalt pavement, making him a wealthy man. The thirty-one-year-old Union commander and expert drillmaster could also whip men into shape. The brigade that he commanded in West Virginia needed it.

After the crushing Union defeat at Chancellorsville in April of that year, in which Lee's badly outnumbered army outmaneuvered General Joseph Hooker's Army of the Potomac, the Union commander looked for scapegoats. He blamed Averell, a Democrat surrounded by Republicans in his chain of command, for his slow performance on a raid on Confederate lines of communication. Averell was relieved of command and exiled to the backwater of West Virginia. Here the Union high command assigned him the 4th Separate Brigade and the daunting task of converting a significant portion of its infantry into cavalry to counter enemy raids on the crucial Union B&O Railroad that ran through West Virginia and required protection at all costs.

In April 1863, Confederates disrupted the line and destroyed a massive amount of war materiel in what would be known as the Jones-Imboden Raid, whose added purpose was to derail the momentum toward statehood in western Virginia, because it was unclear on which side of the slavery issue the area would fall. Snail-like Union foot infantry could not keep up with fast-moving mounted raiders as they pillaged, burned, blew up a railroad bridge, and made off with thousands of cattle and horses. After the raid, Union commanders begged Washington, DC, for additional cavalry to counter future Confederate attacks. There was none to be had—Union horsemen had to be created from the infantry. One officer remembered the pitiful condition of the troops Averell had to transform: "When General Averell assumed command of these troops, he found himself with a brigade of loyal, courageous fighters, scattered through a dozen counties, but who knew little of discipline, or of knowledge of regimental or brigade maneuvers—scantily supplied with approved arms, equipments, clothing, etc. They were inefficient for any reliable defense of the country, and the utter hopelessness of any effort to take the offensive our experience had so recently demonstrated."[1] Luckily, Averell would inherit from the previous commander of the brigade, Major General Robert Huston Milroy, the Jessie Scouts, who acted as Milroy's eyes and ears. Arch Rowand, James White, and the remaining Jessie Scouts, who furnished priceless battlefield intelligence to Milroy, would now give William Averell the edge in battle against his opponents.

Horses and men required lengthy training, but within weeks, Averell, who had a reputation to resurrect, pulled off a minor miracle of organization. Led by the Jessie Scouts, Averell's force left their encampment on August 3 with about 1,500 cavalry, mounted infantry, and a battery of light artillery. Traversing mountains and rugged terrain, they routed a force of Confederates led by Stonewall Jackson's cousin, William L. "Mudwall" Jackson, and destroyed a Rebel saltpeter factory located in a cave. As the men neared White Sulphur Springs, West Virginia, the present-day site of the Greenbriar Hotel, Averell's men ran into a dug-in force led by Colonel George S. Patton, grandfather of the famous World War II general-to-be. The two sides battled for two days starting on August 26, until Averell ran low on ammunition and withdrew. Felling trees behind them to slow the pursuing Confederates, they rode hard back to base "and were mercilessly bushwhacked [by Thurmond's Rangers among others] going into camp weary and sore."[2] The force sustained twenty-seven killed and nearly 200 wounded and captured—costly considering their size—and the law books remained firmly in Confederate hands.

Three months later, not to be outgunned again, Averell set out for the books and the railroad a second time, but with a much larger force. In the first week of November 1863, Averell left Beverly, West Virginia, with Rowand, White, and the Jessie Scouts in Confederate uniforms in advance of about 4,000 Union cavalry and infantry with the mission to march to Dublin, Virginia, and destroy depots, track, and the Virginia and Tennessee Railroad bridge across the New River. The Jessie Scouts relied on speed and deception to lead the raid. Death was always near. "I had a man killed on either side of me,"[3] recalled Rowand. By the very nature of their hazardous duty, most Jessie Scouts would not live to see the war's end.

The attack on the railroad came from multiple forces: Averell's brigade was to link up with Brigadier General Alfred N. Duffié's force, with the Scouts led by Richard Blazer and Otis out front. Duffié was one of the more colorful characters in the Union Army. The French-born officer, a poster boy for stolen valor, made several spurious claims, including that he earned the Légion d'honneur, which he wore in several photographs. Unfortunately, the Union Army did not know he had been tried by the French army in absentia and sentenced to ten years for desertion. Duffié then fled to America, where he married a wealthy aristocratic woman he met in France while she was serving as a nurse.[4] Through her family connections, he secured a position as a colonel in the Union cavalry.

Blazer's men forged ahead of Duffié's force, reconnoitering and determining the location of the Confederates. "It fell to our lot to take the advance all the way, which was just to our hands. We distinguished ourselves by marching and routing Thurmond," Asbe Montgomery recalled.[5] According to one contemporary source, Blazer's Scouts stalked Thurmond's Confederates: "Like the Nomads, [the Scout] reckoned time by nights and not days; he lurks like a wild creature in the darkness when it is in his heart all the while to stand forth like a man in the day."[6]

The Scouts charged into Lewisburg and captured several prisoners and a piece of artillery as they clashed with Confederate troops commanded by Brigadier General John Echols. Despite capturing Lewisburg, the Federals had Echols' force to contend with, and the mission to capture the library and law books had to wait. Before advancing further, the Federals set up camp outside Hillsboro, West Virginia, about thirty miles north of Lewisburg, in the shadow of Echols' Confederate defenses, which bristled above on the rugged face of Droop Mountain. The Confederates managed to maintain the high ground through the morning but, by the afternoon, were overwhelmed by Union infantry who fought their way up the side of the mountain, attacking the Confederates' left flank and forcing Patton and the rest of Echols' troops to retreat south into Virginia. However, the combination of rugged terrain, his burden of prisoners, and foul weather forced Averell to abort the raid without accomplishing his principal mission of severing the vital railway.

After the battle, the weather turned bitter, and it snowed on the long, exhausting westward march back toward Fayetteville. "Cold, snowy morning. All ready to move by daylight, boys anxious to reach camp which is ten miles, slowly traveling, cross by Sewell Mt. . . . Boys [were] never more anxious being worried and having but little sleep during the whole trip. Many of them have worn out their shoes and are barefooted,"[7] Union soldier James Ireland recorded in his November 10, 1863, diary entry.

Despite their success, Blazer and Otis' immediate commanding officer, Colonel Carr B. White, disbanded the Union special operators, likely because skilled men were in short supply and needed in their respective units. But the Scouts' absence from hazardous duty did not last long.

Strategically, the North's approach in the fall of 1863 was about to change. Following the Federals' defeat at Chickamauga, Georgia, on September 18–20, the Army of the Cumberland, under the command of General William Starke Rosecrans, fell back north to the strategic railhead of Chattanooga, in southeastern Tennessee. Hoping to starve out the Federals, the Confederate Army of Tennessee, under the command of Braxton Bragg, besieged the city.

In October 1863, General Ulysses S. Grant was handed command of the disjointed and recently defeated Union forces. Determined to hold Chattanooga, he replaced Rosecrans, who had planned to withdraw from the city, with Major General George Henry Thomas. Grant understood the strategic importance of Chattanooga as a gateway into the heart of the South and a jumping-off point for an attack on Atlanta. Supplying the Union Army became a major factor, and Grant devised a novel solution: the "Cracker Line." Thomas' troops counterattacked and secured a bridgehead on the Confederate side of the Tennessee River. Engineers laid a pontoon bridge over the water, allowing supplies to flow into Chattanooga over a wagon road from a Union supply depot at Bridgeport, in far northern Alabama.

After securing his lines of communication, Grant broke the Confederate siege through a series of bold engagements. The Federals struck after learning that the Confederates had peeled off troops from Chattanooga to attack Knoxville, then in Union control. Shortly after Gettysburg, and despite Longstreet's objection, Lee had dispatched Longstreet's Corps from the Army of Northern Virginia, where it played a key role in the Battle of Chickamauga. Despite Longstreet's objections, who marched north to Knoxville: "We thus expose both to failure, and really take no chance to ourselves of great result," the Confederate general had protested.[8] Union troops then seized the critical high ground at Orchard Knob outside Chattanooga. At the same time, Brigadier General William Tecumseh Sherman maneuvered near the strong Confederate entrenchments on Missionary Ridge, seemingly impregnable high ground overlooking the city. The same day, a Union force of three divisions moved on the Confederates holding the rocky crags of Lookout Mountain, which they overran when Bragg decided to withdraw his troops to secure Missionary Ridge.

On November 25, an attack on the Confederates' right flank made little progress, and Grant ordered Thomas to secure and clear the rifle pits at the base of Missionary Ridge but not advance up the steep mount. After taking the Confederate rifle pits, the Union troops were sitting ducks taking Confederate fire from above. Out of necessity and without orders, the Union troops stormed the ridge in a dramatic assault—one of the few that would succeed against an entrenched enemy holding the high ground during the war. By 4:30 p.m., the center of the Confederate line collapsed, and Bragg's army fell back to Chickamauga Creek and later Dalton, Georgia. Upon hearing of the victory, Lincoln congratulated Grant and urged him to save Burnside: "Well done. Many thanks to all. Remember Burnside."[9]

General Ambrose Everett Burnside commanded the Federal troops at Knoxville in eastern Tennessee, holding out against Longstreet's siege with limited rations. Relieving Burnside became the priority. Jessie Scouts would play a key role in the operations to assist the Union commander.

11. THE SALEM RAID: "LIFE IN ONE HAND AND SEEMING DISHONOR IN THE OTHER"

Desperate to alleviate pressure on Burnside from Longstreet's siege of Knoxville, the Union high command tasked Averell with severing the supply line and interrupting the flow of troops and supplies to the Confederate general, and distracting the Confederates by drawing Southern forces from the siege to defend their supply lines. During the first weeks of December 1863, Averell was ordered to attack the Virginia and Tennessee Railroad once again. The raid had strategic significance[1]—and the Jessie Scouts would lead the advance.

Averell devised a brilliant, complex stratagem involving four different commands raiding multiple enemy territories, three of them distracting the Confederates while Averell's force of mounted men attacked the main railroad at Salem, Virginia. Deep in hostile Southern territory teeming with irregulars and Confederate cavalry in the middle of winter, the men would need to make the ride for their lives and escape across some of the most rugged territory in the United States. Deception, luck, and grit had to align perfectly for the plan to succeed.

Averell ordered Colonel Augustus Moor to march toward Frankford, West Virginia, and approach Lewisburg from the north. General Jeremiah Sullivan and Colonel Joseph Thoburn would threaten Staunton, Virginia, in the Shenandoah Valley, which contained warehouses of Confederate supplies. At the same time, Brigadier General Eliakim P. Scammon was to move out of Kanawha Valley and seize Lewisburg once again, and potentially the law library, by December 12. However, after the earlier Union attempts to seize the law books, the Confederates had moved the tomes to Richmond. The Union command assumed the books would be invaluable to West Virginia's new government. Through the complex nature of the plan, Averell hoped to keep the Confederates guessing as to his true objectives.

The forty-seven-year-old Scammon sported an Amish-like chin-curtain beard and was a seasoned army veteran. The former professor of mathematics required the skills of Richard Blazer to conduct a reconnaissance of Lewisburg, and he cut orders to reconstitute the recently disbanded Scouts: "Send Lieutenant Blazer to Lewisburg to learn the enemy's force and position," he wrote to his staff. "Let him take such men as he wants & do the work quickly and thoroughly—if he succeeds, he shall be rewarded."[2]

Through Scammon's mandate, Blazer quickly reorganized his unit with handpicked men from the 12th and 91st Ohio and 9th West Virginia—men he previously commanded—and new recruits. On foot, Blazer's men, with their own Jessie Scouts out front, would lead Scammon's force. The former joint commander of the Scouts, Harrison Gray Otis, returned to the infantry and led Company A of the 12th Ohio on the raid.

On a freezing wintry morning in early December, all the units in Averell's raid advanced. Eighteen-year-old Archibald Rowand, Old Clayton, James White, and the remaining original Jessie Scouts spearheaded Averell's force from New Creek, West Virginia, located not far from Cumberland, Maryland. The Union general added firepower to the Jessie Scouts' arsenal, as he wrote, "The head of my column was preceded by vigilant scouts, armed with repeating rifles, mounted upon fleet horses, who permitted no one to go ahead of them."[3]

Bone-chilling wind and sleet pelted Rowand and his partner for several hours as they rode toward a creek in the middle of nowhere in West Virginia. Averell had assigned the two Jessie Scouts to conduct a reconnaissance of the area and locate any enemy troops that could impede the unfolding Federal raid. About six miles from the creek, a swarm of Confederate bullets answered the question. Lead tore into Rowand's horse, killing it; other bullets slew his partner riding next to him. Evading the Confederates, Rowand escaped on foot and ran back toward Averell's advancing raiding force. The incident was one of the countless that epitomized the hazardous duty of scouting. Back with the main force, the Jessie Scout made a full report of what transpired to one of Averell's staff officers, found a new horse, and readied himself for another mission.

The precious tactical intelligence furnished by the Scouts became the lifeblood on which crucial decisions flowed. When a raiding force moved behind the lines, it could be ambushed, flanked, or cut off by the Confederates at any time. For some reason, however, Averell initially believed Rowand had submitted an incorrect report of what transpired. With lives at stake, there was no room for error, and the enraged general ordered the West Virginian mustered out of the Jessie Scouts and back to his regiment.

When summoned in front of the general to explain himself, Rowand did not stand down and "wouldn't have it that way." He informed the general of what had happened and that the staff officer to whom he reported had mixed up some facts. Coolly, he told Averell, "The best evidence is you will find my dead horse there and find my partner's body."[4] Another Scout who witnessed Rowand's initial report was brought forward and cleared up the matter. Rowand then told Averell that if he wanted to retain him as a Scout, he would only report to the general in command directly—it would be how Rowand operated for the rest of the war. The following day, Rowand's dead horse and his partner's body were found where Rowand had said they would be.

With the incident behind him, Rowand, White, and the other Jessie Scouts probed deeper in front of Averell's men, sometimes dispatching unsuspecting Rebels or capturing them. Despite Rowand's ambush, the Confederates did not know the full extent or whereabouts of Averell's raiding force. Near the summit of Sweet Springs Mountain in West Virginia, the Jessie Scouts captured a Rebel quartermaster who assured Averell "our advance was unknown yet to the enemy."[5]

The muddy mountain trails and swollen streams proved impassable for the supply train, which could go no farther in these conditions. Many of the horses were poorly shod. Supply troops issued rations, forage, and ammunition to the men, and only the able bodied and well mounted pushed forward. To avoid detection, the Scouts led Averell's troops through the mountainous terrain. At the top of a mountain, "a sublime spectacle was presented to us. Seventy miles to the eastward the Peaks of Otter reared their summits above the Blue Ridge, and all the space between was filled with a billowing ocean of hills and mountains, while behind us the great Alleghenies, coming from the north with the grandeur of innumerable tints, swept past and faded in the southern horizon,"[6] Averell wrote. Hours earlier, the Union general had received word that Scammon, and Blazer's Scouts, had entered Lewisburg.

In the vanguard of Scammons' force, over a dozen of Blazer's men incorporated the tactics of the Jessie Scouts and wore Confederate uniforms to gain an advantage on their adversaries and pass in and out of Confederate lines. Several of Blazer's men had served in Milroy's Jessie Scouts before joining Blazer, bringing with them the Jessie Scouts' tradecraft and tactics.[7] Being a Scout required "the coolest courage, and the clearest head and quickest wit. He passes the enemy's lines, sits at his campfire, penetrates even the presences of the commanding General,"[8] recalled one contemporary historian. Each operation honed the Scouts' experience and tactics as the unit continued to evolve.

Despite their stealth and guile, Blazer's men soon found themselves in a full-blown skirmish with Philip Thurmond's guerrillas on Big Sewell Mountain. After the skirmish, the Rebel partisans realized that Blazer's men were just the tip of a larger spear and quickly melted away. Thurmond reported back to John Echols that a large Union force was advancing on Lewisburg. Echols wisely decided not to contest them directly.

After Blazer's Scouts took the town, a Union report recorded that on December 14, they "reached Lewisburg Saturday, 2 P.M. Duffié in advance with Lieutenant Blazer's Company, Ninety-first. Twelfth and Ninety-first skirmishing in the front. Hayes was with the Fifth West Virginia, a part of the Twenty-third, and [Carr B.] White, with the Twelfth and the Ninety-first, and two sections of the artillery, following. Enemy's scouts [Thurmond's Rangers] assailed our skirmishers [Blazer] on Big Sewell and kept it up from point to point to Greenbrier River, with few casualties."[9]

No longer a Scout but now in command of Company A of the 12th Ohio, Lieutenant Otis also clashed with Thurmond on December 14, 1863, at Blue Sulphur Road near Meadow Bluff, West Virginia. "[I] discovered Rebels lurking in the woods in the rear of my post. I immediately made preparations to receive them, and the post was at once attacked by what afterward proved to be Thurmond's guerrillas, who fired from the cover of trees and bushes, killing 2 and wounding 4 of my command. I promptly returned the fire and very soon drove the Rebels. They retreated through the woods out of sight, leaving behind 1 killed and 1 wounded."[10] Despite the matter-of-fact nature of his report, Otis barely escaped with his life. Several men in his company deserted in the middle of the firefight.

Averell's plan started to unravel. With reports flowing in from men like Otis, General Scammon, fearing that his rear was being overwhelmed by sizable Confederate forces and Thurmond's Rangers, quickly left Lewisburg. Scammon was supposed to hold Lewisburg and keep the Confederates distracted and pinned down while he waited for Moore's forces, who also turned back upon finding that Scammon had retreated. Instead of focusing on Scammon, Echols and other Southern troops could now concentrate on the real threat: Averell's raiders.

Scammon's retreat through the mountains turned into pure misery, Otis recalled: "While crossing Little and Big Sewell Mountains, a blinding snowstorm drove into the faces of the troops, and a piercing cold wind chilled the very marrow of our bones. We bivouacked in the snow on the summit of Big Sewell Mountain, spending a miserable, sleepless night."[11]

After resting his horses and men, Averell received a dispatch telling him Scammon had abandoned Lewisburg. The dashing yet cautious New Yorker nonetheless ordered his men to mount up and put his plan back in motion. With the Jessie Scouts up front, Averell's force rode and marched through rough terrain. Weather made the operation even more treacherous. "This raid was to be attempted in Midwinter, with all the chances of mountainous storms, frosts and snow, as well as swelling floods, against us," wrote Captain J. M. Rife of the 7th West Virginia Cavalry. In the midst of their journey through the sparsely inhabited, dense wilderness, the men suddenly saw signs of civilization: a light from a cabin window shone through the trees. Rife approached, tied up his horse, and entered the cabin, finding a couple and several children by the end of their bed. After the soldier identified himself as a Yankee, the man "looked at me to his heart's content," then asked, "Stranger, whar is your horns?" The woman then responded, "Didn't I tell ye they're human critters like the rest of us." When the officer asked who told him Yankees had horns, he answered, "The men that came round making war speeches and recruiting for the Rebel army!"[12]

Advancing over the mountains, the Scouts later stumbled upon a wedding party. They surrounded the revelers, capturing all, including the bride and groom—a Confederate soldier named John Starks. After the ravenous Union soldiers inhaled the wedding feast, leaving only a small bottle of vinegar behind on the table, the force marched on, taking their prisoners of war with them. When she realized they were taking her groom, the bride insisted on going as well. "She fell into line and marched on and on, in the cold and rain and mud, keeping up with the command until we reached Salem," while the young soldiers "annoy[ed] the poor bride by asking all sorts of questions." Not to be outdone, the feisty bride "often fired back at them so vigorously that one shot would sometimes balance quite an account." Remarkably, the raiders encountered yet another feisty Southern bride when they reached an "old-time Virginia hotel" in White Sulphur Springs. "She was credited with kicking a Yankee soldier down the steps of the house, while he was seeking admission to get a share of the good things usually provided for such occasions."[13]

Dressed in butternut, the Jessie Scouts were able to capture enemy pickets and a Confederate dispatch rider with orders from Major General Samuel Jones, who was based in Staunton. This priceless information was thus never delivered to the telegraph operator, leaving the Confederates blind to the actual whereabouts of Averell's force heading toward the Virginia and Tennessee Railroad depot in Salem, Virginia. By nightfall, however, the Confederates knew where he was headed. The railroad was in the "utmost danger." General Jones sent a message to Richmond: "I cannot throw any of my force here in time to save it. You may be able to do so if you will send a force to check Averell on the railroad."[14]

As the first rays of dawn stretched over the countryside, Jessie Scouts encountered their enemy counterparts, Confederate scouts attempting to find the whereabouts of Averell's command. Bringing them as captives back to Averell, they learned that units commanded by Fitzhugh Lee were dispatched from Charlottesville and a train loaded with Confederate troops from Lynchburg was approaching Salem. The Union commander ordered 350 men and two three-inch guns to meet the threat.

Riding at breakneck speed, Averell's advance troops rushed into Salem, cut the telegraph wires, tore up track near the depot, and set up guns to ambush the trainload of Confederate reinforcements. "A shot was fired at it from one of the guns, which missed; a second went through the train diagonally, which caused it to retire." The engineer threw the train in reverse. "A third and last shot hastened its movements." Around 10 a.m., the bulk of Averell's forces now entered the town and went to work destroying the track and Confederate infrastructure. Groups of men were also sent miles up and down the rail line. They torched bridges and destroyed as much track as possible by removing the rails from the ties, creating massive bonfires, then placing the metal rails on top and attempting to twist them once they were heated. "Five bridges were burned, and the track torn up and destroyed as much as possible in six hours. The 'yanks' [hand levers] with which we had provided ourselves proved too weak to twist the rails, and efforts were made to bend them, by heating the centers, with but partial success."[15]

Now well over a hundred miles behind enemy lines, and with the Confederates fully alerted, Averell later reported that six Confederate commands attempted to block his retreat north. Once again, the Jessie Scouts would help pull off a near-miraculous escape. At Averell's request, the special operators found and hauled in a local doctor, Oscar Wylie, who knew the neighborhood from his rounds through the countryside and presented him to the general.

Averell employed both kind words and a gun in compelling the doctor to guide them. First, he appealed to Wylie's pocketbook, offering him the hefty sum of $500 in gold and conveyance of his family to the North, knowing he would be condemned as a traitor for his service. Wylie flatly refused, prompting Averell to bring out his watch and informed the doctor he had "five minutes to choose between life and death." After a tense ticking of the clock, the doctor succumbed. When asked later by a family friend if he would have shot* the doctor, Averell answered, "Indeed I would, madam."[16]

After Wylie rendered his services to the Scouts, with Confederates still swarming the area hunting the Union raiders, the Jessie Scouts fortuitously found an obscure trail that allowed the command to march literally parallel to Mudwall Jackson's troops without being detected. As the Jessie Scouts and Averell's men raced toward the bridges at Covington, Virginia, that spanned the swollen, raging Jackson River, Confederate newspapers

---

* In fact, the Confederates did brand the doctor who received the $500 in gold from Averell a traitor for his service to the Union. He faded from history after posting bail upon being arrested for murder in Charleston, West Virginia, following the war. He absconded from justice, failing to show up for his trial, and was never to be seen again.

speculated as to the position of Averell's command and opined that the rivers would be unpassable and that he would be severely punished for his temerity and one of the deepest raids in their territory.

Averell kept the campfires lit after they left as a ruse to throw off their pursuers as they continued their desperate ride through Confederate territory. He also sent a detachment of men off in another direction to deceive his enemy. The Confederates set several traps on the bridges in the area, the crucial chokepoints enabling life-and-death egress over the swollen rivers.

Reaching the Island Ford Bridge at Covington, the Jessie Scouts found it miraculously still intact but surrounded by a small party of Confederates prepared to torch the vital wooden structure. In an incredible stroke of luck, however, a single Rebel rider approached the bridge, and the Jessie Scouts asked him where he was going, to which he replied unsuspectingly, "I am going to Colonel Jackson with a dispatch from General Jones."[17] The intercepted dispatch contained the orders to destroy the bridge immediately. Upon reading it, Averell ordered his men to charge ahead. They moved forward carefully at first so as not to be detected, but as their enemies realized the situation, "what a clatter of hooves on the wooden floorboards, and how the horse crowded on the front line!" one Union officer recalled. "I looked for a plunge through the bridge into the waters of the furious stream, for I expected the floor would be torn up at the other end. Fortunately, the floor was all right, the bridge strong, and the enemy, under the command of Major Lady, very kind to give way so that we made a safe landing on solid ground and were in possession of the bridge."[18]

Averell quickly marched his command across the bridge and waited for the baggage train carrying wounded men and prisoners of war, including the Confederate groom captured days earlier, along with their rear guard, the 14th Pennsylvania Cavalry Regiment, all of which lagged several miles behind. The Federal raiders had fought and marched over 150 miles through mountains in snow and rain, on foot, in the most rugged terrain in the United States. Somehow, they would have to traverse approximately the same distance and avoid the Confederates to the safety of a Union garrison. Thousands of Confederates desperately combed the area for Averell. "Not less than 12,000 men were maneuvered to effect my capture,"[19] wrote the general in his official report. Not willing to risk his entire command,

Averell made the heart-wrenching decision to sacrifice his rear guard and torched the bridge to prevent the Confederates from pursuing him.

When the 14th Pennsylvania and other members of the baggage train realized their situation, they burned their wagons, including their rations and other supplies, to lighten their burden. With thousands of Confederates bearing down on them, they feverishly searched for another place to ford the ice-filled swollen Jackson River. The Pennsylvanians pressed a local civilian into service, demanding he show them a suitable place to cross. The first mounted soldier who rode into the whitewater at the indicated point was immediately engulfed by the current and drowned. Furious at the treachery, the Union cavalry threw the local man into the river. He also succumbed to the raging water. At the point of a gun and under threat of torching her house, the Union soldiers compelled another civilian, a woman, to direct them to a crossing point two miles upstream.

In the meantime, a rider from Mudwall Jackson's force under a white flag of truce approached the men with the message that they were surrounded and presented them with an opportunity to surrender. Word of the potential capitulation spread among the regiment and someone cried out, "The 14th Pennsylvania never surrenders!"[20] The commander of the 14th officially responded, "I admit that I am surrounded by your superior forces . . . even under these circumstances . . . I will sacrifice my own life and that of every true and brave soldier under my command before I surrender to a coward and a traitor!"[21] The Confederates tell a different story, that a lack of discipline on the part of Southern troops allowed the Yankees to escape: "[The 14th] regiment hoisted a white flag three times and yet escaped; that instead of gathering up [Union] stragglers the [Confederate] soldiers were running about plundering and gathering up property abandoned by the enemy, and that almost every crime has been perpetrated by the command from burglary down to rape."[22] The distracted Confederates bought the Pennsylvanians precious time to find a fording place. "It was a dismal scene. . . . Low laden clouds overhead; in front, a roaring swishing torrent, carrying drift-ice; behind, and for all we knew, on all sides of us, the human enemy."[23]

"Volunteers!" Shouts went out for the first men to take the plunge.[24] Several men entered the swirling icy water on their mounts. Struggling against the turbulent water, the first man and his horse made it across and received a cheer from the men still on the bank. The rest of the force followed. Several men were swept away by the current, including groom John Starks. Separated from Averell, the 14th Pennsylvania Cavalry and other stragglers made it to yet another bridge burned by Averell and thus had to ford another treacherous river. But without Confederate troops directly on their heels, the men crossed safely. Once the last stragglers in the 14th crossed at Covington, Confederate commands gave up the chase. In terrible shape, barefoot, suffering from frozen limbs and feet, starving, without sleep, and under constant duress from the threat of attack, they would have a long, exhausting march back to Beverly, West Virginia. In uniforms reduced to rags and often shoeless, the men were remarkably expected to replace their worn-out gear using personal funds. Averell defended his men and requested the miserly War Department furnish them with new kit. The department charitably, at least in the eyes of the government, acquiesced and made an exception to their policy.

The 400-mile march in twenty days, mostly in hostile Confederate territory, exacted a high human toll and decimated the men's constitutions for decades after. Total casualties were 138, including 120 captured.[25] Of the captured men, only a handful would survive the horrors and brutal conditions in Libby Prison and Andersonville. Confederate general Jones minimized the raid's impact: "The railroad was rather improved than injured by the raid . . . as the few small bridges burned were in such condition that they were scarcely safe and would require rebuilding very soon."[26] In fact, the mission successfully destroyed countless supplies and shut down the vital supply artery for more than two weeks while the Confederacy struggled to repair it. Averell's superiors deemed the raid a great success, "highly satisfactory and important cutting off [the Confederacy's] most important line of communication."[27]

Averell's raid may well have contributed to breaking Longstreet's siege of Knoxville, as it cut off, at least temporarily, a vital source of supply and egress. After the collapse at Missionary Ridge, Bragg ordered Longstreet to return to the Army of Tennessee, which had now retreated to Georgia. Longstreet demurred and replied that he would maintain the siege on Knoxville as long as possible to prevent Burnside and Grant from linking up and destroying the Army of Tennessee. After failing to break through Burnside's lines at Knoxville with a major assault on one of the city's forts,

Longstreet, on December 4, 1863, abandoned his eighteen-day siege when Grant sent Sherman and a force of 25,000 to relieve the Union forces inside the city. With the Southern army retreating from Chattanooga, both sides held off on major operations during the winter of 1863–1864. However, unlike the conventional forces, Mosby's Rangers would remain active that winter.

12. CRIMSON SNOW

Mosby's latest nemesis emerged in the final days of 1863. About eighty members of Cole's Cavalry[1] led by bugler-turned-officer Captain Albert M. Hunter entered Mosby's Confederacy on December 30 from their base camp nestled on the crags of Loudoun Heights, a few miles from Harpers Ferry. The Union troops hoped to deal a crippling blow to Mosby. Riding over forty miles through sleet and snow and passing through the country hamlets of Hillsboro and Waterford, they halted in Middleburg, where Hunter and his men camped for the evening. During the night, the Northerner experienced a night terror and premonition: "We were in a fight and that a large body of the enemy surrounded us and completely routed us and captured many."[2] Fighting off the ominous sign, Captain Hunter rose the following day, and his command rode to the heart of Mosby's Confederacy: Rectortown.

Hunter was an officer in Cole's Cavalry, or the 1st Regiment Potomac Home Brigade, named after its commander, a brave and seasoned warrior, twenty-nine-year-old Major Henry Cole. The regiment consisted of men from western Maryland; Loudoun County, Virginia; and Pennsylvania. They were "farmers', planters' sons, mainly in good circumstance, who owned good horses."[3] In a deeply divided state such as Maryland, many of them faced hateful discourse, derision, and even physical violence from their neighbors, but as one member of the unit declared, "I loved my country and flag better than my State or section."[4]

Against a dull, gray sky, snow fell as Hunter's men, braving freezing temperatures, cautiously entered an eerily empty Rectortown. Along the way, Mosby's men intimidated their quarry through basic psychological warfare: they "rode around and were seen on every little hill and knoll,"[5] watching the Federals like hawks. A Ranger rendezvous had been scheduled that day, but word got out: "Don't go to Rectortown it is full [of] Yankees."[6] To the invading Union troops, a Ranger seemed to lurk behind every tree and hill. As Hunter scanned the largely deserted town, his men ran out a few Rangers who did not get the word as the troopers occupied Rectortown. Meanwhile, the recently minted commander of Mosby's Company B, Captain Billy Smith, collected nearly three dozen Rangers and went after the Union troopers.

Outgunned and deep in hostile territory, Hunter started the long journey back to Loudoun Heights when he noticed "several blue-coated men riding along." To gain an advantage, deceive their opponents, and approach within pistol range, against the current rules of war, Mosby's men often wore Union uniforms. Hunter continued, "We had not gone a half of a mile when the rear guard notified me that a large force was coming up."[7]

Smith ambushed Hunter at Five Points, a junction where five country lanes converge about four miles from Rectortown. Forming a line of battle, the Union troopers occupied a strong position and fired their carbines at the oncoming horsemen, but many of the cartridges were damp from the inclement weather and misfired. Smith rode in front of his troops and ordered his men to charge to gain "the bulge."

Screaming as they charged into the Union flanks and rear, the Rangers unleashed a torrent of lead from their Colts. Smith's second charge broke Hunter's men. Hunter later remembered his premonition the night before, "dreaming a dream that was realized the next day."[8] The Rangers routed the Federals, "killing, wounding, and capturing 57."[9] In the melee, Hunter was unhorsed and lay wounded and bruised on the ground. Two Rangers with empty pistols stood over him and demanded his weapons. The Union officer pointed to his horse and told them his pistols were on the animal, which had bolted away.[10] The Confederates directed him to join the other prisoners they rounded up. As the Rangers turned their backs to look for his horse, the Union captain hid behind a log and covered himself in leaves. He later reflected, "Here I was alone forty miles from camp on foot considerably hurt, and in an enemy's country, and surrounded by the enemy. It was between 3 and 4 o'clock and in less than an hour turned awful cold."[11] A wet snow fell. Deep in enemy territory at sunset, a scene that would have "enraptured the artist or inspired a poet"[12] unfolded as one Ranger described: "Not a cloud broke the blue sky above as the sun was setting in the west behind its fiery curtains. The mountains seem as one vast sheet of ice, and the reflection of the sun's declining rays on the scene was indeed sublime."[13] But Hunter did not have time to appreciate the natural splendor. Miraculously, the cavalry captain was able to hide from roving bands of Rangers and made the forty-mile trek back to Loudoun Heights on foot in the frigid weather. Within days, he once again would come face-to-face with the Rangers.

Fresh off their victory against Hunter, Mosby sought to vanquish Cole and his cavalry once and for all. An opportunity to destroy their nemesis presented itself in the form of ninety-four-pound Frank Stringfellow. The twentysomething scout and favorite of Jeb Stuart claimed to have disguised himself as a Yankee colonel and had dinner with Union general John Sedgwick, and he later spied for the South undercover as a dental assistant in Alexandria, where he was closer to his beautiful fiancée, Emma Green. His narrow escapes and derring-do were legendary and sometimes sounded too good to be true, because they were. As Mosby remembered, "He was a brave soldier, but a great liar."[14] He was also an elite agent in the Confederate Secret Service.

Assigned to Mosby in the fall of 1863, Stringfellow scouted the area around Cole's headquarters, near the base of Loudoun Heights, and identified a weakness in the encampment: "[Cole had] no supports but infantry, which was about a one-half mile off."[15] Based on the scout's intelligence, Mosby gathered some one hundred men and planned a surprise attack on the freezing night of January 9, 1864, in Upperville.

Wrapped in blankets and bundled clothing to stave off the frigid conditions, the group rode toward the northeast to Round Hill and stopped at Ranger Henry Heaton's commodious estate, Woodgrove. Suffering from frostbitten hands and feet, the men warmed themselves in front of a roaring fire and were fed warm food. Heaton typified many of Mosby's men—wealthy and local, they brought an exceptional knowledge of the area, its customs, and safe houses.

The stars shone brightly through a blue-black sky, and a sharp, cold wind bit into the men's faces and extremities. Rangers occasionally dismounted and stomped their frozen feet to ward off the enveloping frostbite. "No sound broke the stillness of night except the dull, heavy tramp of the horses as they trod the snowy path. Fields, roads, and shrubs were alike clothed in the white robes of winter, and it seemed almost a sacrilege against the beauty and holy stillness of the scene to stain those pure garments with the lifeblood of men, be he friend or foe," recalled James Williamson.[16]

About two miles from the enemy camp, Stringfellow and his scouting party joined Mosby. A frontal assault up Harpers Ferry Road straight into Cole's headquarters would have been a bloodbath. Instead, Stringfellow led the band north to the Potomac. They dismounted and led their horses in single file on foot through deep snow on a treacherous steep, narrow mountain trail following the river. The shrill whistle of a train sounded in the distance as the Rangers navigated the path and spotted Union campfires nearby.

About 200 yards from the sleeping, unsuspecting camp, Mosby paused and ordered Stringfellow and a few other men to stealthily capture Cole and his staff, located in a two-story house[17] one hundred yards from the battalion's bivouac area. Instead, "all of my plans were on the eve of consummation when suddenly the party sent with Stringfellow came dashing over the hill toward the camp, yelling and shooting. They made no attempt to secure Cole,"[18] remembered Mosby. Above the din of battle, Mosby then urged his men to charge Captain Smith, and Lieutenant Thomas Turner shouted:

"Charge them, boys! Charge them!"[19]

Mistaking Stringfellow's men for the enemy, the Rangers fired into the charging Confederates. Simultaneously, Mosby's men fired into Cole's tents. Several of Cole's men sheepishly surrendered in their underwear and nightclothes. Others leaped into action, including Captain Hunter, who recalled, "Gunfire open[ed] my eyes, and in an instant a strange noise had me out of my bunk, also ordnance Sergeant O. A. Horner. I jumped out picked up my boots and stepping out of my tent pulled my boots on outside. Major Horner drew his on inside and had not got out before two or three bullets tore through our blankets on the bunk. Men were all around me, what to do. A carbine was fired just at my side with the words 'get off you son of a bitch,' and I recognized the voice of Charles A. Gilson, who had fired at a man on horseback who was unhitching my horse that was tied just behind my tent."[20]

Cole had issued standing orders that if the Confederates attacked the battalion, his men were not to mount a horse so as to more clearly identify the enemy, and to "shoot every man on horseback."[21]

Cole's men directed deadly carbine fire at the mounted Rangers, seeking cover from the various houses and cabins in the encampment. After urging his men on, one of Cole's officers took a devastating wound to his face, losing his left eye. Hunter described the chaotic nature of the melee: "dark objects moving, some by the flash from the discharge of carbines, that was rapid for a few minutes. I do not think the whole thing lasted more than fifteen minutes, and when quiet was restored, it seemed as if an earthquake or some terrible convulsion of nature had swept over us and tore everything all to pieces."[22]

Crimson blood splattered the white snow. Bullets hit Ranger lieutenant "Fighting Tom" Thomas Turner, one of Mosby's original fifteen. He turned to Walter Frankland and said, "I am shot."[23] Mortally wounded, Turner would die several days later. Mosby's close friend and aide, Fountain Beattie, took a ball to the thigh.

A signal gun from Harpers Ferry discharged, indicating Union reinforcements were on the march toward the besieged camp. Faced with mounting casualties, Mosby ordered his men to retire. As the Rangers tried to evacuate their wounded, more went down, including Billy Smith, who tried to save young Charles Paxson after the latter was unhorsed by a hail of bullets. Alone and dying, Paxson stammered, "Are you going to leave me here on the field?"[24]

Smith rode up and tried to save Paxson, but a shot from a carbine ended Smith's life. "The flash from the volley for a moment blinded me and a feeling of thankfulness that we had escaped possessed me, when suddenly [Smith] leaped upright from the saddle and fell on the right side of his horse, his left foot drawing the stirrup over the right side and both of his feet hung in the stirrups with his head on snow,"[25] remembered William R. Chapman. The Ranger officer pulled Smith's dangling body off the stirrups of his horse and placed his corpse in the snow. Mosby later stated in his report that Captain Smith and Lieutenant Turner were "two of the noblest and bravest officers of this army, who thus sealed a life of devotion and of sacrifice to the cause they loved."[26]

Like mist, the Rangers dissolved into the darkness. Captain Hunter remembered, "A moment's reflection brought us to our senses, and a search for the enemy but always gone."[27]

The retreat to Woodgrove was filled with gloom; "sad and sullen silence pervaded our ranks and found expression in every countenance,"[28] as Williamson ruefully remembered. Mosby called it "one of the worst fights."[29] His Rangers lost many men, eight killed and several wounded who, like Smith and Turner, possessed invaluable leadership and experience. The Rangers' strength stemmed from the exceptional skill and bravery of the men, intangible qualities hard to replace. Williamson recalled Mosby's demeanor: "Even the Major, though he usually appeared cold and unyielding, could not conceal his disappointment [tears ran down his face] and keen regret at the result of this enterprise. He knew and felt that he had suffered a loss which could not well be repaired."[30]

At dawn, the Federals surveyed the carnage. "We found Captain Smith, Mosby's dashing leader, dead in front of Captain Corner's tent, another near and a track of blood from behind my tent toward the road and 100 yd. off we found a dead man. I suppose Charles A. Gilson shots did work for him. A number of our men were wounded. Also, several of Mosby's men fell into our hands," Hunter revealed. One of those men was the mortally wounded Ranger Charlie Paxson. In his dying breath, Paxson asked for a member of Cole's command, Samuel McNair. Months earlier Paxson's mother, an ardent Southerner, had cared for the wounded McNair in their family home after he sustained wounds in a raid. After nursing him back to health, Paxson's mother brought McNair back to Cole with an understanding that if her son, who rode with Mosby, needed the same care he would receive it. Hunter remembered that "Paxton [sic] asked for McNair and stated that fact to him. He got all of the kind attention that could be given to him, but his wound was fatal, and in a short time, he died."[31] A promise had been fulfilled on that cold, bloody night in January 1864.

1864

13. RIVERBOAT GAMBLERS
AND GENERAL CROOK

Dark clouds dappled the evening sky as the Union steamboat *B. C. Levi* chugged down the muddy waters of the Kanawha River bound for Charleston, West Virginia. Brigadier General Eliakim Parker Scammon, a martinet, and disliked by his men, was "anxious to return to his post."[1] Cold rain pelted the boat as the captain of the craft realized the impossibility of running "the chutes" in the Kanawha: whitewater and falls formed around the river's shoals. To wait out the storm, the pilot tied up at the hamlet of Red House Shoals, the oldest community between Point Pleasant and Charleston. Feeling secure in the storm, the Federals did not even bother to post a guard, and Scammon and many members of his staff turned in for the night of February 2–3, 1864.

Word traveled fast that a riverboat with a Yankee general was moored at Red House Shoals, and at dawn, Confederate partisans stormed the boat, rousing nearly forty sleeping Federals out of their slumber at gunpoint. Their "capture [was] no difficult task"—in fact, one reporter called the affair "ridiculous," since fewer than ten Confederates pulled off the caper.[2] At gunpoint, the small band of raiders ordered their prisoners to disembark with their baggage. Generously, the Southerners allowed the men to retain their private property, as they rifled through mailbags and ordered the captain to sail to the opposite side of the river, whereupon the raiders torched the boat.

Union soldiers willing to accept parole (sign a promise, which was generally adhered to, that once they returned to their lines, they would not engage in active service until they were officially exchanged with another prisoner) were released, but the Confederates kept their prizes: Scammon and several members of his staff. With the general and his officers in tow, the Confederates, with assistance from Thurmond's Rangers, began the long journey to Richmond.

Undaunted and on foot, Scouts went on a hot pursuit to rescue Scammon. "After running six miles—and in an almost breathless manner informed the Lieutenant, of what was going on the Kanawha River— and in ten or fifteen minutes he started out with twenty-two of the Independent Scouts, who double-quicked 12 miles to get between the robbers." Amazingly the footrace bore fruit—fleet of foot, the Scouts closed the distance and "got in sight of them and raised the yell, gave chase, ran them two miles, and being entirely exhausted, came to a halt, and then returned, picking up what their flying enemies had thrown away in the race." Leaving a trail of debris in their wake, the Rebels fled into the verdant mountains. Although they could not rescue Scammon, the Scouts recovered about $1,000 worth of arms, tobacco, and dry goods, along with some of the mail, including "about sixty Rebel letters directed at residents of Mason and Putnam counties."[3]

Mercifully, this would be one of the Independent Scouts' last missions on foot. In the wake of the capture of Scammon and his staff came a new commander who saw the enormous benefits of the mounted Jessie Scouts.

Tall and sinewy, with a keen mind, thirty-six-year-old Ohioan George R. Crook sported an unruly beard that could double as a small furry animal. Befitting his mountain-man appearance, their new commander had nearly a decade of experience in the remote northwest territory of Oregon. An Indian fighter, but not an Indian hater, Crook learned Native American languages as well as culture from his time in the wilds of the northwest. Years later, after his death, one Indian chief said, "Then General Crook came; he, at least, never lied to us. His words gave the people hope. He died. Their hope died."[4] One of his aides would later compare Crook to Daniel Boone.[5]

With his mastery of culture, survival skills, and years of battling Native Americans, even wounded by an arrow, Crook brought deep knowledge of what would later be called counterinsurgency, special operations, and an evolving American way of war that he would help usher in. Crook took an immediate liking to Blazer, who retained command of the company and liked the Ohioan's unconventional approach to dealing with partisans; in his autobiography, Crook even took liberties in recounting his role in the Scouts' origin. Crook made the Scouts a high priority and issued General Order 2 on February 8, 1864: "The regimental commanders of this division will select one man from each company . . . to be organized into a body of scouts. . . . One man from each regiment so selected to be a Non-Commissioned Officer. . . . All these scouts then acting together will be under the command of Commissioned Officers. . . . Officers will be particular to select such persons only as are possessed of strong moral courage, personal bravery, and particularly adept for this kind of service. The men selected who are not already mounted will mount themselves in the country by taking animals from disloyal persons in the proper manner . . . providing, however, that sufficient stock is left these people to attend crops with."[6]

However, horses were in short supply, and the loss of a horse could have a devastating impact on a small farm; Crook gave Blazer orders to beat the bushes and procure mounts. He also wisely understood and tried, at least on paper, to practice sound counterinsurgency principles before the term even existed. He hoped not to inflame the local population and push more of them into the arms of the Confederacy. What Crook ordered was not, however, precisely followed. Scout Asbe Montgomery framed the situation bluntly: "The beauty of it was that we were to be mounted on such horses we could get from the Rebs, either citizens or soldiers. Well, you could guess it was not long before we were mounted."[7] Blazer also captured many of their horses and continually upgraded their mounts when opportunities presented themselves: "Then we pick up horses and off to camp, laughing over our fun. Coming into camp we would dismount, and examine who had the worst horse, change off for a better one; so all the time were improving our company's condition in the way of swift and suitable horses for our arduous labors."[8]

Using Averell's Jessie Scouts as a model, and his own experience, Crook attempted to increase the firepower of Blazer's Scouts by pressing the War Department for repeating Spencer and Henry rifles—weapons that could fire as fast as a man could cock the gun's lever and pull the trigger. Some of the men Blazer recruited, such as the 2nd West Virginia Cavalry, had Spencer carbines and brought them to battle, but the Federal bureaucracy dragged its feet on the larger request, claiming none were on hand. Better weapons would take time.

Crook labeled Blazer's company the "Division Scouts." "Each regiment to [contribute] and have a detachment making some eighty men," recalled Montgomery. Sergeants took charge of a squad of men; Montgomery led his "old 9th Virginia boys," which, he said, "I was proud of, as I could eat, fight, and, if necessary, die with them."[9]

With the reorganization of the Scouts, Blazer needed a second in command and leaned on his venerable noncommissioned officer Montgomery, who recommended Lieutenant James Ewing of the 9th West Virginia. Ewing liked to hunt Confederates; "his very soul and strength were all strung at full might as warring against the Rebels." Courageous, and a man who led a "rough and ready life," Ewing attacked Rebels through "quick and active fighting" and demonstrated skill in the saddle: he "put spurs to his horse and [would] make him 'git.'" With his "helper," Ewing and Blazer often divided the company and went after different groups of partisans. In early 1864, they went on a "grand raid" across the mountains for four days and in the Coal River region. With "Old Dick," the men's nickname for their leader, "we thought ourselves 'bully,' and not to be scared of trifles."[10] Deep in largely unfriendly territory, the Scouts remained undaunted. One of those men was Sergeant Joseph Allen Frith, a handsome, twenty-three-year-old, gray-eyed farmer who had recently joined the Scouts from the 34th Regiment Ohio Volunteer Infantry. His fellow soldiers described him as "always ready for any thing, and always in good humor,"[11] and he had many friends, which was indicative of the esprit de corps and cohesion within the unit.

Resting during portions of the day, Blazer's Scouts probed the mountains at night: "[We] mounted, and the Captain, for he had been promoted by this time—going into the enemy's country, riding slowly, not a word to break the silence. On we rode, each comrade holding his gun in hand, not knowing how soon we might need them, as all that country had in it more or less scouts of Thurmond's men; and so used every means to avoid a surprise." The Scouts often surprised the bushwhackers. In one incident Confederates poured out of a house and started firing on Blazer's Scouts. With speed and firepower, the men routed their opponents. Urging his men forward, Montgomery remembered Blazer shouting, "Charge, Boys, give them fits!"[12] The Scouts put spurs to their mounts and rode into a maelstrom of "balls whizzing like hail." Undaunted, they reached the house, sprang from their horses, and "gave them Yankee thunder,"[13] remembered Montgomery.

The few Confederates lucky enough to escape took to the mountains while others fell into Blazer's hands. "You may guess how they fared, as we had refused to take any more of Thurmond's men prisoners, as they had shot some of our men,"[14] wrote Montgomery.

In another incident, Montgomery recalled ambushing Thurmond's men: "Here they are boys! Shoot their hearts out go for them; show no quarter!" A yell rang out along the line of horsemen, "Give it to them don't spare one; remember the bushwhackers have no quarters!"[15] The guerrillas and bushwhackers gave no quarter; they regularly executed captured Scouts. A war of annihilation thus raged in Appalachia.

The labors of Blazer's Scouts bore fruit. In May 1864, a reporter for the *Cincinnati Commercial* recorded, "General [Crook] informed me last night that the bushwhackers have been entirely driven out of the Kanawha Valley, owing to the skill of [Captain] Blazer and a company of picked men. Travel from Gauley to here is now comparatively safe, and immense trains and supplies are continually coming in."[16]

With the Union lines of communication now more secure thanks to Blazer's Scouts, the Federals planned a daring raid.

14. KILL JEFFERSON DAVIS AND BURN RICHMOND: THE KILPATRICK-DAHLGREN RAID

Twenty-one-year-old colonel Ulric Dahlgren rode "on and on, for hours facing the biting storm, feeling the pelting rain, staring with straining eyes into . . . a darkness that could be felt."[1] Beginning on the night of February 28, 1864, the cavalry commander led his all-volunteer command of 500 on what would prove to be one of the most controversial raids of the war. Tucked inside his wooden leg were secret orders from Secretary of War Edwin M. Stanton to burn Richmond and decapitate the Southern leadership.[2]

Nicknamed "Kill Cavalry" for recklessly sacrificing the lives of his men, General H. Judson Kilpatrick masterminded the raid. Union spies had determined the Confederate capitol was vulnerable—only lightly defended after being stripped of troops to supply Lee's army. The plan consisted of attacking Richmond from the north as a decoy, while a smaller detachment struck from the south and pierced Richmond's defenses. The Union raiders would ostensibly free Federal prisoners, execute Davis and his cabinet, and torch the city, thereby ending the war in a masterstroke.

At an extravagant ball, the aggressive, twenty-eight-year-old cavalry leader Kilpatrick tapped an eager Ulric Dahlgren, the son of Union rear admiral John A. Dahlgren, namesake of the Dahlgren gun, to lead the smaller detachment. According to legend, an overly confident Kilpatrick even bet his superior $5,000 that he would personally enter Richmond, and he offered to double the wager a day into the raid.

A magnificent affair held in honor of George Washington's birthday in Culpepper, Virginia, the ball attracted politicians, general officers, and ladies. "The army is overrun with women,"[3] wrote General George Meade. Officers gave up their quarters and treated the women like royalty. The soiree also attracted what appeared to be a twenty-one-year-old maiden with a slim waist and long, flowing hair named Sallie Marsten. At least that was who "she" purported to be. Donning ballgown, powder, and two derringer pistols strapped to the thighs, Sallie was actually ninety-four-pound Confederate spy Benjamin Franklin "Frank" Stringfellow. According to legend, the agent infiltrated the affair by capturing a Yankee officer who planned on bringing the real Sallie, a local Southern woman Stringfellow knew. Frank transformed into Sallie and used her pass to enter the ballroom, where he flirted and danced with the Union officers.[4] As one officer described, "Such flirtations and conversations, flew like musket balls. The sweet strains of music ever rising and falling in rhythmic waves . . . we lived in ecstasy."[5] Stringfellow picked up bits and pieces of intelligence from the chatty officers but nothing on the raid.

Kilpatrick also roamed the floor, "active as a flea and almost as ubiquitous."[6] After making a fiery speech, he waited for the event to conclude before bringing Dahlgren into the fold. The operation's success hinged on Dahlgren piercing Richmond's defenses from the south quickly. If he failed, the mission would fail.

On the night of February 28, 1864, the two Union forces left Stevensburg, Virginia. Dahlgren's volunteers came from several cavalry commands: 3rd Indiana, 1st Maine, 17th Pennsylvania, and 2nd New York. The last two cavalry regiments included several future Jessie Scouts who would escape with their lives and gain invaluable experience on the raid. After cold nights in the saddle dealing with hideous weather on March 1, 1864, Kilpatrick ran into unexpected Southern resistance. His 3,500-strong force was quickly tracked and confronted by Major General Wade Hampton's cavalry. Dahlgren's force from the south continued undetected, but recent heavy rains prevented his 500 men from crossing the James River, forcing them to follow the river and attack from the southwest instead.

Dahlgren, who had lost a leg in the Battle of Gettysburg, blamed a free African American guide for the failure to cross the James. On the recommendation of the Union provost marshal, Dahlgren had promised a freeman named Martin, his last name unknown, a large sum of money to lead the Federals to a suitable ford. When they reached the crossing point, the water was too high, forcing Dahlgren to seek an alternative crossing. The raiders burned property as they went, including Confederate secretary of war James Seddon's mill, stables, barns, and ransacked his home, making the raid personal. When they could not find a crossing point, concerns grew about Martin's credibility. The guide then led them to a fork in the road and brought them down the wrong road, away from Richmond. One of the slaves attached to the column seeking their freedom told Dahlgren they were heading to Ashland instead of Richmond and the guide should have known better.[7] Believing he had been betrayed, "the Colonel then told [Martin] he would have to carry out his part of the contract, to which the guide assented, and admitted that was the agreement and made no objection to his execution. He went along to the tree without any force and submitted to his fate without a murmur," wrote one of Dahlgren's men. Confederate sources claimed the guide was hanged by a leather strap (likely horse reins) and considered it "utterly unjustifiable murder," as there was a ford but "winter rains had swollen the James so that it was, at that time unfordable."[8] Whether the man betrayed the Federals or was simply nervous and accidently went down the wrong road remains a mystery.

The one-legged Dahlgren pressed on, mounting up with the help of one of his men and remarking on the awkwardness of his crippled limb: "We are going on; and if we succeed, I'd gladly lose the other."[9] The small band attacked several Rebel strongpoints near Richmond. Faced with multiple losses—including seasoned noncommissioned officer Sergeant Harrison J. Jack,[10] a twenty-three-year-old volunteer from the 1st Maine Cavalry and a veteran of most of the war's great battles, including Gettysburg—and mounting Confederate resistance, and unable to contact Kilpatrick, Dahlgren ordered his men to retreat and fight back to Union lines. The wounded had to be left behind, along with hundreds of enslaved people who had joined the column seeking freedom. In the darkness, with Confederate patrols hunting them, his command became divided. Dahlgren was killed by five bullets[11] in an ambush by Confederate cavalry and home guard. What was left of the command, low on ammunition, struck out to find Kilpatrick, who had also retreated. Scores of Dahlgren's force were killed or captured while seeking their way to Northern lines.

On Dahlgren's body, a thirteen-year-old member of the Richmond home guard found the handwritten directive to torch the city and assassinate President Jefferson Davis. The controversial orders were photographed and subsequently printed in Southern newspapers, creating a firestorm of rage in North and South alike. The *Richmond Examiner* demanded Davis fight fire with fire and seek revenge: "If the Confederate capital has been in the closest danger of massacre and conflagrations, if the President and the Cabinet have run a serious risk of being hanged at their own door, do we not owe it chiefly to the milk-and-water spirit in which this war has hitherto been conducted?"[12] General Meade personally wrote to General Lee disavowing the divisive order. Evidence, however, indicates the orders were true; Custer would later document that Dahlgren had told him "that he would not take Pres. Davis [prisoner] but would put them to death and he would himself set fire to the first house in Richmond and burn the city."[13] The raid had significant unintended consequences. Although Union leadership claimed the orders were unsanctioned, their revelation put the South on a path of in-kind retribution, and the North would move closer to total war against civilians. The South would also utilize special operations aimed at influencing the looming presidential election through the shadow warriors of the Confederate Secret Service.

II

THE CONFEDERATE
SECRET SERVICE

15. The Department
of Dirty Tricks

A hidden hand lay behind many Confederate operations aimed at altering the course of the war. Facing massive Northern armies, select groups of Southern men and women were forced to innovate and develop unorthodox shadow warfare methods. Collectively, they became the Confederate Secret Service.

Deliberately opaque, the organization was real but unofficial. Some departments were created overnight. Much of the organization remains cloaked in secrecy because its files and records were deliberately burned in the war's final days. By 1864, however, "Confederates had acquired experience in clandestine operations, had developed a body of doctrine concerning such operations, and had created a cluster of organizations that, together, contained a considerable capacity for secret service work,"[1] according to one historian who summed up the clandestine group.

The Confederate Secret Service was obsessed with gadgets and would invent espionage and sabotage devices: for example, the War Department Torpedo Bureau specialized in the groundbreaking technology of land mines.

Most of the devices flowed from the brilliant mind of sixty-one-year-old Gabriel Rains. His younger brother, George Washington Rains, an exceptional chemist and scientist, developed the South's principal source of gunpowder: the massive works in Augusta, Georgia, without which the Confederacy could never have waged a sustained modern war. Together, the two siblings became known as the "bomb brothers."

The "father of modern mine warfare," Gabriel Rains first deployed booby traps, or "improvised explosive devices," against Seminole Indians in Florida in the 1850s—one of their first uses in North America. In one incident, the deadly contraptions failed to detonate on a Native American war party attacking a fort. Rains personally investigated why the bomb failed to explode, and the Indians shot and nearly killed him and several other soldiers. But the mines terrified the Indians, and the fort survived the assault. Resigning from the US Army in 1861, Rains joined the Confederacy. Using pressure-sensitive fuses attached to shells filled with powder, Rains buried "sub terra" torpedoes outside Confederate defenses in Yorktown in 1862, to the great consternation of Union commanders, who called it a "dastardly business."[2]

Rains' Torpedo Bureau, an arm of the Confederate Secret Service, launched a shadow war on the Union. A myriad of cutting-edge "infernal machines" terrorized the North: "coal torpedoes."[3] Seemingly harmless-looking pieces of coal, the mines were actually hollow metal castings filled with gunpowder and coated with coal dust. When the coal torpedoes were tossed in a steamboat's boiler by an unsuspecting tender, the resulting explosion could cause the craft to blow sky-high. The Submarine Bureau developed underwater torpedoes detonated by an electric current that guarded the James River and Southern ports. The bureau outfitted the novel submarine *Hunley* at Charleston with a torpedo, mounting an explosive device on a long wooden pole, or spar, in front of the sub. The *Hunley*'s spar torpedo had a long, barbed spear on the device's business end to affix itself to the wooden hulls of enemy warships. On February 17, 1864, the *Hunley* attacked the USS *Housatonic* in Charleston's outer harbor. The partially submerged vessel pulled away from the Union screw sloop, and once the sub reached the limit of the cord, it released a trigger mechanism that detonated the torpedo and sank the Northern vessel, making it the first combat submarine to sink a warship successfully. On her return to base, the *Hunley* sank, killing all eight crew members; a total of twenty-one died on missions in the vessel.

In 1864, Company A of the Confederate Secret Service pulled off a major coup using one of Rains' "horological torpedoes," better known as a time bomb. Two operatives, John Maxwell and his local guide R. K. Dillard, who reported to Rains, left Richmond and covertly worked their way through Union pickets to City Point, where Grant had a massive munitions depot; they "traveled mostly by night and crawled upon [their] knees to pass the east picket-line." Maxwell disguised twelve pounds of gunpowder in a box of candles. After being halted by one of the wharf sentinels, he described the operation. "I succeeded in passing him by representing that the captain had ordered me to convey the box on board. Hailing a man from the barge, I put the machine in motion and gave it in his charge."[4] Maxwell set the timer on the torpedo for one hour and safely exfiltrated the area—and waited. A massive explosion ripped through the docks and nearly detonated all of the ammunition. A correspondent witnessed the huge mushroom-shaped cloud: "You have read of eruptions of Vesuvius, such as buried Herculaneum and Pompeii. You have seen illustrations of them in the books. This must have been such an explosion as one of these, except that instead of lava and dust and ashes, it rained over the circle of a mile, in whole packages and by piece-meal, everything you can imagine at a military depot. Entire boxes of fixed ammunition came down among the tents in the town, a quarter of a mile distant, and scarcely a tent or house or boat can be found within the circle of a mile that is not riddled by shell and shot, or small ammunition."[5]

Four million dollars in munitions went up in smoke along with the barge, and scores of people, including "a party of ladies [who], it seems, were killed by this explosion. It is saddening to me to realize the fact that the terrible effects of war induce such consequence," wrote Maxwell in his report; "but when I remember the ordeal to which our own women have been subjected, and the barbarities of the enemy's crusade against us and them, my feelings are relieved by the reflection that while this catastrophe was not intended by us, it amounts only, in the providence of God, to just retaliation."[6]

Another arm of the Secret Service was overseen by the State Department headed by Secretary of State Judah P. Benjamin, who had multiple agents at his disposal. Sometimes called the "Brains of the Confederacy," Benjamin was the first Jewish American to be elected a US senator. At the beginning of the war, Jefferson Davis appointed the attorney, railroad founder, and poker player attorney general, and later secretary of war. Benjamin was eventually confirmed by the Confederate Senate as secretary of state in March 1862. Benjamin's State Department trafficked in election interference, bribing members of the Northern press to craft a favorable Southern narrative.

The War Department Signal Bureau and Signal Corps operated a series of covert stations to transmit messages across enemy lines. One signal line sent communications from Richmond to Confederates operating outside Washington, DC. The provost marshal of Richmond, established in 1861 by General John Henry Winder, focused on counterespionage and management of prisoner-of-war camps, as well as the defense of the city. The name "War Department Strategy Bureau" was a clever euphemism for sabotage teams and demolition experts.

While there was no official head of the Secret Service, Jefferson Davis acted as its director, authorizing operations and working closely with Benjamin and a handful of officials. Near the end of the war, the Confederacy was trying to pull the various loose branches and elements together into a central organization, but the war ended before this could be accomplished.

Many Confederate irregulars and partisan units had ties to the Secret Service and the Confederate government or reported directly to General Robert E. Lee. These irregular units would play a crucial role in special operations. Scouts and Signal Corps personnel and other specialists would be detached from the Secret Service for service in irregular units such as the 43rd Virginia Cavalry Battalion, Mosby's Rangers.

Secret Service operations, in conjunction with partisan initiatives, would be part of the South's retaliation in kind for the Dahlgren Raid. But most importantly, the Secret Service would try to influence the 1864 presidential election.

16. CANADA, THE CONFEDERATE SECRET SERVICE, ELECTION INTERFERENCE, AND THE NORTHWEST CONSPIRACY

During the early spring of 1864, Jacob Thompson and Clement Clay boarded a fast steamer, *The Thistle*, off the coast of North Carolina. The iron side-wheel ship would have to be fast and stealthy to avoid dozens of Union ships that blockaded the Confederacy. Thompson carried bank drafts worth $1 million in gold and, with them, the hopes of the Confederacy. The blockade runner successfully pierced the Union encirclement and carried the two men and the enormous sum successfully to Canada. Once there, they hoped to influence an election and launch special operations missions that could potentially change the course of the war. Jefferson Davis knew foreign assistance or domestic assistance from antiwar groups could be crucial to the Confederacy's survival. With Lincoln up for reelection in November, a Peace Democrat on a War Democrat platform or a War Democrat on a peace platform could potentially aid the South's survival and end Lincoln's presidency. Money flowed to Canadians, foreigners, and Democrats alike, critical individuals of influence who could help the cause.

General Robert E. Lee knew the North had superiority in the number of men and resources and the South was losing the war. He wrote Davis, "Under these circumstances, we should neglect no honorable means of dividing and weakening our enemies, that they may feel some of the difficulties experienced by ourselves. It seems to me that the most effectual mode of accomplishing this object, now within our reach, is to give all the encouragement we can, consistent with truth, to the rising peace party of the North."[1]

While the South's fate in fighting a conventional war may have been doomed through today's lens of 160 years of hindsight, many Southern leaders in the spring of 1864 felt differently. The exhausted North, lacking significant progress after three years of war and deeply divided internally, could be made to seek a political solution. Riots in protest of the war roiled many Northern cities, and up to 280,000[2] Northern soldiers would desert from the Union Army during the course of the war. Success mixed with multiple defeats on the battlefield. The seemingly never-ending list of tens of thousands of dead and wounded and the conflict's enormous financial cost formed the sense of a forever war in the minds of many Northerners. Moreover, much of the Northern press, especially Democrat-run newspapers, held an unfavorable view of how Lincoln and his generals conducted the war, and many hated Lincoln himself.

Incurring massive casualties, both Northern and Southern armies still battled on much of the same Virginia ground of 1861, 1862, and 1863. Collectively, the peace movement of Northern Democrats, pejoratively known as "Copperheads," wanted a negotiated peace with the South. The Democratic Party poised to nominate a "peace candidate" in the summer for the 1864 election: a strategic course correction for the party. Democrats reasoned that the war could not be won through a military solution; instead, only a political solution would resolve it. Many Democrats and the Copperheads advocated a conciliatory approach to the war to bring back Southerners, whom some viewed as brothers and not the enemy. Democrats generally thought most Southerners wanted to return to the Union, and Confederates who wanted secession were a small minority.[3] They warned harsh measures would only repel many Southerners and hinder reunification.

For their part, Confederate leaders banked on the remarkable resiliency of the South to outlast the North and lead to a negotiated end to the war that preserved the South's integrity. Davis sent Clay and Thompson as commissioners to Canada to buy influence in North America and abroad and set up a base to conduct Secret Service special operations in the hope of allowing the South to survive the war. Thompson was a former Democratic representative from Mississippi and secretary of the interior under President James Buchanan. Silver-tongued and more slippery than an eel, the fifty-four-year-old Southerner was joined by Clement Claiborne

Clay, a former Democratic US senator and former Confederate senator. His irritable, chronic asthmatic's face adorned the Confederate one-dollar bill. Clay had resigned his seat in the US Senate when war broke out. The ardent white supremacist made an impassioned plea for secession and denunciation of the Republican Party: "No sentiment is more insulting or more hostile to our domestic tranquility, to our social order, and to our social existence, than is contained in the declaration that our negroes are entitled to liberty and equality with the white man."[4]

Operating on verbal orders, each commissioner received a letter from Davis: "Confiding special trust in your zeal, discretion, and patriotism, I hereby direct you to proceed at once to Canada and there carry out such instructions as you have from me verbally, in such a manner as shall seem most likely to conduce to the furtherance of the interests of the Confederate States of America which have been entrusted to you."[5]

Joining Thompson and Clay in Canada was Kentuckian George Nicholas Sanders, who had been appointed consul to London during the Franklin Pierce administration. While in Europe, the fifty-two-year-old dark-haired, bearded Southerner, who reportedly was never without money or beautiful women, entered the same circles as exiled radical revolutionaries such as Giuseppe Mazzini, who advocated insurrection and the "Theory of the Dagger," which justified tyrannicide. "He [Sanders] sees everybody, talks to everybody, high and low. He has little reverence for great men. He would criticize George Washington to his face if he were alive. He was one of the great wire-pullers in the United States," the *London Times* once quipped about the diplomat.[6] He was involved in one plot: "In London, Mr. Sanders fulminated an extraordinary letter advising the killing of Louis Napoleon, by any means, and by any way it could be done."[7]

These men formed the leadership of the Confederate Secret Service in Canada.

The shadowy crew set up operations at the opulent St. Lawrence Hall Hotel in Montreal. The finest lodging in the city boasted a lavish lobby flanked by men's and women's smoking rooms and a telegraph office for the latest news. Guests could saunter down an elegant flight of stairs to plumes of cigar smoke that billowed from the wood-paneled, high-mirrored Dooley's Bar, which served mint juleps year-round. A large billiards room entertained the "secesh," the population of hundreds of Confederate exiles living in Montreal whom the Canadians welcomed. While Canada was officially neutral and part of Great Britain, many Canadians saw value in a divided United States that would be less likely to interfere with Canada, and authorities in Canada turned a blind eye to the Confederate operatives. From the sanctuary of Canada, the Confederate Secret Service hatched plots to rob Northern banks, manipulate US gold and currency markets, burn cities to the ground, free Confederate prisoners, change the election, and influence political will in the North and abroad. Sanders had a grand vision to influence the election, writing to Davis, "We could control the Chicago [Democratic] convention and organize a powerful party, from Portland to San Francisco, that would have the power to stop the war, even should they fail to get possession of the Federal government; and that, after the such organization was promised success, we would have a good prospect of making terms."[8]

But if those influence operations failed, the Secret Service and other Southern irregulars planned to utilize covert operations to unleash a war of terror on the North. After the Kilpatrick-Dahlgren Raid and the failed plot to decapitate the Confederate cabinet, few operations would be out of bounds—including assassination.

In May 1864, Captain Thomas Henry Hines combed Montreal's saloons and boardinghouses to recruit a small army of commandos to execute covert actions for the Secret Service. Arriving in Canada days before Commissioner Thompson, Hines, a member of the Secret Service, devised a plan to foment an insurrection in the Midwest that came to be called the Northwest Conspiracy. The covert operation called for the Secret Service to organize an armed insurrection by tens of thousands of Copperheads and thousands of Confederate prisoners who would be freed from Union prisoner-of-war camps in the Midwest. Directed by the Secret Service, these armed mobs, using smuggled weapons and arms seized from Federal arsenals, would attempt to topple local state governments in Ohio, Indiana, and Illinois.

Hines had reason to be optimistic about the operation's success. Battlefield debacles led to unrest in the Midwest and gains for Democrats in Illinois and Indiana. "The Illinois legislature has been in session, one week, during which the Copperheads have not uttered one loyal word, but have belched treason, day and night,"[9] the *Chicago Tribune* opined. Democrats elected Thomas A. Hendricks, who advocated for a separate Northwest confederacy. Indiana Democrats tried to strip pro-Union governor Oliver Hazard Perry Throck Morton of state troops to keep them out of the war. Republicans barely had enough members to prevent a quorum and dissolved the legislature, blocking the Democrats' efforts. Morton would go to extraordinary efforts to keep Indiana in the war, fighting legislative suppression by financing the state government through private funds and loans. Unrest within the states made Kentucky and Missouri vulnerable to joining the Confederacy.

Lincoln feared an insurrection in the Northwest. Senator Charles Sumner of Massachusetts wrote to a colleague after meeting Lincoln, "These are dark hours. . . . The President tells me he now fears the 'the fire in the rear'—meaning the Democracy [the term often used then by the Democratic Party to describe itself], especially at the Northwest— more than our military chances."[10]

Confederate secretary of state Benjamin summed up exactly what he expected from Hines and Thompson: "[to use the] secret service in the hope of aiding the disruption of the eastern and western states in the approaching election in the North."[11]

Hines found many willing volunteers for his Northwest Conspiracy. Since the earliest days of the war, Confederates had fled to Canada after escaping from Union prisons. Most men barely eked out a living still wearing Confederate uniforms, their only clothes. Despite the risk of being executed as spies, many jumped at the idea of once again fighting for the Confederacy.

Hines appointed twenty-three-year-old captain John Breckinridge Castleman as his second in command. Both men were escape artists. In July 1863 they had been part of General John Hunt Morgan's massive raid into Kentucky, Indiana, and Ohio, which aimed at diverting Union forces from key battlefields and forcing them to defend the Midwest from the raids. Hines led a separate covert mission in Indiana where twenty-five of his men disguised as Union troopers met local Copperhead Peace Democrats. Hines would personally know all the major leaders of the Copperhead movement and become their liaison to the Confederacy.

Morgan's raid had ended in failure, and Union authorities locked up the Confederate cavalry officer and many of his men in the Ohio Penitentiary in Columbus. Drawing inspiration from the escapes through the Parisian sewer system described in Victor Hugo's famous novel *Les*

Misérables, Hines determined a ventilation shaft lay on the other side of cells on the lower level of the prison. Using a system of simple taps that warned them if the guards approached, he and others worked at night for weeks to burrow a tunnel nearly thirty feet long that cut through cell walls and the foundation of the prison. After emerging from the tunnel on a rainy night, Morgan and his men escaped over a wall using a rope made from sheets and a grappling hook fashioned from a poker.

Hines was recaptured soon after, only to break out again and elude the Yankees. He walked into Confederate lines in Dalton, Georgia, in December 1863. A month later, he pitched his plan to Jefferson Davis to set the North ablaze by freeing thousands of Confederates in Union prisoner-of-war camps and sparking an insurrection led by the Copperheads. Secretary of State Benjamin, head of the Secret Service, and Secretary of War James Seddon, whose property had been burned during the Kilpatrick-Dahlgren Raid, approved the plan and allocated $70,000 through the sale of cotton for its execution. The papers found in Colonel Dahlgren's false leg authorizing the assassination of Davis and his cabinet and the burning of Richmond put a plan in motion to meet terror with terror.

17. U. S. GRANT

The spring of 1864 brought a new Union commander and a different strategy to win the war. President Lincoln promoted Ulysses S. Grant to lieutenant general and commander of all Union forces in March, a rank and responsibility last bestowed on George Washington during the Revolutionary War. With it came responsibility for running the war. Grant laid out a crushing plan of constant attack and pressure, "to employ all the force of all the armies continually and concurrently, so that there should be no recuperation on the part of the Rebel, no rest from attack, no opportunity to reinforce first one and then another point with the same troops, at different seasons; no possibility of profiting by the advantages of interior lines; no chance to furlough troops, to reorganize armies, or recreate supplies; no respite of any sort, anywhere, until absolute submission ended the War."[1] Total war.

Born and raised in Ohio and an expert horseman with distinguished experience in the Mexican-American War, Grant proved his abilities as a quartermaster skilled in moving and supplying armies. But his drinking problem led to his resignation from the Army in 1854. He floundered in civilian life, failing in various business ventures. Personally against slavery, at great financial cost, Grant freed an enslaved man, William, whom he had acquired from his father-in-law. The decision created a row in Grant's divided family, and he made it over the strident objections of his father-in-law and wife, who were ardent Democrats and supported slavery.

Grant's life would dramatically change with the onset of war. Initially, failure seemed to follow him when Major General George B. McClellan rejected his efforts to be recommissioned as a captain in the US Army.[2] The governor of Illinois appointed him as a military aide. Grant mustered regiments into the militia and was promoted to colonel of the 21st Illinois

Infantry Regiment. Under the command of Major General John Frémont, Grant's star rose during battles at Fort Donelson and, later, at Shiloh and Vicksburg. Success on the battlefield led to more success and promotion. A genius in war, Grant consistently won battles and campaigns that had been rare in the Union Army during the early years of the conflict. Grant's offensives were not intended to occupy large swaths of Southern territory but instead aimed to destroy the South's armies, the Confederacy's infrastructure, and its ability to wage war.

Once he was appointed overall commander, whether Grant had enough time to influence the looming presidential election via Union victories was in question. Both sides were exhausted from war—the South, like any insurgency, merely needed to survive to outlast the North. Despite its overwhelming troop advantages, the North, like the British nearly a hundred years earlier, never had enough troops to take and hold large amounts of ground and pacify a hostile Southern population. Plus, involvement and aid from France or Britain remained a possibility for the Confederacy. These great powers saw value in a divided United States, hindering its ability to emerge as a rival. Lee, for his part, would fight Grant's strength (far more significant numbers of men and materiel) in a conventional manner—unlike Washington, who changed strategy against the British based on circumstances. Numbers were not Lee's strength; he rarely had superiority in numbers. At the same time, he saw the value of covert operations, but he often viewed them as undisciplined and ungentlemanly.

Despite Lee's bias, Southern guerrillas and Rangers continued to develop an asymmetric form of warfare that favored their smaller forces, tying up large numbers of Union troops as they ambushed their lines of communication. Other Confederate leaders understood that this form of warfare had the potential to prolong the war significantly and enhance the survivability of the South, perhaps making possible a favorable Southern political solution. Political will became paramount to continuing the war. Both sides were locked in a desperate contest of will, a race involving an evolving form of special operations and unconventional warfare that would play a crucial role in determining the course of the war.

18. The Scout toward Aldie

Embedded with the Union cavalry, on April 18, 1864, forty-four-year-old author Herman Melville rode through the twilight on a scouting mission probing Mosby's Confederacy. Nearly thirteen years had passed since the publication of *Moby Dick*, a book that was not considered a critical or commercial success during Melville's lifetime. Before the Civil War, Melville tried his hand at poetry and submitted a book of verse to his publisher. The manuscript had been rejected months earlier. To resurrect his career and eke out a living as a writer, he thrust himself into the war as a civilian and observer, capturing the conflict with his pen in a book of poetry titled *Battle Pieces and Aspects of the War*. On that day, Melville rode with the 2nd Massachusetts Cavalry.

The latest group intent on eliminating Mosby's Rangers, the 2nd Massachusetts Cavalry, was not a typical Northern regiment. Recruitment of Union soldiers had slowed. Despite the threat of the draft and bounty hunters, the average desertion rates for Massachusetts recruits within sixty days of receiving their bonuses still topped 40 percent. So the core and leadership of the 2nd Massachusetts were Californians, including the "California One Hundred" and the California battalion—volunteers so eager to join the fight that they had used their enlistment bonuses to purchase their passage via ship to the East Coast. The energy and patriotism of the Californians had a positive effect on the malaise of the East Coast recruits; their desertion rates dropped to 12 percent when placed with Californians.[1] This Massachusetts-California conglomeration was led by Massachusetts colonel Charles Russell Lowell III, a scion from Boston, Harvard graduate, and industrialist. Lowell was Melville's nephew and had recently married Josephine "Effie" Shaw, the sister of Robert Gould Shaw, who had famously led the 54th Massachusetts, America's first all-Black regiment raised in the North during the Civil War. Although killed during their attack on Fort Wagner outside Charleston, South Carolina, in 1863, Shaw inspired thousands with his leadership.

Despite Lowell's courage, he "was not universally loved by the enlisted men. . . . They endangered their lives because they knew his worth to the regiment. Officers and men strove to match his courage and zeal for the cause. He was a strict disciplinarian, a patrician, and an elitist—none of which were admirable traits to the independent-minded Californians. Nevertheless, they followed him through the smoke, fire, and sheer terror of battle—wherever he led them,"[2] wrote one historian.

Weeks earlier in 1864, Mosby had launched a devastating ambush on Lowell's troopers at Anker's blacksmith shop about two miles from Dranesville, Virginia, and not far from Miskel Farm. Hiding in a pine thicket, Mosby relayed his orders: "Men, the Yankees are coming, and it is very likely we will have a hard fight. When you are ordered to charge, I want you to go right through them. Reserve your fire until you get close enough to see clearly what you are shooting at, and then let every shot tell."[3]

Tension gripped the Rangers as the Californians approached. "We sat motionless on our horses, holding our breaths, with heads thrown forward and our ears strained, watching and waiting in anxious expectation for the approach of the enemy and the signal for the attack," remembered Ranger James Williamson.[4]

An eerie silence and stillness enveloped the pine grove. The shrill shriek of Mosby's whistle pierced the air.

The Rangers obtained the bulge and ran through the stunned 150-trooper patrol from the 2nd Massachusetts Cavalry and the 16th New York Cavalry, then led by Captain J. Sewall Reed.

"I got the drop on a Californian with my last shot. He threw up his pistol and exclaimed, 'I surrender.' I took it for granted that he meant what he said and rode past him, firing at a man beyond who was trying to work his way through a wedge of his men on the roadside. Then the man who so readily surrendered turned and shot me in the back as I passed him. I don't blame him in the least, for I ought to have had the sense to take his pistol from him when he held it up,"[5] recalled John Munson.

Baron Robert Von Massow dashed into the melee. One of several foreign Confederate volunteers like Bradford Hoskins, the Prussian came to America "to see something of actual war." The striking German "wore a steel gray uniform with green trimmings, [redlined cape and plumed hat], and carried a huge saber."[6] Fearless, the baron preferred the saber; on a previous operation, one of the Rangers suggested the Prussian use his Colts: "Baron unless you are ready to die this morning, use your pistols and put back that sabre." The baron demurred and replied, "A soldier should always be ready to die."[7]

Massow charged Reed with his sword. With the Prussian's cold steel bearing down on him, the Yankee motioned to surrender by putting his pistol in the air. The baron did not disarm Reed, and he spared the officer by lowering his sword and moving on to other Federals. Reed subsequently shot Massow in the back. William H. Chapman watched in horror as he saw his friend fall to the ground. Reed put spurs to his horse and tried to flee. Chapman caught up to him and killed the Yankee officer. Chapman returned to Massow and said, "'Baron, I shot and killed the man who shot you.' [Reed] had told me he would surrender. I am much obliged to you,'"[8] Massow grittily responded.*

In total, the Rangers lost one man but killed over a dozen Federals and captured over fifty more and scores of their horses.

Charley Binns, a Ranger deserter, had guided Reed's patrol that day. Binns, a native of Loudoun County, fled Mosby's command after the guerrilla leader had him arrested for attempting to kidnap two free Black women and sell them into slavery. Another account describes Binns as "guilty of an outrage at a farm near Salem."[9] After Binns' escape and betrayal, Mosby's men could not wait to get their hands on him, so he skedaddled during the action: "When the first shot was fired, Charley started to run and was never heard of by the Californians or our men." Munson humorously quipped, "It was said that he stopped for one night in Winnipeg to get a bite and then went on towards the North Pole."[10]

Adapting from the loss of his men during the ambush at Anker's, Lowell determined to go after Mosby again with a larger force. He invited Melville to join what the latter would immortalize as *The Scout toward Aldie*. Lowell went in big: 250 troopers and 250 infantry. The Union commander knew

---

* The baron would later recover from his wounds and go on to command German cavalry as a general officer.

Mosby would always shy away from infantry, with their deadly massed rifle fire that could kill from a distance. The slow-moving force cautiously entered Mosby's realm even though Washington, DC, loomed in the distance. Rangers seemed behind every tree.

Melville's elegant stanza captured the mood:

As glides in seas the shark,
Rides Mosby through green dark.

All spake of him, but few had seen
Except the maimed ones or the low;
Yet rumor made him every thing—
A farmer—woodman—refugee—
The man who crossed the field but now;
  A spell about his life did cling—
  Who to the ground shall Mosby bring?[11]

As Lowell's men left their camp near Centreville and rode toward Aldie, Mosby's men took potshots at the column but wisely avoided a direct engagement with the Union commander's superior numbers. The first day of the mission was a bust. As bugles sounded "boots and saddles," the 2nd Massachusetts and other troopers beat the bushes only to find that the Rangers had vanished in the mist. One step ahead, Mosby's men continued to slip in and out of the darkness beyond the Federals' grasp.

Mosby used psychological warfare and played on the fears of all those who entered his realm, which Melville described in verse:

An outpost in the perilous wilds
Which ever are lone and still;
  But Mosby's men are there—
  Of Mosby best beware.[12]

The frustration and futility of war are captured in Melville's account of the raid, as the Federals chased ghosts and were haunted by their own fears.

On the second day of the mission, Lowell received a tip that the Rangers planned to attend a wedding in Leesburg that evening. Lowell divided his force and boldly sent part of it on foot to the town. The men arrived shortly after the wedding, where they engaged the Rangers in a gun battle. The Rangers wounded several of Lowell's men and killed another before disappearing into Mosby's Confederacy. The next morning, Lowell rode up to Leesburg with ambulance wagons and carefully moved his men back to their camp that evening. Fittingly, Melville closed his poem with "To Mosby-land the dirges cling."[13]

Success fueled the expansion of the 43rd Virginia Cavalry Battalion, and Mosby added Company D. The other companies often referred to it as "Company Darling" because many of the men were dandies and finely dressed. John Munson called the men of Company D "the flower of the battalion."[14] Rising from private to captain, Richard Paul Montjoy was picked by Mosby to lead Company D. Despite their finery and aristocratic airs, they proved to be fierce fighters.

Along with a new company came new leadership. A Yankee trooper mortally wounded Mosby's friend Jeb Stuart on May 12, 1864, during an engagement at Yellow Tavern, Virginia. The news devastated Mosby personally and changed his chain of command. He now reported directly to the Confederacy's commander in chief, General Robert E. Lee. As Mosby continued to expand his command and operations in Virginia, Blazer's Scouts in West Virginia spearheaded a diversion.

19. THE DUBLIN RAID

In the first week of May 1864, the band struck up such a loud tune of martial music that the melodies echoed off the West Virginia mountains. In full splendor, the musical ensemble of the 5th West Virginia Infantry marched while Blazer's Scouts, who remarkably, as an elite unit, also had a few musical instruments, rode down the Kanawha Turnpike straight into the heart of Thurmond's Appalachia, making as much racket as possible. At night, the Federal troops stoked the flames of massive bonfires; unlike in the stealth missions of the past, General George Crook wanted the Confederates to know that his army had taken the offensive.

A roving martial symphony musical display was part of Crook's genius for unconventional warfare: the 5th West Virginia Infantry deployed to distract and mislead the enemy in a feint with Blazer's Scouts in the van. The ruse worked—confused Confederates took the bait and initially focused their attention on the small force, while Crook marched toward his objectives on the Virginia and Tennessee Railroad. The raid on the railroad was part of Grant's overarching strategy to bring pressure on the Confederacy on multiple fronts. Crook's raid on Dublin was equally complex. The primary attack involved the bulk of Crook's Kanawha Division marching 140-plus miles over winding mountain trails and swollen streams behind enemy lines, to attack Dublin Depot and the New River Bridge on the Virginia and Tennessee Railroad a few miles away from the depot. The object of multiple previous, unsuccessful Union operations, the 780-foot covered railway bridge was a vital strategic artery and difficult for the Confederates to replace. To confuse the Rebels, General William Averell, led by the Jessie Scouts, aimed to destroy the Confederate saltworks at Saltville as well as the lead mines in Wythe County, Virginia, some forty miles west. At the same time, Blazer's Scouts and the 5th West

Virginia marched toward Lewisburg in a feint to divert Confederates away from Crook. Another force, under Major General Franz Sigel, a German American immigrant, targeted Staunton, a critical supply base and railhead for the Confederacy.

The operations dovetailed into Grant's master stratagem. For the first time in the war, Union armies coordinated their offensives across numerous theaters. Recognizing that Richmond would fall with the loss of Lee's army, Grant ordered the Army of the Potomac to target the Army of Northern Virginia, beginning first at what would become known as the Battle of the Wilderness in early May. Grant ordered Meade, "Wherever Lee goes, there you will go also."[1] Simultaneously, Major General Benjamin Butler's forces marched from the Virginia Peninsula to attack Lee and Richmond from the east. Sherman's army, meanwhile, invaded Georgia and attacked the Confederate forces led by Joe Johnston, who retreated before the advancing Union Army, to seize the vital railhead and industrial area of Atlanta. Nathaniel Banks led a force assigned to the capture of Mobile, Alabama.

In Lewisburg, West Virginia, the musical ruse employed by the 5th West Virginia and Blazer's Scouts proved effective. Confederates reported an entire Union division near Lewisburg, and Thurmond's men attacked Blazer's Scouts and the Union decoy force instead of Crook's division, which advanced largely unmolested over the mountains toward Dublin. The now-expert Blazer's Scouts stealthily made their way over Sewell Mountain. "When we started, the Rebs learned of our coming, and blockaded the road over those mountains, so no wagon or horse could pass," one Scout recalled. "But our horses were too well used to the woods to be stopped." They concealed themselves during the day and traveled at night by main roads. Blazer's Scouts "wound their way through brush and over logs."[2] Despite their stealth, Thurmond still attacked, and the Scouts sustained several killed and wounded.

Freezing rain and even snow pelted man, beast, and wagon as Crook's main force of 6,000 fought through a quagmire of soupy mud. The raiders paralleled the New River, marching along remote trails in the mountains of West Virginia before they emerged near the Virginia border at Princeton Court House. Here, a small Rebel cavalry force fired on them and quickly retreated.

Continuing the footslog to Dublin, Crook ordered his men to wiretap the Confederate telegraph lines near the route of the raid. The Southern operator at Dublin immediately discerned Federal interlopers trying to read his signals. He tapped out in Morse code, "Hello Yank," and snarkily invited General Crook to dinner. Crook had a sense of humor and accepted the invitation but added that he would regrettably be a day late.[3]

The electric telegraph was one of the most underappreciated technological advancements that changed the face of warfare during the Civil War. It transformed the nature of leadership, allowing unprecedented, almost instantaneous communication not only between officers but also to their commanders in chief. Lincoln often huddled in the telegraph room of the White House getting real-time updates from field commanders as to the status of troop movements—the country's first wired president.

By 1861, telegraph cables connected almost all major cities in the Union with more than 50,000 miles of wire, while far fewer lines connected the South. Though they improved communication, they could also be a liability; lines were vulnerable to being tapped, as Crook demonstrated.

Caught by surprise, Confederate general Albert Gallatin Jenkins constructed his battle lines with less than forty-eight hours to prepare. Commanding a hodgepodge force consisting mainly of old men and boys from the home guards, Jenkins built a hasty defensive line of logs, rail fences, and earth, stretching about a half mile along a ridge between Cloyd's Mountain and the town of Dublin, to block the path to warehouses and the major depot of the Virginia and Tennessee Railroad. A large meadow about 500 yards long and a winding muddy creek lay in front of the Rebel defenses.

The harsh crackle of musket fire and boom of cannons peppered the lines of blue as Crook's men charged across the meadow on the sunny morning of May 9. Outnumbered by nearly three to one, the home guard and other Confederate troops unleashed a withering volley on the Union attackers. Five Federal flag bearers went down in the melee as the attack faltered. Men retreated and looked for cover. Seeing the unfolding disorder, Crook leaped from his horse and led his troops forward into the storm of lead and iron. Despite the dashing charge, the general floundered in the mud and water of the creek and had to be helped out by his men. The Federals descended on the Confederate breastworks. Fighting became hand to hand and raged for a little under an hour. One Ohioan later wrote about the intensity of the battle, "Old soldiers say that it was one of the hardest of the war for the time it lasted." Crook lost 10 percent of his men killed and wounded. Confederates under Jenkins' command lost 23 percent of their force, a massive number considering the duration of the fight—Jenkins himself suffered a wound that would prove mortal. Captured by Crook's men, the former Democratic congressman, a wealthy planter and slave owner, died a dozen days later at the hands of a careless orderly who ruptured an artery from the wound at the base of his amputated arm, causing him to bleed out.

With Jenkins' force cleared from the ridge, Crook rumbled toward Dublin, where his men tore up nine miles of railroad track and put to the torch warehouses full of priceless war materiel and supplies as they moved on to their most prized main objective—the destruction of the long-sought-after New River Bridge.

Crook placed the Jessie Scouts out front, along with a company of skirmishers led by Captain Michael Eagan; they approached the crucial bridge and supply artery. "A cannon-ball . . . struck deep in the ground right in front of me, stunning me severely for a few minutes," remembered Eagan.[4] Confederate and Union artillery dueled from opposite sides of the bridge. Motivated by an aide who "said that whoever would burn the bridge would be remembered," Eagan took some matches and climbed up one of the piers. He "broke off some dry pine from the side works and ignited the bundle in the west end of the bridge." Flames quickly engulfed the timber-covered railroad bridge, and within minutes the trestle seemed to leap from its stone pylons as it plunged into the river below.* Future president, and at the time regimental commander of the 23rd Ohio, Colonel Rutherford B. Hayes savored the moment. "A fine scene it was, my band playing [Yankee Doodle] and all the regiments marching onto the beautiful hills hurrahing and enjoyed the triumph."[5]

---

* Remarkably, the Confederacy rebuilt the bridge within a month. Unfortunately, the Union failed to bring the explosives needed to destroy the stone pylons.

Moving up and down precipitous mountains and across "tortuous streams" for nearly a week, Arch Rowand and the Jessie Scouts rode ahead of Averell's force of 2,000 mounted troops, charged with attacking the Confederate saltworks and lead mines. They found the Confederates on May 7. "Captured scouts of the enemy and one company of the Eighth Virginia (Confederate) Cavalry on picket," wrote Averell.[6] The Confederates gleaned accurate information from their scouts that a Union force was advancing but were uncertain whether the raid would target the lead mines or the saltworks.

General John Hunt Morgan, back in command after his 1863 arrest and imprisonment following his raid in Ohio, correctly guessed Saltville and dug in his force of 4,000 troops. Outnumbered by two to one, Averell attempted to skirt around Morgan and attack Wytheville, though they nevertheless collided. "At [Wytheville] we ran into Morgan's men, too heavy for us to tackle, and we got back. The Confederates got my horse; they shot him from under me," remembered Arch Rowand. Averell's force barely escaped with their lives. "Averell was wounded that day with a bullet on the top of his head which disabled him for a little while."[7] The two sides battled for over four hours, and Averell lost more than one hundred men and officers. In the dead of night, the raiders escaped by crossing the swollen New River. When Confederates hot on their heels arrived soon after, the river had miraculously risen to impassable levels. "Had their designs been accomplished in reaching the river before me the success of the expedition might have been varied," Averell laconically reported.[8]

Averell's men destroyed track and other critical infrastructure as they moved to join Crook's force. With the bridges burned behind them and the river swollen, the two commands began the long journey back to West Virginia together. Hundreds of enslaved men, women, and children seeking their freedom flocked to the two Union commanders. Low on supplies and food, Crook nonetheless mercifully accepted them into his protection even though being bogged down by civilians could jeopardize his escape from the Confederates. Denying them passage could have resulted in their death or severe punishment, and the Union commander also saw an indirect benefit of removing a portion of the Confederate labor force.

Snow, mud, and rugged terrain combined with worn-out horses and mules made for a difficult journey. Thurmond's Rangers sniped at them along the way. After they had run the gauntlet forged by Mother Nature and Confederate bushwhackers, all that stood between the raiders and their destination, Meadow Bluff, West Virginia, was the swollen Greenbrier River. Crook improvised and converted supply wagons into barges—jumping in to guide stalled horses and mules across the river. Harassed by Thurmond's men, the general was grazed by a stray bullet. Unflinching, he continued to press forward.

With all the commands united at Meadow Bluff, Crook ordered Blazer and his men to "forage in the vicinity of Lewisburg and take everything. In two days had ten wagons loaded and sent to the army," Asbe Montgomery recalled.[9]

Blazer's Scouts and the Jessie Scouts did not rest long. Once again, the men would traverse the same ground to attack Staunton in the Shenandoah Valley.

THE SHENANDOAH VALLEY

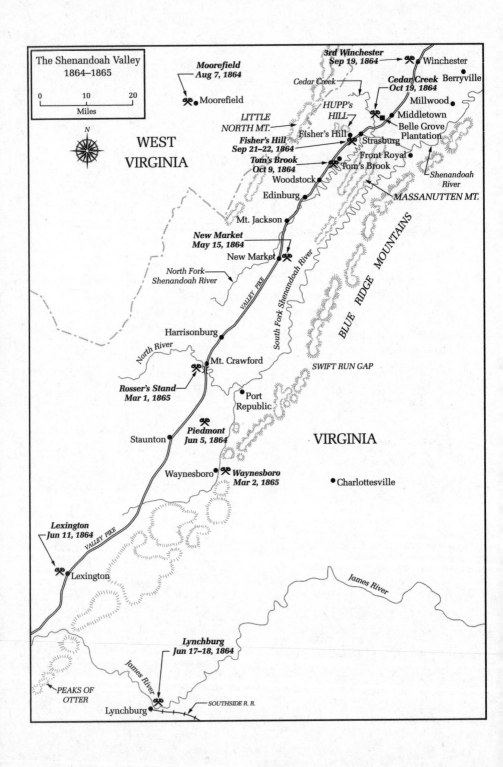

20. INTO THE VALLEY: STAUNTON AND LEXINGTON

A small party of Confederate scouts rode down the side of the mountain. Off in the distance, they spied a group of riders moving toward them. The Southerners drew their pistols and rode toward the column. Within fifty yards, Rebel scout James M'Chesney let out a sigh of relief, realizing the men in front of him were clad in gray. *These are our men*, he thought. He and his fellow Confederate scout, William I. Kunkle, rode to the officer in the group and called out, "Good morning, gentlemen." When asked if they had seen any Yankees, the captain responded, "No."

M'Chesney's gaze turned to the men in front of him. "Observing for the first time that the whole party, some twenty in all, had their pistols in hand as if expecting an enemy from our direction, I said to the captain that they had evidently taken us for enemies, to which he agreed." The captain tersely asked where the Confederate scouts had come from while the men continued advancing in groups of four until they nearly surrounded the Confederates, so close their horses almost brushed one another. But the captain's tone soon aroused the scout's suspicions. "My eyes quickly took in the situation, and I observed that, while they wore gray coats or jackets and slouch hats like our men, they all wore blue pants, their horses were branded 'U.S.,' and their saddles, bridles, and all their equipment were such as the Yankee cavalry used." The scout knew at once he was amid Jessie Scouts. He thought, "Either Camp Chase or the grave had opened before me." The scout's mind worked rapidly. By this time in the war, the Jessie Scouts had become renowned for their prowess, the name having been used for any Union scout wearing a Confederate uniform. As his fellow Confederate continued conversing with no idea of who they were speaking with,

M'Chesney played along, answering Captain Richard Blazer's questions. Having determined not to surrender, he slowly started to back up his mare and declared loudly that it would be useless to go any further since they hadn't seen any Yankees. "My face-to-face talk and manner had made him careless, as he was sure that he had me." As M'Chesney turned his back, he heard the captain shout, "Halt!"[1]

The Confederate spurred his horse and dashed through "a shower of bullets." More than two dozen shots were fired at the fleeing Confederate, including several from less than ten feet away, all failing to reach their mark. Kunkle wasn't so lucky. One bullet grazed the top of his head. "Fortunately, it was a pointed ball and striking obliquely the round surface of the skull, it did little damage." Another bullet shattered one arm, and a final ball passed through his elbow. Unable to escape, Kunkle was captured, and the Yankees brought him before Blazer, who threatened, "Now, old fellow, we have you safe; and if you don't tell me where [y]our general is and the number of his forces, I'll damn soon put you up the spout." Kunkle appealed to Blazer's honor in pleading for his life: "Captain, I am a Confederate soldier, and as a natural consequence I intend to be true to my country. I have had the pleasure of guarding some of your men, and I have never spoken an unkind word to one of them; and if you were a gentleman and a brave man, you would not do it either."[2] The appeal worked. Despite being raw from losing several men days earlier, Blazer simply turned his horse and left the uncooperative Confederate scout to his captors, who took him to the rear.

The incident occurred while Blazer's Scouts were in the vanguard of Crook's forces. Once again, Blazer's Scouts served as the general's eyes and ears, leading his troops in a Federal advance on Staunton in the Shenandoah Valley.

The Shenandoah Valley stretches over 150 miles from the Potomac River in the North to the James River in the South. The rugged Alleghenies create the western wall of the valley, while the Blue Ridge forms the eastern border. The valley was the breadbasket of the Confederacy, critical for its farms, granaries, and depots. Both sides vied for control of the numerous passes and gaps that enabled points of egress into the valley. From March to June 1862, Major General Thomas J. "Stonewall" Jackson conducted his successful Shenandoah Valley campaign. Winning numerous battles, his smaller force of roughly 17,000 troops engaged multiple Union armies, preventing their deployment in a Union offensive on Richmond.

Most importantly, the valley acted as a back door to the North's capital, Washington, DC, a route of invasion to the North: Lee's campaigns that ended at Antietam and Gettysburg flowed through it.

"Here comes the main 'tug of war.' . . . We did not know how nigh was one of the hardest marches ever any set of men endured," recalled Asbe Montgomery. "The time had come for all our skill and bravery to be tested. But our country lay bleeding before us, and we felt like offering our lives on its altar as a sacrifice if needs be. The time came, struck tents, the bugle sounded, and off for Staunton, through Lewisburg, and across the Greenbrier River. The scouts to the advance to clear anything that might be in the way."[3]

Immediately after they raided the Virginia and Tennessee Railroad in May, Blazer's Scouts and the Jessie Scouts were back on the move to the Shenandoah Valley. The Army of West Virginia had a new commander, Major General David Hunter, known to his troops as "Black Dave." Hunter was appointed to command on May 21, 1864, following the disastrous Battle of New Market on May 15, where the former youngest-ever vice president of the United States, John Breckinridge, now a Confederate general, defeated Union general Franz Sigel with the assistance of Virginia Military Institute (VMI) cadets. Despite his superior numbers, Sigel lost the battle, prompting Grant, when asked for Sigel's replacement, to tersely respond, "By all means, I would say appoint General Hunter, or anyone else, to the command of West Virginia."[4]

Hunter hated secessionists, despite having deep family ties in Virginia. His appearance reflected his demeanor. He sported a coal-black wig and dyed his mustache. Somewhat a loose cannon, when in command of the southern districts of Florida, Georgia, and South Carolina in 1862, Hunter issued General Order 11 emancipating enslaved individuals in those territories four months before President Lincoln issued the Emancipation Proclamation. Lincoln rescinded and publicly repudiated the order as part of his effort to hold slaveholding border states in the Union. Order 11 also made Hunter a marked man in the South, a "felon to be executed if captured."[5] The radical ideologue, ahead of his time, also advocated for Black units within the Union Army.

Grant envisioned that Hunter, now in command of the Army of the Shenandoah, which included General Crook's division and Averell's forces, would then march on Staunton, Virginia, and go about dismantling the

Confederates' rail and supply lines as well as other critical infrastructure, ordering essentially a scorched-earth policy on May 21. Blazer's Scouts led Crook's division, while the Jessie Scouts and Arch Rowand spearheaded Averell's 2nd Cavalry Division.

Once the commands united, Hunter divided his men into columns to confuse the Confederates regarding their intentions. As they pushed toward Staunton, they left a path of destruction in their wake, controversially burning homes and private property as well. Staying in contact with the other commands was essential; Averell sent out four men, including Rowand, before nightfall to find General Alfred Duffié, who was leading his brigade in one of the columns. Riding deep into Southern territory, they spied the light from a house as they searched for the Frenchman. Wearing Confederate uniforms, the Scouts offered to pay a woman tending to a sick child for something to eat. "Her eyes shining, 'Pay?' she said. 'I do not charge our boys anything!'" Ravenous from the long ride, the men wolfed down bread and cold milk until jarred by the order, "Surrender!" Staring down a dozen gleaming carbine barrels a few feet away, Rowand called out, "Are you Yanks?" "No!" came the reply. "'Oh' as though relieved. 'That's all right, then; we surrender!'"[6] he answered.

As the Confederates removed the Jessie Scouts' weapons, Rowand concealed evidence that would have unmasked him as a Union Scout in his shirt sleeve. "I remembered that in my pocket there was a pass, naming me as a scout and passing me through the Union lines at all times; I managed to get the small pocketbook and, by a flip of my fingers, shoot it up my sleeve and hold it in the hollow of my arm. Then they took us into the house, and the inquisition began."[7]

As Rowand recalled, the Confederates carefully placed the Scouts with the light of the fire "strong on my face, so that they could see the flicker of an eyelid or the twitch of a muscle, and the captain, with his back to the light, sits facing me, with our chairs close together." Fortunately, Rowand and his fellow Scouts were close enough they could hear and coordinate their stories. "Townsend and I never even glanced at one another, but each strained his ear for the other's answers."[8] The men would have been executed on the spot if they had contradicted each other's stories.

Remarkably, one Scout, Townsend, had in fact deserted from Confederate general Jenkins' command, which would have made him a traitor in their eyes and put him in especially "grave danger" of revealing their true identity as he was questioned by one of the Confederates. Surprisingly, however, "that very fact saved him."[9]

"This man is all right, Captain," his interrogator called out. Still unsure, the captain then turned to Rowand and grilled him about his background. Because he had been posted in West Virginia, Rowand was able to respond with great detail to the inquiry. Rowand then asked, "What is wrong with me?" The Confederate officer responded, "That is what puzzles me. You have answered all of my questions satisfactorily. You are a Southerner. I know you are not a Yankee." With stunning confidence, Rowand brazenly laughed in the officer's face and suggested, "Then to make sure what we are, you had better send us under guard to Breckinridge's headquarters." That comment melted the captain's final doubts. He abruptly handed the Scout a letter saying, "For General Breckinridge. Take it and get through as quick as you can. Hurry."[10]

"Hurry!" Rowand said with a sneer. "We'll need to!—you've kept us here an hour and a half now."[11]

The four Scouts rode as quickly as they could back to Union lines but ran into trouble when they were confronted by a picket of Ohio militia who could not fathom why a Scout would be in a Confederate uniform. A militia officer sized the two men up and down, swore, and threatened to hang them. Rowand sat on a tree stump and told the officer, "If he didn't get us to headquarters, forthwith, he himself would be in trouble." The officer made the Scouts walk to headquarters. Upon arrival the Jessie Scouts were recognized, and Rowand gleefully gave the Breckinridge letter to General Averell.* Rowand then told the general how the Union pickets treated them and "then somebody else got a scolding, and a pretty severe one."[12]

Maintaining lines of communication among the commands, General Hunter sent Jessie Scout James White on a mission moving through Confederate territory to deliver cipher-coded dispatches to General Crook. Early in the journey, White killed a Confederate scout carrying messages but soon ran across a Rebel officer and four men. The Scout rode up to the party. White took on the identity of the Confederate scout he had recently killed, and displayed the papers he had just captured. The following day, while "leisurely riding along the road and thanking

* The Confederate letter that Rowand handed Averell is in the *Official Records of the Union and Confederate Armies (OR)*.

Dame Fortune," he heard the men he encountered the day before shout, "Halt!" White put spurs to horse and galloped into West Virginia's rugged Allegheny Mountains. The men followed "so closely" that, while riding, he intentionally tore off the address from Hunter's dispatch. But amid "the dark screen of the forest trees," White escaped from the Confederates. Avoiding roving patrols, bushwhackers, and Confederates on leave, he "plodded wearily up the mountain side, scrambling through briars and underbrush and over fallen and decayed timber." Tired, wet, cold, and starving, White followed the Cheat River. Days passed until he encountered "ten of as villainous looking renegades as ever went unhung." White knew to recognize a "foe and what he had to deal with, and scarcely had the echo of their voices died out amid the mountains,"[13] when White jumped off his horse and ran for his life. Exhausted and emaciated, the Jessie Scout finally stumbled into Union-controlled Meadow Bluff, West Virginia, after a journey of nine days that spanned well over a hundred miles.

Back at camp, Scouts' duties could include unsavory tasks. Arch Rowand recalled being ordered by an officer to execute Southern civilian David S. Creigh, who, months earlier, had killed a Union soldier with an axe who was ransacking his home. Creigh hid the corpse in a well. A court-martial found Creigh guilty. One of Averell's staff officers palmed off the execution on the Jessie Scout.

"Rowand, you hang the prisoner."[14]

"I'm not going to do anything of the kind, I didn't enlist for an executioner," Rowand responded. The captain angrily insisted that the orders were from General Averell, so the reluctant Scout obeyed. Using a rope from a bed, they hung the prisoner from a nearby tree. "I have witnessed civil executions since, but then [I] didn't know enough to tie the hands and feet of the condemned."[15] Only later did the Scout discover that the captain had been ordered to perform the dreaded duty himself but foisted it on Rowand.

Creigh was not the only man executed during the raid. General Averell reported "a spy from the enemy who came into my camp shortly after my arrival and was killed by my order."[16] The Confederate made the mistake of claiming to be a Jessie Scout, and "he was executed by shooting without the formality of a drum-head court martial,"[17] recalled Rowand. Life and death behind the lines could rest on a razor's edge.

Far ahead of Crook's army, wearing Confederate uniforms, Blazer's Scouts skirmished with the enemy. "Come on, boys!" shouted Blazer. At full speed, wielding their Colt pistols to deadly effect, they dashed in and among a contingent of Confederate troops. "Some of them fall and breaking like quarter horses the rest took to the brush, but not til several had been killed, and several more taken prisoner," Asbe Montgomery recalled.[18]

During the advance, Blazer's Scouts sustained casualties, one of whom left a massive hole in the company. Sergeant Joseph Frith, while skirmishing with the enemy, died from an accidental discharge from an untrained fellow Yankee soldier, a clerk who had "no business" riding with the Scouts and who carelessly carried his "revolver in hand, directly in the rear of Joe. His horse stumbled and fell, causing the discharge of his pistol. The ball entered poor Joe's back coming out at the pit of his stomach," wrote one of the Scouts in a letter to Frith's father. The surgeon examining Frith's wound told him he would recover. "Joe would not believe it; he said he could not live. He did not fear to die but regretted to be shot by one of his own men." Like many dying men, he spoke of his mother and "wanted to let her know he died like a soldier." After an agonizing night, the next day seemed not as painful: "At seven o'clock he folded his arms across his breast, turning over on his side, and seemed to fall asleep—he was gone to his rest." His father reflected on Joseph's death, the second son he had lost during the war, sending a letter with these powerful words to the local newspaper: "In his own pure and unselfish life, he taught you a lesson *how to live*, and in his calm composure in the hour of death,* he has left you his example of *how to die*."[19]

At Staunton, in southwestern Virginia, Crook's forces combined with those of Averell and Hunter. Lacking discipline and leadership, Hunter's men ravaged the town, destroying the railroad and warehouses. To Crook's utter disgust, Hunter's men committed many acts that he considered disgraceful. Staunton also contained one of the larger hospitals of the

---

* Tragically, Joseph Frith's body is buried in an unmarked grave, likely near where he spent his final moments in this world.

Confederacy and its patients bore the scars of war: Confederate soldiers missing arms and legs watched the destruction inflicted by the Yankees.

While Hunter's men destroyed Staunton, Grant suggested that Hunter next attack Lynchburg, a vital rail hub, supply center, and hospital town over one hundred miles west of Richmond. For three days, Hunter dithered, waiting for supplies and ammunition. Crook urged Hunter to attack immediately—"Celerity was more important than numbers or ammunition"—and offered to lead the attack himself.[20] Hunter dismissed the idea. Once he finally got underway, Hunter put Blazer's Scouts in the vanguard, moving first to Lexington, Virginia. Here the Scouts faced more skirmishes: "We dismounted and deployed, and had some heavy firing, and as usual left some of them to lay quiet." In the melee, Asbe Montgomery had "the best horse . . . I ever rode" shot from underneath him. "His loss to me was great."[21]

The first to advance into Lexington, the Scouts received word from an enslaved individual that Confederate canal boats laden with artillery and supplies lay hidden nine miles away on the Maury River. Crook dispatched the Scouts on a mission to seize them that made national headlines. The *Chicago Tribune* reported, "To secure these, Capt. Blazer with his scouts was sent out, and, skirmishing the whole route, he found the boats as reported. Burning five of them, he dismounted his men and hauled the remaining two to Lexington. In them were six cannons—two six-pounders, one twelve-pounder, and three mountain howitzers." The haul also included half a ton of powder, 9,000 rounds of artillery ammunition, and provisions.[22]

Returning from missions was dangerous since the Scouts had to pass through their own lines wearing the uniform of the enemy. One Union soldier recalled an incident seared in his mind: "We were ordered to open ranks to let Blazer's Scouts pass through and then occurred another singular but ghastly event that will never leave my memory. While the Scouts were passing through our ranks the Rebel scouts [shot a Scout] in the forehead killing him instantly and knocking him from his horse so that he tumbled over on me, his crushed and mangled head striking my shoulder and smearing the blood and brains over my coat. I tell you that looked like war. I'll never forget it."[23]

A small Confederate force tried to save Lexington and VMI by burning the bridge over the Maury River, but Averell's force forded the waterway and entered Lexington, where they torched numerous residences and VMI in revenge for their role in the Battle of New Market. Crook was aghast: "Hunter would have burned the Natural Bridge could he have compassed it."[24] One man who tried to stop the burning of VMI had a connection to it. Lieutenant William Henry Gillespie was a member of VMI class of 1862 and had served on Stonewall Jackson's staff, but after he learned that Confederate authorities had arrested his father, he deserted and was now a member of Hunter's staff. His appeal failed, and VMI went up in smoke.

With the Scouts in the lead, Hunter, Crook, Averell, and Duffié made their way toward Lynchburg, clashing with and pushing aside smaller Confederate forces. The Federals marched through the Blue Ridge Mountains at the Peaks of Otter. The rhododendrons were in full bloom, and the men plucked them and placed them in their hats and rifle barrels, creating the spectral appearance of a moving column of flowers. Hunter's cavalry reached the outskirts of Lynchburg, which pushed the Confederates into their thinly manned defensive works. Yet the precious time Hunter had wasted in Staunton would catch up to him. Nearly one hundred miles away, Robert E. Lee determined to prevent Lynchburg from falling into enemy hands along with its military warehouses and vital rail junction.

For the previous forty days, Lee had been battling Grant in the tangled brambles of the Wilderness and later the bloodbath of Cold Harbor. Lee audaciously dispatched Lieutenant General Jubal A. Early, in command of the Army of Virginia's II Corps. Early was one of Lee's most talented and able battle commanders. Known for snarling at his subordinates, "Old Jube," or "Lee's bad old man," had rheumatoid arthritis, which bowed his shoulders and, along with a hairy beard and shining eyes, gave him the appearance of a "malignant and very hairy spider."[25] Under his command, approximately 9,000 men marched and raced by rail to Lynchburg to halt Hunter's army. Jessie Scouts warned Averell that the Confederates were railing reinforcements into Lynchburg. "Hunter would neither believe his own or the [Jessie Scouts],"[26] recalled Rowand.

Hunter's men assembled for battle against the undermanned defenders. The fighting commenced the morning of June 18, 1864. "The air was full of lead and shells flying, while Orderlies and Aids were loping in every direction, carrying orders. Every brave man was at his post, some dealing out death to the foe, while others were waiting with anxiety for orders. So desperate was the struggle that no man seemed to desire to speak,"

Montgomery recalled. In the midst of the action, Early's reinforcements arrived in the nick of time. "Constantly cheers were sent up from the Rebel lines, telling us that they were gaining in number."[27]

The Confederates counterattacked. "So they formed in mass, thickly as stubble on a newly-cut harvest field—charged our little lines, and came driving our men back, with fiendish looks and savage screams—the air dark with lead, smoke, and dust—and the ground strewn with the slain and stained with blood. They forced our lines back by inches."[28] Hunter's men in turn checked the Confederate attack and advanced. Some of Crook's men penetrated Lynchburg's outer defenses, but Hunter was convinced he was vastly outnumbered by Early's II Corps and other Confederate reinforcements. Hunter was running low on ammunition and other supplies since Confederate guerrillas, including Mosby's Rangers, had harried his supply lines.

The partisans had captured or disrupted numerous supply trains on the Valley Pike, the macadamized road that ran down the Shenandoah Valley from Winchester to Lexington and connected the Federal supply centers at Martinsburg and Harpers Ferry. It was vital to supplying any Federal army operating in the valley. Consequently, most of the major battles in the valley were fought alongside and near the Valley Pike. Convinced Early commanded a force much larger than his own and fearing Confederate guerrillas in his rear if he retreated to Washington, Hunter decided to fall back to West Virginia. It was one of the most difficult retreats of the war, as the men faced the blazing sun, severe weather, empty stomachs, and the Confederates. "I think it was the most disastrous retreat by the Union forces. It was simply demoralizing. I saw two men fall down and die of starvation and fatigue,"[29] remembered Rowand.

Lee's route of invasion to the north passed through the Shenandoah followed by the bloody battles of Antietam and Gettysburg. Hunter's retreat to the west instead of the north left the Shenandoah Valley, the back door to the nation's capital, open to Jubal Early's army. While the path of invasion to the north lay open, another path to seizing control of the Federal government and ending the war germinated in the Confederate Secret Service headquarters in Canada.

21. SHADOW WAR CANADA: INFLUENCING THE DEMOCRACY

Piratical, fat, and restless, Secret Service operative George Nicholas Sanders puffed on his cigar with "furious, incessant whiffs."[1] He was on a crusade to influence and control "the Democracy," the Democratic Party's term for itself at the time. Shortly after his arrival at the St. Lawrence Hall Hotel in Montreal, he "obtained control of [Commissioners] Clay and Holcombe and might get anyone in trouble by his active brain and tireless scheming,"[2] remembered operative John Castleman. Pragmatic and ruthless, Sanders thought the covert action and insurrection Hines and Castleman planned to ignite in the Northwest Conspiracy had a limited chance of success. He saw that influence and money would have a better chance of success of stopping the war. Sanders moved Commissioner Clay away from Thompson's and Hines' plans, to help in his own effort to control the Democratic convention mainly through Peace Democrats but also through more mainstream Democrats, including New York governor Horatio Seymour. In a letter to Jefferson Davis, Sanders laid out his plan to "form an alliance with the Northern Democracy [Northern Democratic Party]." He stated, "Clay, Holcomb, and I endeavored to show [Thompson, Hines, and Castleman] the impossibility of the success of any movement not open and general in character—that the Northern people could not be induced to rise either by states or by sections, but that we could control the Chicago [Democratic] convention."[3] The Confederate Secret Service hoped to do this by funding the Democratic peace movement and encouraging it by appealing to the anger generated from the loss of civil liberties, such as the suspension of habeas corpus, and the yearning for peace in a forever war with endless casualties. Horace Greeley, the influential editor of the *New York Tribune*, was an antislavery crusader who supported the war but was horrified by its aftermath and the stalled Union offensives that seemed to go nowhere. He summed up the mood of the country in writing to Lincoln, "Nine-tenths of the whole American people, North and South, are anxious for peace—peace on almost any terms—and utterly sick of human slaughter and devastation."[4]

In early June, in Canada, Hines, Castleman, Sanders, and Commissioner Thompson met[5] former Ohio Democratic congressman Clement Laird Vallandigham and put both plans in motion. Sanders' scheme called for gold to influence, build, and fortify Vallandigham's peace movement within the Democratic Party, while Hines' bold plan used violence to create an insurrection in the North.

Embittered from his recent election loss, the forty-four-year-old congressman was a dynamic lawyer and had mesmerizing oratorical skills that drew huge crowds. On January 14, 1863, Vallandigham had delivered a speech that hit both parties like a tsunami. He focused on Lincoln's unconstitutional acts and the hundreds of thousands of dead and wounded, and the treasure spent on what he described as a failed war. He believed the Southern states would never return "back into the fellowship and love at the point of a bayonet." The Ohioan called for an armistice and an "honorable peace,"[6] which struck a chord. "'Peace' is on a million lips,"[7] trumpeted one newspaper. A powerful movement was born that Sanders and the Confederate Secret Service planned to harness.

Vallandigham argued that the First Amendment protected his activities. On May 1, 1863, the Copperhead leader had addressed a crowd of 10,000 jammed into the tiny town square of Mount Vernon, Ohio. He railed against the war, urged the throng not to support it, and expressed sympathy for the Confederacy. The Ohioan and the movement he led publicly encouraged Union soldiers to desert.[8] He also infused his speeches with outrage at the loss of civil rights from the war, which appealed to many midwesterners. He feared that anarchy and a reign of terror could take place in the North, similar to internecine fighting in Missouri. Rousing racist diatribes laced Vallandigham's speech that day, like the one he had delivered in the halls of Congress before the war broke out. "[The Constitution] means white—pure white!—and not any shade. The term 'white' is a word of exclusion against the whole negro race, in every degree. Whoever has a distinct and visible admixture of the blood of that race is not white;

and it is an utter confusion of language to call him white."[9] Vallandigham harangued that the war was not about preserving the Union but about freeing enslaved people and destroying white liberties.

President Lincoln viewed internal dissent as one of the greatest threats to the Union, the so-called fire in the rear. Using the authority from his controversial 1861 suspension of the writ of habeas corpus, Lincoln ordered the Ohioan's arrest, and a military tribunal sentenced him to prison. Upon the congressman's arrest, his supporters firebombed several buildings in Dayton and killed a young infantry officer who tried to quell the mob. Responding to calls from Democrats and even some Republicans outraged by the arrest of a former member of Congress, Lincoln commuted the sentence and settled on exiling the firebrand to the South. Vallandigham left the South, evaded Federal forces, and escaped to Canada during the summer of 1863. From there, he won the Democratic nomination and campaigned in absentia for the governorship of Ohio in the fall of 1863. He also led a secret organization with shadowy ties to the Confederacy known as the Sons of Liberty.

In the parlor of a house in Ontario, Vallandigham told Hines and Thompson in the summer of 1864 that the Sons of Liberty were over a quarter of a million strong and growing. The organization drew men mainly from Illinois, Indiana, and Ohio. Semi-military in structure (organized into companies, regiments, brigades, and divisions) and for states' rights and personal liberties, the organization, above all, hated the war, and its members were willing to offer "their lives, fortunes, and sacred honor" to end it. He claimed the Sons of Liberty had 85,000 men in Illinois, 50,000 in Indiana, and 40,000 in Ohio. Castleman wrote, "Mr. Vallandigham advised purchase of arms for the Sons of Liberty, expressed the opinion that judicious expenditure of money would vastly increase the efficiency of this order." Seditiously, Vallandigham told the Southerners he "favored the formation of a 'Western Confederacy.' He also favored 'Sons of Liberty' displacing [executing] the governing officials in Illinois, Indiana, Ohio, and Kentucky." As the armed wing of the Copperheads, Vallandigham offered two regiments "practically armed"[10] to protect the looming Democratic National Convention scheduled for August in Chicago.

According to Thompson, the Sons of Liberty prepared for insurrection: "The universal feeling among its members, leaders, privates was that it was useless to hold a presidential election. Lincoln had the power and would certainly re-elect himself, and there was no hope but in force. The belief was entertained and freely expressed that by a bold, vigorous, and concerted movement the three great Northwestern States of Illinois, Indiana, and Ohio could be seized and held. This being done, the States of Kentucky and Missouri could easily be lifted from their prostrate condition and placed on their feet, this in sixty days would end the war."[11]

A few days later, in June, Vallandigham and the Confederate Secret Service met the other leaders of the Copperhead movement, a catchall term for the radical, rising, dominant wing of the Democratic Party that included secret groups such as the Knights of the Golden Circle and the Sons of Liberty. In St. Catharines, Ontario, near Niagara Falls, they bought into Hines' Northwest Conspiracy. The radical and violent groups had surreptitious signs, symbols, and handshakes and armed guards at their meetings. Over the past two years, mobs and individuals within the groups had unleashed violence, murder, sabotage, and arson: burning government warehouses and Unionists' homes and snipping telegraph wires. Hines and Castleman hoped to harness this violence and bring it to another level to create an insurrection.

In the coming weeks, Sanders, Clay, and the other commissioners would focus on their influence operations. They continued to meet various Democratic leaders and Copperheads on the Canadian side of Niagara Falls, often at the Clifton House hotel, including the fifth governor of California, former US senator John B. Weller, who advocated that California become a separate republic and an ally of the Confederacy. In these meetings, Sanders and Clay would help craft with Vallandigham the Secret Service's masterstroke: the bones of the Democratic platform. At the convention in Chicago, they would call for an armistice to end the war.

George Sanders also understood information warfare and the power of the media. He bragged to Jefferson Davis that his goal was "the Democracy [the Democratic Party] having possession of the press,"[12] making it his next target. Accordingly, the Confederate Secret Service plied Northern newspapers with cash to shape the Confederacy's narrative of how hopeless and fruitless the war had become. Among other initiatives, the Secret Service sent tens of thousands of dollars to the owner of the *New York Daily News*.[13]

The Secret Service continued to expand its influence operations outside the Sons of Liberty and funded the Democratic candidate for

governor in Illinois. The "Official Journal" of the commissions recorded
a meeting with the governor regarding his need for campaign funds for
his reelection. "When Mr. J. A. Barrett of Illinois and B. P. Churchill of
Cincinnati visited Mr. Thompson, bringing . . . assurances . . . to secure
the election of Mr. Robinson as governor of Illinois, and asking that money
should be advanced for that purpose, stating that Robinson had pledged
himself to them, that if elected he would place the control of the militia
and its 60,000 [troops at their disposal]." Thompson furnished tens of
thousands of dollars on behalf of Robinson's campaign.[14]

For Hines and Thompson, the Democratic convention in Chicago
in late August seemed like a golden opportunity to utilize Vallandigham's
Sons of Liberty to incite an uprising and free Confederate prisoners at
nearby Camp Douglas. Arms and money continued to flow to the Sons
of Liberty from the Confederate Secret Service along with operatives.
The insurrection, or Northwest Conspiracy, moved forward, as did the
Confederates' efforts to fund and grow the peace movement. For his part,
Thompson had "no confidence in political movements"[15] and sent a chilling
note to Confederate secretary of state Judah Benjamin stating, "Nothing
but violence can terminate the war."[16]

22. "To Threaten Washington"

As the Secret Service schemed and plotted in Canada, one of the Confederacy's most significant missed opportunities of the war began on June 28, 1864, when Jubal Early started marching his army toward the nation's capital dozens of miles north. With Hunter fleeing to West Virginia, Early's army had a clear path on the Valley Pike in the Shenandoah Valley and into Maryland. The original objective of Early's mission was multifold: to draw Union troops away from Grant's devastating siege of Petersburg, to disrupt the B&O railway lines, to free thousands of Confederates held captive in the Point Lookout prison camp southeast of Washington, DC, and finally to threaten and potentially seize the capital. Early promised Lee on June 28 "to threaten Washington" and, if an opportunity presented itself, "find an opportunity to take it."[1]

Early's march on Washington had its origins weeks earlier. After sustaining massive casualties at the Battle of Cold Harbor on May 31–June 12, Grant—unlike his predecessors, who, after defeat, retreated to Washington—kept marching around Lee's lines at Richmond to strike the vital railhead at Petersburg some twenty miles south of the Southern capital. The battle unfolded on June 9, when Union forces under General Benjamin Butler attacked Petersburg but failed to seize the town, giving Lee precious time to reinforce and entrench his troops in the area. Over the coming days, Grant moved his army over a pontoon bridge on the James River toward Petersburg. Both sides dug in with trenches that eventually stretched over thirty miles from Richmond to the eastern and southern portions of Petersburg in the Union's attempt to sever the rail lines into and out of Richmond. Desperate to relieve pressure on Petersburg, Lee dispatched Early to save Lynchburg from Hunter and draw Union troops away from the siege of Petersburg and, if the opportunity presented itself, threaten Washington.

For days Early marched his 14,000-man-strong army north from Lynchburg with almost no resistance. The opportunity to capture the Union's capital city became a more realistic possibility. Early kept Union authorities guessing on his target: the B&O Railroad, Baltimore, or Washington. Grant knew Early's force was meant as a distraction and an attempt to bleed off Union troops from his siege at Petersburg. But the distraction proved potentially devastating: Early had an uninhibited path to the capital, its resources, and the president.

On July 6 Captain Robert E. Lee Jr., General Robert E. Lee's youngest son, arrived in Early's camp outside Frederick, Maryland, with orders from his father for Early to launch one of the most daring special operations missions of the war: free the prisoners at Point Lookout, some 10,000 men. Initially hatched by Lee in the winter of 1863, the plan accelerated when Lee wrote Davis on June 26 urging, "Great benefit can be drawn from the release of our prisoners at Point Lookout. The number of men employed for this purpose would necessarily be small. . . . I think the guard might be overpowered, the prisoners liberated and organized, and marched immediately on the route to Washington."[2]

Early ordered Marylander brigadier general Bradley Tyler Johnson to head east toward Baltimore, cutting telegraph lines and burning bridges as he went to stall Union communication and troop movements. The former Maryland politician had raised and formed his own company at the beginning of the war and later led plans to form a Maryland Line (regiments composed of Marylanders), and now he commanded his own brigade. Early's plan then called for Johnson to head south toward Point Lookout on the southeastern side of Washington by the morning of July 12, in time to conduct a simultaneous assault with troops from an amphibious force that included operatives in the Confederate Secret Service sailing up the Chesapeake Bay from Wilmington, North Carolina, carrying thousands of arms for the freed prisoners.

Despite Johnson's men successfully executing their first objective, multiple events resulted in Jefferson Davis aborting the operation before it fully unfolded on July 12. Johnson took longer than anticipated in his almost impossible task of traveling over 200 miles through enemy territory in such a tight time frame. Davis feared that the Union fleet would destroy the amphibious force at the mouth of the Chesapeake. And finally, details of the operation had leaked out to Union authorities, jeopardizing the entire mission. Had freeing the Confederate prisoners ranked as a higher priority or Johnson been sent on a more direct path, the plan might have succeeded; the impact of thousands of troops to replenish and reinforce Early's Army of the Valley District could hardly be calculated. In truth, this operation that one Confederate officer referred to as "decidedly the most brilliant idea of the war"[3] could probably have moved forward even without the naval component of the plan. Point Lookout's defenses—the feebly manned Union garrison—could hardly have withstood an onslaught from a brigade of seasoned Confederate veterans while also maintaining control of thousands of angry Southern prisoners.

At the same time as Johnson moved toward Point Lookout, Major Harry Gilmor and his band of roughly 175 men went on a rampage through Union territory to divert their enemy's attention from the prison break and the attack on the capital. A member of an elite Baltimore family, the dashing Gilmor was imprisoned for his staunch Southern sympathies by the Federal government when the war broke out. After his release, he joined the Confederate Army as a private, although he was quickly promoted to sergeant major and raised his own company, where he earned his reputation as a scout for various Confederate commands. In 1863, he organized the 2nd Maryland Cavalry, also known as "The Band" or Gilmor's Partisan Raiders,[4] who used unconventional tactics to harass Yankee targets, cutting telegraph lines, tearing up track, even burning Maryland governor Augustus Bradford's summer home in retaliation for Hunter's burning of the former Virginia governor's home in Lexington.

In one instance, on July 11, Gilmor used a flaming captured train emptied of passengers from the Philadelphia, Wilmington, and Baltimore Railroad to set a bridge over the Gunpowder River on fire. In addition to destroying the bridge, he also snared a high-value target in passenger Major General William B. Franklin, the commander of XIX Corps. "I backed the whole flaming mass down on the bridge, catching some of the infantry a little way from shore upon the structure and compelling them to jump into the water. The train was running slowly, and stopped right on the draw, where it burned and fell through communicating the fire and destroying the most important part of the bridge."[5] After burning the trestle, Gilmor and his men headed toward Towsontown (presently Towson), where he stopped off at Ady's Hotel and cavalierly downed a glass of ale. When he received word of a large Union cavalry detachment arriving from Baltimore, he instructed several men to guard their prisoner, General Franklin, and several Union officers. But their captors had passed out from exhaustion and the prisoners slipped away in the dead of night.

Gilmor and his men acted as Early's scouts as they marched north through the Shenandoah, but when Early tapped the Marylander for the special operations mission, Early and Johnson deprived themselves of one of their best eyes and ears. Old Jube also failed to utilize fully the war's master spy, John Singleton Mosby, and his Rangers.

23. Mosby's Calico Raid and Showdown at Mount Zion Church

Mosby and his Rangers were ideally positioned to play a critical role in the attack on Washington, DC. They could impede the movement of Federal troops while also tying up as many of them as possible, further clearing the path to Washington. It would have made sense for Early and Mosby to work closely together, but that was not to be.

Cantankerous, "mean as a dog," and an officer Robert E. Lee dubbed "my bad old man," Early was difficult to work with, as Mosby found out firsthand.* Early failed to notify the partisan leader of his plans or order him to coordinate. Mosby found out about Early's invasion of the North, and a potential attack on Washington, only after Mosby's men accidentally ran into Early's quartermaster in Middleburg, Virginia. Mosby felt snubbed by Early, and their resulting actions and inactions may have influenced the course of history.

Despite the lack of camaraderie and coordination between the two Confederates, Mosby, on his own initiative, prepared to launch a raid at Point of Rocks, Maryland. The goal of what became known as the Calico Raid was to cut the Northern line of communications by severing the Baltimore and Ohio Railroad and telegraph lines. The operation began

---

* Noted for his prickly personality, Early rebuffed Mosby's requests for direction and coordination multiple times. Mosby wanted to coordinate with Early. The Rangers in front of Early's army as a recon force or used to disrupt Union response could have been a force multiplier. Mosby's postwar letters indicate he hated Early.

on July 3 when 250 Rangers assembled at Upperville. Armed to the teeth and equipped with empty sacks for stuffing with Union loot, the Rangers rode a mile in the sweltering heat to Green Garden Mill, located next to Ranger Dolly Richards' elegant family mansion,* to water their horses.

In the coming months, Richards would play an outsize leadership role in the battalion. The Confederate officer, exquisitely dressed, handsome, fearless, and only nineteen years old, possessed sagacity and coolness under pressure that belied his years.

After satiating the thirst of animal and man alike, the Rangers resumed their journey to Point of Rocks. The town, a key hub for the Baltimore and Ohio Railroad, was also a connection to the Chesapeake and Ohio Canal (C&O) and a Union supply depot. Two hundred and fifty Northerners—infantry and two companies of Loudoun Rangers—guarded the town.

The Loudoun Rangers were an independent cavalry unit drawn from the Quaker and German populations and the largely staunch Unionist towns of Waterford and Lovettsville. On June 20, 1862, the Loudoun Rangers mustered two small cavalry companies, making them one of the few Union units raised in Confederate Virginia. The unit never numbered over 200 men and largely operated as a home guard along the Potomac River, protecting Union residents of upper Loudoun County. Led by Waterford miller Samuel Means, the Loudoun Rangers would be a nuisance to Mosby's Rangers by occasionally raiding Mosby's Confederacy.

Weeks earlier, Mosby's men had easily captured Duffields Depot farther west on the Baltimore and Ohio Railroad line in a bloodless battle, never needing the artillery they brought that day. But on July 4, Mosby would need all the resources at his disposal to overcome his Union foes, including his artillery and his tactics for shocking the enemy.

Through the dust and oppressive heat, a team of horses dragged a twelve-pound Napoleon up the high ground on the Virginia side of the river. The hot, sweaty work would pay off, for from that vantage, Sam Chapman, who led the crew of artillerists, would overlook the entire field of battle.

---

* The Rangers would use Green Garden, a brick home built in the Greek Revival style owned by Dolly Richards' family, as one of their safe houses during the war. The mansion contains a secret trapdoor and hiding space that still exist today.

The rest of Mosby's Rangers began the tricky business of crossing the Potomac. Loudoun Ranger sharpshooters lay in wait, concealed in bushes on the bank and a strategically located island in the center of the river. A phalanx of Confederates dismounted and waded cautiously into the muddy waters, uncertain of their footing. Almost immediately, the Northerners began taking aim, attempting to pick off Mosby's men.

"We floundered through the water shooting, yelling stumbling over the round river stones and getting ducked overhead, rising and sputtering and firing again, the boom of our artillery proclaimed the celebration was on,"[1] remembered one of Mosby's Rangers.

If any of Mosby's Rangers considered turning around, their own artillery quickly dissuaded them. A round from Chapman's gun fell short and exploded immediately behind the Rangers. Caught between the "devil and the deep sea," the Rangers surged forward. At least one Ranger considered "the enemy the lesser of the two evils."[2]

As the water grew deeper, the Southerners struggled. "The higher the water came up around them, the more exasperated they became," Ranger Private John Munson recalled.

After one shot came "annoyingly near" the Rangers, Mosby rode up to one of his men who was armed with a carbine and asked, "Pitts, can you stop that Yankee over there from sucking eggs?"

"I'll try," responded Pitts, who had water up to his breast.

Raising his carbine, the far too modest Pitts aimed and fired, killing the Loudoun Ranger.[3]

From overhead, Sam Chapman's Napoleon boomed. Led by Dolly Richards, Company A crossed from the island to the Maryland side and onto the towpath near the C&O, which ran parallel to the river on the northern side.

Raising the Napoleon's trajectory, Chapman fired, and again, Union troops scattered. They scrambled across a small wooden bridge over the canal, tearing up the wooden floorboards as they crossed. The Federals then hunkered down in a small earthen redoubt perched on a small hill on the northern side of the C&O. Sheltered there from the artillery fire, they peppered Mosby's command as his men forded the river from the island and worked their way up the riverbank to the canal.

But their gunfire was not enough to quell the spirit of the Southerners. Braving a hail of bullets, Lieutenant Harry "Deadly" Hatcher dashed across the bare support timbers on the bridge and seized the Union garrison's flag on the other side of the canal. Meanwhile, Dolly Richards tore wooden planks from a nearby building. As the Napoleon belched to provide cover, Mosby's Rangers used the planks to repair the bridge. Lewis Powell and others surged forward across the canal as artillery rounds arched overhead. In the face of the onslaught, the Loudoun Rangers fell back.

The Confederates pursued them and captured a few of their men and an officer. One of Mosby's Rangers later remarked, "I have never understood why the taking of the Point of Rocks that day was such an easy job. When you recall that our only approach to them was over a narrow towpath and which we could ride only two abreast, that we were on the farther side of a rock-ribbed canal over which it was impossible for us to charge them, it is inscrutable that they did not get into that railroad tunnel and just shoot us down as fast as we showed ourselves. But the facts are that less than two hundred and fifty cavalry rode down on them in broad daylight, re-laid the flooring on the bridge before their eyes, crossed over it, and ran them as far as the eye could reach, without loss or injury to a single man or horse. This sounds like a fairy tale, but it is literally true."[4]

With the Northerners out of the way, Mosby's Rangers ransacked Point of Rocks; they severed telegraph lines and cut poles. Soon their empty sacks burst with dry goods, "bolts of cloth . . . [some] of the gaudiest prints, served as sashes which streamed from the shoulders of the wearers . . . boots and shoes, for both sexes, hung from the saddles and horse's necks; and various kinds of tin-ware flashed back the sunlight."[5]

The men remained mindful of the "girls they left behind" and gathered up hats, hoops, and flashy ribbons, looking like a "parade of Fantastics." Eventually, a considerable wagon train loaded to the gills with booty rolled to the Fauquier hills, leading one Ranger to quip, "This was quite a novel attachment to Mosby's men, their specialty being to attach themselves to the other fellow's wagon train."[6]

After the Rangers picked Point of Rocks clean, Mosby sent Henry Heaton, who had been one of Early's aides, and Fountain Beattie to find Early and deliver a written message: "I will obey any order you send me." On July 7, the two Rangers found Early in Sharpsburg, Maryland. Early made no mention of the raid and requested that Mosby support him by once again cutting the railroad and telegraph lines and reconnoitering toward Washington.[7] Early made this a verbal request instead of a written order.

Mosby chose not to comply, and this, combined with a lack of coordination between the commands, potentially impacted history.

Mosby's men recrossed the Potomac before Union reinforcements arrived. Back in Virginia, the Ranger leader sent his best scrounger, Major Hibbs, to find forage for horses and detailed scouts to track any Northern troops venturing into Confederate territory. About 2 p.m. on July 5, hundreds of Loudoun Rangers and men from the 8th Illinois Cavalry poured into Point of Rocks and Maryland Heights outside Harpers Ferry. In all, a total of 2,800 reinforcements moved from Washington, DC's defenses—one-third of its force.[8]

Mosby's Rangers took cover on the Virginia side of the Potomac, where their leader hatched a plan to keep the Union troops tied down for as long as possible. Creating the illusion of vast numbers of Confederates, the Rangers rode around, creating clouds of dust and occasionally parading in front of the Federals. From time to time, they pretended that they intended to recross the river, engaging the Northerners in a series of skirmishes. As one Ranger remembered, "It was a kind of endless chain business by which regiment after regiment was paraded across the stage. . . . Of course, our commander had to refrain from overdoing the thing, and see to it that the program was duly varied, lest the fake should be discovered."[9]

During the back-and-forth across the river, the scouts led by Lieutenant Harry Hatcher returned, and so did Major Hibbs. The major, with his "famous Corn Detail[,] secured the sinews of war and undoubtedly secured a still filled with alcohol. Though the men might go without rations, and perhaps fought all the more savagely when hungry, the horses had to be kept in prime condition, and whatever happened, fed."[10] As the horses grazed on Hibbs' scrounged corn, Hatcher reported that a large force of 150 handpicked men, the 2nd Massachusetts Cavalry and 13th New York, commanded by Major William H. Forbes, scion of a wealthy abolitionist family in Boston, was prowling the neighborhood and looking for the Rangers, having recently left Leesburg, heading south toward Aldie.

After dispatching men to ride shotgun to guard the four wagons of booty as they headed back to Fauquier County for safekeeping, Mosby had 175 men remaining in his command to deal with Forbes. Mosby ordered his men to mount up, and they rode south through Leesburg. Locals greeted the Rangers with a triumphant welcome. "The pretty girls of Leesburg lined the streets as we passed through the town and presented us trays laden with the most acceptable breakfasts,"[11] recalled one of the Rangers.

Riding down several obscure country lanes, the Rangers traveled southeast from Leesburg and emerged behind Forbes, who had his horses grazing in a field by a farm across from the Mount Zion Church (near the present-day junction of Route 50 and Route 15). Strategically, on July 6, 1864, Mosby placed his men to block the Federals' route of escape to their base camp at Falls Church, Virginia, and personally scouted the Union position. After finding Forbes half a mile west up the Little River Pike, he had his men stealthily move into position. They crept to within half a mile when a sharp-eyed Union picket spotted them and fired a signal gun.

Having lost the element of surprise, Mosby led his men into the open. At the same time, Forbes drew up his men in formation. "Their alignment was as perfect as if on dress parade."[12] The two commands faced each other across the field, several hundred yards apart.

Once again relying on his shock tactics, Mosby responded with a frontal attack, "a straight charge over an open road upon an enemy who was fully prepared for us,"[13] recalled Ranger John Henry Alexander.

Sam Chapman yanked the lanyard on the Napoleon. The gun barked, and a shell sailed over the heads of the Union cavalrymen. It exploded too high to cause any damage; however, their horses, unfamiliar with exploding artillery shells, panicked.

Dolly Richards' Company A charged on horseback in a sweeping gallop, firing their carbines. The Rangers let out blood-curdling yells and screams, a crucial part of their tactics to intimidate their opponents. Mosby swept their line "like a hurricane."[14]

One Union officer recalled seeing them "swooping down like Indians, yelling like fiends, discharging their pistols with fearful rapidity, and threatening to completely envelop our little band."[15]

It was too much for the Northerners to bear. "Unable to stand the shock, they broke and ran some distance, but rallied and formed again behind a fence."[16]

"Form in the woods,"[17] yelled Forbes.

Mosby's men crashed into the Californians and New Yorkers, and brutal hand-to-hand combat ensued. Rangers' Colts, carbines, and sawed-off shotguns blasted the Bluejackets at point-blank range as Yankee sabers clanged, and other Federals fired their carbines, pistols, and revolvers.

Californian private Nathan Fogg defended himself with a .44-caliber Colt Army while Sergeant Edward Tyrell, a native of New Bedford, Massachusetts, hacked with his saber.[18] Fogg received a wound in the leg during the melee but escaped to safety.

Dashing between Mosby's men, "Forbes occupied the center of the action" and tried to rally his men, barking, "Follow your leader!" Like a bloodhound, he tracked down Mosby in the whirling mass of bodies and horses. Blue and gray uniforms became so "interwoven" that the Californians used their Spencers as clubs, bludgeoning one of the Rangers "insensibly."[19] Standing on his stirrups with his saber drawn, Forbes thrust the sword at the Gray Ghost with his full weight and momentum. But Ranger Tom Richards took the blow intended for his commander, and the blade sliced through Richards' meaty shoulder.

Still standing, Richards "snapped his pistol in the major's face,"[20] but it misfired.

Simultaneously, a bullet felled Forbes' horse, bringing down its rider, pinning him to the ground, and forcing the Union major to yield.

With Forbes' surrender, his men scattered. "Mosby pressed on and drove them in disorder."[21] The Federals galloped for their lives down Braddock Road toward the safety of their camp in Fairfax. An "exciting" adrenaline-charged horse race unfolded. One Ranger recalled, the Federals "poured into us Mr. Spencer's *unpalatable pills* [bullets] the whole distance."[22] But Mosby, Private John Munson, and other Rangers nipped at their heels, catching several men as far as ten miles away, at Sudley Church. Munson remembered, "We found a man kneeling near the fence by the roadside, with his head bent forward touching the rail in front of him and his left hand clutching a gaping wound in his side."[23]

Once again, the Rangers had defeated their adversary, killing or wounding eighty of Forbes' men and capturing fifty-seven prisoners, including the major himself. But afterward, Mosby ensured that Forbes was well treated, so well, in fact, that the two men would become close friends after the war.[24]

24. "I Don't Think Many People, North or South, Realize How Close Washington Came to Falling"

Once the Union realized the Confederate Army was headed to Washington, time was of the essence. Initially, the Union high command had been unsure of Early's objective. Johnson's and Gilmor's raids suggested Baltimore or the main Union railroads were the probable Confederate objectives. Grant himself was preoccupied with Petersburg and slow to react. The only thing standing in Old Jube's way was about 7,500 troops commanded by Union major general Lew Wallace.* Ordered to hold the iron B&O railway bridge across the Monocacy River, Wallace telegraphed back, "I will hold the bridge at all hazards. Send on the troops as rapidly as possible."[1] True to his word, Wallace and his valiant men, many inexperienced recruits, took a stand on July 9, against Early's superior force in the bloody Battle of Monocacy, outside Frederick, Maryland.

Wallace understood his role—to buy time and delay Early. As Wallace's troops battled, he eyed his watch, writing years after the war, "Five hours from my very able antagonist, General Early! I counted them, beginning at seven o'clock, not once but many times, much as I fancy a miser counts his gold pieces."[2] Nonetheless, Wallace's telegram to headquarters later on July 9 sounded an ominous alarm: "I have been defeated . . . the enemy are not pursuing me, from which I infer they are marching on

---

* After the war, Wallace authored the epic novel *Ben-Hur*.

Washington."[3] After defeating Wallace, the Confederates torched the buildings around the railway trestle but did not have enough powder to blow it up. They also made a feeble attempt to blast the bridge and sever the vital B&O Railroad trestle with solid shot from a cannon, resulting in only minor damage to the stout iron structure. But most importantly, Early's battle with Wallace would cost the Confederates a precious day on the road to Washington.

Battle-weary, Early and his men continued their long, hot march on July 10 another thirty miles before reaching Rockville, Maryland, about twelve miles from Washington. "[The day] was an exceedingly hot one, and there was no air stirring. . . . [We] were enveloped in a suffocating cloud of dust, and many of them fell by the way of exhaustion."[4] The sun and scorching heat had a debilitating effect on man and beast alike. Early rode ahead of his men and through his field glasses could see the Capitol dome in the distance and the Union defenses in front of him "but feebly manned."[5]

Riding from Rockville to Washington's Tenleytown, Brigadier General "Tiger" John McCausland and over a thousand of his cavalrymen probed the Union defenses in advance of Early's main force. Hailing from the Kanawha Valley, where Thurmond's Rangers operated, ardent Confederate McCausland before the war taught at VMI with Stonewall Jackson. He was nicknamed "Tiger John" because of the aggressive pressure he placed on his men. That day and night he pushed his men into Washington. Lacking some of the Confederacy's best scouts, such as Mosby or Gilmor, the Southerner hunted for weaknesses in the capital's inner belt of defenses, looking for a clear avenue of advance.

McCausland later revealed, "I don't think many people, North or South, realize how close Washington came to falling into Rebel hands that summer. . . . I rode with my staff into the defenses. . . . Your capital was practically undefended! I sat there on a big gun and looked at the lights and wished I had men enough to go ahead and capture the place and end the damned war!"[6] While no one knows exactly where McCausland allegedly looked at the lights of Washington, it most likely occurred at Fort Gaines, the present-day location of the American University campus, which was on reserve status, making it largely devoid of a garrison.

One of Lee's most trusted generals and future Democratic senator from Georgia John Brown Gordon confirmed the gaps in Union defenses:

"I myself rode to a point on those breastworks at which there was no force whatever. The unprotected space was broad enough for the easy passage of Early's army without resistance."[7]

Compounding matters, the Union lacked a unified command. No one seemed to want to take responsibility for the potential unfolding debacle. Union chief of staff Major General Henry "Old Brains" Halleck, in a dereliction of duty, ducked directly commanding the Union forces defending the capital. He acknowledged weakness in the Federal fortifications in his correspondence to Grant: "The forces in some parts of the entrenchments, and they are no means reliable, being made up of all kinds of fragments, should give away before they can be re-enforced from other points. A line thirty-seven miles in length is very difficult to guard at all points with an inferior force."[8]

Despite McCausland's potential opportunity near Fort Gaines, Early directed his effort at Fort Stevens, which defended the northern and one of the main approaches into the city—the Seventh Street Pike. Only a total of 209 souls manned the ramparts, and they were all that stood in the way of Early's corps of combat veterans.[9] The delay at Monocacy, a lack of scouts, and the weather all played a role in delaying Early's potential attack. Those Union troops included one-hundred-days men, National Guard troops from the 150th Ohio Volunteer Infantry who had been federalized two months earlier to serve only one hundred days. The green Ohioans, who had been initially promised duty in a safe area, now bought precious time for the arrival of Union reinforcements. Skirmishing hundreds of yards in front of the fort, the men slowly fell back as Early's massive forces moved into position.* To augment the citizen-soldiers from Ohio, the Federals recruited anyone possible. "Every available man in Baltimore and Washington put in the trenches," recalled one participant.[10] Secretary of War Edwin Stanton ordered all military-age men to man fortifications, including soldiers convalescing in the city's hospitals. Clerks, messengers, invalids, "military riffraff . . . a sorry lot they were . . . laid down their pens, and off they went to 'report' for military duty," explained one Federal official.[11] Lincoln remarked that he doubted there were enough troops to hold the Union defenses and that

---

* One of those guardians of the city who put his life on the line to save the capital was my great, great uncle, twenty-two-year-old Solon farmer Orrin Mills.

the reinforcements on the way "will scarcely be worth counting. Let us be vigilant and cool. I hope neither Baltimore nor Washington will be sacked."[12] But the valiant Ohioans, later reinforced by dismounted Union cavalry, skirmished just long enough for advance elements of the VI Corps to arrive in the nick of time to augment the fort's measly garrison.

Fortuitously, steamboats carrying the desperately needed Union reinforcements from the VI and XIX Corps began to arrive on the afternoon of July 11. Lincoln stood on the wharf on the Potomac and greeted thousands of troops as they marched toward Fort Stevens. Advance elements of Major General Horatio Wright's VI Corps arrived at the fort around 3 p.m. As both sides clashed, Lincoln himself fearlessly stood on a parapet to view the action as bullets flew from both sides, becoming the only sitting US president in history to come under enemy fire during a time of war. Wright later recalled, "When the surgeon was shot after I had cleared the parapet of everyone else, [Lincoln] still maintained his ground till I told him I should have to remove him forcibly. . . . He agreed to compromise by sitting behind the parapet instead of standing upon it. . . . He did so rather in deference to my earnestly expressed wishes, than from any considerations of personal safety."[13]

As the sun went down, the Confederacy's window for seizing the capital also closed. Had the Southern general attacked as soon as he arrived at the fort or had better intelligence on Union weak points, his forces could possibly have pierced the Federal defenses and altered the course of history. Early could have also dispatched smaller parties of Confederate troops to incinerate the capital. His raid had already placed in doubt Lincoln's chances for reelection; his success might have sealed the president's fate. The capture or burning of Washington could have been the death blow to the political will in the North, which had waned after the slew of Southern victories.

The exhaustion of his men, who had been fighting and marching for days, combined with the arrival of Union reinforcements, caused the Confederate general to break off the engagement and withdraw his forces from the capital on the evening of July 12, crossing the Potomac at White's Ferry. The Federals hoped to catch the cantankerous Confederate before he escaped to the relative safety of the Shenandoah Valley. But lacking confidence in Hunter, General Halleck dispatched George Crook to command Hunter's Army of West Virginia to join with Wright's VI Corps to smash the Southern army. Plodding through Virginia, the combined force failed to intercept the bulk of Early's troops as the Rebels passed through Snickers Gap in the Blue Ridge Mountains, which led to the Shenandoah. Crook's force collided with Early's rear guard on July 17 at Cool Spring, Virginia. Leading Crook's troops, Blazer's Scouts found the area "infested with Rebs." Blazer's men "served as sharpshooters and got highly complimented,"[14] recalled Asbe Montgomery. Despite the Scouts' success, the Battle of Cool Spring was a Confederate victory that forced a Union withdrawal.

Early's raid shocked public opinion in the North to its core. The fall of the capital could have opened the door to foreign intervention or recognition of the Confederacy from England or France. The United States had carefully been watching France after it initiated regime change in Mexico with the installation in 1864 of Maximilian von Habsburg as emperor and his tens of thousands of occupying troops. Across multiple fronts, over the course of several months, the Union strategy to win the war stalled. Outside Petersburg, Lee kept Grant's massive army at bay. Grant's losses against Lee were appalling: 70,000 were killed, wounded, or captured. Grant's multipronged offensive against the Confederacy seemed stymied.

Bond sales on government debt to finance the war provided half the amount needed. Financially, the value of the dollar plummeted while gold skyrocketed.[15] The Confederate Secret Service also had an operation to accelerate the dollar's decline. Thompson set up an arbitrage scheme by sending an agent to New York who would purchase gold and export it overseas, "selling it for sterling bills of exchange, and then again converting the exchange into gold." The scheme, according to Thompson, had "a marked effect on the market,"[16] until the Secret Service agent's former partner was arrested, which caused the agent to shut down the operation and flee to Canada. Thompson also urged the Sons of Liberty and others to convert their paper money into gold. As the greenback sank, the Democratic Party's stock continued to rise.

In the lead-up to Early's attack, George Sanders dropped another bomb on the Lincoln administration: a phony peace conference. Sanders set up a trap to create a fake peace conference with the influential editor of the *New York Tribune*, Horace Greeley, an antislavery crusader who largely supported the war but now was horrified by the massive numbers of killed and wounded that had resulted from the stalled Union offensives.

During the summer of 1864, Greeley called for negotiations and an armistice and was invited to attend a peace conference set up by Sanders and the commissioners. Most Democrats saw an armistice and cooling-off period as the key to negotiations, while the Confederates knew that once an armistice began, the war would never be restarted. Lincoln reluctantly allowed Greeley to attend, along with his private secretary John Hay, and met the Southerners in Niagara Falls, Canada, in the middle of July. Through clever machinations, Sanders tricked Lincoln into admitting the war would not end until the Confederates surrendered and slavery was abolished. The Confederates then portrayed Lincoln as uncompromising and as a saboteur of the negotiations.

Next, the oily Confederate sent a statement to the Associated Press that hit hundreds of other papers and turned the media against Lincoln, painting the president as a monster: "All the Democratic press denounce Lincoln's manifesto in strong terms, and many Republican presses admit it was a blunder." Sanders was overjoyed with the resulting propaganda victory for the South. Thompson described how "Lincoln's manifesto shocked the country. The belief, in some way, prevailed that North and South would agree to a reconstruction, and the politicians, especially the leading ones, conceived the idea that on such an issue, Lincoln could be beaten at the ballot box." The conference had a chilling effect on the Sons of Liberty also, as Thompson noted: "A lot of arms were purchased by [the Secret Service] and sent to Indianapolis." The Sons of Liberty changed their tune from violence and insurrection to voting Lincoln out of office. With the prospects for the Northwest Conspiracy greatly diminished, "the trial of the ballot box should be made before a resort to force,"[17] wrote Thompson.

Lincoln was despondent about the upcoming election: "I cannot but feel that the weal or woe of this great nation will be decided in the approaching canvass. My own experience has proven to me, that there is no program intended by the Democratic Party but that will result in the dismemberment of the Union." Lincoln added, "You think I don't know I am going to be beaten, but I do and unless some great change takes place badly beaten."[18]

25. THE HIGH-WATER MARK: CHAMBERSBURG BURNS

Convinced Early had withdrawn the bulk of his troops back to Petersburg, Grant ordered the VI and XIX Corps back to the besieged city, leaving only Crook's 8,000-strong Army of West Virginia in the valley. Sensing blood, Early pounced and routed the Federals in what would become known as the Second Battle of Kernstown on July 24, 1864. Colonel Rutherford B. Hayes helped stave off disaster: "It was now discovered that the enemy, with his greatly superior forces, enveloped the troops on our right, and that they had been driven back. The First Brigade moved back up the hill, when I was ordered by Major-General Crook in person to hold the enemy in check long enough to enable one of our batteries, which was very much exposed to withdraw, and then fall back slowly, bearing to the right of Winchester going north, and protect the line of retreat on the Martinsburg Road."[1] Former Blazer's Scout Harrison Gray Otis also found himself in the heart of combat: "Men were falling by the scores on all sides. I saw [one of the men] go down within a few rods of where I stood, pierced by five balls. Lt. Col. Comly fell by my side, stunned by a shot in the head but giving him a helping hand he soon rose again."[2] Withering fire and overwhelming Confederate numbers forced Otis' line to falter as he received a musket ball to the right leg. The Confederates forced Crook to retreat across the Potomac into Maryland, opening a path for the South's last major raid into northern Union territory.

Days earlier, on July 17, Hunter was given orders by General Halleck to burn Confederate infrastructure in the Shenandoah Valley. "He was to devastate the valley south of the railroad as far as possible so that crows flying over would have to carry knapsacks. This need not involve the burning of houses, dwellings."³ But Hunter went after dwellings, torching even the home of his cousin Andrew Hunter, a Confederate sympathizer.

Hunter's pyromania—burning mills, farms, and other structures— moved the Union toward total war in the Shenandoah Valley, a war directed not only at the Confederacy's armed forces but also at civilians. The burnings hit a nerve with the Confederates. Early dispatched Brigadier General John McCausland to Chambersburg, Pennsylvania. McCausland recalled opening and reading the order: "I nearly fell out of the saddle. He ordered me in a very few words to make a retaliatory raid and give the Yankees a taste of their own medicine. The job wasn't pleasant to contemplate."⁴

McCausland and Bradley Johnson's Virginia and Maryland cavalry brigades surrounded Chambersburg on July 30 and demanded $100,000 in gold or $500,000 in US dollars or they would torch the town, but the town leaders were unable to pay.

Archibald Rowand and another Scout had a bird's-eye view of the raid. Hiding in a clump of bushes on a little knoll at the edge of town, the two men "stayed within half a mile of the town when it was burning, and then followed the enemy back till we found to a certainty which way he was going, then we got back to Gen. Averell."⁵

Harry Gilmor recalled in his autobiography sparing the home of one Union woman: "I went in and told the lady who came to the door that I was there to perform the extremely unpleasant duty of burning her house." According to the major, she did not beg for her home but only requested time to remove some belongings. "Breakfast was on the table, and she asked me to eat something while she was getting her things together." When he realized he had fought against her husband and knew of his kindness and honor, he decided, "Then, madam, your house shall not be destroyed."⁶

After burning Chambersburg, McCausland then rode west to threaten more Northern towns and the Baltimore and Ohio Railroad. The Confederates planned to burn McConnellsburg, Pennsylvania, but its citizens ponied up enough rations to prevent their town from being torched. With Averell in pursuit, the Confederates rode to Hancock, Maryland, and demanded $30,000 and 5,000 rations for the hungry cavalry force. When the town's residents had trouble furnishing the ransom, Marylanders Bradley Johnson and Harry Gilmor stepped in and tried to stop McCausland from incinerating the town. "I and my men objected, saying that too much

Maryland blood had been shed in defense of the South for her towns to be laid under contribution or burned." McCausland was not deterred and pressed on with plans to torch Hancock. Gilmor and Bradley effectively mutinied against their superior officer, as Gilmor revealed: "I perceived, too, that [McCausland's] men were inclined to plunder. After a consultation with General Johnson, I brought in my whole command and stationed two men at each house and store for their protection."[7] Averell's cavalry decided the issue by attacking McCausland, and rather than fight a pitched battle with the Yankee cavalry, he retreated to Cumberland, Maryland. There the Confederates encountered a makeshift force assembled by General Benjamin Kelley, which convinced McCausland to avoid the city and move to Moorefield, West Virginia. Having moved over eighty miles from Hancock, McCausland felt he could rest his exhausted force. Camping along the South Branch of the Potomac River, an area ideally suited for grazing and resting their horses but poor for security, the exhausted Confederates turned in for the night. According to one account, a citizen whose horse was stolen by the Confederates gave the precise location of the Southern cavalry on August 6 to the Jessie Scouts. Armed with this intelligence, Averell aimed to destroy McCausland's unsuspecting cavalry, using the Jessie Scouts to lead the way as the rest of his force followed behind.

26. MOOREFIELD

"Halt!"[1] "Who comes there?" challenged the Confederate picket as the Jessie Scouts, including Archibald Rowand and James White, approached in their butternut uniforms.

"A Friend,"[2] answered one of the Jessie Scouts.

"A friend of whom?"

"A friend of the Confederacy. Who do you suppose?"[3]

"Advance one and give the countersign." When one Jessie Scout advanced, "the Confederate picket sort of recognized him and addressed him as Major Gilmor and asked if he had heard anything of where the Yankees were."[4]

The Jessie Scout responded that the Yankees were south of Romney. While the pickets conversed, the remaining Scouts surrounded the Rebels.

"Yet, thinking that we were his own men, he told us where the other pickets were and they thought we were the relief guard and allowed us to approach without the countersign."[5]

As the lead Scout parlayed with the picket, the other Jessie Scouts "dismounted, tightened their saddle girths, and, acting in a careless manner, walked up to the pickets. At a given signal, they each seized a bridle rein, and with cocked pistols, took the two outposts prisoner."[6]

With the valuable information, the Jessie Scouts, leading Averell's cavalry, stealthily approached McCausland's sleeping Confederate camp. On the morning of August 7, 1864, as the sun came up over the Shenandoah Mountains, thousands of Confederate cavalrymen lay sleeping on the ground. Brigadier General McCausland's Rebels had crossed back into Southern territory and had little fear of Union reprisal on this peaceful morning. Most slept near wooden fences with their horses tied loosely so they could forage in the idyllic green pastures along the South Branch of the Potomac River near Moorefield, West Virginia. The men and their horses could both use the rest after their raid into Northern territory and the burning of Chambersburg days earlier. They believed the Federal cavalry was over eighty miles away in Hancock, and the Confederate cavalry outnumbered Averell's force by two to one.

With the pickets dispatched, Averell's cavalry descended on the unsuspecting slumbering Confederates, using the tactical intelligence the Jessie Scouts gathered. Little did they realize that the Federals would give them the surprise of their lives.

Bivouacked in the camp was partisan officer Major Harry Gilmor. The Marylander found himself thrust into the action.

"Get up, damn you!" a voice barked at Gilmor.

"[I] recognized the *twang* at once; at the same instant, a shot was fired by the speaker, the ball striking the rail on which my head was resting. There were two mounted men in the field, and I saw the head of a column on the road, all dressed in gray. I was somewhat confused. As I rose to my feet the trooper nearest fired at me again, defenseless as I seemed to be, crying 'Surrender!'"[7]

Confused, Gilmor pulled his pistol and shot the gray-clad mounted trooper. "His comrade sang out so that all could hear, 'What in the hell are you doing? you are killing your own men.' I stood thunderstruck. As the fellow was in full Confederate uniform, I asked him what he belonged to; he replied, 'To Captain Harry Gilmor's command.' Had he given me my proper rank, he might have fooled me; but when he said *captain*, I told him he was a lying scoundrel, and fired two shots before he fell. I knew these men must be Jessie Scouts."[8]

Sabers slashed, pistols and carbines cracked, and Union cavalry screamed, "Remember Chambersburg! 'Surrender, you house-burning scoundrels!' others, 'Kill every damned one of them,'"[9] as they descended on the Confederates.

Jessie Scout James White led one of the charges, "causing the surprise of the enemy."[10] Several men tried to put up a fight, but unable to saddle their horses, they were easy prey for the attacking troops. The Jessie Scouts had orders to capture John McCausland and Bradley Johnston, but did not get either,[11] but the Jessie Scouts came close, seizing Johnston's saddle.

In the unfolding chaos, Harry Gilmor mounted a horse and shot and hacked his way through the Jessie Scouts and Union cavalry. In the melee, Gilmor tried to save one of his close friends, Lieutenant William Kemp: "I had to cut my way to him, had raised myself in the stirrups with uplifted sabre to cleave the fellow's skull when [Kemp] discharged his pistol into [the Union trooper's] stomach, and he was free." Seconds earlier in the gunfight, one of Kemp's pistols failed to discharge, so he hurled it into a trooper's chest. Freedom was short-lived for the two men as they bolted over a fence with their horses. The Federals shot Kemp's mount. Thrown from his horse, he was quickly surrounded by Yankees. Gilmor tried to rescue his friend: "I shot one, and he knocked down two before they killed him."[12] Wearing dark-blue pants and a US military hat with his gray frock coat strapped to his saddle, Gilmor looked like a Union officer as he sped down a narrow farm lane to safety.

Averell's force and the Jessie Scouts killed or captured over 400 Confederates and snared 400 horses at Moorefield.[13] The decisive victory degraded Early's eyes and ears: "The balance of the command made its way to Mount Jackson in great disorder, and much weakened. This affair had a very damaging effect upon my cavalry for the rest of the campaign,"[14] Early later wrote.

After the Battle of Moorefield, three Jessie Scouts and Archibald Rowand reconnoitered the enemy near Bunker Hill, Virginia. The Scouts spotted a bullfrog entangled with a black snake and made wagers. For a moment, the men of war reverted back to boys. "A lonely duel in the middle of a great, sunny field. There was neither sight nor sound of armies nor of war: only summer sights and sounds—wind in the long grass, and bees," Rowand fondly remembered. The brief window into their childhood ended abruptly as a volley sounded, interrupting the contest. One of the Scouts' horses was shot, dismounting him. Rowand grabbed him "by the collar and dragged him across his own big gray horse; then, firing as they rode, they all dashed for the ford."[15]

The ebb and flow of scouting continued. Near Martinsburg, West Virginia, Rowand and several Jessie Scouts were riding through a wood searching for the Confederate cavalry when they found themselves in the midst of it. "There sounded the Rebel Yell behind them, and the [Confederate] cavalry came charging through. They were swept in the charge against their own men."[16] Each of the Scouts sounded out the blood-curdling

Rebel yell. "We went into the charge"[17] and "yelled as loud as anyone."[18] The Scouts edged toward the flank of the cavalry charge, looking for the first opportunity to exit. Escaping with their lives, Rowand and the Scouts concluded their last mission under General Averell.

Hunter failed to stop the burning of Chambersburg. Making matters worse, when Grant asked him where Early's army was located, he responded that he had lost all trace of the bulk of it.

The time period around the burning of Chambersburg, not Gettysburg, arguably represented the high-water mark for the Confederacy. Lincoln's campaign remained in serious peril. He needed military victories. Grant's army had stalled in its siege of Petersburg, and Sherman's army still had many miles of hard fighting between them and Atlanta. Crook's army had been defeated and routed at Kernstown. The war seemed on the verge of failure. The back door to the nation's capital, the Shenandoah Valley, remained open. The time had come for a leadership change. In August, Grant appointed a new Union commander: Philip Henry Sheridan. Bypassing Crook and Averell, Grant turned to his friend and George Meade's cavalry commander to lead what would become known as the Middle Military Division and the Army of the Shenandoah. Consisting of approximately 45,000 men, the army included Crook's Army of West Virginia, two infantry divisions from the XIX Corps, the VI Corps, and two cavalry divisions. With a new organization and army, Grant hoped to permanently shut the back door to the US capital.

27. An Embedded Combat Artist, General Sheridan, and Mosby's Great Berryville Wagon Raid

Special artist James E. Taylor embarked on the assignment of his life: capture the exploits and battles of the recently formed Army of the Shenandoah and its new commander, Major General Philip Sheridan.

As a civilian, Taylor placed himself at great risk by embedding as an illustrator with the Union Army in the heart of combat, capturing the images of war and its aftermath. The twenty-five-year-old graduated from the University of Notre Dame when only sixteen. A gifted artist, Taylor enlisted in the 10th New York Infantry, fought in numerous battles, and sent his drawings to *Frank Leslie's Illustrated Newspaper*. After his enlistment expired, the newspaper hired him full time, and he embedded in various commands.

Photography was in its infancy, and bulky equipment did not transport well on the battlefield. Photographs required chemicals, darkrooms, and lots of time. Taylor's magnificent hand-drawn, detailed scenes captured history in pencil on his sketchpad practically in real time. After Taylor completed his work, an express rider delivered his drawings to his publisher, who reproduced etchings from the hand-drawn originals. Hundreds of thousands would see Taylor's work every week.

The Northern press's coverage of the war, which was often critical, was augmented by the Confederate Secret Service's covert funding of negative stories, all of which fueled the War Department's attempts at censorship. Throughout the war, the Lincoln administration shut down numerous newspapers, exiled and arrested editors, and shuttered presses, all without due process. Offenses included printing stories that encouraged resisting the draft, discouraging enlistment, and printing material that was deemed treasonable. Another tool of censorship the Lincoln administration wielded was the postal service. The postmaster general in early 1863 suspended the *New York Daily News* from use of mail for distribution— effectively shuttering the newspaper for months. On the battlefield, Union field censors attempted to restrict and edit stories, enforced blackout periods, and wielded other heavy-handed restrictions, but reporters found ways around the censorship. As opposition to the war grew louder and casualties mounted from Grant's offensives, the War Department tried to limit the number of reporters in the field in a "growing reluctance at this critical stage of affairs to issue passes to the press and other non-combatants,"[1] recalled Taylor.

In early August, Taylor reported to General Lew Wallace to obtain a rare press pass. Wallace's "name was on every tongue at this minute" for his stand at Monocacy. On that day, Wallace made an exception, and with the precious document in hand, Taylor struck out for Sheridan's current headquarters at Harpers Ferry, West Virginia. Steaming down the tracks of the Baltimore and Ohio Railroad, Taylor traveled over the iron bridge Wallace had vainly defended weeks earlier. Taylor's hand went into action as he captured the trestle and debris of the epic battle. Joining Taylor in the railcar were Union officers, civilians, and an "excess of the fair sex." As the train hurtled toward Frederick, Maryland, the women aggressively foisted their politics on their "disapproving chaperons," waving small Confederate flags and boisterously shouting songs like "Maryland My Maryland" and "Southern Rights, Hurrah." One Union artillery officer who stood in the aisle of the car and rested his arm on a wooden seat bore the brunt of their insults. A "saucy bevy of minx and venomous spitfires," Southern women hurled degrading and racist epithets, calling the officer, "Lincoln hireling!" and "you Black worshiper!" Taylor remembered the Northerner took it "like a man and bore up heroically under the ordeal while exercising the only weapon available, good-natured banter, a personal encounter being out of the question with women."[2]

Having withstood the withering and obnoxious abuse from the Maryland women, Taylor finally arrived in Harpers Ferry after stopping overnight at Frederick. Whipping out his pad and pencil, he sketched the ruins of the Federal arsenal there, which had been destroyed by Confederates during their occupation of the facility in the spring of 1861. After memorializing the works, he moved to the brick engine house known as John Brown's Fort, where the abolitionist and his men had holed up during his famous 1858 raid. As Taylor's pencil formed the image of the fort, a cavalry column materialized and headed toward the front. Taylor instantly recognized its leader, Brigadier General George Armstrong Custer, by his distinctive "yellow hair." The commander of the Michigan Cavalry Brigade cut a dashing figure riding a "coal-black charger," adorned in a "jacket of velvet with a tracery of bullion." Taylor's pencil captured Custer's spiral locks as they tossed in the breeze and his knotted scarlet scarf, which barely concealed Custer's enormous Adam's apple—a strange juxtaposition to all his finery.[3]

Rising early the next day, Taylor made his way to General Sheridan's headquarters, located in an old government building atop a summit known as Camp Hill, and passed outgoing army commander General David Hunter along the way. Taylor later noted, "Though not for him a triumph of arms, [the Lynchburg Campaign] bore his enemies bitter fruit and their intensified hatred for the 'renegade Virginian.' . . . Especially strong was the feeling against him in this county of Jefferson, the home of his relatives who were made to doubly feel the force of his 'mailed hand' for their disloyalty, and going to the extreme with his cousin Judge Hunter, to whose beautiful home near Charles Town, he applied the torch."[4]

Passing a guard, Taylor entered Sheridan's office, where the general and his chief of staff were seated at a camp table scrutinizing a topographical map of the valley. Despite Taylor's intrusion, Sheridan greeted him "civilly" and inspected the artist's papers. Taylor later used his keen skills of observation and attention to detail to describe the man in front of him: "Small in stature and about 135 pounds. His head was abnormally large with projecting bumps which from a phrenologist's view denoted combativeness. His body and arms were long while his pedals were disproportionately short, 'duck legs' in fact. . . . The general's voice was anything but musical and when exercised under excitement, had a rasping sound, and croaking intonation when in its normal key. Sheridan's stature was far from commensurate with his ability and brain. In that little body, there was tremendous energy and untiring vigilance that carried him to victory."[5]

After Sheridan read the press pass and a letter from Frank Leslie, Taylor posed an awkward question: Could the general spare a horse? "A ghostly smile lit his features" as Sheridan responded, "Now young man, look at the appearance of this room with my effects yet unpacked. You see we are all in confusion, having but the day before moved in bag and baggage, and cannot tell what minute I will depart for the front. It might be within an hour or a day." Little Phil then explained his headquarters was short on horses and no mounts could be spared. Taylor gracefully accepted the response but the artist's "chagrin could hardly have escaped Sheridan's dark penetrating glance,"[6] thought the combat illustrator.

Within hours after the meeting, the general and his staff did indeed depart to the front, riding down the Valley Pike toward Winchester. Eventually procuring a horse, Taylor followed the army. Near Winchester, Mosby's Rangers were waiting for the general's supply train and would soon send a message to the Army of the Shenandoah.

> As glides in seas the shark,
> Rides Mosby through green dark.
>
> All spake of him, but few had seen
> Except the maimed ones or the low;
> Yet rumor made him every thing—
> A farmer—woodman—refugee—
> The man who crossed the field but now;
>   A spell about his life did cling—
>   Who to the ground shall Mosby bring?[7]

Riding through the green dark, John Singleton Mosby led about 300 of his Rangers and two small mountain howitzers, their largest group of men for a single engagement to date. Mosby's Rangers emerged from their safe houses in Fauquier County to ride all night through remote mountain trails to stalk their prey outside Berryville, Virginia, a small town several miles east of Winchester. They set their sights on Sheridan's massive three-mile-long wagon train winding down the Berryville Pike. A dense fog cloaked the Rangers' movement as the train lumbered forward, taking two and a half hours, from end to end, to reach any given point on its route.

"Saddle up, Munson, and come along with me." Ranger John W. Munson's hope for sleep had been dashed by orders directly from Mosby to gather a few men and scout the wagon train to gather intelligence. The disciplined, eighteen-year-old trooper knew Mosby led by example and never would ask one of his men to go where he would not go himself. But arguably the greatest American guerrilla leader in history did not look the part. The teenager from Richmond remembered the first time he met the hatchet-faced, brilliant leader of the 43rd. "The shock was something considerable . . . a small plainly attired man, fair in complexion, slight but wiry, standing with his arms behind his back, talking quietly to one of his men. . . . The visions of splendor and magnificence that had filled my mind swept away. The total absence of might, the lack of swagger, and the quiet demeanor of the man, all contributed to my astonishment and chagrin. He did not even strut," recalled Munson. Mosby's piercing blue eyes were something to behold and held sway over his men. When Mosby spoke, "they flashed the punctuations of his sentences,"[8] and when he was angry, they could make the hair stand up on one's neck. Mosby's blue eyes flashed as he directed his men toward the wagon train.

"We struck out in the stillness of the night, came the rumbling echoes of the heavily laden wagons. . . . We found the long line of wagons as far as the eye could reach." Wearing raincoats and in some cases pieces of Yankee uniforms, Mosby, Munson, and others were able to ride among the drivers and cavalrymen, chatting "in a friendly way."[9] The drivers thought they were just Union cavalry guarding the train. The Confederates plumbed the drivers for information to discover the train was hundreds of wagons long, guarded by several regiments of infantry and cavalry distributed along the route. Outnumbered ten to one, Mosby recalled, "I was about to do what all men would say, if I failed, was an act of desperation. A successful blow struck then at Sheridan's communication would, I knew make a deep impression on him and have much influence on the result of the campaign."[10] Munson boldly asked one of the cavalrymen for a match to light his pipe. "When I struck it, revealing his face and mine by its light, he did not know I was pretty soon going to begin chasing him."[11] Then Mosby and the others melted away back to their men.

On August 13, 1864, the rays of dawn cut through the fog and clouds of dust as a giant serpent of white-covered wagons emerged. "The flash of morning began to blow over the beautiful valley landscape—there are no lovelier spots than the Valley of Virginia around Berryville,"[12] recalled Munson. Mosby positioned his guns on a small hill that overlooked the rolling train. On Mosby's command, a Ranger fired a round from the howitzer that exploded like a clap of thunder near the wagons, marking the start of the battle.

"Then we rushed them, the whole of Command charging from the slope, not in columns, but spread all over creation, each man doing his best to out yell his comrade and emptying revolvers when we got among them, right and left. The whole train was thrown into panic. Teamsters wheeled their horses and mules into the road and, plying their black-snake whips, sent the animals galloping madly down the pike, crashing into other teams which, in turn, ran away,"[13] wrote Munson. The Union cavalry bolted. The infantry retreated behind any cover they could find.

An unexpected enemy soon emerged on the field of battle: thousands of angry yellow jackets. "The gun was in a position over their nest. They were home-rulers like the Boars, and instantly a swarm flew out to repel the invasion of their territory,"[14] Mosby quipped. The cloud of stinging pests forced the Confederates to briefly abandon the guns they had captured as they rode off with the caisson and limber chests. Eventually, one of Mosby's men rescued the guns from the wasps and brought them back into action. Rangers continued to assail the wagons. "Our men were yelling, galloping, charging, firing, stampeding mules and horses, and creating pandemonium everywhere,"[15] remembered Munson. The melee to subdue the wagon train spanned a mile and a half. With the Federals in retreat, the Rangers descended on the spoils. They burned wagons, took prisoners, and rounded up Union horses, mules, and hundreds of beef cattle. In their victory, the Rangers yelled and whooped for joy, competing with braying from the mules. In the excitement, the Rangers missed a lucrative prize, a paymaster's chest that contained tens of thousands of dollars in greenbacks.

Mosby's men donned some of the blue Union uniforms piled in the wagons. "[One Ranger,] decked out in a major's suit, was swearing at the mules and at the same time playing 'Dixie' on a fiddle he found in the wagon," remembered Mosby. The Rangers' haul was tremendous. Mosby reported to General Lee that he had captured and destroyed seventy-five loaded wagons, secured 200 prisoners, and seized between 500 and 600 horses and mules, 200 cattle, and other stores.[16] Only two Rangers died in the ambush.

An army fights on its stomach, as Napoleon has noted. Supplies and logistics are crucial to any modern army. While it is said that amateurs talk tactics, professionals discuss logistics. Sheridan made a fatal mistake in not moving the wagon train along with his army and instead rushing it forward without adequate defenses, and the exploit was magnified in the Northern press.

Mosby's main goal was to tie up numbers of Federal troops many times larger than his own. Federal troops guarding supply lines could not be used in battle. A "natural" and a master of unconventional warfare, the partisan leader explained, "One of the most effective ways of impeding the march of an army is by cutting off its supplies; and this is just as legitimate as to attack it in a line of battle. Jomini* says that the irregular warfare of the Cossacks did more to destroy the French army on the expedition to Moscow than the elite regiments of the Russian guard."[17] In this instance, roughly ten times the number of Sheridan's men was not enough to protect the wagon train. The threat of future raids would keep even more troops bottled up in protecting supply lines instead of fighting on the front lines.

Rubbing salt in an already open wound, the Rangers attempted to kidnap Sheridan. After ascertaining the location of Sheridan's headquarters from Union prisoners, Mosby and a small group of Rangers hoped to repeat the success of the earlier high-value capture at Fairfax Courthouse. Mosby went forward to reconnoiter and found the house illuminated by campfires but not guarded by many troops. He returned to his men and ordered another Ranger forward, but the Ranger accidently found himself in the midst of six sleeping Union soldiers who awoke and roused the camp, forcing the Ranger and Mosby to retreat without securing the diminutive general.[18]

* Antoine-Henri Jomini was a Swiss officer who served in Napoleon's army and Russian Imperial forces. He was one of the most celebrated writers of his age and may have coined the term "logistics."

III

SHERIDAN'S SCOUTS AND
"COME RETRIBUTION"

28. "I Have 100 Men Who Will Take the Contract to Clean Out Mosby's Gang"

Sheridan's headquarters in the Shenandoah
Valley, August 16, 1864

"The families of most of Mosby's men are known and can be collected," Ulysses S. Grant brutally telegraphed Sheridan on August 16, 1864. The general further suggested the families could be held hostage at Fort McHenry "for the good conduct" of Mosby and his men. Perhaps most shocking, Grant ended the communication with the order, "Where any of Mosby's men are caught hang them without trial."[1] After Mosby's Great Berryville Wagon Train Raid, Grant threw down an iron fist.

Grant followed up with another telegram to Sheridan two hours later, instructing him to send a division of cavalry to Loudoun County, Virginia, "to destroy and carry off the crops, animals, negroes, and all men under fifty years of age capable of bearing arms. In this way, you will get many of Mosby's men. All male citizens under fifty can fairly be held as prisoners of war."[2]

Sheridan partially complied with the scorched-earth policy, issuing orders for Union troops to destroy all "wheat and hay south of a line from Millwood to Winchester. You will seize all mules, horses and cattle that may be useful to our army. Loyal citizens can bring in claims against the government for this necessary destruction."[3] Lacking the extra troops to pull away from the threat of Early's Army of the Valley District, the Union general demurred and did not carry out Grant's brutal order to round up families related to the Rangers. Sheridan was also sensitive to the 1864 political climate. Every report of another successful wagon raid by Mosby's Rangers made Northern victory seem an increasingly elusive goal. The Democrats used the house burnings and loss of personal property that made headlines in Northern newspapers as a cudgel in their campaign against Lincoln. The Shenandoah Valley had become a political and strategic epicenter of the Civil War.

Perhaps to placate Grant's wrath, Sheridan sent a message to the general the next day claiming to have killed some of Mosby's Rangers. The report proved false, however, as the men were not Mosby's. Sheridan deceitfully wrote Grant a day later, "Guerrillas give me great annoyance, and captured a few wagons." He chillingly added, "I am quietly disposing of numbers of them." Sheridan later noted, "We hung one and shot six of his men yesterday."[4]

On August 18, however, an incident with far-reaching consequences did involve a small group of Mosby's Rangers. They attacked a four-man Union picket near Castleman's Ferry—killing one, Corporal Alpheus Day, wounding another, and capturing the remaining two.

To avenge the attack, the commander of the Michigan Brigade, Brigadier General George Armstrong Custer, ordered several family homes of Rangers burned. Over fifty Wolverines rode to obey the directive. By the light of dawn on the morning of August 19, William H. Chapman and a group of Mosby's Rangers saw the flames and smoke rising from Ranger Province McCormick's home and found his family weeping outside. The Confederates then rode on to find the wife of Ranger William Sowers and her children sobbing as they watched their home burn. "Those helpless non-combatants crouching in the rain, weeping over their burning homes, wrought up the resentment of the men and we started out to even things up in real guerrilla fashion,"[5] wrote Ranger John Munson. The homeless civilians sent the Rangers in the direction of advancing Federals and urged the Rangers to "smite and spare not!"[6]

"Like bloodhounds on the trail,"[7] the Rangers rode toward Confederate colonel Benjamin Morgan's one-hundred-plus-year-old estate. Chapman urged his fellow Rangers forward: "No quarter! No quarter!"[8] Around two in the afternoon, they caught up with the unsuspecting Union soldiers, who were still busy with the burning of Morgan's estate. The Federals failed to guard against a surprise attack. Stalking their quarry, the Rangers rode slowly down the only entrance and exit—a quarter-mile, tree-lined lane that led to the plantation—then charged when they were within one hundred yards. A bloodbath ensued.

Trapped, the Federals had no way of escape, surrounded as they were by stone fences in a lane accessed by a single gate. As the Rangers descended on the soldiers burning the barn, haystacks, house, and other outbuild-ings, they refused to give quarter, even when the men begged for their lives. The furious Rangers shot even those taken prisoner. "Ten men were murdered on the ground after surrendering, nearly all of whom were shot through the head. Four have since died and two more cannot live. Some of the fiends, appalled at the bloody agonies, did not shoot their prisoners until ordered to 'shoot the d—n Yankee son of a b—" by their officers," the *New York Times* later reported.[9]

Mosby sent word to his superiors that "about 25 of them were shot to death for their villainy."[10] And thus began an even more grisly cycle of vio-lence as the *Times* story and other reports of the incident further inflamed Union forces and begat retaliatory attacks. The *Times* noted that "Mosby practically raised the black flag"[11] in the valley, and the retribution killings continued. Mosby had to be stopped.

The Great Berryville Wagon Train Raid and the killing of the house-burning soldiers triggered an intensive manhunt to kill or capture Mosby and his Rangers. An election year loomed, and the press magnified Mosby's achievements. Sheridan had to neutralize the Gray Ghost, protect the Army of the Shenandoah's supply lines, and halt the embarrassing headlines that aided the South's information war on the North. Seeking a solution, Sheridan turned to his former West Point roommate and friend George Crook, who offered him the unit he took much credit for shaping: Blazer's Independent Scouts. The mission to neutralize Mosby fell on the shoulders of thirty-five-year-old Captain Richard Blazer.

The Scouts had been operating without rest for months. "In moving with the army . . . we were constantly in motion and fighting all the time from Winchester to Berryville; hence to Cedar Creek; capturing numbers of Johnnies—then falling back to Winchester and Halltown,"[12] recalled Montgomery. The incessant battle had reduced the Scouts' numbers. At Halltown, West Virginia, Blazer received orders to fill the unit to one hundred Scouts. Men from various units volunteered for the hazardous duty, and from these volunteers, Blazer hand-selected the most qualified men. Sheridan activated Blazer's hunter-killer team with the sole mission of eliminating the South's most dangerous men, thereby pioneering the US Army's counterinsurgency warfare.

Breaking through the bureaucracy that Crook failed to penetrate months earlier, Sheridan ordered these chosen men supplied with the finest rifle in the Civil War arsenal: the Spencer. "I have 100 men who will take the contract to clean out Mosby's gang. I want 100 Spencer rifles for them. Send them to me if they can be found in Washington,"[13] Sheridan wrote in orders to Washington on August 20, 1864.[14]

The Spencer repeating rifle and shorter-barreled carbine were some of the most advanced small arms in the world at the time. The Spencer Model 1860, the first operational lever-action rifle, fired a .56-56 rimfire metallic cartridge—groundbreaking at a time when most weapons utilized paper cartridges. In the stock, a tube contained a seven-round, spring-loaded magazine that fed cartridges into a breech-loading chamber by cocking and replacing a lever. Now a soldier no longer had to stand up and ram a bullet down the barrel of a rifle. A Spencer had a rate of fire of over twenty rounds per minute; a traditional musket in the hands of a trained soldier could fire only two or three shots a minute.

Department of War chief of ordnance General James Ripley considered the rifles "newfangled gimcracks" and opposed the pioneering technology because the weapon's rate of fire could waste ammunition. Additionally, the Federal supply system, already overburdened, could not maintain enough ammunition in the field for repeating weapons to be used by the entire Federal force. The repeater was also several times more expensive than a traditional rifled musket. The Confederates did not field a similar counterpart. Among other factors, the rimfire metallic cartridge ammunition was difficult to manufacture. Christopher Miner Spencer, the rifle's inventor, finally broke through bureaucratic red tape by gaining an audience directly with Abraham Lincoln, a fellow inventor and the only commander in chief to hold a patent in his name, for a device to lift boats over shoals in rivers. He personally test-fired the Spencer near the partially completed Washington Monument on August 18, 1863. On the walk over to the makeshift target range, the group passed by the War Department, and the president sent his son to see if the secretary of war would like to join them. While waiting for a response, the president noticed a tear in his black alpaca coat. He pulled out a needle and started to mend the rip, musing, "It seems to me this don't look quite right for the chief magistrate of this mighty republic, ha, ha, ha!"[15]

When Lincoln received word that Secretary of War Edwin Stanton was too busy to join the demonstration, he quipped, "Well, they do pretty much as they have a mind to over there."[16] Spencer handed the rifle to Lincoln, who proceeded to aim.

"The target was a board about six inches wide and three feet high, with a black spot on each end, about forty yards away. The rifle contained seven cartridges. Mr. Lincoln's first shot was about five inches low, but the next shot hit the bull's-eye, and the other five were close around it. 'Now,' said Mr. Lincoln, 'we will see the inventor try it.' The board was reversed, and I fired at the other bull's-eye, beating the President a little. 'Well,' said he, 'you are younger than I am and have a better eye and a steadier nerve.'"[17]

The Spencer rifle so impressed Lincoln that he directed the War Department to place more orders for the gun.[18]

Armed with their Spencer rifles and carbines,[19] each Scout also had at least a Colt Navy or Army revolver—most men had two pistols. Although Blazer's men were armed to the teeth, Mosby's men still significantly outnumbered them. Undaunted, "we felt like trying him" and "flaxing him out," remembered one Scout. Blazer's men had spent months honing their skills battling Thurmond's partisan Rangers and other irregulars, and they felt prepared to battle a foe they considered ruthless, "cutthroats" yet "well trained," "bound to their oaths to never yield to the Yankee forces, also sworn to spare no energies, going through all the hardships of guerrilla warfare, destroying even home friends to carry the point," recalled Asbe Montgomery. "[Mosby's men] became a source of terror, not only to small bodies of the army but to all travelers, and even to some of their own friends." Sergeant Montgomery was gung ho: "[Taking out Mosby] that was just what we wanted to do."[20]

Once the Scouts received their Spencers and provisions, Blazer announced their goal of defeating Mosby. Morale within the Scouts remained sky-high, but many of the men did not fully appreciate just how perilous the manhunt would prove to be. Most of the Scouts had read about Mosby's exploits, the stuff of legend: raids, train derailments, and high-value captures—the missions appeared in headlines across the North and the South. Mosby's Rangers had first captivated both populations' attention in the cold, wintery months of 1863.

Despite the threat to his supply lines, Sheridan still pursued Early, but the wily Confederate general retreated deeper into the valley onto the defensible high ground at Fisher's Hill. Lee soon reinforced Early's army. Mistakenly believing Early's army was larger than his, embarrassingly, on August 21, Sheridan retreated toward Harpers Ferry.

In that third week of August, Sheridan unleashed Blazer's Scouts. They left Sheridan's army and set out alone, "struck for tall timber," as they called it, and infiltrated Mosby's Confederacy. They entered an area where most forces their size, roughly one hundred men, had been crushed countless times in the past year. But the Scouts operated like the men they hunted. "We moved cautiously, watching every bird, almost, that flew across our path,"[21] wrote Asbe Montgomery. In particular, the Scouts monitored the fords, ferries, and crossing points of the rivers.

Building on the Scouts' months of experience in hunting Thurmond's Rangers, Montgomery observed that "Mosby learned that somebody else could hide, shoot, and dash, and swim rivers as well as his fellows."[22] In this type of guerrilla warfare, a fast horse became paramount. Scouts seized the best horses they could find; speed, agility, and how a steed performed in combat became matters of life and death for the rider.

A smaller echelon of twelve to sixteen Jessie Scouts roamed ahead of Blazer's main column as an advance reconnaissance element.

As Montgomery wrote, their mission was hazardous: "Sometimes our small squads ventured further than prudent and this caused us to have to get up the 'dust' sometimes like a streak of lighting, for three or four miles. Go out and leave the company four or five miles, and the first thing would be: 'Halt, you d—d Yankees!' Then we knew what to do. It was 'git.'"[23]

On August 25, the Scouts routed a force of renegade partisans under the command of nineteen-year-old John Mobberly. The teen had deserted from Elijah V. White's 35th Virginia Cavalry, also known as White's Comanches. The Comanches recruited from Loudoun County and campaigned with the regular army but returned home when not in service. Mobberly deserted from White and set up his own gang. Sadistic, cruel, and "reckless beyond reason and fearless of danger . . . [Mobberly] courted it."[24] Union brigadier general John Stevenson described Mobberly as a villain in charge of "a gang of murderers infesting Loudoun."[25] While Mobberly is known to have participated in at least one operation with Mosby, the Ranger leader did not tolerate his barbaric methods, especially when it came to those he captured. Mobberly rarely took prisoners, but he savagely transported those he did take to the mountains. He maliciously placed these defenseless individuals supine and mounted boulders on their limbs. The men died of exposure, starvation, or wild animals, and he left their bodies to rot.[26] Another atrocity involved Mobberly riding his horse over severely wounded Union soldier Charles Stewart and joyfully firing his pistol into his hapless torso. After firing all six barrels, he loudly laughed and stripped the boots off Stewart's mangled body. Preternaturally, Stewart would live to tell the tale and even seek vengeance.

But on that late August day, Mobberly's men met their match. Blazer demolished an element of the cutthroat's gang. The Scouts had "quite a skirmish" and took six of Mobberly's guerrillas and "five or six good horses," after which they felt they were gaining control of the valley, "calling ourselves Boss,"[27] remembered Montgomery.

"Every day brought fresh scenes. Almost every day we crossed the river and mountains to hinder the reb cavalry from cutting us off, and Moseby [sic] in the same valley that we were, made pretty scaly times." The Scouts rode up and down the bucolic Blue Ridge Mountains, forested with verdant pine and hemlock trees. Mountain streams and open meadows were sprinkled throughout the hard rides up and down rugged trails. Despite the paradise-like surrounds of nature's lush bounty, the land Blazer's Scouts dared to cross into was some of the most dangerous Confederate territory. Outnumbered and undaunted, they hunted the hunters. The Federals were painfully aware of the annihilation of their predecessors, and yet they believed in the nobility of their cause. Much like today's special forces, they would operate alone, deep in enemy territory. To prevail they would rely on their own grit and resourcefulness. "Moseby [sic] and his men outnumbered us so materially that we had to look sharp, to save our necks, for it was no use to talk of being captured unless we wanted our throats cut from ear to ear, or to be swung up by the neck,"[28] Montgomery recalled.

The eyes from North and South focused on events in the Shenandoah, where unconventional warfare would continue to play a crucial role as the election of 1864 loomed.

29. THE MOST IMPORTANT ELECTION IN AMERICAN HISTORY

Democratic National Convention, Chicago, August 29–31, 1864

The delegates cheered as the band struck up "Dixie."[1]

Powerbrokers of the Democratic Party roamed the Amphitheatre in Chicago. Democrats had delayed their convention for two months in the hope that public opinion would continue to shift in their favor in arguably one of the most critical elections in American history. While the party was divided, Peace Democrats dominated the convention. They believed a course correction was needed to resolve the war and proposed an immediate armistice, followed by negotiations and a willingness to grant the South their independence to achieve peace.

Another wing of the party, the War Democrats, believed in continuing the war, vying for power in a den of asps—the Peace Democrats were pejoratively named "Copperheads" for the poisonous snake that silently sneaks up and strikes its prey without warning, as well as the copper pennies they wore on their lapels designating their affiliation. One Copperhead acidly described the opposing faction: "There is not a difference between a War Democrat and an Abolitionist. They are both links in the same sausage, made from the same dog."[2] Despite their differences, both sides agreed that Lincoln and the Republicans had destroyed the country, and ending slavery was off the table. The war being waged in the Shenandoah played a crucial role. Discussion of house burnings and other potential violations of constitutional rights and civil liberties took center stage.

Racist rants coursed through many speeches. "This war is an unholy fight. Soon the net is to be drawn that will gather in its half-million more to feed the insatiable thirst for blood of the Negro God. Let us demand a cessation of the sacrifice until the people shall pronounce their great and emphatic verdict for peace, and let the tyrant understand that the demand comes from earnest men and must be respected,"[3] one delegate spewed.

Another delegate, G. C. Sanderson of Pennsylvania, argued that the war was not being fought to preserve the Union: "What is this war for? The n—er. It is for the n—er against the white man. I think we don't want our bosoms stuffed so much with damned n—ers this warm weather. I don't believe the negro is equal to the white man. Is it not high time that this infernal war was stopped?"[4]

The Copperheads' leader, Clement Laird Vallandigham, drove the convention's agenda. One contemporary newspaper reported, "The truth is, the masses of the party sympathize with radical men like Vallandigham. He is today the idol of the crowds. He is the great favorite of the masses of the country precincts, who crowd the convention and the city. Today, were they allowed their preference, they would nominate him unanimously for their presidency."[5]

Weeks before the convention, Vallandigham illegally returned to the United States under a phony name and emerged as one of the Democrats' most powerful voices. Despite the calls from the governor of Indiana and other politicians to lock up the Ohioan, Lincoln wisely deferred, allowing him to freely mingle in Chicago, as his arrest itself could have sparked a rebellion in the Northwest. Lincoln saw value in Vallandigham's presence in further dividing the Democrats at the convention.

Swashbuckling captain Thomas Hines, Kentuckian John B. Castleman, and sixty Confederates covertly traveled to the Windy City and executed the first phase of the so-called Northern Conspiracy with Vallandigham's Sons of Liberty. To aid in inciting an insurrection, the Confederate Secret Service and the Sons of Liberty planned on freeing nearly 8,000 Confederate prisoners from nearby Camp Douglas. "Our operation shall be confined to and directed against railroads, public stores, steamers, buildings in the public use, and such things and property as are of benefit to the enemy and the destruction of which will advance the interests of the Confederacy." For the past several months, the Secret Service had plied the Sons of Liberty with tens of thousands in cash and had covertly run thousands of pistols and rifles through Northern lines or purchased them in the North to arm the Copperhead groups. Castleman and Hines also planned to hit the Federal arsenal in Springfield. But to Hines and Castleman's utter dismay, when the time came for the uprising, the Sons of Liberty got cold feet. Castleman bemoaned their "obvious timidity." The Sons of Liberty put their influence behind the ballot box, for now. The best the Confederate operatives could secure were promises from them to implement the plan after the election. Had the operation proceeded as planned, the result could have been devasting, as one newspaper article months after the plot related: "The consequence would be that the whole character of the war would be changed, its theater would be shifted from the border to the heart of the free states."[6]

Instead of fomenting insurrection, Vallandigham emerged as the force behind the party's major political planks on August 30—a crucial victory of the Confederate Secret Service's influence operations. Through their asset, they had effectively written the Democratic Party's campaign platform. Significantly, the committee that Vallandigham chaired resolved to "demand that immediate efforts be made for a cessation of hostilities."[7]

The delegates assembled to nominate a presidential candidate on the steamy day of August 31, 1864. War Democrats put forth George McClellan, fearful that if he was not the nominee, he might run as an independent and split the Democratic vote. The Peace Democrats put forth the governor of New York, Horatio Seymour, a frequent guest of the Confederate Secret Service at St. Lawrence Hall.[8] The Copperheads even proposed the toxic Vallandigham amid cheers from the crowds and an occasional hiss. Some members also suggested former president Franklin Pierce. McClellan was the Democratic front-runner. As Lincoln predicted, the Copperheads knew their best chance of winning was to promote a War Democrat on a peace platform, but numerous Copperhead speakers complained about the general's activities during the war. One angry Marylander decried, "What you ask me to do is, in reality, to support the man who stabbed my own mother; and I for one—and I believe I speak for the whole delegation of Maryland—will never do it. . . . In September 1861 [McClellan] broke up the Legislature of a sovereign State, deliberately and with full purpose, to exercise tyranny and oppression in advance of Abraham Lincoln. Now here is the man who has dealt a fatal blow to the institutions of our country."[9] After the second round of ballots, McClellan secured the nomination. Vallandigham dramatically stepped up to the rostrum and asked that McClellan's nomination be made unanimous. The address

stunned reporters in the audience: a seemingly bitter pill for the Ohioan
to swallow. But behind the scenes, Vallandigham had crafted a deal that
ensured that he would become McClellan's secretary of war. Undoubtedly, the very man who so stridently opposed the war from its start could
hardly be expected to carry on Grant's total war. Installing Vallandigham
as secretary of war demonstrated that the Democrats intended not to win
the war but to end it through a platform that called for an armistice.

Copperheads balanced the ticket by installing as vice-presidential
nominee Vallandigham's right-hand man, Congressman George H. Pendleton from Ohio, a hardcore Copperhead who had voiced sympathy for
the Confederacy. While not a Copperhead, McClellan regurgitated the
Democrats' central plank, telling an associate on August 23, "If I am elected,
I will recommend an immediate armistice and a call for a convention of
all the states and insist upon exhausting all, and every means to secure
peace without further bloodshed."[10] Commissioner Clay wrote to Secretary
of State Judah Benjamin on the success of the Secret Service's influence
operations: "Peace may be made with him on terms you may accept. He is
committed to the platform to cease hostilities and try negotiations. That
is a great concession for him and the War Democracy. An armistice will
result in peace." Clay hammered home a crucial point: "The platform means
peace, unconditionally. The war cannot be renewed if once stopped, even
for a short time." Clay stressed that "McClellan will be under the control of
the true peace men. Horatio, or T.H. Seymour is to be Secretary of State,
Vallandigham Secretary of War. McClellan is privately pledged to make
peace even at the expense of separation, if the South cannot be induced to
reconstruct any common government."[11]

During the final weeks of summer, Abraham Lincoln was convinced he
would lose the election. History was not on the president's side; for thirty-
two years, through eight presidential administrations, only Andrew Jackson
had won reelection to a second term. On August 23, Lincoln asked his
cabinet members to sign an envelope that contained a memorandum he
would not allow them to see until after the election. Known as the Blind
Memorandum, it read, "This morning, as for some days past, it seems
exceedingly probable that this Administration will not be reelected. Then
it will be my duty to so co-operate with the President elect, as to save the

Union between the election and the inauguration as he will have secured his election on such ground that he cannot possibly save it afterwards. LINCOLN."[12] Lincoln acknowledged that his chances for reelection seemed hopeless, but he determined to do everything in his and his cabinet's power to win the war before March 4, 1865, and the inauguration of a president McClellan.

Although Lincoln predicted failure at the polls in November, he adamantly advocated for their necessity the day after he was elected. "But the election was a necessity. We cannot have free Government without elections, and if the rebellion could force us to forego or postpone a national election, it might fairly claim to have already conquered and ruined us."[13] He believed in the will of the American people.

Others earlier had called for the postponement of the election, maintaining that if the election were held during a civil war, "the vote would be fraudulent." The country would "flame up in revolution, and the streets of our cities would run with blood."[14] Lincoln trusted in the inherent wisdom of the American people. The wartime president later eloquently stated, "It has long been a grave question whether any government not too strong for the liberties of the people can be strong enough to maintain its own existence in great emergencies. On this point, the present rebellion brought our Republic to a severe test, and a Presidential election occurring in regular course during the rebellion, added not a little to the strain. If the loyal people, united, were put to the utmost of their strength by the rebellion, must they not fall when divided and partially paralyzed by a political war among themselves?"[15]

The founder of the Jessie Scouts, John Frémont, also threw his hat in the ring as a third-party candidate and threatened to split the Republican base. A faction known as Radical Republicans questioned Lincoln's commitment to Black civil rights and attracted high-profile abolitionists like Frederick Douglass, but within weeks Frémont dropped out of the race.

Shrewdly, Lincoln ran under the banner of the National Union Party to garner both Republican and Democratic voters. In that vein, he jettisoned his current vice president, Hannibal Hamlin, and brought on a Democrat, Andrew Johnson, Lincoln's appointee as military governor of Tennessee, as his running mate.

The platforms of the two parties could not have been more diametrically opposed. When read out loud at the earlier Republican convention in

June in Baltimore, each of the eleven planks resonated with the audience there:

> Resolved, that as Slavery was the cause, and now constitutes the strength, of this Rebellion, and as it must be, always and every-where, hostile to the principles of Republican Government, justice and the National safety demand its utter and complete extirpation from the soil of the Republic [applause]:—and that, while we uphold and maintain the acts and proclamations by which the Government, in its own defense, has aimed a death-blow at this gigantic evil, we are in favor, furthermore, of such an amendment* to the Constitution, to be made by the people in conformity with its provisions, as shall terminate and forever prohibit the existence of Slavery within the limits or the jurisdic-tion of the United States. [Tremendous applause, the delegates rising and waving their hats.][16]

One plank lauded Union men in uniform: "Resolved, That the thanks of the American people are due to the soldiers and sailors of the Army and Navy [applause], who have periled their lives in defense of their country and in vindication of the honor of its flag; that the nation owes to them some permanent recognition of their patriotism and their valor." Another called for honoring soldiers regardless of color: "That the Government owes to all men employed in its armies, without regard to distinction of color, the full protection of the laws of war."[17] Calls went out for a transcontinental railroad that would unite the American coasts. Finally, the National Union Party had grave concern for the borders of the United States and foreign encroachment in North America and called for enforcement of the Monroe Doctrine. France had invaded Mexico in 1862 and installed Maximilian I after conquering portions of the country. With regime change also came a country favorable to the Confederacy.

---

* In April 1864, the Thirteenth Amendment ending slavery in the United States sailed through the Republican-controlled Senate. In Congress, Democrats in the House of Repre-sentatives blocked the amendment when it failed to reach the required two-thirds majority in June 1864. The Thirteenth Amendment was passed by Congress on January 31, 1865, and ratified on December 6, 1865.

192 PATRICK K. O'DONNELL

Nevertheless, an insurgency still raged in Mexico, and with the Union fully engaged in civil war, the country could do little to oppose a potentially hostile European power on the southern border.

Regardless of the Republicans' platform, the Democrats argued that the time had come for a new approach to the war. Endless casualties in a forever war that would eventually bankrupt the treasury was the current prospect. The South, in their view, did not need to win the war, only survive it. Political will wavered, many feeling a military solution was not viable. Democrats offered a new path—a course correction—through an armistice, a very likely by-product of which would have been a peace agreement to grant the Confederacy what it long sought: independence.

30. Takedown at Myer's Ford

*Early September 1864, near the Virginia
and West Virginia border*

Sixteen Jessie Scouts took the lead: dressed in butternut and impersonating Confederate cavalry, they rode in the vanguard of Blazer's Scouts. The Scouts picked up the tracks of scores of horsemen in ground soggy from the previous night's rain. Blazer's men doggedly pursued the Rangers, who outnumbered the Federals by nearly two to one.

"Old Dick," as Blazer's men called him, "was not a man to rest when his country was bleeding, so he would ride, sick or well. I have known him to ride days and nights, and not eat one bit, and scarcely sleep, only when halted in the daytime, lay down and sleep again. He would risk health, and everything for his country," recalled Asbe Montgomery. Contrasting with his ardor and resolve to bring down Mosby, Richard Blazer possessed "heart"—a kindness that he extended to his men, "always looking after their interests." Blazer treated the Southerners he encountered with fairness. He was also generally "kind to prisoners—to those who were entitled to be recognized as prisoners of war, and you could plainly see it pained him to do anything else."[1]

Blazer's rapport with strangers paid dividends as well. A day earlier, an African American man risked his life to furnish information to the Union captain that Mosby lurked nearby. The Confederate leader considered informants traitors and swiftly dealt with them in a harsh manner. Black residents in Mosby's Confederacy, whether enslaved or free, faced violence and death if they collaborated with the Union.

Blazer's Scouts rode up a winding trail on the side of the mountain to a pasture where they fed their horses. Expert woodsmen and trackers, the

Scouts sized up their opponents' numbers from the tracks and droppings from the Confederates' mounts. The bluecoats rode down the mountain following between 150 and 200 Rangers. Riding slowly and cautiously for two miles, the cavalcade halted at the bottom of a hill and "sat listening a short time,"[2] recalled Montgomery. Through the trees, they heard voices. Blazer ordered a detail of his men to dismount and creep up on the Confederates. Spencer rifles in hand, the Scouts expected to pour a volley of lead into the unsuspecting Rebels; instead, they found two men swilling applejack near a still.

Blazer's men seized the two inebriated fellows, and maybe the applejack,[3] and accused them of belonging to Mosby's command. "Alarmed," they denied the charges and promised to aid in the search if they were not harmed. Blazer gave the Southerners a chance to lead them to the Rangers and "mounted slowly and carefully so as to not be led into a snare by the young men."[4]

The bluecoats rode two abreast along a narrow lane bordering the eastern side of the Shenandoah River. The country road spilled into the open field of a large farm where Ranger companies A and B, under the command of Lieutenant Joseph N. Nelson, dozed and their horses leisurely grazed. "I could not imagine there was an enemy on our side of the river and thought the only danger would be from the other side at the ford, where I had been stationed,"[5] recalled Ranger James Williamson.

A crackle of Colts and the whine of horses signaled the start of the battle. Blazer's men emerged from the woods behind the encamped Confederates like avenging wraiths as the Rangers scrambled to mount their horses. Within seconds, several of the Rebels found a way to "form four deep."[6]

"They are thick as fleas," Sergeant Montgomery exclaimed to Blazer as the Scouts charged into the melee. Blazer turned around to view his galloping men descending into the maelstrom, and Montgomery yelled, "Come on boys, charge them and face them."[7]

Putting spurs to their horses, the men fired their pistols and Spencers into the Rangers' ranks. "Yelling like a madman," Montgomery screamed, "You scoundrels; we will give you something else to do besides taking ambulances and wagon trains."[8]

Nelson tried to rally his men and initially drove some of Blazer's Scouts back.[9]

The two sides bunched together: a mass of horses and armed men firing at each other at close range.

Confederate Emory Pitts, who had assailed the Loudoun Rangers at Point of Rocks, found one of the Scouts pointing a pistol at his face. It misfired, and Pitts "leaned from his saddle, seized his antagonist by the scruff of the neck with his left hand, lifted the man from his saddle almost over on to his own lap, and with his right hand held a revolver under his captive's breast and fired a bullet through him, dropping the corpse to the ground as he galloped away. The soldier happened to fall on one of our men who had been unhorsed, half hidden among the rocks, playing possum."[10]

A bullet grazed Williamson's ribs. As he gasped for air, Ranger William Walston asked him, "Are you hurt much?"[11]

"I don't think it is much,"[12] Williamson stoically but breathlessly responded.

Bullets whistled near the men's ears as the two Rangers fled. "Hold on to old Bob," Walston shouted, referring to the Ranger's venerable mount, which had been in countless skirmishes. Williamson sped off on Old Bob, and as he panned the area, he saw "our men were completely demoralized and fleeing in all directions."[13]

Blazer's momentum seized the bulge. Fighting like the men they hunted, "we were all in a heap in a moment, shooting them off, none of our men having yet fallen, they began to fall back."[14] Lieutenant Nelson fell from his horse and took a bullet in the thigh. Like a dam that suddenly burst wide open, the Rangers fled in the direction of the river to escape from the Scouts.

"Soon everything was on our side," recalled Montgomery. But the battle took its toll; a bullet slammed into Montgomery's horse, and several of his fellow Scouts were wounded in the melee. A Ranger felled a Scout to Montgomery's right and now turned his Colt on the sergeant's face. "Luckily, I saw it just about two feet from me. Not having time to pull the hammer back [on my Colt] I aimed a blow at his arm and sent his revolver over his head." "My time next," Montgomery shouted over the din of battle and put a bullet in the Ranger, sending him "whirling"[15] out of his saddle. With two Navy Colts and a Spencer, Montgomery and Blazer's Scouts went to work in the thick of the Rangers' ranks until a ball burrowed into Montgomery's shoulder blade.

Blazer's men had overwhelmed a larger force; as Blazer wrote, "I came upon Mosby's guerrillas, 200 strong,[16] and after a sharp fight of thirty minutes, we succeeded in routing him, driving them three miles, over fences and through cornfields. They fought with will, but the seven shooters [the Spencers] proved to be too much for them."[17]

After gathering the wounded from both sides, including a Ranger "who had his arm shot off," the Scouts crossed the Potomac at Myer's Ford and rode into Myerstown, West Virginia. Blazer's command suffered five casualties—one dead, four wounded—and claimed to have killed six of Mosby's men and one officer, wounded four more, and captured six Rangers.

A spirit of humanity pervaded the way Blazer's men conducted themselves; as Ranger J. Marshall Crawford wrote, "although these Yankees were drunk" (some of the Scouts likely drank the applejack), "they carried our wounded to houses in the neighborhood, and requested every attention to be shown to them until removed. I must say they had more of the instincts of humanity about them on that day than any [Yankee] we ever met before."[18]

31. SHERIDAN'S SCOUTS:
THE TIDE TURNS

Sheridan's headquarters in the field, Shenandoah Valley,
late August 1864

"I asked General Averell for his oldest scout." The five-foot, five-inch Sheridan looked the six-foot-tall, 140-pound Scout up and down.

"I am his oldest in point of service—in knowledge of the Valley," responded Jessie Scout Archibald Rowand.

"How old are you? How long have you been a scout?" the general asked in disbelief.

Rowand recounted his two years of service. He was nineteen years old and knew the valley like the back of his hand. The general took the Scout into his headquarters and "pumped"[1] him for information and his bona fides for an hour and a half.

Sheridan then ordered Rowand to bring in his fellow Jessie Scouts: Jack Riley, Dominick Fannin, Jim White, Alvin Stearns, and John Dunn. While Blazer was tasked with hunting Mosby full time, these Jessie Scouts would form the nucleus of what would become known as Sheridan's Scouts.

Rowand and the other Scouts would come to love Sheridan, who "stood by his scouts in everything, and they one and all would have gone to any ends to get for him the information that he desired. He himself gave his orders to us—his 'old' scouts . . . and he personally received our reports."[2]

Sheridan's congenial nature and sense of humor set the men at ease. Months later, when Rowand asked Sheridan about his first impression of the young Scout, he responded, "Two big brown eyes and a mouth, Rowand; that was all."[3]

Lincoln had staked the Republican Party's political future on a military victory to crush the Confederacy. Another military disaster on the battlefield could have dire consequences and result in the South once again threatening Washington. The outcome on the battlefield often depended on the quality of the intelligence Sheridan received. To that end, Sheridan needed the best eyes and ears in the field and leaned on the Jessie Scouts and Blazer's Scouts to deal with Mosby and other Confederate irregulars. As Sheridan recalled, "My retrograde move from Strasburg to Halltown caused considerable alarm in the North. . . . Mutters of dissatisfaction reached me from many sources, and loud calls were made for my removal. . . . The difference of strength between the two armies was considerably in my favor; but the conditions attending my situation in a hostile region necessitated so much detached service to protect trains, and to secure Maryland and Pennsylvania from raids, that my excess in numbers was almost canceled by those incidental demands that could not be avoided."[4] Mosby's and the other Confederate irregulars' strategy was working—large numbers of Sheridan's troops had to be diverted for security.

"War is a mere continuation of policy by other means,"[5] as Prussian general and military theorist Carl von Clausewitz famously noted. "I knew that I was strong, yet in consequence of the injunctions of General Grant, I deemed it necessary to be very cautious," Sheridan later observed, "and the fact that the Presidential election was impending made me doubly so, the authorities at Washington having impressed upon me that the defeat of my army might be followed by the overthrow of the party in power, which event, it was believed, would at least retard, if, indeed, it did not lead to the complete abandonment of all coercive measures."[6]

Sheridan's solution to the problem in large part depended on the intelligence his Scouts could provide.

"I could not risk disaster. . . . I determined to take all the time necessary to equip myself with the fullest information, and then seize an opportunity under such conditions that I could not well fail of success."[7] Sheridan remembered, "I felt the need of an efficient body of Scouts to collect information regarding the enemy, for the defective intelligence-establishment with which I started out from Harper's Ferry early in August had not proved satisfactory. I, therefore, began to organize my Scouts on a system which I hoped would give better results than had the method hitherto pursued in the department, which was to employ on this service doubtful citizens and Confederate deserters. If these should turn out untrustworthy, the mischief they might do us gave me grave apprehension, and I finally concluded that those of our own soldiers who should volunteer for the delicate and hazardous service duty would be the most valuable material."[8]

Maintaining their existing tradecraft, the Scouts were walking arsenals and "were disguised in Confederate uniforms whenever necessary." Sheridan paid them, often in gold, "in proportion to the value of the intelligence they furnished." That actionable intelligence "often stood us in good stead in checking the forays of Gilmor, Mosby, and other irregulars."[9] The intelligence came in many forms—some that could change the course of battle and the war.

The Scouts' intelligence work involved forging connections and building relationships. "They learned that just outside of my lines, near Millwood, there was living an old colored man [Thomas Laws], who had a permit from the Confederate commander to go into Winchester and return three times a week for the purpose of selling vegetables to the inhabitants."[10] Sheridan's Scout private James Campbell found the man. An older scout, at least in terms of service, Campbell had accompanied Sheridan when he arrived in the Shenandoah Valley and had been with him through many battles. The five-foot-six former sailor had enlisted in the Union Army on September 8, 1862, with the 2nd New York Cavalry. His eventual battle history would be remarkable and include an astonishing number of the major and minor battles of the war, as well as experience behind lines. Sheridan would say on his death, "This country will never know how much it owes to James A. Campbell."[11]

The same can be said about Thomas Laws, one of the bravest unsung heroes of the Civil War.* One Sunday evening, Campbell and another Scout approached the enslaved African American Laws and his wife as they were sitting on the steps of their cabin. "Two unknown men came through the yard and struck up a conversation with me about Winchester. I told them I could go to Winchester any time I choose as my master lived there, that was, in Berryville." The two Scouts returned to Sheridan's headquarters with the information about their potentially valuable informant. The general

---

* Combat artist James E. Taylor, who embedded with Sheridan's army, reached out to Laws after the war and maintained the only written correspondence with the enslaved African American.

wanted to determine whether Laws was reliable. Campbell returned to the cabin with an invitation for Laws: "The general wants to see you tonight."[12]

"They carried me to the general," Laws recalled. "When I got there, the general and I took our seats on an old log that was laying by the camp."[13] Among other inquiries, Sheridan asked Laws if he knew Rebecca Wright. The twenty-six-year-old Winchester native was a Quaker schoolteacher, Union supporter, and ardent abolitionist recommended by General Crook as a possible informant.

Wright lived in a divided house. Her sister Hannah was a "dyed-in-the-wool Rebel,"[14] and her brother David was conscripted into the Confederate Army. At the same time, the Confederates imprisoned her father for his fervent Unionist beliefs. "After a little persuasion,"[15] Laws agreed to carry a message to Wright for the general. Campbell carried Sheridan's letter behind enemy lines to Laws and stayed at Laws' cabin until he returned from his mission. "[Laws'] message was prepared by writing it on tissue paper, which was then compressed into a small pellet, and protected by wrapping it in tin-foil so that it could be safely carried in the man's mouth," or swallowed if the Confederates searched him.[16]

Rebecca Wright remembered the middle-aged Laws as a "quiet, dignified" man, "very" well dressed in a white shirt, coat, and tie, who approached her in her yard asking if he could see her privately. She took him into the school room where she taught, and he asked if she was "a Union lady" and if she knew General Sheridan.

"When she said she did not, I thought I was between Heaven and Earth," remembered Laws. Risking his life, Laws "ventured anyhow and gave her the letter."

Understanding the gravity of the situation and her actions, Wright took the letter. "I turned to my mother for guidance, not taking my sister into my secret for, that I knew would be fatal." Wright remembered saying to herself, "I will pay no attention to the letter." She showed the missive to her mother, stating, "The Rebels would kill us if they should find out."

"That is true," Wright's mother responded. "But men are dying for their country, and thy life and my life may be needed, too. I would not persuade thee. Settle it with thy conscience. Go to thy room and give thyself to prayer."[17] Rebecca Wright thought deeply about what she was about to embark on and prayed.

Finally, according to Sheridan, "the brave girl resolved to comply with my request, notwithstanding it might jeopardize her life."[18] Wright not only took on the task at great peril, but after the war, she would be spit on, ostracized, and hated by her neighbors, and her life would be threatened.

In a reply sent via the Scouts Laws, Wright informed Sheridan of a convalescing Confederate officer who had visited her mother's boarding house the night before and casually revealed that a division of infantry and a battalion of artillery commanded by Major General Joseph B. Kershaw had started back toward Richmond to join General Lee. "Her answer proved of more value to me than she anticipated,"[19] recounted Sheridan in his memoirs. The crucial intelligence gave the general confidence in the weakened strength of Early's army coiled in and around Winchester. After the war, Sheridan wrote to Wright, "It was on this information the battle was fought, and probably won."[20]

With the critical intelligence in hand, Sheridan approached Grant. "[I] pointed out with so much confidence the chances of a complete victory should I throw my army across the Valley Pike near Newtown that he fell in with the plan at once, authorized me to resume the offensive, and to attack Early as I deemed it most propitious to do so."[21]

The Third Battle of Winchester, or the Battle of Opequon, unfolded on September 19, 1864. The Union general launched his attack at 2 a.m. Despite the Union's advantage in numbers, portions of the attack began to falter. In typical form, the Confederates, though fewer, used the favorable terrain to their advantage. Early's deft reaction to the attack and miscalculations in Union troop movements and placements on Sheridan's part nearly resulted in disaster. Sheridan hit the Confederates with infantry and cavalry, but Early parried each attack. By midmorning, the tide of battle appeared to be shifting toward the Confederates. General Crook then spotted and exploited a weakness in the Confederate lines and hit their left flank with infantry and a cavalry assault, collapsing it. Confederate colonel George S. Patton Sr., the savior of the Battle of White Sulphur Springs over a year earlier, was mortally wounded in the battle. Blazer's Scouts had a bird's-eye view of the battle from a distant mountaintop as Asbe Montgomery wrote: "We saw the blaze of guns, and soon heard the booming of the cannon, which told us plainly what was going on. So desperate the engagement, and the firing so heavy though we were three or four miles off. We waited for the signal of victory some time, for sometimes the forces on both sides would cheer; you could tell from the sound of the small arms when either side was falling back. While everyone stood holding his horse, with anxious looks, and panting to hear our boys give the victorious cheers, that our comrades so often were permitted to do by Him who holds the destinies of men. Finally, we heard the yells start off at the head of the lines, and like a telegraphic dispatch, it flew from one to the other regiments. It was a terrific yet cheering sound, and we all knew the battle was won."[22]

Sheridan's forces drove Early's army through the streets of Winchester, the vital Virginia town at the top of the Shenandoah Valley that had changed hands dozens of times. Elements of Early's retreating army made a final stand in what is now known as Winchester National Cemetery while the rest of the army fell back. Crook launched an attack to crush the retreating Confederates. Sheridan, riding his massive black gelding, Rienzi, dashed behind the advancing Union troops with saber in hand, urging the men forward. The "whole army" gave up a wild cheer and "shouted itself hoarse." Another soldier exuberantly exclaimed on seeing the officer, "We were not used to seeing a commanding general on the front line of battle, and the exploding shells and whistling bullets added to the excitement of the scene."[23]

After being pushed out of Winchester, Early's troops fled the battle-field south on the Valley Pike toward their prepared defenses at Fisher's Hill, renowned for its seemingly impenetrable topography. Once again, Crook's troops played a decisive role when he turned Early's left flank in a surprise attack led by the Scouts. Federal troops had stealthily marched unobserved along the side of Little North Mountain led by Jessie Scout James White. He "ascertained and communicated the exact position of the enemy to General Crook."[24] Crook's men "rushed with unwonted fury down the mountainside, a living avalanche with impetuosity that was useless to resist."[25] White's horse was shot from under him and he was badly wounded. Crook's brilliant surprise flanking attack resulted in a rout that could have destroyed Early's army, but instead the army suc-cessfully retreated with heavy losses. Sheridan would later blame General William Averell for failure to pursue Early with alacrity and relieved him of his command, ending Averell's otherwise illustrious career and his role in enhancing the Jessie Scouts.

Combat artist James E. Taylor illustrated the battle and its grisly aftermath. Picking his way through a labyrinth of dead bodies, he heard a dog barking. "A Confederate soldier lay dead and by his side in an attitude of defiance his faithful canine friend who shared with him the hardships of the march and risks of the battlefield, resisting fiercely the friendly overtures of the touched Federals, allowing none to approach, while keeping a steadfast watch over the dead."[26]

The Third Battle of Winchester and subsequent action at Fisher's Hill "electrified the country,"[27] Grant later wrote in his memoir. The engagements gave the Union a decisive victory exactly when it needed it most. The battles were the bloodiest of any in the Shenandoah to this point, with high casualties on both sides.* The battles also demonstrated how a small group of determined and thoughtful men and women, acting with courage, could change the course of history.

Success on the battlefield at Winchester and at Fisher's Hill, where the Jessie Scouts played a crucial role, combined with William Tecumseh Sherman's victory in Atlanta days earlier, shifted the war's momentum and with it the political will of the nation as well as the needle at the polls. The Democrats' peace platform was determined on the battlefield as the *New York Times* proclaimed, "Peace is being negotiated now every day, by every victory."[28]

Days later, the *Daily National Republican* crowed, "When Sheridan advances, McClellan goes backward."[29]

* At the Third Battle of Winchester, Early lost nearly 4,000 killed, wounded, and missing. Sheridan had nearly 5,000 of the same. At Fisher's Hill, nearly 900 of Early's men were captured and about 300 more were wounded and killed. Sheridan had roughly 520 killed, wounded, and missing.

32. RANGER LEWIS POWELL

Despite Sheridan's victory at Winchester and Blazer's manhunt, Mosby continued to hit Federal supply lines. Three days after the battle, on September 22, 1864, a large force of Rangers, led by Sam Chapman, unexpectedly collided with nearly an entire brigade of Yankee cavalry. A desperate firefight and chase ensued; Lewis Powell, riding his favorite blood bay, fled the scene. According to one account, "The speed of Powell's mare was all that saved his neck from being stretched on that occasion. He escaped with seventeen bullet holes through his clothing."[1] Six other Rangers weren't as lucky. In the melee, one Union officer tried to surrender and was allegedly shot down by the Rangers. Remarkably all but six Rangers were able to shoot their way out of the hoard of Federal soldiers.

Boiling with rage from the perceived murder of the officer, some Union soldiers pushed three of the Rangers behind the Front Royal courthouse and, while their superiors looked the other way, shot them. While Custer may not have directly ordered their execution, he commanded the brigade. Two other Rangers were questioned and then hanged, and a sign attached to one read, "Such is the fate of all Mosby's men."[2]

Most tragically, sixteen-year-old Henry Rhodes was caught running down a stream bed and dragged behind Union cavalry horses through the streets into Front Royal with his wailing mother following behind, pleading for his life. He had never ridden with the Rangers before this day and had gone this time hoping to find a mount. A soldier ordered the bleeding, battered Rhodes to stand and, while he was struggling to do so, executed him with a pistol shot to the face.

In a ravine shrouded by a canopy of conifers outside Salem, Virginia,* Lieutenant Ed Thompson had gathered his Rangers in early autumn. The officer addressed his men and asked for three volunteers "to undertake the rather risky job." Without hesitation, Lewis Powell and two other men stepped forward "before the others could answer."[3]

Within the confines of Salem and along a route that stretched for miles, pockets of hundreds of Union troops guarded gangs of workers as they painstakingly laid steel rails. The fresh track was part of efforts to complete the unfinished Manassas Gap Railroad, a supply line for Sheridan's army into the Shenandoah Valley and to support its advance south. In September 1864, Sheridan focused on the Manassas Gap, which would terminate in Strasburg and allow his forces to be supplied by rail instead of the long, tortuous wagon route that first went to Harpers Ferry and then through territory infested by Mosby's Rangers.

Mosby made disruption of the rails his top priority. In one of the countless engagements that made up Mosby's war on the Manassas Gap, Thompson wanted to draw the Federals out of Salem and into an ambush. The incessant attacks were working, and progress on the iron road slowed to a snail's pace. Union losses mounted, and the Rangers cowed some Federals into submission. Casualties and lack of progress forced General Henry Halleck, the chief of staff, to consider depopulating Mosby's Confederacy of Rebel inhabitants and sending them south as he urged Sheridan to deploy his cavalry to "clean out Mosby's gang of robbers."[4] Sheridan felt he could not spare the troops. He still had to not only guard outposts and supply lines but also fight Early's considerable army. His plan remained to employ Blazer's Scouts to contend with Mosby. In desperation, the Union used civilians as human shields. "Your plan of putting prominent citizens on trains is approved, and you will carry it into effect. They shall be so confined as to render escape impossible, and yet be exposed to the fire of the enemy,"[5] Halleck callously wrote. The ploy failed to deter the attacks, and the Rangers continued to rip up rails at night.

Thompson's three volunteers did their part in the war on the rails on that autumn day. The "first class men, always ready for any duty and

---

* Salem has been renamed Marshall, Virginia.

game," acted as bait to lure the Yankee cavalry out of Salem. Powell itched for action, "always keyed up for any new sensation,"[6] wrote one Ranger. His blood bay had a menacing "habit of foaming at the mouth and exposing the white of her eyes."[7] That day, Powell rode right into scores of Yankee cavalry bristling with weapons. The three Rangers fired on the Federal pickets and made the ride of their lives as a swarm of mounted Yankees sped off in hot pursuit of the riders.

Concealed in bushes, the balance of the Rangers waited for Thompson's signal for the trap to be sprung. Attacking the front and back of the column of Union riders, Munson recalled, "our men got them . . . and killed, wounded, and captured all but one of them."[8] A lone trooper escaped. Thompson killed the Union trooper's horse, but the Federal jumped a fence and scampered away.

The violence surrounding the rails continued. On October 8,* near Piedmont,† Big Yankee Ames, now promoted to second lieutenant in F Company, rode off to gather more of his men to counter an approaching Federal patrol bearing down on them. For Ames, war was kill or be killed—if captured, he knew he would be executed on the spot for desertion and the path of Union dead bodies he left in his wake. A year and a half in the saddle riding into the heart of the Ranger's fiercest engagements had hardened the New Englander into a ruthless and efficient killer.

Likely a lone Jessie Scout spotted Ames. Getting an advantage, from the Confederate butternut he wore, the Scout mortally wounded Big Yankee. Ames' men heard the pop from the Jessie Scout's weapon, saw the smoke rising in Shacklett's orchard, and spotted Ames' riderless horse running down the lane from the house. William Chapman caught the animal, and several Rangers galloped toward the house, where they saw the Jessie Scout's horse tied at the gate. They quietly approached to find him rifling through Ames' pocket and called out, "Are you a Yankee?"[9]

The Jessie Scout jumped up and shouted "no" but ran down toward his horse. One of the Rangers dismounted and ran after the Scout and shot

---

* Varying sources report Ames' death on October 8 or 9, 1864. The individual who killed Ames could have also been a member of the 8th Illinois Cavalry.

† It is now known as Delaplane, Virginia.

him as he tried unsuccessfully to vault over a fence.[10] Rangers tearfully buried the thirty-eight-year-old Ames under a large oak tree nearby.*

Eventually, Mosby's war on the rails caused the exasperated Federals to abandon the completion of the Manassas Gap Railroad. Instead, they continued funneling supplies through Harpers Ferry and overland to the valley rather than through Manassas Junction. Thousands of troops had to be moved off the main battle line to guard the effort. Most importantly, from the Confederates' perspective, Mosby and Early helped delay Sheridan's army from joining Grant in Petersburg. As Sheridan conceded in his later memoir, "During the entire campaign, I had been annoyed by guerrilla bands under such partisan chiefs as Mosby, White, Gilmore [sic], and others, and this had considerably depleted my line of battle strength, necessitating as it did, large escorts from my supply trains. The most redoubtable of these leaders was Mosby."[11]

---

* I frequently travel by a roadside marker designating the site of his death located at Winchester Road in Delaplane, Virginia. Decades after the war, his comrade-in-arms Ranger A. G. Babcock removed his remains from the spot where he fell and reinterred him in Hollywood Cemetery in Richmond, Virginia, where a granite marker memorializes his service to Mosby's Rangers.

33. EARLY STRIKES BACK: CEDAR CREEK

On a routine scouting mission on October 18, Jessie Scouts Dominick Fannin and Alvin Stearns rode up to several stragglers from Jubal Early's army and used the cover of darkness to work their way deeper into the Confederate lines. Wearing butternut, the two blended in and discovered to their alarm that the Southerners were heading northward instead of retreating south. Thousands of Confederate troops marched toward the slumbering Union Army camped at Cedar Creek, just southwest of Winchester.

The two Scouts had already spent nearly three years battling in the saddle. The twenty-one-year-old Stearns was born in Ohio, but the blue-eyed, dark-haired, freckle-faced Scout had been a farmer in New York before enlisting. He was attached as a Scout from Company E, 8th New York Cavalry. His eighteen-year-old companion Fannin, a former blacksmith, enlisted as a private on January 8, 1862, in Company L, 12th Pennsylvania Volunteer Cavalry Regiment.[1]

The two Jessie Scouts exfiltrated the enemy lines and made their way "with all speed" back to Union headquarters at Belle Grove Plantation near Cedar Creek, south of Middleton, Virginia. Since Sheridan had left the camp for a meeting in Washington, they reported the impending attack to General Crook. "The enemy will attack at dawn!"[2] the two men implored.

Since Winchester, Early's army had endured a series of defeats but planned to change the course of the campaign in the Shenandoah, right before the election. Most recently, Early's cavalry had suffered a stinging loss several miles away at Toms Brook, Virginia. The Federals considered Early's Army of the Shenandoah a spent force incapable of mounting an effective counteroffensive. That evening, Crook's reconnaissance parties incorrectly confirmed to the general that the Confederates had departed their camps and retreated farther down the valley.

Back at a ramshackle cabin ensconced behind Union lines that served as the Jessie Scouts' headquarters, Fannin told Rowand and his fellow Scouts how Crook dismissed their intelligence and "made them feel like a five-cent shinplaster." They excitedly warned, "We'll be attacked at daylight—you'll see!" The two men swore, decried Crook's dismissiveness, and bemoaned that Sheridan hadn't been present to receive their report. Rowand, tired and sick of the Scouts' carping, finally turned to the men and said, "Lie down, you two fools, and let me sleep. If Crook can stand it, we ought to!"[3]

Days earlier, Confederate general John Brown Gordon had scaled a nearby mountain. Considered one of Lee's finest battle captains who moved with "splendid audacity which characterized him,"[4] the charismatic self-taught officer and future US Democratic senator, who had no formal military training before the conflict, proved to be a genius at war. Scanning the entirety of Sheridan's positions, Gordon picked up the most minute details through his field glasses: each gun emplacement, position, and unit flags. He spotted a glaring weakness in the Federal lines: they had left their left flank exposed. The Federals had falsely assumed that Massanutten Mountain would be too rugged for any force to surmount and attack the Union line undetected. The Confederates scouted the area and found a narrow path that skirted the forested mountain and paralleled the Shenandoah River.

On the night of October 18, using the light of the moon, thousands of Confederate troops, stripped of canteens and anything else that could make noise, made their way along the remote trail around the Union left flank. At the same time, Kershaw's Division, which had just returned from Petersburg, moved toward the Union front, and another portion of Early's army advanced down the Valley Pike toward the XIX and VI Corps. Early and Gordon hoped to reverse their losses at Winchester and Fisher's Hill with a crushing Confederate victory on the eve of the election. In one of the most audacious attacks of the war, roughly 14,000 Confederates barreled down on 32,000 Union troops.

"They're coming!" shrieked one groggy Union soldier around 5:00 a.m. The buzz of a bullet pierced a blanket that covered the window of the Scouts' cabin, signaling impending doom as thousands of wraithlike men clad in ragged butternut descended on the slumbering VIII Corps, the Army of West Virginia. "We gave a Rebel yell and ran right in on them and scattered them like chaff before the wind,"[5] recalled one of Kershaw's soldiers.

The Jessie Scouts mounted their horses and soon ran into General Horatio Wright, commander of VI Corps, who said, "You Scouts better fall back. This will be no place for those uniforms in a few minutes,"[6] remembered Rowand. The frigid autumn fog of October 19 had screened the Confederates until their shrill Rebel yells reached the Federals' ears as the troops hit the Federal lines. Utter pandemonium gripped many Union regiments and brigades as they disintegrated and fled northward to Middletown. Union soldiers were bayoneted while slumbering in their tents. Hordes of gray swept through the quickly disintegrating Federal lines. Some Northern troops fought in pockets of resistance. The Confederates demanded the surrender of the 8th Vermont and tried to seize their regimental flags. But the proud New Englanders defiantly shouted back, "Never!" and savagely fought hand to hand. Three color bearers fell, and the flags changed hands as "skulls were crushed with clubbed muskets; bayonets dripped with blood. Men clenched up and rolled upon the ground in the desperate frenzy of the contest for the flags,"[7] recalled one combatant. Thousands of Federals fell back in a panic-stricken mob. The "wounded, frantic at being left behind, struggled to keep up, there rose one long wail of pain and terror. From behind, there came ever the roar of battle where the Confederates who would not pillage fought the Federals who would not run."[8]

Hungry, shoeless Confederates attacked not only the Federals but their rations. After hours of bloody battle, much of it hand to hand, the fatigued and ravenous Confederates slowed their attack. The slight pause allowed Crook to stiffen Union defenses. Early arrived at the front around 10:30 and declared,

"Well, Gordon, this is glory enough for one day. This is the 19th. Precisely one month ago today we were going in the opposite direction."[9]

Early believed that the Federals were defeated and about to abandon the field. Recognizing that his men were exhausted, hungry, and thirsty, he planned to re-form his lines and consolidate his gains. Gordon implored Early to launch another attack immediately and pointed to VI Corps. "I felt sure we would compass the capture of that corps—certainly its destruction. When I had finished, he said: 'No use in that; they will all go directly.'"

Astounded, Gordon replied, "That is the VI Corps, general. It will not go, unless we drive it from the field."

"Yes, it will go too, directly," Early retorted.

Gordon later recalled, "My heart went into my boots. Visions of the fatal halt on the first day at Gettysburg."[10]

History would record the controversial pause as the Fatal Halt.

From the Union lines shortly after the halt, Early's men heard excited, loud cheers. Many of the Federal troops and Confederates believed powerful Union reinforcements had arrived. Indeed, they had. They were in the form of one man: General Philip Henry Sheridan himself had appeared.

"There comes the 'Old Man,'" said Arch Rowand, spotting General Sheridan on his black horse.

"Can't be; he's in Washington," exclaimed another.

"It's him; there come a couple of his staff officers a hundred yards behind."

"Boys, how is it?" The general had stopped and pulled up beside the Scouts.

"General, it's a rout!"

"Not quite that bad!" Sheridan reassured them. "The Eighth and Nineteenth are scattered, but the Sixth is solid!"

A passing lieutenant exchanged a few words with the five-foot-five officer straddling the enormous black horse, then asked Rowand, "Who was that, Scout?"

"That was General Sheridan."[11]

Departing around 8:30 a.m. from Winchester, he had galloped on his massive, jet-black, white-fetlocked gelding named Rienzi for the epic ride of the Civil War. Sheridan had received the three-year-old horse as a gift from the men of the 2nd Michigan Cavalry in 1862, and he named the beast after a town in Mississippi. Despite being previously wounded multiple times in battle, the horse brought Sheridan through numerous engagements, most famously that day.* Embedded combat

* The gallant warhorse survived scores of battles and passed away in 1878. A taxidermist preserved the animal for posterity; Rienzi, renamed Winchester, is on display at the Smithsonian's National Museum of American History.

artist James Taylor witnessed the ride, recalling, "[Sheridan] thunders by like a whirlwind. He braced well back in his saddle, his body forward bent and his feet in the hooded stirrup. . . . And I never shall forget the look his face wore which was of the intense anxiety, such to mark the features of one about to face a fateful crisis."[12] The ride and rally would be the stuff of legend and the rally would go down as an epic comeback in military history. And later, a famous poem by Thomas Buchanan Read titled "Sheridan's Ride" featured prominently during Lincoln's campaign of 1864 and reinforced the campaign slogan of "Don't swap horses in midstream."[13]

As Sheridan approached the front lines, one of his men shouted, "General, where will we sleep tonight?" A hush fell over the men as they waited for his answer. "We'll sleep in our old camps tonight, or we'll sleep in hell!" he answered, and the men responded by "cheering like mad."[14]

By noon, the Federals had held up the Confederate advance, checking several charges.

Sheridan also paused. A rumor lingered that Longstreet and his corps had arrived to deliver a crushing blow. The delay favored the Northern general, who reorganized his retreating army after confirming from captured Confederate prisoners that Longstreet was not in the Shenandoah.

Around 4:00 p.m., 200 buglers signaled "forward" in the all-out Union counterattack. Colonel Charles Russell Lowell, who now led a brigade and was the previous commander of the 2nd Massachusetts Cavalry, pointed his saber at the enemy and charged, though he was suffering from excruciating pain from an earlier wound. With their colors fluttering in the breeze, 3,000 cavalry also charged, along with thousands of Sheridan's men. Throughout the war and in his effort against Mosby, Lowell had had twelve horses shot from under him. At Cedar Creek, on his thirteenth horse, a Confederate bullet hit Lowell while in the saddle, and it would prove mortal.

Nonetheless, the blue lines inexorably surged onward. "It was a glorious sight to see that magnificent line sweeping onward in the charge," recalled one trooper. Sheridan committed his entire army; as one soldier remarked, "There was no reserves, no plans for retreat, only one grand, grand absorbing thought—to drive them back and retake the camps."[15] The Confederate lines held and repulsed several charges, leading Early to initially believe "the day is finally ours."[16] But by 5:30 p.m., under a shower of lead and iron, the Federals pierced Early's left. "We are flanked!" Cries rose above the din of battle and the smoke and thunder of cannon; the Confederate lines collapsed and fled in disorder southwest toward Fisher's Hill. Expending their ammunition during the rout, the Federals picked up cartridge boxes from the dead and wounded as they pursued the retreating Southerners and soon regained the Union camps and Sheridan's headquarters at Belle Grove Plantation. Fuming from defeat and cantankerous as ever, Early characteristically blamed his men for the loss, which had been bloody: the Confederates lost more than 3,100 men they could not easily replace,[17] while Union casualties amounted to 5,700.

In a personal act to immortalize the great victory, Sheridan renamed Rienzi Winchester. Jubal Early's army would never threaten Washington or Sheridan's army again. Crucially, Sheridan's victory on October 19 at Cedar Creek lifted Northern morale and greatly boosted Lincoln's chances of reelection.

34. THE GREENBACK RAID

Mid-October 1864, Valley Pike, Virginia

Despite being pursued by Blazer's Scouts, Mosby's Rangers were constantly in the saddle terrorizing Union positions and conducting raids on the rails. One attack, known as the Greenback Raid, garnered national attention before the election. Departing from a blacksmith shop near Middleburg, Virginia, led by Mosby himself, the Rangers set out toward Duffields Depot along the Baltimore and Ohio Railroad, located north of Charles Town, West Virginia. Traveling along the Valley Pike, Mosby's men encountered a small party of Jessie Scouts. As the Rangers charged, the Scouts fled, but one unfortunate Union soldier dressed in butternut was captured.

Ranger Ewell Atwell was given the unenviable duty of executing the Jessie Scout. Wearing a Confederate uniform made him a spy, a capital offense. "Ewell had a record for killing men in a fight," recalled Ranger John Alexander, "but he told me that he just did not have the nerve to take that fellow out under the stars and all alone by themselves stand him up and shoot the life out of him. So he told him to turn his back and run for it and he would give him five steps start. How much that was worth to him in front of Attwell's [*sic*] revolver, God knows. Attwell [*sic*] swore to the men that he did not know."[1] Rangers rarely missed their targets at close range.

After their encounter with the Jessie Scouts, the Rangers picked their way in the night through a gap in enemy lines to an undefended stretch of the railroad near Duffields Depot without being detected by patrols or reported to any of the nearby enemy camps. A bright, clear moon shone down on Mosby and approximately eighty of his Rangers as they lay exhausted, sleeping on a steep frost-covered bank next to the railway track they had sabotaged. The Rangers were jarred from their slumber by the screech of steel brakes, a deafening explosion, and showers of red-hot cinders, steam, and ash. "A good description of the scene can be found in Dante's *Inferno*," quipped the erudite Mosby in his memoirs.[2]

"Above all could be heard the screams of the passengers—especially women." Mosby had specifically selected the 2:00 a.m. western-bound passenger train for sabotage from the timetable provided by Jim Wiltshire, the same Ranger who, Mosby claimed, informed him of the gap in enemy lines, knowing "it would create a greater sensation to burn it than any other." The presidential election loomed in November, and every attack on railroads and wagon trains that made headlines in the Northern newspapers damaged public opinion of the Lincoln administration's handling of the war. The colonel had timed their arrival to the minute to minimize the danger of the "extremely hazardous enterprise." Mosby justified the risk: "I knew it would injure Sheridan to destroy a train and compel him to place stronger guards on the road." Mosby also carefully selected the location of the attack to minimize injury to the passengers: "I preferred derailing the train in a cut to running it off an embankment, because there would be less danger of passengers being hurt."[3]

As the massive black locomotive veered off the displaced track and into the deep cut in the earth, the boiler exploded, creating mayhem and confusion. Mosby jumped up from his sleep, literally pushed his men down the steep bank, and ordered them to pull the frantic travelers from the train before setting fire to the ten passenger cars.

When a car full of German immigrants traveling west to get homesteads refused to leave their seats, Mosby suggested they set fire to the coach to encourage them. "They don't understand English, perhaps they understand fire," said one Ranger as he threw a parcel of lighted *New York Herald*s into the train.[4]

"The Germans now took in the situation and came tumbling, all in a pile, out of the flames. I hope they all lived to be naturalized and get homes. They ought not to blame me, but Sheridan; it was his business, not mine, to protect them," Mosby later wrote.[5]

Mosby remained atop the bank, as he had been injured a few weeks earlier in a skirmish when his horse was shot and his foot trampled by a Yankee cavalryman's horse. Leaning on a cane and able to wear only one boot, he directed the Rangers as they helped the passengers out of the train and up the steep bank. One participant described the scene as "a romantic situation." He expressed jealousy of his fellow Ranger, Jim Wiltshire, "the luckiest dog on earth with the ladies," when a young woman of "remarkable beauty" begged him, "Oh, captain, protect me, for I am a Mason's daughter!" Reportedly the gallant Wiltshire replied, "And I, miss, am a Mason's son. Be not alarmed," then swooped her up as she fainted in his arms and took her to safety.[6]

Another woman attempted the same tactic, insisting a Ranger inform Colonel Mosby, "My father is a Mason!" Mosby only wryly responded, "Well, tell her I can't help it."[7]

"As soon as the passengers had gathered on the railroad bank, and the ladies were assured of their personal safety, their spirits revived, and they appeared to enjoy the adventure," one contemporary chronicler recalled. The ever-silver-tongued Mosby mingled with the passengers, assuring them, "[The Federals] will not guard the railroad, and I am determined to make [them] perform [their] duty."[8]

The attack resulted in only one casualty—a Federal officer who was shot as he attempted to escape. Mosby and his men left the civilians "to keep warm by the burning cars" while they took fifteen horses and twenty soldiers as prisoners, including the two US paymasters carrying satchels of greenbacks totaling over $168,000. At Ebenezer Church near Bloomfield, Virginia, Mosby would later divide the enormous bounty equally among his men while eschewing any portion for himself. He immediately sent the satchels ahead with a small party of three men to more easily evade the enemy.

On the return march, Mosby rode next to one prisoner, a well-dressed German lieutenant in a beaver overcoat and high boots on his way to join Sheridan's army. The Confederate colonel inquired, "We have done you no harm. Why did you come over here to fight us?" The German replied, "Oh, I only come to learn de art of war." A bit later, the same man came riding up to Mosby dressed in old clothes to complain of having been relieved of all his finery by one of the Rangers. "I asked him if he had not told me that he came to Virginia to learn the art of war. . . . Very well, this is your first lesson."[9] The German was not the only prisoner captured; Ranger Lewis Powell also took a prisoner.[10]

The Gray Ghost had the Yankees playing constant catch-up. Not content with their enormously successful Greenback Raid, two companies of Mosby's Rangers crossed the Potomac and struck the canal and B&O

Railroad in Maryland. Once again, the Union Army would be forced to divert troops from many other areas to more closely guard the railroad and the canal to ensure lines of communication and supplies between Shenandoah, Baltimore, and Washington were not disrupted.

"My object had then been accomplished,"[11] concluded Mosby. Military communications from the field to Halleck revealed the extent of Yankee anxiety: "At least 1,000 good cavalry should be attached to this command to protect us against the sudden dashes of the guerrilla forces infesting this part of the country."[12]

A two-horse buggy jostled up and down on the bumpy Valley Pike on October 25. Riding in the carriage, General Alfred Duffié, one of the war's poster boys for stolen valor, felt secure, flanked by an escort of over fifty cavalry troopers. The Army had recently reassigned him to a new command. Impatient with the slow pace of the escort, Duffié rushed ahead of the convoy in the carriage with a ten-trooper escort.

Nearby, Mosby and several companies of Rangers hovered, waiting like hawks for a larger wagon train slowly approaching from Martinsburg in the distance. The Rangers prepared another familiar ambush with their mountain howitzers. Unexpectedly, Duffié's carriage suddenly entered their sights.

The Rangers' guns barked. "Killing several, we dispersed the cavalry . . . under heavy fire of shell and musketry," remembered one Ranger. Duffié immediately knew the peril he faced and ordered the driver to ride to the safety of the larger approaching Union wagon train.

Duffié's carriage moved at "breakneck speed . . . the general and his adjutant tossing from one side to the other—over the top of each other—hats off—now down, then up. Every few moments, a shell would burst close to the carriage—down their heads would duck to the bottom of the carriage."[13]

Riding for his life, Duffié came within 200 yards of the larger wagon train when two Rangers swooped down, secured the carriage's horses, and, under the barrels of their guns, presented the prisoners to Mosby.

"Who are you?" Mosby asked his latest captive.

"General Duffié," the Frenchman responded.

Apparently, Duffié's reputation preceded him, and Mosby dismissively ordered, "Take him to the rear."[14]

Things turned personal on their way back to Mosby's Confederacy when the Rangers learned that Captain Blazer and his Scouts had encamped near Kabletown and they turned from their destination to hunt Blazer. The Rangers rushed into Blazer's camp only to discover that the Union Scouts had left shortly before their arrival, though "his fires were still burning brightly."[15]

35. ARTIST AND RETRIBUTION

Morning in the Shenandoah Valley dawned with an overcast of clouds. James E. Taylor felt the raw, crisp early November air as he leisurely rode on a Union wagon supply train from Berryville north to Summit Point, Virginia. One of the war's greatest combat artists knew better than to ride alone and risk his "scalp at the hands of the ubiquitous Mosby." A company of riders soon overtook Taylor's wagon train, "proceeding at a trot, who proved to be the famous, 'Blazer Scouts' and as the captain slackened up to converse with the commander of the train with whom I rode, I was not long in gleaning that the Scouts were starting on an expedition in quest of Mosby, to wipe out his command or getting wiped out,"[1] Taylor wrote in his sketchbook journal.

The combat artist sensed the opportunity of a lifetime: ride and sketch Blazer and obtain safe passage to Charles Town, West Virginia, his destination. Humble, self-effacing, and not seeking publicity, Blazer assented to Taylor's request, but only after the artist assured him he understood the grave danger he faced by riding with the Scouts.

Taylor knew full well the risks—he had placed his life on the line for his profession for years, producing some of the most exceptional battlefield art. Combat artists "braved every hardship and peril of the war, often under fire and in the most dangerous positions during battle in the business of their vocation as observers and recorders of events," and they "justly rank among the heroes of the war,"[2] one historian of the time explained.

Taylor embodied keen skills of observation and attention to detail in describing Blazer: "high cheekbones, straight, outshooting sandy hair, mustache and chin whiskers, eyelids slanting downward to the nose in which set steel gray eyes of eagle sharpness, marred somewhat by a kink or cross in one, but to judge by their glitter, vision evidently flawless. If he possessed the power of vision of his chief [General George Crook], he certainly had a great advantage in detecting from afar the stealthy approach of the meteoric Mosby."[3]

Blazer had esotropia, which caused one of his eyes to point inward, but his leadership, presence, and handsome features more than made up for the physical flaw. With a hunter's sense, "[he] was celerity itself, and like the Prussian [cavalry general] Seyderlitz was constantly turning up at the most unseasonable hours where least expected, and when least desired by the partisans."[4] The Scouts traveled down the Berryville Pike, looking for trouble, "proceeding leisurely to Charles Town over open ground as if courting attention from Mosby's lookouts in the ridge, and doubtless, a glass was trained on them from thence, as desired."[5] They passed a landscape touched by war: a solitary lime kiln standing upright in a field, coupled with the remains of a torched railroad bridge, alongside countless scars of conflict. Riding in closed ranks to prevent being flanked, rushed, and ambushed by Mosby, the Scouts generally conducted missions that spanned three days. They hunted all day, set up their camp in remote areas late at night, and saddled up before dawn to look for Mosby.

That afternoon, the Scouts dismounted in a grove. "The troopers throw their bridles over their horses' necks, seek the shade to lay by till summoned to the saddle,"[6] as Taylor described, a scene he immortalized on his sketchpad.

Eventually, the cavalcade reached Taylor's destination, and he shook Captain Richard Blazer's and the "brave and courteous" first lieutenant Thomas K. Coles' hands. After they parted, Taylor ominously wrote, "I quickly pass from the presence of the gallant band. . . . Where one seeks fight, he generally finds it."[7]

In the middle of October, a soldier fitted a leather strap, a noose, around Private Albert Gallatin Willis' neck as several troopers clambered up a poplar tree behind him. The troopers walked across a branch and their combined body weight brought the limb closer to the ground. The twenty-year-old only had seconds left on earth as he courageously faced his executioners.

Before the war, Willis had been a Baptist divinity student who later boarded with Confederate preacher Thaddeus Herndon in the tiny hamlet of Scuffleburg, nestled in a remote area in the Blue Ridge Mountains. After joining Company C of the 43rd Battalion in December 1863, his life dramatically changed. At Scuffleburg, months later, Willis escaped a Union dragnet that stormed the parson's home. Ranger Frank Rahm, who would later also have his own remarkable escape, recalled that night: "Kemper and Willis [the two Rangers slept in the same room] heard the commotion and soon had their door rapped on, with a demand to open, which they refused to do when the Yankees began firing through the door. The house was situated on an incline; hence it was some distance to the ground, being on the third floor. As soon as firing commenced, although in their 'evening apparel' they raised their window and out they went." Since the Federals occupied the front of the house, Willis made his way for the hayloft behind the home, "where he burrowed deep in the hay." The Union troopers stormed the barn and searched the loft, "and hunted every square inch in the place as they thought, but to no avail. Willis told me of their having probed the hay with their sabres, and many times, in guarding his front, he would gently guide the sabre so as to throw it on one or the other side of him."[8] Willis escaped capture, and so did Kemper, who nearly froze to death hiding behind a tree stump on the side of the mountain after eluding his pursuers. The incident was not Willis' first—he had survived other skirmishes and narrow escapes. He earned some much-needed rest in October when Mosby granted him a furlough and he and another, unknown Ranger traveled south toward Willis' home in Culpeper, Virginia, for downtime away from the war.

Fall in the eastern foothills of the Blue Ridge is beautiful: leaves turn brilliant hues of orange and red, vibrantly bathed in color. The faint scent of burning embers lingered in the air as Willis' horse went lame outside a patchwork of houses called Gaines Crossroads, the present-day Ben Venue. A local blacksmith's hammer and anvil masked the clatter of the approaching Union troops of the 2nd West Virginia Cavalry as they bore down on the two unsuspecting Confederates. Overwhelmed by numbers, Willis and the other Ranger surrendered without a fight, and the troopers from 2nd West Virginia (a unit that supplied many men to Blazer's Scouts) took the two men to Colonel William Henry Powell's headquarters located north of the tiny hamlet of Flint Hill. Powell explained, "Having learned of the willful and cold-blooded murder of a United States soldier by two men (Chancellor and Meyers, members of Mosby's gang of cutthroats and robbers) some two miles from my camp a few days previous, I ordered the execution of one of Mosby's gang whom I had captured."[9]

Days earlier, the Union soldier Powell referenced had wandered into Flint Hill (a Confederate area) dressed in civilian clothes. The individual claimed to be a deserter and asked for work. Meyers, a civilian, spent several days with the man and a Confederate soldier named Chancellor, who had returned to Flint Hill to visit his father, Meyers' neighbor. Meyers and Chancellor became convinced the man was a "spy feigning desertion" and placed him in custody. The three men started riding to Gordonsville, northwest of Richmond. Chancellor and Meyers planned to deliver him to Confederate authorities. According to Mosby, the individual was a spy; he could have been a Jessie Scout.[10] After traveling ten miles, the "spy" attempted to escape several times. Chancellor warned him that his next escape attempt would be his last. The spy attempted yet again; Chancellor stopped him with a bullet. While both men were Confederates, neither man was a Ranger. Nevertheless, Colonel William Powell blamed Mosby's men for killing the probable Jessie Scout.

After Powell found the man's body, he ordered his men to torch "the residence, barn, and all buildings and forage on the premises of Mr. Chancellor."[11] Next, the Union colonel wanted to make examples out of Mosby's men. But after he found out Willis was a divinity student, he told the young Ranger he could claim an exemption as a chaplain. Willis refused. Powell then ordered the two prisoners to draw straws to determine who went to the gallows. The other Ranger drew the shorter straw and burst into tears. "I have a wife and children, I am not a Christian and am afraid to die," the unlucky man pleaded. Willis replied, "I have no family, I am a Christian, and not afraid to die."[12]

Willis prayed as the noose was fitted around his neck. Suddenly, the branch violently arced skyward, and the noose tightened. Willis' lifeless body swung from the tree limb. A placard attached to his corpse read, "Hung in retaliation for a Union soldier said to have been killed by one of Mosby's men."[13] Willis would not be the last man executed, as a deadly series of slayings and retribution followed in his wake.

Seeking guidance to combat the cycle of violence, Mosby wrote to Lee, "During my absence from my command, the enemy captured six of my men near Front Royal. These were immediately hanged by order and

John C. Frémont, a Union general and politician whose experience with Scouts in the American West prior to the Civil War inspired the formation of the Jessie Scouts, named them in honor of his wife, Jessie. Initially, the Scouts had a checkered background, stealing anything not nailed down; but after the removal of their first commander, Charles Carpenter, they developed into a potent force, Lincoln's special forces. (*Source: Library of Congress Prints and Photographs Division.*)

Twenty-year-old Medal of Honor recipient and Union Jessie Scout Archibald Hamilton Rowand, Jr. wearing a Confederate uniform. Jessie Scouts often wore the uniform of their enemies to accomplish their missions behind the lines and the Union commandos conducted some of the Civil War's most hazardous duty. Many would not survive, one reason their story remained untold. Daring and bold, they were predecessors to America's special operations forces, which the Office of Strategic Services (OSS) studied and analyzed before America entered World War II. (*Source: NARA via Wikimedia Commons.*)

Thurmond's Rangers and Blazer's Scouts initially operated in some of the most beautiful and rugged terrain in the United States near the New River Gorge. (*Source: Wikimedia Commons.*)

Captain Richard Blazer commanded a unique company of Jessie Scouts known as Blazer's Independent Scouts. An elite hand-picked troop of volunteers comprised of the best woodsmen, marksmen, and trackers, Blazer's Scouts hunted irregular Confederate troops and especially the South's most dangerous men, including Mosby's Rangers. (*Source: Ohio History Connection.*)

Colonel John Singleton Mosby, nicknamed the "Gray Ghost," was the commander of the 43rd Virginia Cavalry Battalion known as Mosby's Rangers. Considered by many to be the greatest guerrilla leader in American history, Mosby tied up tens of thousands of Union troops and pioneered a modern form of guerrilla warfare the OSS would incorporate behind the lines in World War II. (*Source: Author collection.*)

William Dabney Thurmond co-founded Thurmond's Rangers with his brother Philip. The guerrilla or partisan group operated out of the mountains of West Virginia. Ruthless and deadly, Thurmond's Rangers were Blazer's Scouts' first opponents. A Confederate to the end, Thurmond would never sign an oath of allegiance to the Union after the war. He founded the town of Thurmond, West Virginia. (*Source: Online West Virginia Encyclopedia.*)

Image of a tremendous explosion at a Union munitions depot caused by a covert operation conducted by the Confederate Secret Service. Facing massive Northern armies, select groups of Southern men and women were forced to innovate and develop unorthodox shadow warfare methods. Decades ahead of their time, they excelled at election interference, explosives, and assassination. (*Source: Library of Congress Prints and Photographs Division.*)

A coal torpedo developed by the Confederate Secret Service. Seemingly harmless-looking pieces of coal, these mines were actually hollow metal castings filled with gunpowder and coated with coal dust. When the coal torpedoes were tossed in a steamboat's boiler by an unsuspecting stoker, the resulting explosion could cause the craft to blow sky-high. (*Source: Wikimedia Commons.*)

Most engagements between Scouts and irregular forces were sudden and violent. Their weapons of choice were .36 caliber 1851 Colt Navy, six-shot revolvers (top: serial number #156131 inscribed to Confederate Cavalryman Ben D. Barnes) or .44 caliber 1860 Colt Army revolvers (bottom: serial number #108524 used by 2nd Massachusetts Cavalryman Nathan Fogg against Mosby's Rangers at the battle of Mount Zion Church). The saber was carried by Sergeant Edward Tyrell at the clash at Mount Zion. (*Source: Author collection.*)

A haunting image of Blazer's Scout Sergeant Joseph Frith, who died in the service of his country. Sergeant Frith is buried in an unknown and unmarked grave, reportedly behind the Dickinson family home near Callaghan and Covington, Virginia. If you have any information on his possible grave, please contact the author directly by email via his website. (*Source: Art Frith.*)

Major General Philip Henry Sheridan, nicknamed "Little Phil," was one of the Civil War's most significant generals whose Jessie Scouts led the North to victory. (*Source: Library of Congress Prints and Photographs Division.*)

Brevet Major General William Woods Averell deployed the Jessie Scouts to lead his forces. He conducted several daring and epic raids against the Virginia and Tennessee Railroad and later attacked Southern troops in the Shenandoah Valley. (*Source: Library of Congress Prints and Photographs Division.*)

Major General George Crook, the "Gray Wolf," mastered wilderness skills, fighting tactics, and culture from Native Americans, which he imbued in Blazer's Scouts. (*Source: Library of Congress Prints and Photographs Division.*)

The Dahlgren-Kilpatrick Raid was a Union attack on Richmond on March 1, 1864, with purported and controversial plans to burn the city and execute Confederate leaders such as Jefferson Davis. The raid triggered Confederate plans to utilize their Secret Service and irregular operations to alter the trajectory of the war. (*Source:* Harper's Weekly *via Wikimedia Commons.*)

The Confederate Secret Service set up operations at the opulent St. Lawrence Hall Hotel in Montreal. Guests could saunter down an elegant flight of stairs to plumes of cigar smoke that billowed from the wood-paneled, high-mirrored Dooley's bar, which served mint juleps year-round. A large billiard room entertained the "secesh," the population of hundreds of Confederate exiles living in Montreal whom the Canadians welcomed. From the sanctuary of Canada, the Confederate Secret Service hatched plots to rob Northern banks, manipulate U.S. gold and currency markets, burn cities to the ground, free Confederate prisoners, conduct influence operations on the election of 1864, plot insurrections and assassinations, and influence political will in the North and abroad. (*Source: McCord Stewart Museum.*)

George Nicholas Sanders, a member of the Confederate Secret Service in Montreal, understood information warfare and the power of the media. He bragged to Jefferson Davis that his goal was "The Democracy [The Democratic Party] having possession of the press…" making it his next target. Accordingly, the Confederate Secret Service plied Northern newspapers with cash to shape the Confederacy's narrative of how hopeless and fruitless the war had become. (*Source:* Harper's Weekly *via Wikimedia Commons.*)

Clement Laird Vallandigham, racist former Ohio congressman, was head of the Copperhead movement of the anti-war Democrat Party. Powerful and influential, he was an asset of the Confederate Secret Service and played a crucial role in their attempts to interfere in the election of 1864. (*Source: Library of Congress Prints and Photographs Division.*)

An original Copperhead penny with holes drilled in it to be worn on the lapel to identify a Copperhead supporter. The Copperhead peace movement was the dominant force in the Democrat Party during the 1864 election. The Confederate Secret Service funded the movement and planned an insurrection with it in the Midwest. (*Source: Author collection.*)

Lieutenant General Jubal Early. "Lee's Bad Old Man" wreaked havoc in the Shenandoah Valley and came within an eyelash of capturing Washington, DC, on July 10-11, 1864, setting up one of the greatest "what if" questions of the Civil War. (*Source: Library of Congress Prints and Photographs Division.*)

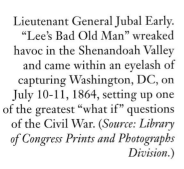

A breakthrough weapon, the Spencer was the world's first military metallic cartridge repeating rifle. This Spencer repeating carbine was carried by Sgt. Herman Richards of Co. B. 5th New York Cavalry, who fought Mosby's Rangers at the Grape Wood Farm Engagement. Blazer's Scouts were armed with the Spencer rifle and the Spencer repeating carbine. Richards carved his name and company in the stock of the weapon. (*Source: Author collection.*)

Mosby (standing middle) and some of his Rangers, also known as the 43rd Virginia Cavalry Battalion, were Sheridan's nemeses during 1864 and 1865. These elite soldiers rode into combat and ambushed wagon trains, railroad tracks, and engines. The Rangers tied up thousands of Union troops and defeated many Union units deployed against them. (*Source: Library of Congress Prints and Photographs Division.*)

Major Henry Harrison Young, a fearless Rhode Island officer born for war, was the commander of Sheridan's Jessie Scouts. (*Source: U.S. Army Heritage and Education Center.*)

Major HENRY H. YOUNG
Chief of Scouts, Staff of Gen. Sheridan

Sheridan's Jessie Scouts played a crucial role in gathering intelligence, establishing sources, and obtaining critical battlefield intelligence that turned the tide at the Third Battle of Winchester, which was instrumental in changing the momentum of the 1864 presidential election. (*Source: Library of Congress Prints and Photographs Division.*)

Combat artist James E. Taylor was briefly embedded with the Jessie Scouts. His dramatic drawing captures the frantic Confederate retreat through the streets of Winchester, Virginia, on September 19, 1864. "We have just sent the Rebels whirling through Winchester," his

Captain Nicholas Badger was an unscrupulous Union officer who escaped from Mosby's Rangers. (*Source: Author collection.*)

The author visiting the grave of African American Thomas Laws, one of the great unsung heroes of the Civil War, who worked with Jessie Scouts to ferry crucial intelligence on Confederate troop strength obtained from Union sympathizer Rebecca Wright. The intelligence shifted the course of the Third Battle of Winchester and the war. (*Source: Author photo.*)

Major General Sheridan's epic ride turned the tide at the Battle of Cedar Creek on October 19, 1864, which helped seal Lincoln's victory at the polls in November that year. Sheridan was a hands-on general who would also change the course of the Battle of Five Forks through his personal courage. He later credited his Jessie Scouts for much of his success since they provided invaluable tactical battlefield intelligence. (*Source: Library of Congress Prints and Photographs Division.*)

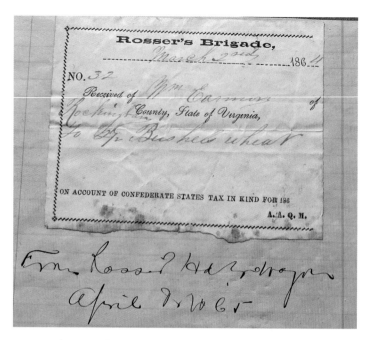

Random events and actions from a single individual can change the course of history. Above is a rare one-of-a-kind artifact, a receipt from Confederate General "Tex" Rosser's headquarters wagon captured by a Union officer at Appomattox. Prior to the Battle of Five Forks, Rosser fished the local river for shad and decided to have a fish fry for two other Confederate generals defending Five Forks. Crucially, the generals failed to tell their seconds where they would be located far behind the line. While they dined on fish and spirits, Sheridan attacked. They listened for gunfire but heard none. A natural phenomenon known as an acoustic echo canceled the thunderous sounds of battle, causing the generals to miss one of the most crucial battles of the war and contributing to the Confederate defeat. (*Source: Author collection.*)

The Battle of Five Forks proved to be one of the most crucial battles of the Civil War since it forced a premature evacuation of Confederate troops from Petersburg and Richmond. General Sheridan personally led the attack using priceless intelligence gathered from the Jessie Scouts. Scouts accompanied their leader on the attack. (*Source: Library of Congress Prints and Photographs Division.*)

High Bridge rose 126 feet above the Appomattox River and spanned half a mile of the valley. A wagon bridge below also spanned the river. The crucial choke point became an objective of both armies during Lee's escape from Petersburg. (*Source: Library of Congress Prints and Photographs Division.*)

Lieutenant Allen F. Belcher, whose frock coat is also pictured here, was one of eighty cavalrymen who, in a near-suicidal attack, charged the High Bridge. The cavalry found themselves thrust into mortal hand-to-hand combat during which Belcher received a severe saber slash across his face. The Confederates annihilated Belcher's force, seizing nearly eight hundred prisoners, six battle flags, and a brass band of musicians. The Confederates torched the railroad bridge but failed to destroy a critical wagon bridge below. With the wagon bridge in Union hands, hardly anything stopped the Federal army from pursuing Lee's ragged, hungry, and diminished force. (*Source: Author collection.*)

Lewis Powell, one of Mosby's Rangers, was also an operative for the Confederate Secret Service and a key member of the Lincoln Conspiracy. Known for his charm and dash, he was also an escape artist. (*Source: Library of Congress Prints and Photographs Division.*)

Lewis Powell was a member of the plot first to kidnap Lincoln and later to kill the president and decapitate Union leadership. After his pistol jammed, Powell brutally attacked Union Secretary of State William H. Seward with a knife and nearly killed him on April 14, 1865, just before John Wilkes Booth shot Lincoln at Ford's Theatre. (*Source: National Police Gazette via Wikimedia Commons.*)

During Lee's retreat, Sheridan's Jessie Scouts located Lee's crucial supply trains at Appomattox needed to fuel his hungry and exhausted troops. The operation helped seal the fate of the Army of Northern Virginia and thwarted Confederate aspirations for guerrilla warfare that could have led to one of the bloodiest insurgencies in history. The reunification of America after years of horrific Civil War began at Appomattox as Grant and Lee met face to face, depicted here by artist Louis Guillaume. (*Source: Granger Historical Picture Archive.*)

Emperor Maximilian I of Mexico. In the final months of the Civil War, Sheridan's Jessie Scouts were sent to the Mexico border, from which they conducted covert operations in Mexico during one of America's first proxy wars against a European power, France. The Scouts helped arm the resistance against the tens of thousands of French troops in Mexico. Thousands of Confederates fled to Mexico to aid Maximilian. Many Jessie Scouts would never return home from what would be their final mission. (*Source: Library of Congress Prints and Photographs Division.*)

The author was present when members of SOCOM recreated in June 2019 the parachute jump of Operational Group PAT on a remote WWII mountain drop zone into what was then German-occupied Southern France. The OSS Operational Groups, forerunners of the U.S. Army Special Forces, ambushed German convoys, blew up bridges, and captured thousands of German troops, much like the Jessie Scouts and Mosby's Rangers they studied when forming modern special operations forces during WWII. (*Source: Author photo.*)

in the presence of General Custer.* They also [hanged] another [Willis] lately in Rappahannock. It is my purpose to hang an equal number of Custer's men whenever I capture them."[14]

Lee concurred with Mosby's approach and said, "I do not know how to prevent the cruel conduct of the enemy toward our citizens. I have directed Colonel Mosby, through the adjutant to hang an equal number of Custer's men in retaliation for those executed by him."[15]

On November 4, each Union prisoner pulled a scrap of white paper from a hat. Twenty-seven slips of paper. Twenty blanks. Seven marked. Drawing one of the unlucky seven would equal execution.[16] Mosby planned to carry out Lee's orders as a reprisal for the killing of Mosby's men.

Several of Custer's men prayed aloud. One by one, each gingerly plucked a slip of paper. Some exhaled sighs of relief; others cried, "Oh God, spare me!" One drummer boy became hysterical before extracting a blank slip, to his great relief.

But the second drummer boy was not so lucky.

Upon hearing that a young man stood among the condemned, John Singleton Mosby immediately ordered his release. Both drummer boys were excluded as the nineteen men who earlier thought they had cheated death again drew lots. One selected the mark of death.

The Confederates soberly bound the condemned and mounted them on horses. As lightning arced across a dark sky and cold rain fell, the prisoners and Mosby's Rangers rode toward the Shenandoah Valley. Mosby ordered four men to be shot and three hanged.

The Rangers marched the seven prisoners into the Shenandoah through Ashby's Gap, where they crossed paths with Ranger captain Richard Montjoy, who also had prisoners in tow from an earlier engagement. One of Mosby's prisoners noticed Montjoy's Masonic ring and entreated the officer for his life. Montjoy obliged and exchanged one of his prisoners for the condemned Mason.

---

* Custer did not directly give the order, but members of his 5th Michigan were involved in the murder of two of Mosby's men.

Yet all did not go according to plan. One of the prisoners asked for time to pray. Kneeling down, he managed to free his hands, jump to his feet, punch the nearest captor in the face, and escape into the woods. Surprised by the sudden turn of events, the Confederate soldiers immediately fired their pistols at three other men sentenced to death. However, one of the revolvers misfired, and a second of Custer's men escaped into the night. The Confederates hanged the remaining three prisoners, adorning one with a note that read, "These men have been hung in retaliation for an equal number of Colonel Mosby's men hung by the order of General Custer, at Front Royal. Measure for measure."[17]

When Mosby's men returned and explained that two of the prisoners had escaped, the Gray Ghost was unperturbed by the news. Instead of executing more men, he decided to send John Russell to Winchester under a white flag with a letter for Sheridan. Mosby detailed the facts and stated, "Since the murder of my men not less than 700 prisoners, including many officers of high rank, captured from your army by this command, have been forwarded to Richmond, but the execution of my purpose of retaliation was deferred in order, as far as possible, to confine its operation to the men of Custer and Powell. Accordingly, on the 6th instant, seven of your men were, by my order, executed on the Valley Pike, your highway of travel. Hereafter any prisoners falling into my hands will be treated with the kindness due to their condition, unless some new act of barbarity shall compel me reluctantly to adopt a course of policy repulsive to humanity."[18] Russell returned with a letter from Sheridan. Neither man ever discussed its contents, but the reprisal killings halted.

36. DOPPELGANGERS

Harry Gilmor and several of his men rode down the Valley Pike to "take a look at Sheridan's camp." Avoiding Union patrols and Jessie Scouts, several handpicked men from the 2nd Maryland Cavalry, also known as Gilmor's Raiders, traveled north for two days to glean intelligence at the behest of Early. Gilmor's men operated independently of Mosby and were one of Early's favorite reconnaissance units. The Southerners dressed in Union blue avoided fighting since they were mainly "a party of observation," unless the right opportunity arose and the Raiders had the edge over the enemy; as Gilmor noted, "We gave them a turn, just to keep our hands in." On that dark and rainy fall night, the riders spotted a column of Federal cavalry. One of Gilmor's men, wearing a blue overcoat, rode up to the rear of the column and offered his canteen to an officer. Stunned, the Federal officer drew his sword and ordered, "Take your place in the ranks." Gilmor's man "politely touched his hat, saying that he did not belong to the squadron, but was one of Blazer's Scouts."[1] The irregular nature of Blazer's operations, and use of enemy uniforms, made imitation the highest form of compliment and the perfect cover story. The Confederate then convinced the officer that if the Federal dropped back a little, he would fill his canteen. Thirsty, the man complied—and soon found a cocked pistol in his face and an audience with Gilmor as a prisoner.

After resting and sending the prisoner back to Southern lines under guard, Gilmor and a smaller group of his men once again donned Union blue overcoats and set out for Sheridan's camp near Winchester, where they passed through pickets and "ascertained to a certainty that no troops had gone to Grant."[2]

On a new mission, the doppelgangers suddenly found themselves face-to-face with the real deal: four of Blazer's Scouts. Wearing a blue overcoat that matched theirs, Gilmor convinced the Scouts they were part of Major General Alfred Thomas Archimedes Torbert's cavalry as the group rode toward camp to vote in the presidential election. Gilmor smiled and made small talk. He asked, "I suppose you will vote for Lincoln?" Blazer's men replied in the affirmative and showed the Confederate irregulars their "tickets" to cast ballots. The Marylander motioned, and on his silent signal, the Scouts had pistols in their faces, surrendering without firing a shot. Gilmor took the tickets and nonchalantly rode into the lions' den of thousands of Union troops. "We took their papers and tickets to Sheridan's camp, and there voted for Lincoln! This gave us every facility for gaining information, for of course no one could object to us after voting for Lincoln!"[3]

Not only did Blazer's men and Gilmor's Raiders vote in arguably the most consequential election in history, but the Jessie Scouts, including Arch Rowand, also did. He fondly wrote to a fellow Scout years later, "Each of us having two years' experience as Scouts. And I may say we are both hard-shelled republicans. I voted for Abe Lincoln in 64, at Martinsburg, when I was nineteen, and have never strayed from that path since."[4]

Because of the massive number of Union soldiers in the field and away from their home states, absentee ballots were allowed for the first time in the 1864 presidential election. The Union Army permitted many men to go on furlough and return to their home states to vote. Others voted in their camps and mailed in their ballots. The mail-in ballots were controversial, and fraud was suspected. Orville Wood, a county official from upstate New York, would uncover one of the most elaborate electoral conspiracies in American history.

Traveling from upstate New York to ensure that the votes of his county's soldiers were being counted properly, Wood arrived in Baltimore to monitor the mail-in ballots. While visiting convalescing soldiers at Fort McHenry, one of America's most sacred sites, the home of the "Star-Spangled Banner," Wood's "suspicions were aroused." Soldiers were "checker playing" with the ballots. The ballots required a series of forged signatures. To gain access to the process and the trust of the supervisor involved in the conspiracy, Wood insinuated that he was a Democrat and McClellan supporter. "McClellan received 400 votes and Lincoln

11. [Wood] expressed surprise at the small number of votes polled for Lincoln, when Mr. Ferry [the supervisor] said that, when Union votes came into that office, they were all right when they went out, and that they were doing more here than he thought of."[5] Wood played into the scheme and was brought into the fold by Ferry, personally taking part in the fraud by altering thousands of ballots to make them votes for McClellan. Wood brought evidence to authorities, exposing the entire operation. Ferry provided a full confession of his illicit activity in a military court, and a military commission was called by General Abner Doubleday to rectify the process. The committee's bombshell findings came out just before the election.

Other forms of election fraud or vote tampering were also attempted. Mosby and other Confederate irregulars received orders to capture ballot boxes to disrupt the election, but most of their efforts failed. Seven out of ten Union troops would vote for Lincoln and to continue the war.[6]

Despite a promising start with the success of the election influence operation, the Northwest Conspiracy insurrection hatched from Montreal sputtered before the election. The Sons of Liberty, for a second time, got cold feet and did not unleash their insurrection before the election. The armed rebellion would have involved tens of thousands of Copperheads and thousands of freed Confederate prisoners of war whom the Confederate Secret Service planned to unleash in the Midwest. Hines plotted to execute the Northern leadership of several states: "The State governments of Indiana, Ohio, and Illinois will be seized and their executive heads disposed of," he had written Seddon the previous June.[7] Battlefield success at Winchester, Cedar Creek, and Atlanta had altered the course of the war and, with it, hearts and minds at the ballot box and damped the ardor of many Copperheads. In the early fall, a government agent penetrated the Sons of Liberty, which led to the arrest of some of its prominent members, an event that "totally demoralized the Sons of Liberty."[8] Thomas Hines had to pull another remarkable vanishing act as Federal detectives surrounded the Chicago house he operated from, forcing him to hide in a mattress box spring for nearly a day as they fruitlessly searched the dwelling. He escaped shortly thereafter. Spending a month on the run en route to Richmond, Hines dodged Union detectives, broke his sweetheart out of a convent, and found time to have a honeymoon in Cincinnati before returning to Richmond on December 12.*

In testimony in Federal court, witnesses revealed that secret groups with ties to the Confederate Secret Service undermined the government through various seditious oaths: "I promise and swear that I will bring all loyal Democrats into this Circle of Hosts. I further promise and swear that I will do all in my power against the present Yankee-abolition-disunion administration; so, help me God." A similar offshoot was disclosed in Federal court in Des Moines: "I will resist draft either by State or Federal authorities; and I will do all in my power to unite the States of the Northwest with the Southern Confederacy."[9] Despite the setbacks, the Confederate Secret Service's influence operations to control the narrative by funding elements of the Northern press proved successful. The Secret Service also influenced the peace platform for the Democratic Party and encouraged the armistice, which would have likely ended the war had it not been for crucial victories in Atlanta and in the Shenandoah Valley. Weeks later, Jacob Thompson would write a letter to Jefferson Davis asserting that the shadowy group's efforts were not in vain. Union fear of a "fire in the rear" through the threat of insurrection and prisoner-of-war camp raids extracted a large cost to the Union for a small investment in gold and personnel on the part of the Secret Service: "The apprehensions of the enemy have caused him to bring back and keep from the field in front at least 60,000 to watch and browbeat the people at home," wrote Thompson. Despite the setbacks, the Secret Service did not give up on the Copperheads and funded and supported a new group of leaders, the Order of the White Star.[10]

On Tuesday, November 8, 1864, Americans voted. Even though the Electoral College votes reflected a landslide for Lincoln of 212 to 21, the popular vote was much closer, 55 percent to 45 percent.[11] Despite the recent Union victories, remarkably almost 2 million Americans—45 percent of voters—still cast ballots for the Democrats and against the war, illustrating how precarious the situation remained. A shift of 80,000 votes in key states would have generated a McClellan victory.[12] Union general Benjamin Butler stated, "Votes in three great states could change the late presidential election. " Most importantly, Butler stressed,

---

* Thomas Hines later put himself through law school and would emerge as the chief justice of the Kentucky Court of Appeals.

"a single disaster or a single victory . . . may turn your majority."[13] The Confederates' roll of the dice and near victory at Cedar Creek might have been that event, but Federal military successes had shifted the will of the country. Sherman's capture of Atlanta after the Confederates abandoned the city and the decisive naval Battle of Mobile Bay, which sealed off the port from blockade runners, helped turn the tide. However, Sheridan's victory in the valley, the Third Battle of Winchester, led by the Jessie Scouts, and the Battle of Cedar Creek, offered the bookend that would tip the scales in favor of Lincoln.

With their election interference operations blunted by the Union victories, the Confederate Secret Service was compelled to seek radical, violent covert operations to change the course of the war. Almost a month before the election, on October 13, the commissioners had composed a letter in coded cipher to Richmond: "We again urge the immense necessity of our gaining immediate advantages. Strain every nerve for victory. We now look upon the re-election in November as almost certain. . . . Our friends shall be immediately set to work as you direct."[14] The ciphered letter intimated a new course of action. Planning for one such operation had gained momentum in mid-October.

37. John Wilkes Booth and Special Operations That "Would Make the World Shudder"

Hundreds of miles away from Virginia, John Wilkes Booth was on a mission. Ostensibly going to Canada to enhance his theatrical wardrobe, Booth visited the unofficial headquarters for the Confederate Secret Service, the St. Lawrence Hall Hotel in Montreal, and checked into room number 150 on October 18.[1]

The twenty-six-year-old, a popular stage actor from a family of actors, was described by some as the "handsomest man in America." Booth led a double life. His sister kept a secret memoir that was published upon her death. In it, she described her brother as "a spy, a blockade-runner, a rebel! . . . He has been from childhood, an ardent lover of the South and her policy."[2] Renowned for his keen mind and charisma, John Wilkes Booth was not a madman.

During the time of Booth's stay, Confederate saboteurs had sallied out of their lair in Canada on October 19 to raid the town of St. Albans, Vermont, and hold up three banks, making off with over $200,000. The personnel and plans for the raid flowed from Montreal and George Sanders and company. One of the raid's goals was to create an incident that would draw the British, who had Southern sympathies, into the war on the side of the Confederacy. They also hoped to force the Union to place more troops on the northern border to guard against future raids. The Confederates almost succeeded in creating an international incident when a local posse of Northern townspeople pursued the men who fled to Canada. Instead, Canadian authorities rounded up approximately a dozen raiders and recovered and returned over $80,000 of the stolen money.

After the raid, Sanders, who ascribed to the "theory of the dagger" and was a proponent of political assassinations, checked into room 169, just down the hall from Booth. Three credible eyewitnesses saw the two men together. One of them later recalled under oath, "They were talking confidentially, and drinking together. I saw them go into Dowley's [the hotel bar] and have a drink together."[3]

According to St. Lawrence Hall's guest book, another crucial Confederate Secret Service operative checked in during Booth's stay: John Harrison Surratt.[4] He frequently stayed at the hotel; the guest book and arrival book have entries under his name and various aliases more than a dozen times. Only twenty when the war broke out, the divinity student abandoned his studies for the priesthood and became a Confederate courier and spy. Upon his father's death, he assumed the role of postmaster and innkeeper of Surratt's Tavern in Clinton, Maryland. His mother, Mary, had a boarding house in Washington, DC. Both destinations were safe houses for the Confederate Secret Service. Surratt would emerge as an essential member of Booth's team and one of the South's most significant operators.

Spy vixen Sarah Antoinette Slater often accompanied Surratt. The black-eyed, fair-complexioned, slim twentysomething[5] got bored sitting around waiting for her husband to return from the war, so she volunteered for Secret Service work and was tied to some of their most important missions. Months later, Slater helped rescue the St. Albans raiders who had been rounded up by Canadian authorities. Often wearing a veil and speaking perfect French, she covertly carried papers from Richmond stating the men were not criminals but agents acting on behalf of their government, which halted their extradition to the United States. Adopting various aliases, among them Kate Brown and Kate Thompson, and referred to as the "the French Woman," Slater captured the attention of those around her; Surratt confided to one man that he had "woman on the brain."[6]

Booth's diary revealed what they were planning. "For six months we had worked to capture [Lincoln],"[7] Booth wrote in early April 1865. His diary entry placed the origins of Booth's planning in Montreal in October and explained the plans to capture versus kill. Capturing Lincoln had advantages over assassination: the president could be used as political leverage in negotiations. Seizing the leader of the Union could destabilize Federal operations and war plans. After the Dahlgren Raid, Federal house burnings, and advancement toward total war, Lincoln had become a more palatable military target, since the Federals had planned to decapitate Confederate leadership during the Dahlgren Raid.

Confederates and Mosby demonstrated expertise in the capture of high-value targets, such as snaring General Stoughton. And Lincoln's personal security remained surprisingly lax, as he often traveled with only a small escort. The Rangers could provide security for the capture team through hostile territory and bring Lincoln and the team to the safety of Richmond.

Parallel to the unfolding operation involving Booth, the Confederate Secret Service had another team also looking at kidnapping Lincoln. It is unclear whether this was an operation occurring concurrently or perhaps a feasibility group under the command of Captain Thomas Nelson Conrad. Confederate topographic experts and mapmakers went to work to examine egress routes from Washington to Richmond. Confederate secretary of war James Seddon cut orders in September that "Lt. Col. Mosby and Lieutenant Cawood are hereby directed to facilitate the movements of Captain Conrad."[8]

A preacher and principal at Georgetown Institute, Conrad revealed his loyalties in 1861 when he ordered a band to play "Dixie" at commencement. Federal authorities soon arrested Conrad and threw him into Washington's Capitol Prison but later released the fiery preacher in a prisoner exchange. Joining J. E. B. Stuart's cavalry, Conrad took on the dangerous occupation of scout but never shed his religious calling. He assumed the role of chaplain. At the end of September 1864, the preacher spy infiltrated back into Washington, where he went to work for the Confederate Secret Service and was given $500 in gold, which Jefferson Davis authorized from Secret Service funds via Request No. 47.[9] "I had reached Washington safely and begun to reconnoiter the White House. . . . I had to ascertain Mr. Lincoln's customary movements." At Lafayette Park, "only a stone's throw from the White House," Conrad observed for days: "Officials' ingress and egress, noting about what hours of the day he might venture forth, size of the accompanying escort if any: and all other details. . . . We had to determine at what point it would be most expedient to capture the carriage and take possession of Mr. Lincoln; and then whether to move with him through Maryland to the lower Potomac and cross or the upper Potomac and deliver the prisoner to Mosby's Confederacy for transportation to Richmond. To secure the points necessary for reaching a proper conclusion about all these things, required days of careful work and observation. . . . Having scouted the country pretty thoroughly . . . we finally concluded to take the lower Potomac route."[10]

Testing the feasibility of this route became a priority. Months later, following the assassination, Booth would take the same route to escape from Washington and into Virginia. The path involved moving from Washington through southern Maryland using covert lines established by the Confederate Secret Service, crossing the Potomac, landing near Mathias Point, and traversing a peninsula known as the Northern Neck to the safety of Richmond. The Confederate Secret Service signals officer in the Northern Neck ordered to work with Mosby and Conrad was Lieutenant Charles Cawood. Mosby also had two Secret Service Signal Corps personnel assigned to his command.[11]

During this time frame, Mosby conducted a raid that, while not stated, was likely intended to test whether taking Lincoln across the lower Potomac would work. Mosby tapped Walter Bowie, one of his best Rangers, who was from a distinguished Prince William County family and knew the area like the back of his hand. Bowie also had ties to the Confederate Secret Service. The Scout led a band of twenty-five Rangers through the Northern Neck to Mathias Point, with the ostensible, likely bogus, cover story of aiming to capture the governor of Maryland. Their route of egress makes little sense for capturing the governor in Annapolis, which would have been easier to accomplish from the north. After capturing over a dozen Union soldiers and horses, Bowie's men moved to Sandy Springs, a few miles from Rockville. Here a group of citizens and Union cavalry tracked them down and shot and mortally wounded Bowie as most of the remainder of his team escaped to Mosby's Confederacy.

Booth fit right in at St. Lawrence Hall. As one witness, John Deveney, later swore under oath, "[Booth] was then in company with Sanders, Thompson, and others of that class. He seemed well received by these men and was on familiar and intimate terms with them."[12]

Booth also racked and broke balls in the billiards room next to Dooley's Bar. Drinks flowed freely as the game unfolded. Politics swirled in the air, and Booth is said to have exclaimed, "It made d—d little difference [who was elected], head or tail—Abe's contract was near up, and whether elected or not, he would get his goose cooked." Later, Booth boasted, "Do you know I have the sharpest play laid out ever done in America? I can bag the biggest game this side of—. You'll hear of a double carom one of these days."[13]

An eyewitness under oath later testified that, before he departed Canada, Booth went to the Ontario Bank, deposited money, and obtained a bill of exchange that could be cashed at other banks. The teller believed Booth might have been introduced to a "Mr. P. Martin," a known Confederate agent with expert knowledge of the Confederate secret routes in southern Maryland. Martin also provided Booth with a Secret Service letter of introduction to contacts in southern Maryland, the "Doctor's Courier Line," that included ardent Southern operative Dr. Samuel Mudd, men who would abet Booth and his team in their flight from Washington to Maryland and across the Potomac to Virginia. The Secret Service's underground lines in southern Maryland were essential to Booth's mission. When the assassination option was introduced is not known, but the Confederates' plans for kidnapping the president, and perhaps a deadlier operation, moved forward. During Booth's stay, George Sanders proclaimed to a London-based *Daily Telegraph* correspondent that the Confederate Secret Service would conduct covert missions that "would make the world shudder."[14]

The Confederate Secret Service planned to roll out a war of terror in the North from Montreal in conjunction with the kidnapping plot. The organization teemed with novel and groundbreaking ideas on how to survive the war and kill Yankees. One plot involved biological warfare. Within the group, Dr. Luke Pryor Blackburn, an expert on infectious diseases, gathered bales of infected clothing from yellow fever patients who died in Bermuda that he planned to distribute in Northern cities. The Confederate Secret Service plotted to poison New York's water supply in another deadly operation. Neither operation got too far beyond the planning phase.

After spending nearly ten days in Montreal, Booth traveled by train to New York City, which was teeming with Confederate operatives. He would visit the city a dozen times, presumably meeting his Confederate handlers. There, Booth stocked up on weapons, ammo, and two pairs of handcuffs. He undoubtedly had help from the Confederate Secret Service to obtain two Spencer carbines, a cutting-edge weapon for the time.

Among other shadowy characters, the actor met with his good friend and fellow actor Samuel Knapp Chester. "After considerable conversation," Booth attempted to enlist him in the plot to kidnap the president. "He finally opened the whole affair to him and stated there was a plot to kidnap the president and cabinet and take them to Richmond; and there were 50 to a hundred engaged in the plot and they have all taken the oath of secrecy, and that the plot was completed."[15] Here, Booth revealed the extent of the plot and its size; this was not a small group of conspirators. Booth promised Chester thousands of dollars for his involvement. When Chester demurred, Booth threatened to kill him if he went to the authorities, claiming he carried a derringer pistol to shoot anyone who betrayed him.

The clandestine organization also had operatives in place to burn New York to the ground. Initially scheduled to occur before the election, the plan to burn the city was delayed until November 25, the day after Thanksgiving; President Lincoln in 1863 had officially proclaimed the fourth Thursday of November a national day of thanks. Following the plot hatched in Montreal, eight operatives set fire to nineteen hotels throughout the city in addition to P. T. Barnum's Museum. They rented rooms and then doused the mattresses with scores of bottles of "Greek fire," a supposedly highly flammable liquid mixed by a sympathetic chemist. However, the Greek fire proved more difficult to ignite than they expected; simple matches would have been more effective. Moreover, many operatives failed to leave the windows of their hotel rooms open to feed oxygen to the flames.

Local authorities quickly recognized the fires as a Confederate plot and miraculously deployed fire departments and local citizens to douse the flames. Barnum's museum, with its hay for the animals, proved their biggest challenge. As New Yorkers doused the flames, the perpetrators escaped back to their Confederate headquarters in St. Lawrence Hall. Only one arsonist was later captured in February 1865.

The operation to capture the president moved to the next phase: assembling an action team of operatives including John Surratt and John Wilkes Booth, as well as one of Mosby's best Rangers.

38. BLAZER STRIKES AGAIN: BATTLE IN THE VINEYARD

Captain Richard Montjoy's Company D experienced the Shenandoah Valley's bone-chilling temperatures of mid-November as they cautiously rode northwest toward Winchester from Paris, Virginia, through Ashby's Gap. The Rangers hit the backcountry trails most of the day. After concealing themselves in a wooded area one evening, the company set back on the Valley Pike at sunrise the following day, looking for trouble.

Montjoy received word that a group of Federal cavalry was "carelessly" trotting down the pike. The five-foot-eight former machinist ordered Company D to conceal themselves behind a barn and wait. Seconds ticked by. Montjoy had fearlessly led his men in battle many times—earning a rare accolade from Mosby: "one of the bravest of the brave."[1]

When the Union cavalry reached the barn, a squad of Montjoy's men revealed themselves and ordered the Federals to surrender.[2] Sergeant Martin Schaffer resolutely refused to be taken alive. The Federal enlisted man commanded the seventeen-man detachment, coincidentally from the 17th Pennsylvania Cavalry. That morning he had orders to take dispatches to a nearby rail station. Only two weeks earlier, Schaffer had boldly escaped captivity by two Confederate guards. After his traumatic experience, Schaffer openly talked to his men about never being captured again. The Union sergeant vowed to go down fighting.

Ranger steeds thrust into the flank and rear of the Union cavalcade and disrupted the bluecoats. Montjoy's men rapidly emptied the barrels of their Colts as an occasional double-barreled sawed-off shotgun thundered: the deadly weapon could tear apart flesh and bone and blow men off their horses at close range. Violent and swift, the Rangers' charge once again proved decisive. Most of the Union troops quickly put spurs to their horses in an attempt to flee, but several men "bit the dust in the space of about one mile,"[3] wrote Ranger J. Marshall Crawford. Montjoy's men made short work of the seventeen-man party: seven were killed or wounded, including Sergeant Schaffer, who died of his wounds, and nine men were taken prisoner. One man, Martin Morgan Tyler, the detachment's rear guard, escaped to tell the tale, and according to a report, "R.W. Moll, wounded, was shot after he had surrendered."[4]

Following the ambush, Montjoy split his command. Rangers who boarded in Loudoun County made their way toward Castleman's Ferry[5] to return home. At the same time, the prisoners and the remainder of Company D headed toward Berry's Ferry to cross the Shenandoah River and travel back to their lairs in Fauquier County. With a frigid wind nipping their faces, the Confederates and their prisoners rode down a long country lane in front of a mansion known as Clay Hill.[6] The Confederates suddenly ran into over a dozen riders,[7] cloaked in butternut.

Startled by the unexpected encounter with Blazer's Jessie Scouts who moved ahead of the main column, the Confederates must have halted briefly, just enough time for Blazer's men to get the bulge as they swarmed and charged Montjoy using the same tactics the Louisianan had employed hours earlier.

Montjoy tried to rally his fleeing men, but the Rangers skedaddled and fled toward the Shenandoah River and west as fast as their horses could carry them. Lieutenant Edward Bredell of St. Louis, who had joined Mosby and assumed the rank of private, lay dead in front of Clay Hill mansion. William Armstrong Braxton received a mortal wound[8] but attempted to escape on his mount.

Under hot pursuit from Blazer's men, with lead flying and the crack of pistol fire, the Rangers sped off to the southwest. At the Vineyard, home of the widow of Philip Pendleton Cooke, a poet, the two forces clashed again. The Vineyard was located a couple of miles from Millwood, Virginia, and took its name from a network of wild grapevines. The brick house was situated atop a commanding hill and overlooked a beautiful landscape.[9] The Rangers and Scouts battled in the pastures around the estate.

Once again, Captain Montjoy and Lieutenant Charles E. Grogan, who "had little sense of fear and danger,"[10] attempted to rally their men.

Grogan boasted an epic record. He first battled at Bull Run and later sustained wounds at Chancellorsville and at Gettysburg, where the Union captured him. They sent Grogan to Fort McHenry and later Johnson's Island, located in Lake Erie near Sandusky, Ohio. An escape artist, Grogan absconded from the island by hiding in a barge filled with hay.[11] From Ohio, Grogan somehow made his way to Mosby, likely walking and riding hundreds of miles from Ohio to Virginia.

Despite Grogan and Montjoy's efforts, the Rangers broke and galloped headlong into the Shenandoah River with the Scouts on their tails. They plunged into the icy water and set out toward Burwell's Island,[12] a sandy area of land in the middle of the river. A young, Southern boy identified only as L.M.L. decades later described the action that followed: "A merry group of youngsters of which I was a member, were grazing and secreting from the Yankee army a very valuable lot of horses on Burwell's Island [only hundreds of yards from the Vineyard] when suddenly Mosby's battalion dashed into us, being hotly pursued by Captain Blazer."[13]

As Blazer's Scouts raced toward the Rangers onto the island and over to the eastern bank of the river, a running gun battle raged with "bullets flying as thick as gnats in August." Fearing for his life, L.M.L. made "a dive for east side of the Shenandoah, eventually after being closely pursued I became frightened and jumped my steed and ran to the bushes; my horse wheeled and ran back to the enemy."[14]

Montjoy escaped, only to be killed weeks later in another gun battle in Loudoun County. Blazer's Scouts rounded up several prisoners during the chase and brought the mortally wounded Ranger William Armstrong Braxton into the Vineyard. The Scouts had battled with partisans for over a year but retained their spirit of humanity. "As [Braxton] lay on a sofa, Lieutenant Coles, [Blazer's second], of Blazer's command entered the house, and approaching the dying soldier, expressed commiseration for his condition, and offered such religious consolation as [he] could command."[15]

When the dust settled on Burwell's Island, "a deathlike sentence prevailed."[16]

During the eerie silence, L.M.L.'s comrades brought forth "the lifeless body of a stately-looking gentleman, a stranger [Ranger Edward Bredell]. He was laid out at my uncle's house; the night I shall never forget; the sad expression on his face, and how I felt for his loved ones at home. He was buried the next day on the bank of the river."[17]

39. SHOOTOUT AT KABLETOWN

"You let the Yankees whip you? I'll get hoop skirts for you! I'll send you into the first Yankee regiment we come across!" Mosby had acidly remarked after the defeat Blazer had inflicted recently on Montjoy at the Vineyard. "The cutting words used by Mosby . . . still rang in their ears,"[1] recalled James Williamson. The time was now ripe for vengeance.

"Wipe Blazer out! Go through him!"[2] snapped Mosby, as he issued orders to Dolly Richards from his lair at Brookside, a home in Delaplane, located in northern Fauquier Country. On November 16, between 200 and 300 men of Richards' force, which included Companies A, B, and D, rode toward the West Virginia border in search of Blazer.

"When both sides were out for scalps and each was looking for the other, the end could not be far off,"[3] Ranger John Munson later observed. The next day, fighting through a "terrible rain," Richards' Rangers crossed the mountains and the Shenandoah River. Riding through the day, they bivouacked without shelter or fires at "Castleman's big woods"[4] located northeast of Berryville. Despite the wind and bone-chilling rain, the riders continued the hunt for their quarry.

Only a few miles away from Mosby's men, Richard Blazer and his Scouts broke camp before dawn, as they always did in order to not give the enemy any advantage in tracking them. According to Ranger John Henry Alexander, Blazer "had pretty accurate information about our numbers," and they knew the Rangers were searching for the Scouts. Both sides wanted the edge and the opportunity to ambush the other, to get "the bulge."[5]

Donning the butternut-dyed uniform of the enemy, Henry Pancake probed into the predawn darkness, pushing ahead of his fellow Scouts. Sixteen Jessie Scouts, including Pancake, led the vanguard. Exhausted from having ridden for two days and two nights after a foray into the Luray Valley, they started to make their way north toward their familiar base around Kabletown in northeast West Virginia. Their horses crossed the icy Shenandoah at Jackson's Ford. In the cold early-morning fog, two shadowy riders approached Pancake.

Richards had sent Rangers Charles McDonough and John Puryear to scout around Charles Town for Blazer. As the two men rode toward Kabletown, they spotted a column of apparent Confederates. McDonough had a price on his head and was labeled a "bushwhacker and assassin,"[6] accused of killing a Federal captain. Fearing capture by unknown riders, McDonough held back as Puryear, a youth in his teens who "was brave [and] who bore a heart always ready for a soldier's fate, and he bowed to the inevitable with the best grace he could,"[7] rode toward Henry Pancake and other Jessie Scouts. One of them addressed the Ranger, "Hello Johnny." The tone of the greeting "disarmed any suspicion which [Puryear] may have had,"[8] and Pancake and his fellow Scouts pounced and seized the Confederate. Stunned by the capture, McDonough put spurs to his horse and sped off toward Richards.

According to several Rangers' accounts, the Scouts brought Puryear to Lieutenant Coles. Renowned for his fairness and compassion, having just tended to a mortally wounded Ranger after the Vineyard gunfight, Coles did something out of character and allegedly tortured the Ranger. "He was brow-beaten, cuffed and threatened in a fruitless effort to loosen his tongue," recalled one Ranger. Supposedly, Scouts placed a noose around the Ranger's neck and raised him in the air. With his legs dangling and the rope biting into his neck, they lifted and lowered him several times, but Puryear refused to talk. After failing to glean intelligence from the tight-lipped Ranger, the Scouts mounted up and ordered Puryear on "the worst horse." The animal refused to move, and Puryear requested a large stick to compel the horse forward. Remarkably, the Scouts assented, and Puryear "had a club that was about right for the plans that were forming in his mind."[9] With the captured Ranger in tow, the column of Blazer's Scouts rode off hunting for Mosby's Rangers.

After McDonough escaped and rode in a "circuitous route," he found Richards and alerted him. Richards ordered the men to regroup near a house concealed under a cliff near the Shenandoah.[10] The Rangers then went on the move.

Less than half a mile away, Blazer's Scouts stopped to eat a quick breakfast. Henry Pancake stood next to Lieutenant Coles and Captain Blazer as they boiled coffee when a young African American boy suddenly ran into the Scouts' camp. A Union woman had sent the young man, who risked life and limb, to apprise the Scouts that a large force of Confederates had crossed the ford "and were watching us."[11] If captured, the boy faced death since Union collaborators were dealt with harshly, part of the effective intimidation campaign that silenced civilians. But Kabletown, West Virginia, was not in Mosby's Confederacy, and Blazer had gained the trust and loyalty of many Union families who were willing to risk their lives for his Scouts.

Blazer broke camp and ordered Coles and Pancake on a reconnaissance to locate the Rangers' position. Peering through binoculars atop a hill halfway between the two forces, they found Dolly Richards.

As Richards searched for Blazer, he told his men, "Blazer is now camped near Kabletown; as soon as you come in sight of his pickets, draw your pistols and move off at a gallop, but don't fire a shot or raise a yell until you hear the shooting in front. Don't shoot until you get close to them. They've got Puryear and four other prisoners, and you may kill some of them."[12]

Missing each other by minutes, Rangers and Scouts hunted each other in "opposite directions of a circle."[13] Rangers soon stumbled upon Blazer's empty camp and found the burning fires, a pile of corn, and bundles of newspapers. Richards planned to fight on the ground of his choosing. Rangers reported Blazer moving southward along the Charlestown Road, which Myers Town* intersects, and another road running east to the Shenandoah River. One Ranger described the field of battle, "which borders the road to the south and runs parallel with it a considerable distance. Just back of them was an open field, which sloped rather abruptly from the woods into a deep valley that rises toward the south in full view of the road at this time of the year. Along the top of this back hill, on the southern boundary of the field, ran an old rail fence. From the fence to

* During the Civil War, the town was known as Myers Town; it is now Meyerstown. The unfolding action predominantly occurs in Myers Town, even though the skirmish is often called the Battle of Kabletown.

the road, the distance was perhaps three hundred yards." Richards left a few men scattered in the woods in a depression below a hill. Company B formed in a battle line "under the brow of the hill . . . facing the road, so disposed that the enemy would not see them until one or the other should reach the top of the hill."[14] The Rangers waited.

"We proceeded to the hill and got a good view of the rebs and confirmed all of the intelligence given by the colored boy," recalled Pancake. Wasting no time, Pancake and Coles sped off to Blazer, who had formed his command and advanced toward the Rangers, flush with a string of victories and naturally aggressive, if outnumbered. Amid the advance, Pancake and Coles caught up with Blazer and reported "that they were in a good position and it wouldn't do to attack them with our little force amounting to 65 men all told."[15]

"Fall in!" Blazer yelled at his command. "Away we went,"[16] as they galloped toward the Rangers, remembered Pancake.

Richards positioned his companies across a dirt road in a rolling field skirted by woods with Company A in plain sight while Company B lay hidden at the bottom of the hill. The trap was set. Richards' carefully crafted plan unfolded as planned until a drunken Ranger dashed into the woods near the Scouts' position, fired a shot, and galloped back to Lieutenant Hatcher, who angrily yelled at him. Blazer's Scouts crossed the road and started to rip down two big rail fences. The Rangers coiled for their attack. Armed with their Spencer carbines and rifles, the Scouts hoped to kill from a distance. Pancake scanned the field: "The rebs were in plain view . . . it was a desperately daring deed, and we hurried up the job, coming around into line like whip cracker."[17]

"Harry, they are dismounting," yelled Dolly Richards to Hatcher.

"Seeing Blazer's men taking down the fence and dismounting, Captain Richards thought they intended to dismount and fight us at long range, which would give them every advantage, with their guns—they being sheltered by the woods and we being exposed to their fire in the open field,"[18] recalled one Ranger.

Charging into Blazer's line would have been devastating, so Richards implemented a ruse to draw the Scouts into a trap. Hatcher ordered a few men to pull down a fence in their rear and prepare to feint a retreat moving his company off the field.[19] Perhaps Blazer thought Company A was the entire Ranger force—in any event, taking the bait, he fatefully threw caution to the wind and ordered his men to charge.

Blazer's men fired a volley from their Spencers. Releasing blood-curdling Rebel yells, Company B surged forward from behind the hill. "The rebs were right with us, shooting our boys down and hacking our ranks to pieces,"[20] recalled Pancake. Hatcher then reversed course and charged at full speed into Blazer's left flank. "Hand to hand combat ensued."[21] The Scouts "were of the true metal, however, and stood the surprise and the shock like true heroes," recalled Ranger John Henry Alexander. Time stood still for a "minute" that lasted for what seemed like an eternity, as both sides emptied "their revolvers into each other's faces."[22] Wearing Confederate butternut, Blazer's Jessie Scouts knew that if captured, they would be considered spies and face immediate execution. Bodies hit the cold, muddy field.

During the fighting, "Puryear rose in his stirrups, let out a rebel yell and, with a swinging, back-handed movement, dealt his guard a killing blow in the face with his club. Then he slipped from his horse in the thick of the melee, and stripped his fallen enemy of his pistols, remounted on the fellow's horse, and lit into the ranks of Blazer's crowd that surrounded him with an expression of ferocity that is impossible to describe. His black eyes blazed and, with the perspiration standing on his forehead, his jaws set, and his whole face started an errand of vengeance,"[23] recalled Ranger John Munson.

"Lieutenant Coles became the single object of his pursuit, and, his eye falling upon him, he followed him like a Nemesis,"[24] remembered Alexander.

Blazer tried to rally his men and "stood his ground among the last desperate fighters."[25] One Ranger remembered, "They fought desperately, but our men pressed on, broke them, and finally drove them from the field."[26] It was every man for himself as the Rangers hit the Scouts like an angry swarm of bees.

Many of the Scouts fell in the field, but Pancake, Coles, Blazer, and others fled down the road past a blacksmith shop in Myers Town. Pancake's uniform aided his escape, but the other Jessie Scouts rode for their lives. Then Lieutenant Coles broke from the main body of the "flying men to seek his own salvation"[27] with Puryear in hot pursuit.

John Alexander caught up to Coles, who raised both hands and sur-rendered. Alexander leaned over to unbuckle the Union officer's belt that contained his pistols, and as he bent over, he heard horses' hooves behind him—it was Puryear. Rage and excitement marked the teen's countenance. He pointed a cocked pistol at Coles' head.

"Don't shoot this man; he surrendered!"[28]

"The rascal tried to hang me this morning!" retorted Puryear. Alexander asked Coles, who had been bleeding profusely from a chest wound caused by Puryear, if the statement was true. Silence. As Alexander moved, "[Coles] rolled his dying eyes toward me with a look I shall never forget, and I would gladly have tarried to give him such comfort as I could. But this was no time for sympathy, and I hurried back to the road."[29] Days later, Alexander found out Coles had stashed $1,800 in his clothing, and the Ranger wondered if Coles, through his stare, had attempted to give it to him for trying to save his life.

Henry Pancake galloped past Puryear as "balls whizzed all around"; looking back, he saw the teen shoot the Union officer. "Only Captain Blazer and myself were left on the road, and there were 30 to 40 of Mosby's men after us,"[30] recalled Pancake. Within the throng, four men broke out to pursue Blazer and Pancake, "the best soldiers in Mosby's command, Sam Alexander, Syd Ferguson, Cab Maddux, and Terrible [Lewis] Powell."[31] Ferguson rode Fashion, "one of the fastest and fleetest and hardiest animals in the battalion."[32]

Blazer and Pancake sped north toward the tiny hamlet of Rippon, not far from the Berryville Pike, where Pancake gained on the Ohioan and finally caught up to him.

"Where's the boys?" Blazer asked.

"All I know is just one behind, and I guess they've got him by this time," replied Pancake. Blazer, willing to make one final sacrifice for his men, looked at Pancake and said, "I'm going to surrender."[33]

"I am going to get out of this," stammered Pancake, knowing if captured he would be executed. From about thirty yards, the Rangers were "peppering away" at the group with their revolvers when Ferguson caught up with Blazer. According to the Rangers, who may have embellished the incident, Ferguson, whose pistols had been emptied, allegedly called on the Yankee officer to surrender. Blazer did not, and Ferguson knocked him off his horse with the butt of his pistol. Blazer appeared dead on the ground, but when Ferguson examined him, "he got up smiling" and "admitted he was stunned," then "took his medicine cheerfully" and asked that his men be treated fairly.[34] Blazer complimented Richards "highly for his bravery and skill in the management of his men, saying he never saw men fight better, and that he had been whipped fairly, a compliment that affected Harry Hatcher so sensibly, that he would not refrain from embracing the old soldier, although he was a foe,"[35] recalled Ranger J. Marshall Crawford. Blazer's surrender bought Pancake precious seconds to put more yards between him and his pursuers. The Jessie Scout made the ride of his life for two more miles; more men dropped out of the manhunt. "The chase was different from that after Captain Blazer. He could surrender and live; I couldn't. I had to beat in that horse race or die, and as there were 40 horses on the track after me." The Rangers fired "a volley that whizzed all around me," a last gasp as their horses wore out. Pancake looked back. Later he recalled, "I never felt so happy in my life."[36]

Relieved, Pancake rode leisurely for a mile and saw a man leading a horse down the road. The Scout recognized one of his own, wounded from the gunfight. The two survivors together, exhausted but alive, limped into Union pickets at Winchester. Seeing a soldier in Confederate uniform, naturally, the pickets did not believe Pancake's story, and they detained him. Of the sixteen Jessie Scouts who rode in Blazer's Scouts, Pancake was one of the few survivors—the rest died in the fields and roads around Kabletown or Myers Town or were captured. The Federals determined Pancake's account to be true and released him around 11:00 that evening.

The following day, the lone Jessie Scout rode back to Myers Town with a cavalry company. Twenty-two bodies* were hastily buried in shallow graves† near the blacksmith's shop.[37]

The hunter had become the hunted. Blazer's Scouts had been created to hunt and kill the Rangers, but now most of them lay dead or captured by their prey.

---

* John Opie, a Confederate cavalryman, reported the same number.

† I have visited the graves of many of the men in this book. The *Roll of Honor*, 15:234–236, details the men buried in Winchester Military Cemetery. Sixteen men from Blazer's command who died on November 18, 1864, are buried in lot 20. Number 2001 is listed as "colored." It is highly likely that Mosby's men hanged the boy, and he was buried in a place of honor with the rest of the soldiers in Blazer's command. The body could also have been Blazer's African American aide. I have an original expense report signed by Blazer listing the aide. Lieutenant Thomas Coles was removed to Woodland Cemetery near Ironton, Ohio. Several other families brought their sons' remains home.

40. The Road South and Rising from the Ashes

Rangers rounded up the captured and wounded Scouts and moved the most severely injured to a church near Kabletown. Local families took in others. Richard Blazer received special treatment. After his capture, Dolly Richards' men took $152 from Blazer. The Union Scout also carried Confederate script that "was of no use to [the Rangers]," and they allowed him to keep it along with $12 they "afterward generously returned to him."[1] The money would save his life.

After the shakedown, the Rangers detailed a special guard to the Federal commander, which included Ranger Lewis Powell, to travel to Richmond, the location of the infamous Libby Prison and the headquarters of the Confederate Secret Service. Richard Blazer remembered Lewis Powell escorted him on his long journey to prison in Richmond. As a third party related, "Captain Dick Blazer of the Blazer Scouts was captured . . . taken to Richmond by one Payne* [Powell], belonging to Mosby's gang. Captain Blazer is well-acquainted with the man."[2] One of the very men Blazer's Scouts was formed to capture or kill now escorted the chief of Blazer's Scouts to Richmond. Here, Powell would receive orders for his next mission.

Blazer's men were not afforded the comfort of horses and arduously walked to Richmond via another route.[3] It was the beginning of another long journey.

Along the way south to Richmond, the guards and Blazer stopped at the home of a lawyer and "violent secessionist" for dinner. The slaveholder went on a racist, curse-filled rant directed at Blazer and African Americans.

* Blazer referred to Powell by the alias he assumed: Payne.

Blazer inquired what he had ever done to him and why he was so "bitter against the race." The lawyer responded, "Oh! [I] lost one hundred and twenty n—ers." "How many do you have left?" asked Blazer. "About twenty," responded the secessionist. Blazer acidly retorted, "Well, you have twenty more to lose."[4] The men got back on the trail to Richmond after their tension-filled dinner.

Hundreds of men captured by Mosby made the long journey to Richmond down winding mountain trails. Weeks earlier, the Rangers had snared six-foot-tall, gray-eyed Private Joseph A. Brown of Blazer's Scouts, who provided a detailed version of the sojourn, the same route to Richmond that Powell would travel with Richard Blazer as his prisoner.

"I bridled and saddled my horse called 'Mosby' having captured him at Meyer's Ford. . . . I had ridden about four miles, or a little beyond Warrenton when I saw five soldiers about one-fourth of a mile ahead of me." Passing a man with a cartload of sugar cane, Brown asked him if the five men were Yanks. He responded affirmatively. "Fearing treachery, I pulled my revolvers around to the front and opened the holsters." The five riders, wearing Federal overcoats, approached and called out, "Good Day." "Their response was three cocked revolvers at my head."[5] Outgunned and knowing the result of noncompliance, Brown surrendered.

The Rangers took Brown's revolvers, Spencer rifle, and cartridge box. After riding into the woods east of the pike and unloading the weapon, the Confederates handed Brown his Spencer: "This is no good without ammunition." Brown's captors pressed him, asking if he was a Scout, and informed him that he was headed toward Confederate cavalry headquarters for the area under the command of Major General Thomas Lafayette "Tex" Rosser. Armed to the teeth, more than a common soldier, and knowing the penalty of being caught as Scout or spy, Brown told them he was a "safeguard at Winchester."[6] Amid Brown's interrogation by Rosser's staff, Mosby's men brought in several new prisoners: Captain Nicholas Badger and his orderly, as well as a free African American civilian named George Washington, or "Wash," who acted as a paid servant for Badger. The haul also included an aging mail carrier of General Powell's division; Thomas Green and Curt McIntosh of Company I, 23rd Ohio; Bill Tatman and Tom Wilson of the 2nd West Virginia Cavalry; and George Johnson.

Brown was no longer the only Scout. The Rangers also brought in George McCauley, formerly from the 9th West Virginia.[7]

As the throng of prisoners filed in, Mosby made a grand appearance. Standing apart from his men and the Federals, Mosby grasped the bridle rein of his "splendid gray horse." Badger vividly described Mosby: "His forearm resting on the saddle's pommel, his left arm akimbo, and his foot thrown across the ankle and resting on its toe. He is a slight, medium-sized man, sharp of feature, quick of sight, lithe of limb, with a bronzed face, the color and tension of whipcord; his hair a yellow-brown, with full but light beard, and mustache of the same. A straight Grecian nose, firm-set expressive mouth, large ears, deep-gray eyes, high forehead, large well-shaped head, and his whole expression denoting hard services, energy."[8]

Mosby wore "top-boots and a civilian's overcoat—black, lined with red—and beneath it the complete gray uniform of a Confederate lieutenant-colonel, with its two stars on the sides of the standing collar, and the whole surmounted by the inevitable slouched hat of the whole Southern race." Badger also noted how Mosby's men often gained the element of surprise: "His men were about half in blue and half in butternut."[9]

As Mosby passed Badger, "he scarcely noticed [him]" but noticed the Federal officer's prized horse, Belle. After Badger dismounted, Mosby said to his manservant, "Take that horse."[10]

Enslaved body servant, friend, and Ranger Aaron Burton went to war with John Mosby. A slave of Mosby's father, Burton raised Mosby and was by Mosby's side through the entire war. As Burton noted, "I loved him and was with him in all his battles. . . . He was a good man and was a great fighter." Mosby had the "greatest confidence in his body servant, and he was frequently left in charge of all the booty that was captured from the Union soldiers." One individual described Burton as "the perfection of politeness . . . with a sweet musical voice"[11] and fond of singing to himself.

Badger, heartbroken from the loss of his beloved Belle, a horse he had ridden for three years "through many a bloody and hair's breadth escape, who loved me with almost human love," recollected, "I could not refrain from throwing my arms around Belle's neck and tenderly caressing her for the last time before she was led away."[12]

As Burton led the horse away, an unfortunate Ranger lieutenant protested, wanting to keep the animal for himself, mumbling something about the rules of dividing the booty. He "was promptly silenced" and put in his place, ordered to choose from among the other captured horses. Meanwhile, Mosby, perhaps with a cup of coffee in hand, busied himself reading the paperwork of the captured men. The Gray Ghost had a nose for fine coffee and would always find the best, according to John Munson. Real coffee was scarce after the second year of the war, and most people drank "decoctions of roasted peanuts, or beans, or sweet potatoes, or almost anything that would look black, and taste burnt. Mosby would not drink a drop of any such sham coffee, and he could distinguish the slightest adulterated article from the real bean."[13]

He approached Badger with "a peculiar gleam of satisfaction on his face and said, 'Oh! Captain Badger, inspector-general of the cavalry! Good-morning, Captain. Glad to see you, sir. Indeed, there is but one man I would prefer to see this morning to yourself, and that is your commander [Brigadier General Armstrong Custer].'"

Mosby acidly added, "Were you present, sir, the other day, at the hanging of eight of my men as guerrillas at Front Royal?"[14]

It was the one question Badger dreaded. "[It] pierced me like a sword," recalled the Federal officer, as he had been present during the hanging. Believing it might make matters worse if he timidly claimed he tried to "save the lives of the wretched men," Badger boldly and firmly proclaimed, "I was present, sir, and, like you, have only to regret that it was not the commander instead of his unfortunate men."[15]

Expecting a denial, the answer Badger relayed "seemed to please Mosby. . . . With a grim smile," the guerrilla leader then directed another officer to search Badger and the prisoners. The Rangers purloined the Federals' belongings. "A board of officers was assembled to appraise their value . . . the rules of the gang requiring that all captures shall be thus disposed of, or sold, and their value distributed, or sold, and their value distributed proportionally among the captors."[16] Boots, a gold watch, $300 in greenback, rings, a Bible, and a Masonic pin all went to the board for accounting.

The Rangers considered Wash contraband and "raffled" him for $2,000, a free man enslaved and trafficked like livestock. He was "very indignant that he should be thought worth only two thousand dollars Confederate." Wash then extolled the men with his accomplishments. He could make the best milk punch of any man in the Confederacy. "This hit at the poverty of their resources," remembered Badger. Perhaps in an act of kindness or a show of plenty, Aaron Burton offered Wash a drink. Despite being parched, Wash "stubbornly refused," his pride intact. Badger privately asked Wash why he turned down the drink; "You know, too much freer breeds despise!"[17]

Mosby then returned Badger's Bible, letters, and Masonic pin, telling him, "You may as well keep this; it may be of use to you somewhere. Some of my men pay some attention to that sort of thing. Your people greatly err in thinking us merely guerrillas. Every man of mine is a duly enlisted soldier and detailed to my command from various Confederate regiments. They are picked men, selected from the whole army for their intelligence and courage. We plunder the enemy, as the rules clearly allow. To the victors belong the spoils, has been the maxim of war in all the ages."[18]

After the Confederates finished searching the other prisoners, a Ranger the Scouts nicknamed Jim Crow searched Private Joseph A. Brown for valuables, but the Scout concealed his money in a hidden slit in his waistband. As Crow frisked him, Brown handed over his personal letters. "A dead giveaway," the letters were each addressed, "In care of Captain Blazer, commanding scouts." Unflinching, Brown "coolly remarked, those are from my girl." Remarkably, Crow returned them. The Scout realized Crow could not read.

After the shakedown, the men set out in an easterly direction. Rangers led and flanked the group. As Brown rode, he chewed on the letters' envelopes to destroy the evidence. After crossing the Shenandoah, the band traveled through Ashby's Gap and spent the night in an abandoned schoolhouse, the "sole relic left of a former civilization."[19] Badger surmised that Mosby used the dilapidated and unpainted structure as a way station. To guard the prisoners, Mosby's men ringed the schoolhouse's interior. Brown built a small fire to warm the room using a Bible he found and, conveniently, the incriminating letters as kindling. Mosby's men, meanwhile, opened a mailbag captured from the courier and entertained themselves reading love letters. The men slept in the schoolhouse until dawn, when they mounted up and continued their journey to Richmond.

As the band ambled along, Brown whispered to fellow Scout George McCauley, also known as Mack, that he had cartridges that the Confederates had failed to find for their unloaded Spencer rifles in saddlebags on their horses. They conspired to load their guns covertly and make their escape when they entered the Luray Valley. Riding up a steep, winding trail in the

Blue Ridge Mountains, the men beheld a spectacular autumn vista: brilliant yellow-, orange-, and red-infused forest, rivers, and mountains. Mosby turned to Badger and said, "This is a favorite promenade of mine. I love to see your people sending out their almost daily raids after me. Here comes one of them now, almost towards us. If you please, we will step behind this point and see them pass. It may be the last sight you will have of your old friends for some time."[20]

"The coolness of his speech enraged me," thought Badger, yet the Union officer also "admired" Mosby's "quiet and unostentatious audacity."[21] Badger claimed briefly to have considered rushing the guerrilla leader but checked his anger as the Yankee patrol passed within half a mile of them at the bottom of the mountain.

"Mosby stood with folded arms on a rock above them, the very picture of stoical pride and defiance, or, as Mack whispered: 'Like patience on a monument smiling at grief.'"[22]

As the men moved into the Luray Valley, Mosby told them they were inside Confederate lines and "the first effort of escape would be death,"[23] then he bid the party farewell. Several heavily armed men guarded the prisoners' caravan as they headed south to Richmond. Brown rode up toward Badger and whispered to him of his plans and asked him to take command once they attacked the guards.

Brown rode next to McCauley and handed him several precious brass Spencer cartridges as rain fell. After the exchange, the private reached back to grab his rifle, his bulky rain poncho obscuring his movement; next, he attempted to load the weapon but found "one cartridge in the cylinder [magazine] that failed to drop out." Each Spencer had a seven-round tube magazine with a spring that led the cartridges into the rifle's chamber. "Expecting every minute to be detected," Brown found a small piece of a lead pencil that he used to extract the jammed round. The spring now operated properly. With his heart pounding in his breast, "and not in the mouth as a few minutes before,"[24] the Scout rode up to McCauley and whispered that he would touch his left foot as a signal to start shooting.

With the foothills of a mountain 200 yards in front of the group and woods to their left, the caravan approached ever closer to their first stop: Confederate general Rosser's camp, where Brown suspected he would be unmasked as a Scout. A ranger rode in front of Brown. Jim Crow rode

in front of McCauley and another Ranger. A final Ranger held the column's rear. Brown asked how far Rosser's camp was. One of the Rangers responded that it was about two and a half miles. He then turned to
Crow and casually commented, "I would just as soon have a good navy
revolver as a hundred-dollar greenback." Just then, Brown touched McCauley's foot, and both men fired their Spencers. Brown killed one Confederate,
and McCauley's shot struck Crow, dropping him from his horse. The
Ranger fell and landed in a sitting position, catatonically holding the bridle
of his horse. Badger "vamoosed" after the first shot. Brown spun around
and jumped off his horse to shoot another one of the Ranger guards, who
had been grabbed by one of the prisoners and was being held "securely,"
as Brown approached within fifteen feet. The Ranger blasted him with
his revolver. The bullet grazed the Scout's shoulder. Brown raised his gun
"and fired, the ball taking him above the left eye, killing him instantly, the
blood and brain-matter spattering [prisoner] Green in the face."[25] Green
held on to the corpse as both men dropped to the ground together. The
dead Ranger's revolver was at half-cock, a split second away from firing
a second potentially deadly shot at Brown. The single surviving Ranger
guard escaped, galloping half a mile away at full speed, "firing his pistols
to alarm the country."[26]

Brown scrambled over to Jim Crow, whose rain overcoat had covered
his head after he fell off the horse. "I shot him through the cape. I took
four revolvers from him, and jumping on his horse, commenced to fasten
the revolvers around me, but one of them fell out of the scabbard when I
jumped down to get it, the horse becoming frightened ran away."[27]

The prisoners scattered behind Confederate lines and in a countryside
soon to be crawling with angry Southerners hunting for them. Brown ran
on foot toward the mountain and caught up with Green and Tatman. They
fled about three miles until, remarkably, they encountered Wash. When
two Rebels fired on the band, Brown and the other men separated from
Wash as they moved from one wood to another.

Brown's group hid in bushes till about 8 or 9 p.m., and "all the while we
could hear their horses walking on the stony road, patrolling and watching
for us." With revolvers in hand, the men cautiously made their way through
the countryside. Listening carefully, Brown and the group approached a
road and crawled through a hole in a fence. After running all night, they

briefly rested to catch their breath. In the morning, they finally heard the water of the Shenandoah River, accompanied by the terrifying barking of bloodhounds.

As Brown and the men knew it would be difficult to outrun the hounds, they "backed up against a large oak tree side by side," with the intent "to sell our lives as dearly as possible."[28] As they saw the dogs pass them in the distance, Brown and the others crossed their trail and took to the river to throw off the dogs. The Scout led the band down the river for about half a mile until they came to a small log cabin. By now, the men had not eaten for two days.

"With one revolver in my bosom," Brown approached the house and told a woman he was a Confederate soldier who escaped Federal troops from Front Royal. He asked how far it was to Front Royal, asked if she had anything to eat, and offered to pay her.

"You are no Rebel," she insisted, then turned to a ten-year-old boy and told him to run and inform the authorities. Brown pulled out his revolver and threatened to kill the child if he moved. The Scout then demanded food, and she went into the house and returned with bacon fat and cornbread. "Fearing it might be poisoned, I made her eat some of both to satisfy myself." Brown snatched the food and made his way back to Green and Tatman, telling the woman that he "belonged to General Rosser's command on the way out of the cabin, and if she thought I was a Yankee and wanted me recaptured, she could tell."[29]

They wolfed down the food and continued moving toward Front Royal, about thirteen miles away. Avoiding patrols, the men stumbled upon two boys working a sugar cane patch. "We played Rebels and asked if any Yankees were around?" "None nearer than Front Royal but seven of your boys went along the road a few minutes ago."[30]

The men followed the river, looking for a ford, when they came across a cabbage patch. "We thought we struck oil," recalled Brown. Each man devoured a head the size of a "wooden pail."[31] Not long after the cabbage patch, the men's luck continued, and they found a ford. Wading through the cold water of the river up to their arms, they made it to the other side and kept to the woods, avoiding all roads. Brilliant orange and crimson hues from the trees, combined with an abundance of black haws and persimmons, assaulted the men's eyes as they advanced.

As darkness fell, the men stumbled across Union pickets, finally safe. Badger's party was not.

Badger, McCauley, and Wash would spend seven more days behind Confederate lines. One man not joining them, the old mail carrier, "was never seen again" and likely was recaptured by the Rebels. After separating from Brown, somehow Wash miraculously linked back up with Badger's party. Badger remembers going through one of the Ranger's saddlebag and finding his gold watch and $1,100—"doubles of their robberies of our men." The cash evoked a snarky response: "Not quite nuff," said Wash, "showing his ivories from ear to ear" as he demanded full value of the enslaved person of $2,000.[32]

An expert woodsman, the Scout led the group in the direction the enemy would least expect—South—directly into their lines. After first heading to the mountain, where they linked up with Wash, the group rode for hours "directly into the enemy's country as fast as we could ride, and before complete darkness intervened, we made thirty miles from the place of our escape." Pushing the horses as far as they could endure up the summit of the Blue Ridge, the men would "see the Rebel campfires . . . and view their entire lines"[33] by morning.

Led by McCauley, the men avoided Confederates sent to recapture them. Pangs of hunger and thirst gnawed at the Federals as they maneuvered away from Confederate pickets. The men had not eaten for three days, and desperation set in. "We even ate a poor little dog which had followed our fortunes to his untimely end." Barbarically, even cannibalism was considered. Badger considered sacrificing poor Wash: "[We] were thinking seriously of eating negro Wash, when he, to save himself from so unsavory a fate, ventured down the darkness to a cornfield and brought us three ears of corn apiece which we ate voraciously."[34]

Starving and on a mountain near Rebel lines, the men decided to head farther south and struck the Shenandoah twenty miles behind Early's army. Using the cover of night to cloak their movements, they built a raft "and floated by night forty miles down that memorable stream through his crafty pickets." Using all their knowledge and skills from nearly a year of service as Scouts, they used their Union uniforms "and after that passed for Rebel scouts earnestly 'looking for Yanks' until we found them."[35]

Against all odds, McCauley led Badger and Wash home. Union forces, fearing Brown and his party were Confederate spies, initially detained them after their escape. The wily Scout was able to avoid his Union captors and first reported to his old officer Colonel Rutherford B. Hayes, who verified Brown's identity. He reported directly to Sheridan.

Badger also made a report and told his story to the press, to whom he embellished and exaggerated his role in the escape. McCauley returned to the Scouts and the other men to their respective units. Despite so many close brushes with death, Wash survived and remained a free man.

41. HENRY HARRISON YOUNG: A MAN BORN FOR WAR

Union major Henry Harrison Young was born for war. "It was very rare to find a man who found in the most deadly peril his greatest pleasure, and who sought out danger not only in the line of duty, but because he reveled in it." Young thrived in battle and lived for it. His commanding officer, Colonel Oliver Edwards, later wrote, "We had many officers who in civil life had shown nothing above average ability, that in the hour of trial, amidst the carnage of battle, proved themselves possessed of heroic quality, yet these gallant men were not fearless; they loved life, and they knew the danger they were going to meet, and could be relied upon to charge up to certain death without faltering."[1]

Young, however, was truly fearless, a five-foot-five, wiry Rhode Islander who relished the thrill of combat. Mustering into Company B of the 2nd Rhode Island Volunteer Infantry as a second lieutenant in 1861, Young fought through many battles, his first being at Bull Run in July 1861. Writing to his mother, Young described how combat at Manassas changed him: "You say you think it [the suffering] would discourage anyone from going to war. The fact is, no one knows what fighting is till they have seen it; and they that have, after it is over and they think about it, there is a longing for it again that no one knows who has not experienced it."[2]

Young thrived in the chaos of battle and sought out the rush of adrenaline that combat generated. His brigade commander remembered, "He was always ready to dash through the hottest place, to cheer on a wavering regiment or to rally a disorganized one." During the Battle of Fredericksburg in mid-December 1862 and the slaughter of frontal assaults on Confederate positions at Marye's Heights, Young would leave no man behind. "He discovered a wounded soldier of the 2nd Rhode Island in such a position that he was exposed to the fire of both sides. Leaping from his horse amid a shower of bullets, he was himself wounded in the arm, but dragged the poor fellow to the shelter of a tree; it was but the work of a moment, yet amid the noise and confusion of battle seemed wonderfully cool and deliberate."[3] After completing a dangerous mission in which Young obtained intelligence that even Sheridan's own elite Jessie Scouts had failed to produce, Young captured the general's attention: "I have been looking for that man for two years, and I want him."[4]

Young's current boss, Edwards, the provost marshal of the area, where the impressive Rhode Islander was his inspector general, adamantly protested the transfer: "I would rather you would take my right arm than to take him from me."[5]

"I will not take an officer of your staff from you without your consent," Sheridan replied, "but I want him and will make him Major and personal Aide-de-Camp on my staff. I will let him pick one hundred men from my command, arm them and command them as he likes, and report to me."[6]

Believing the change to be in the best interest of the Union, Edwards reluctantly relented. But surprisingly, Young did not immediately jump at Sheridan's prestigious offer. "It required almost coldness as well as entreaty to send him from me,"[7] Edwards recalled.

Sheridan wanted to expand his Jessie Scouts and put them under leadership that was not a desk-bound supervisor but a hands-on, fighting officer. Young fit the bill perfectly. As an inspector general, Young loved to be in the thick of things. To penetrate enemy lines, he would don a Confederate uniform. Much of his tradecraft came from riding with Blazer's Scouts. "Young at every opportunity rode out at the side of Captain Blazer and learned much of the methods of such irregular warfare, much that must afterward have proved of incalculable value."[8]

Young's mount matched his rider. The expert horseman preferred a "little gray horse, a special favorite, on which he placed a great reliance, for by its matchless speed and noble work it had several times extricated him from positions of extreme peril."[9] A contemporary who interviewed Young's men and relatives wrote of the dashing officer that he was "imperturbably cool, patient, shrewd, and with a quiet way about him, yet frank and ingenious—it seemed that there was nothing he could not accomplish."[10]

One incident revealed his ingenuity and humor. Once while scouting, he came upon a Confederate recruiting station and allowed himself to be recruited. "'Come here! You're a likely-lookin' young feller—how about enlistin'?' Young listened to the sergeant's pleading—'didn't know but what he would someday—well, mebbe he would then.' More argument; suddenly the sergeant had him—enlisted." Young showed up on the appointed day, but instead of joining the Confederate Army, he captured the sergeant, all his "hard-earned recruits, and the entire contents of the office."[11]

In pursuit of one notoriously dangerous bushwhacker who "boasted that he never was so happy as when he let out the life-blood of a Union prisoner,"[12] Young requested three Confederate uniforms and two soldiers. They tracked and found the man, who wounded one pursuer and shot the horse out from under the other, leaving the diminutive, wiry Young to battle the man in hand-to-hand combat alone. Somehow, the Rhode Islander single-handedly managed to bind and bring the murderous thug back to headquarters.

Young worked hand-in-glove with his right-hand man, Sergeant J. E. McCabe. The twenty-three-year-old Pennsylvania native had already weathered a slew of battles with Company A, 17th Pennsylvania Volunteer Cavalry Regiment, including Gettysburg, Brandy Station, and Cold Harbor, and had been on the doomed Kilpatrick-Dahlgren Raid in Richmond. McCabe caught Colonel Oliver Edwards' attention after the cavalryman survived a mission where he shot his way out of an ambush with Mosby's Rangers. Outnumbered three to one, McCabe "was attacked by about thirty men of Mosby's guerrillas. I fought my way through without losing a man and got back to Winchester with my return dispatches."[13] Edwards placed Young and McCabe on a joint mission that forged their friendship and trust in each other. After leading several dozen cavalrymen behind enemy lines, engaging in several successful skirmishes with the enemy, and capturing multiple prisoners, the indomitable Young paid McCabe the ultimate compliment when he told the sergeant as they approached Winchester, "'Sergeant McCabe, you understand better how to handle this affair than I do; I wish you would take charge from now on.' I took charge and we captured several more Rebels that day. By the time we got back to Colonel Edwards' headquarters, we had in all seventeen Rebel prisoners and one of them was [a] notorious guerrilla."[14]

Once Sheridan had found the man to lead the Jessie Scouts, Henry Young, he decided to once again make it a larger organization. Realizing the news would leak to the Confederates, the general called it a battalion of Scouts when it was, in fact, only a company. McCabe reflected, "[Sheridan] suggested that we should organize a full company of a hundred men for scouting purposes. So we picked the men we wanted, mounted them and furnished them with grey uniforms and two revolvers each," often carried in the top of their high boots. The men were sometimes armed with seven-shot Spencer carbines depending on the mission. Merging the existing Jessie Scouts, such as Arch Rowand, James White, Dominick Fannin, Alvin Stearns, James Campbell, and others into the new company, Young adopted the tradecraft developed by the Scouts as well as Richard Blazer. "We frequently went into the Rebel line, learned to talk the Southern language and became familiar with each regiment, brigade, division, and corps of the Rebel army, and after that went among them as full-fledged Rebels." McCabe acted as a true noncommissioned officer. The sergeant conveyed Young's orders to the men. "We had fifty-eight to sixty men all the time, and every day and night some of our men were within the Confederate lines. . . . I had charge of the men, and any orders that were given to the men were given by me."[15]

Young and McCabe picked some extraordinary individuals for the elite unit that would become known as Sheridan's Scouts. One of those men, William H. Woodall, was a Confederate deserter who became a civilian Scout. The twenty-one-year-old "killed his superior officer for making an insulting remark about his (Woodall's) sister, and fled the Confederate lines and came into ours at Winchester," remembered Rowand. "He told his story to General Sheridan, gave valuable information, offered his services as a scout, which was accepted, and although tested and watched, under orders from the General, by the balance of us, he proved true in every instance."[16]

After the disaster at Kabletown, and with Blazer himself captured, McCabe also integrated some of the remaining members of Blazer's Scouts into the unit. As with Blazer's Scouts and Mosby's Rangers, their training was on the job. After his Scouts received weapons and Confederate uniforms, Young decided an exceptionally difficult mission was needed to forge unit cohesion and discipline—if it didn't get them all killed. Young planned to have his tiny band ambush a large unit of Confederate cavalry many times the Scouts' numbers. Young had his men positioned on horses behind trees where the Confederates often passed, creating a kill zone.

They waited and waited for what seemed like an eternity in the frigid November air until the Confederate cavalry rode into sight.

On Young's "shrill signal, [he] whirled his horse about, and fired his [Spencer] carbine in the faces of the Confederate troops. His men followed him; the carbines roared like artillery; bullets raked the column, down whose bloody lanes the Yankees rode at the charge, firing their revolvers on either side without mercy." The charge routed the massive Confederate force and created "pandemonium," while Young lost only one man.[17] Like Mosby, Young employed psychological warfare, and fear of the unseen enemy would wear on the Confederates.

Along with a mastery of psychological warfare, Young was a chameleon. A master of disguise, the Rhode Islander served behind the lines so often that "his disguises had to be changed and varied constantly; now it was one role, now another—private soldier, deserter, countryman, peddler, Confederate officer." Young allegedly went after Mosby himself under cover. One scheme involved infiltrating Federal men who claimed to be deserters into Mosby's camp. "But [the deserters] must have been the wrong men for their opportunity, for nothing seems to have come of it."[18]

As winter approached, Grant's army was stalemated in Petersburg. Grant had attempted to cut off Richmond from the south at the vital supply center and railhead of Petersburg, located some twenty miles south of the Confederate capital, after the bloody battles at Cold Harbor and Lee's stand at North Anna. The attack on Petersburg had begun in the middle of June. Grant hoped to quickly storm the city but was thwarted by the Confederates, and a bitter siege ensued as both sides had battled in trenches and fortifications ever since. In Georgia, Sherman had begun his infamous March to the Sea on November 15, during which he aimed to cripple the South by destroying their industrial base and means of transportation. Sheridan, however, continued to conduct intelligence operations in the Shenandoah Valley even while settling down for the winter, as he realized the value of his Jessie Scouts. "I now realized more than I had done hitherto how efficient my scouts had become since under control of [Major] Young, for not only did they bring me almost everyday intelligence from within Early's lines, but they also operated efficiently against the guerrillas infesting West Virginia."[19]

42. "The Devil Takes Care of His Own"

Captain Richard Blazer could see his breath in the frigid air as he lay side by side on the cold ground in the vast, low-ceilinged room with scores of other Union prisoners of war. Given no coverings except their clothing and only practically inedible bricks of ground cornbread for rations, the men counted the days, hoping they would survive until their release. Many didn't. A contemporary newspaper account reported that 158 of the 1,500 men imprisoned at Danville in 1865 died in January alone.[1]

After his capture on November 18, 1864, Blazer was initially confined in Libby Prison in Richmond, where he confirmed "the old story of the horrors" regarding the three-story brick warehouse–turned–Confederation prisoner-of-war camp on the banks of a canal beside the James River. But Libby Prison was "a palace compared with the prison at Danville," where he was transferred on December 11 and remained confined until February 17. "When he came back to us, he was very much emaciated, having lost a considerable amount of flesh," testified one soldier, in addition to developing rheumatism and kidney disease, which would plague him "until he died."[2] One saving grace for Blazer would be the $12 he smuggled in and used to purchase extra food. The ability of Union prisoners to purchase supplemental food caused the *Gallipolis Journal* to proclaim that "fiendish malignity" and "settled determination to destroy the lives of as many Yankees as possible by starvation"[3] rather than scarcity fueled the Union prisoners' treatment.

Around the same time Blazer languished in Libby Prison, his Confederate nemesis suffered brief capture and one of his closest brushes with death. It seemed the gates of hell opened on Mosby's Confederacy. For much of December, Mosby found Loudoun County in smoking ruins and subject to Sheridan's scorched-earth policy. "I will soon commence on Loudoun County and let them know there is a God in Israel. Mosby has annoyed me considerably, but the people are beginning to see he does not injure me a great deal but causes a loss to them of all they have spent their lives accumulating. . . . But when they have to bear their burden by loss of property and comforts, they will cry for peace,"[4] Sheridan wrote to Halleck on November 26. In what would become known as the Burning Raid, he ordered his cavalry regiments who had battled Mosby for months to burn all mills and barns, destroy all forage and subsistence, and drive off and kill livestock. Homes were to be spared. With the division's massive numbers, Mosby could only attack rear elements of the unit but could not stop the swath of destruction they cut across the county.

Mosby, coming from a wedding near Glen Welby farm on a cold early December night, arrayed in his finest—with heavy black, scarlet-lined cape, ostrich-plumed hat, gold cords, tall boots, and two stars gleaming on his collar indicating his rank—stopped with fellow Ranger Tom Love at a friendly home for a late supper. Believing themselves safe, they left their horses and pistols secured outside. However, amid their dinner, scores of Union troops descended on them and their hosts.

When Union officers entered the dining room of Lakeland,* Mosby quickly covered the stars on his collar with his hands. "I knew that if they discovered my rank, to say nothing of my name, they would guard me more carefully." As he stood by a Union officer, a stray bullet from outside struck the Confederate guerrilla leader in the stomach. He gasped, "I am shot!"[5]

Chaos ensued. "In the confusion to get out of the way, there was a sort of hurdle race, in which the supper table was knocked over, and the tallow lights put out," wrote Mosby in his memoir. "In a few seconds, I was left in the room with no one but Love, Lake [their host], and his daughter." Still bleeding profusely, Mosby walked into the adjoining bedroom and hid his coat with its telltale stars, then he lay on the floor, "determined to play the part of a dying man." When the Union soldiers returned, they questioned a guest at the dinner who knew Mosby well, and whose brother was in his command, about the fallen man's identity. Mosby "listened with fear and trembling for her answer" until he heard her declare she had never seen

---

* The beautiful two-story stone mansion still stands.

him before. "I am sure that in the eternal records, there is nothing registered against that good woman who denied my name and saved my life."[6]

Mosby himself gave the soldiers a false name and false command when they interrogated him and examined his wound. A doctor declared his wound to be mortal, shot through the heart. "He located the heart rather low down, and even in that supreme moment, I felt tempted to laugh at his ignorance of human anatomy. I only gasped a few words and affected to be dying."[7] The soldiers left after stripping him of his fine boots and trousers, thinking a dead man would have no further need of them.

"Although I was a prisoner at the time, I have never complained of [the bullet], for it proved to be a lucky shot for me. It was the means of my escape." After waiting to be sure his enemies had left, Mosby rose from the pool of blood and walked into the other room, greatly astonishing his hosts. "They were as much astonished to see me as if I had risen from the tomb." Even Mosby still thought he might have one foot in the grave: "My own belief was that the wound was mortal; that the bullet was in me." Wrapped in quilts and placed in the back of an oxcart, Mosby was transported to a safe house in the middle of a fierce storm, where doctors removed the bullet before he was further transported to his father's house in Lynchburg to convalesce. In the meantime, Northern and Southern press falsely reported his death, but eventually a Northern paper retracted with the commentary that "the devil takes care of his own."[8]

When Mosby recovered from his wounds and grew strong enough to travel, he rode by rail from Lynchburg to Richmond, where he made an appearance at the Confederate Congress in late December, which gave him an overwhelming reception. Before returning to his Rangers, he visited General Lee in Petersburg, where the two men had dinner. No record of their conversation exists, but later events strongly indicate that the two men discussed a special mission that involved kidnapping Abraham Lincoln. Fittingly, a month later, Confederate Secret Service ciphers changed to the keywords, Come Retribution.

Earlier in December, Lee ordered Mosby, at the suggestion of Confederate secretary of war James A. Seddon, to send four of his seven Ranger companies to an area known as the Northern Neck. This northernmost of three Virginia peninsulas consists of portions of Westmoreland, Richmond,

Northumberland, and Lancaster Counties. The eastern part of the neck faces the Potomac River and Chesapeake Bay, with southern Maryland located directly across the waterways. On the surface, the move appeared bizarre. These four companies, under the command of Lieutenant Colonel William Henry Chapman, were being placed far outside their normal area of operations and safe houses. Ostensibly, the Rangers who had been deployed to the Northern Neck after Sheridan's Burning Raid on Mosby's Confederacy lacked food and forage to counter roving Union marauders. This was most likely a cover story for why they were operating so far away from Mosby's Confederacy. Spurred on by the Dahlgren Raid and the failed mission to capture and kill Jefferson Davis and his cabinet, the Confederate Secret Service planned to kidnap President Lincoln and use him as a bargaining chip in future peace negotiations. After capturing the president, a team of operatives could move Lincoln south through Washington along their secret line of Confederate agents in southern Maryland, across the Potomac to the Northern Neck, and into a secure location. Mosby's men in the Northern Neck would be in an ideal position to screen the operation from pursuing Union cavalry and bring Lincoln to Richmond.

To what extent Mosby knew about the operation remains a mystery; his knowledge could have been compartmentalized. An ideal spy, Mosby never put anything of operational value in writing in the event it could fall into enemy hands. The Gray Ghost kept his men in the dark; as he quipped to John Munson, "Only three men in the Confederate Army knew what I was doing or intended to do; they were Lee and Stuart and myself; so don't feel lonesome about it."[9] With Stuart dead, that left two men who knew Mosby's plans. Coincidentally, or by design, when Mosby visited Richmond, another shadowy figure emerged in the capital: John Surratt.

Combat artist James E. Taylor enjoyed the warmth of a fire and the banter of friendly conversation on one of his final nights in the Shenandoah Valley. Operations there were winding down for the winter. A division of Sheridan's VI Corps had already moved out of the valley to join Grant at Petersburg, and the rest of Sheridan's infantry support would soon do so while the plucky general retained the cavalry. Moving his correspondent with the pace of the war, Frank Leslie recalled Taylor back to Baltimore for reassignment. The otherwise uneventful evening at the tavern where Taylor lodged shifted when "two mysterious visitors equipped for the warpath" sidled up to bathe in the heat generated from the flames of the fireplace. In whispered tones, the tavern keeper revealed to Taylor that the strangers were Jessie Scouts and explained their role in Sheridan's army. Minding their own business, the "reticent men" bided their time till midnight, when they would "steal away to their perilous mission." Besides his times riding with Blazer's men, this was Taylor's first contact with Sheridan's Jessie Scouts, and he reflected on their duty. "They carried their lives in their hands, and as they sat there in the play of the firelight, with lips sealed, for instinctively none questioned them, they riveted my gaze and started my fancy, and they arose in my minds as heroes of the highest magnitude for the spy must of necessity be a noble and courageous character. He must be patriotic, quick-witted, intelligent, and terribly in earnest, or he will never undertake the Secret Service of the Army."[10]

Taylor wondered whether this would "be their last mission in their country's cause; whether a rope or a volley from a file of men."[11]

43. "A Changed Man"

Lewis Powell returned to Mosby's Confederacy after escorting Richard Blazer and the other Scout prisoners to Richmond. "Leaving Richmond, Powell returned to the Piedmont a changed man. He often spoke of his visit to Richmond and his intention. Powell soon began to sell off his horses and dispose of his effects, saying that he would be gone on his Maryland expedition," wrote Lewis Edmonds Payne, describing Powell's demeanor when he returned late in the fall of 1864. Only a teen during the war, the young man lived with Powell, who boarded in the Payne family home near Warrenton.* Payne recalled that when the topic of politics came up, especially Lincoln, Powell would rant about Secretary of State William Seward: "Seward is the man; he furnishes the brains. He's the power behind the throne itself."[1]

Powell stayed out of harm's way. After returning from Richmond, he "never went on any raid, but was continually talking about a visit or raid into Maryland, and he and other soldiers would go off to the stables or woods and have long talks and seem to be particularly anxious that no one should know what they were talking about," recalled Payne.[2] Powell's behavior stemmed from his service and upcoming mission with the Confederate Secret Service, which he met with in Richmond after delivering Blazer.[3] Powell's friends and fellow Rangers, Captain R. S. Walker and Lieutenant W. Ben Palmer, describe the night in January 1865 that Powell embarked on his mission and left Mosby's Confederacy: "[We] found the young man dressed in a badly fitting suit of citizen's clothes and with a black slouch hat pulled down over his eyes. He was in high

---

* Powell would steal Payne's identity and use it as his own for his mission. Payne later became a US attorney.

spirits and talked of plans." The Ranger officers said Powell talked about his mission. "He said that they intended to kidnap Lincoln and bring him South. No mention was made of killing anyone."[4] If junior officers knew Powell's mission, seemingly an open secret, Mosby undoubtedly would have been aware of it.

Clearly, Powell had more extensive plans in Maryland and a rendezvous through the Secret Service with John Wilkes Booth. As one of Mosby's best Rangers, Powell would be the trained soldier on the Secret Service's action team to capture the president. Yet, before leaving Mosby's Confederacy, in one incident, the fearless Powell went out of his way to save Union lives rather than take them.

Around Christmas, several Union soldiers were captured near Warrenton, Virginia, after looting and sacking a local's home. The civilians seethed, killed one man, and wanted to execute the remaining men. Powell jumped on his horse and rode into the violent scene. One local woman witnessed Powell in action: "I saw him in his saddle-stirrups; and he told them that whilst he was a gentleman, and wished to be treated as one, though he could not defend all, if they killed or captured the one, he had in his charge, they would do it at the peril of their lives."[5] The mob dispersed.

A couple of weeks later, Powell would leave Mosby's Rangers for a mission that would change history. The tale most modern authors would recount is that Powell deserted Mosby's Rangers, simply walking away from them to become a civilian, and coincidentally met Booth in Baltimore. The explanation is preposterous. Very few men in Mosby's command left the war and returned to life as civilians. The tiny number who did turned coat and fought for the Union; they did *not* join an operation that would prove to be one of the most perilous of the war.

On January 13, 1865, Powell walked into Union lines in his disheveled civilian clothes, told what had to be a whale of a story to Union soldiers—that he was a refugee fleeing the South—took the Oath of Allegiance to the Union, and proceeded to Baltimore and his Secret Service handlers as Lewis Payne.

1865

44. Young's Scouts
and the Journey

Pelted by rain, sleet, and snow, Major Henry Young, along with seventeen[1] Jessie Scouts and fifty raw cavalry troops from the 5th New York under the command of a sergeant, rode all night. Exhausted, Arch Rowand and the Scouts were asleep in their saddles. At 3 a.m. Rowand jolted from his slumber and "felt instinctively something was wrong," remembered the Scout. In the pitch-black night, not a star twinkled in the sky. Rowand pulled out a match to check his compass. The horses, finding their riders asleep in their saddles, had "concluded to go back to Winchester," and on their own rode back to the Yankee town. Rowand rode up to Young and asked if he planned on going to Winchester. The officer answered sharply, "No." "That's where we are headed for," the West Virginian responded. After showing the commanding officer his compass, Young angrily retorted, "Take the lead." The young Scout sped into the darkness; they had to reach Edinburg before dawn. Since some of the men were unhorsed, a "great deal of foul language was used at the speed I was going,"[2] recalled Rowand. Finally, the cavalcade approached a small Confederate outpost guarding the bridge on the Valley Pike at Edinburg located next to a sprawling mill. The picket was under the command of Shenandoah Valley native Captain George J. Grandstaff of the 12th Virginia Cavalry. Rowand rode up far ahead of the group and, cloaked in butternut, fooled the Confederate sentries by saying he "belonged to Major Gilmor's command." With a pistol in their faces, the Federals apprehended the first of dozens of prisoners they would take that day. Once the party reached Woodstock,

Major Young, "against Campbell's protest and mine, determined to stay at Woodstock to get something to eat."[3]

A reliable Union informant, a one-armed butcher whom the Jessie Scouts befriended, warned them of 200 Rebel cavalry only three miles away on the Back Road.*

Within an hour, the Confederates "came charging into us and we had to get out." The fresh recruits withered in the face of an enemy several times their number. After losing a Jessie Scout, twenty cavalrymen, and their prisoners, the Union cavalrymen fled for their lives. Young had requested seasoned troops, "but through some misinterpretation of the order, or carelessness," he had received green cavalrymen.[4]

"For God's sake, stop the cavalry!" Young yelled to Rowand.[5]

Although Rowand threatened the fleeing sergeant with death, stopping the flight of the green troops "was impossible . . . seeing they were demoralized I started back to the scouts, it was then Campbell yelled to me."[6]

"Young's down!"[7]

The intrepid Young, whose horse had been shot out from under him, was fighting on foot surrounded by Rebel cavalrymen calling for him to surrender. Pistols blazing, James Campbell and Rowand boldly charged into the melee. Campbell scooped their commander up onto the back of his horse while Rowand "protected the rear," and all three rode off under a hail of gunfire. "Campbell got two bullets through his clothes," and Rowand's horse was "slightly wounded."[8]

Three decades later, in a letter of recommendation for a Medal of Honor, Brigadier General Horace Porter said of Campbell, "He had so many hair-breadth escapes and showed such coolness and true heroism on all occasions, that he commanded the admiration of all the officers who knew him."[9] Rowand responded to Porter's praise by saying, "It is hardly necessary for me to say to you that Campbell is one of the bravest of the brave."[10]

John Riley, one of the Jessie Scouts captured by the Confederates that day, escaped from his captors by jumping over a wall just above Fisher's Hill. Riley "went through the top of a pine tree, breaking the branches and all." The Scout then crossed a river and showed up at camp late the next morning. The first thing Riley said to Rowand, who was

---

* The Back Road is the formal name of the road; it still exists today and is a scenic drive.

nicknamed Barefoot, was, "Jesus, Barefoot, it was lucky they did not get you; that picket you captured came back looking for the Scout that rode up with him, and he had his gun cocked, and had you been there he would have blown your head off."[11] The enraged Confederate lost his brother that evening, as Rowand would soon find out.

However, Thomas Cassidy, another Scout who had been captured, did not escape his captors; the Confederates planned to hang him. Resourceful and possibly a double agent, Cassidy may have convinced the Confederates he was a deserter or enlisted as a Scout in one of Young's phony Confederate recruiting schemes weeks earlier, as evidenced by the pass he carried: "December 1, 1864—Pass Thomas Cassidy, scout at these headquarters through the lines at any point. By order of Lieutenant-General Early. S. J.C. Moore, A.A.G."*

Sheridan immediately sent a staff officer under a flag of truce to the Confederate lines to save the Scout's life by offering a prisoner exchange. Ditching his Confederate uniform, Rowand donned Union blues and fell in with the escort led by a Union major. Sheridan hoped Rowand's trained eyes might pick up some intelligence along the route.

The party arrived at Woodstock and the major approached Grandstaff as a crowd of locals gathered around the men.

"This man was dressed in Confederate uniform and will be hanged."[12]

The two men parlayed. The argument went nowhere.

"There will be a hanging going on in Winchester then,"[13] retorted the Union officer.

The tension was broken by a young girl who yelled, "Hang him, too. He's one of their Jessie Scouts."[14] A livid Confederate cavalryman pushed his way through the throng of spectators and snarled that his brother had been killed the day before and he would kill Rowand on the spot. Rowand pulled out his revolver and told the men to move aside from the crowd, and they "would settle it." Fortunately, Grandstaff rode between the glowering men and tersely asked the Union officer if Rowand was a Jessie Scout.

Before the major could answer the question, Rowand responded, "You know, or ought to know, that I belong to the 1st West Virginia Cavalry."[15]

---

* Sergeant Joseph McCabe possessed Cassidy's pass after the war. Cassidy's pass and McCabe's pass from General Sheridan were reprinted in a newspaper article, "A Soldier's Double Duty," *Daily News* (Lebanon, PA), May 29, 1883, 1.

"Why?" Grandstaff asked inquisitively.

"I was one of the thirteen men under Lieutenant Smith that charged through your command on top of Fisher's Hill. We didn't whip you fellows, but you killed two of our boys."[16]

The powerful and swift answer shut down the negotiations, and the imminent shootout between the two men ceased as the Federal party slowly backed up and rode out of Woodstock without Cassidy. Grandstaff sent the Scout to Richmond, where the Confederates exchanged him weeks later for a Confederate officer. Cassidy returned a changed man from his near-death experience—"he had lost his nerve after looking at the noose for 30 days,"[17] remembered Rowand. The Scout asked to return to regular duty; hesitant to lose one of his best men, Sheridan reluctantly agreed to the request.

After the incident, "the Rebels were very anxious to capture the Jessie Scouts," recalled one Scout. James Campbell and Sonny Crissman rode up the valley on one wintry day into an ambush. A dozen Confederates surrounded the men, with four taking the bridle reins of their horses. "Crissman shot the man dead who took hold of his bridle rein, wheeling around, miraculously escaped without a wound." Campbell was not so lucky; the Confederates seized the Jessie Scout and stripped him to "all but his underclothing." Amid the deep snow in the bitter cold, the "Johnnies thought Jim would not attempt to get away, but Jim preferred a cold walk to stretched hemp."[18]

45. To Catch a Partisan Chief

In early February 1865, Jessie Scout Arch Rowand traveled through enemy territory on a mission to find the lair of partisan leader Harry Gilmor. "On Tuesday, I was ordered with one man to go to Moorefield. By Order of Gen. Sheridan." Braving the bitterly cold weather, snow drifts, and icy roads of the Shenandoah Valley and smooth-talking their way through Confederate pickets, the two Scouts, dressed in Confederate uniforms, accomplished their arduous task in just forty-eight hours. "Returned on Thursday, reported to the General the whereabouts of Harry Gilmor and command."[1]

Sheridan wasted no time in following up on the critical intelligence from Rowand and swiftly assembled a force of 300 cavalry under the command of Lieutenant Colonel Edward W. Whitaker of the 1st Connecticut Cavalry, tasking a group of twenty of Young's Jessie Scouts, dressed in butternut, to ride ahead and "pass off as a body of recruits for Gilmor coming from Maryland."[2] Sheridan conceived the ruse to have them inform Gilmor's men deceptively that a large Union force of cavalry was just behind them so as to discern the exact whereabouts of Gilmor.

"On Saturday morning, a force of cavalry (300) and twenty Scouts left this place [Winchester] for Moorefield, a distant fifty-eight miles. Traveling all Saturday night, we arrived at Moorefield Sunday morning just before day. Leaving the town surrounded by a strong picket, we struck South Fork River Road. I advanced with five Scouts. Two miles from the town, we came in sight of two large, fine houses: Williams and Randolph's,"[3] recalled Rowand.

Seeing a large group of horses in the stable, Rowand and the other Scouts surrounded Randolph's house while Young knocked on the front door.

"What soldiers in the houses?"

The servant woman shocked the Union Scouts when she innocently gave them the exact location of their prey: "Major Gilmor is upstairs."

Hearts pounding with excitement at being so close to securing their prize, Young and four Jessie Scouts crept upstairs with pistols drawn. After entering the room where Gilmor and his cousin slumbered, Young pressed the barrel of his pistol against the sleeping man's head and demanded more than once,

"Are you Colonel Gilmor?"

"Yes, and who in the devil's name are you?" replied Gilmor, who later wrote, "Although dressed as Confederates, I saw at a glance what they were. But it was too late for a fight, for they had seized my pistols, lying on a chair under my uniform."

"Major Young of General Sheridan's staff."

"All right. I suppose you want me to go with you?"

"I shall be happy to have your company to Winchester, as General Sheridan wishes to consult you about some important military affairs," answered the Union officer.[4]

Even as the Confederate guerrilla was held at gunpoint and saw from the window swarms of Union cavalrymen gathering outside, he still held out hope for escape. "I had intended never to be taken alive," he later wrote. He dawdled in getting dressed, "hoping my men would make a diversion in my favor." Then, when hurried outside and mounted on his black mare, he "was already on the lookout for a break in the fence to make the effort."[5] Jessie Scout Sergeant G. D. Mullihan complained, "As soon as Major Gilmor was in the saddle, he made an attempt to escape. I suspected this and was prepared for him. I caught his horse by the bridle rein. He made a second attempt. Again, I caught his horse." Finally, the exasperated Scout threatened that if Young did not put their prisoner on an inferior horse, he would shoot Gilmor's horse from under him. "Now that we had him, I was not going to let him escape."[6]

Gray-eyed, five-foot-three William E. Hart, of Company B, 8th New York Volunteer Cavalry, was instrumental in capturing Gilmor and received the Medal of Honor for "gallant conduct and services as a scout in connection with the capture of the guerrilla Harry Gilmor and other daring acts"[7] in the Shenandoah Valley.

On the journey back to Winchester, while the Jessie Scouts and Young guarded Gilmor, the notorious Confederate captain George W. Stump fell into the hands of Mullihan and four of his fellow Scouts.

Spying a nearby house, Mullihan, his stomach empty, rode over to it in search of something to eat. The woman who served the Jessie Scout food revealed the house belonged to Stump, an independent partisan who worked with Confederate leaders and was known as "Stump's Battery" because of numerous revolvers and carbines he kept with him at all times. "Knowing that Captain Stump . . . [had a] reputation of hanging and cutting the throats of Union prisoners, I made a further inquiry about him, telling the colored woman that I had important dispatches and must see him at once."[8] Going first to the church, then being informed the captain was visiting at his brother's house a short distance down the road, Mullihan and another Scout made their way to the residence.

"We discovered Captain Stump in the act of mounting his horse, I ordered him to surrender . . . we fired several shots, and he fell forward to the ground. He tried to regain his feet and reached for his revolver. But we were upon him before he could use it, and I pointed my revolver in his face and forced him to his knees. We immediately disarmed him." Stump lived up to his moniker of "Stump's Battery." "His belt was supported with two straps over his shoulders, and on that belt he carried three pistols, and on his saddle he had a pistol and a seven-shot carbine."[9]

After disarming him, Mullihan inquired, "Where are you hurt?" The Confederate captain pointed to his thigh.

"Are you Captain Stump?"

The Confederate obfuscated and claimed to be his brother. As they walked down the road, Stump lunged and attempted to grab Jessie Scout Nick Carlisle's revolver. At that, Mullihan dryly responded that he "would make a sieve out of him" if he tried that again.

When the group rejoined Young's column, Mullihan informed the major that they had captured "Captain Stump, but he will not own up to it." When Stump finally capitulated and admitted his true identity, Young served the Confederate an ultimatum. "I suppose you know that we will kill you. But we will not serve you as you have served our men, cut your throat or hang you. We will give you a chance for your life. We will give you ten rods start on your own horse, with your spurs on. If you get away,

all right. But remember, my men are dead shots." Captain Stump stoically "smiled, rode out, and we gave him the word 'Go.' We allowed him
about ten rods start, then our pistols cracked, and he fell forward, dead,"
remembered Mullihan.[10]

The journey continued. Remarkably, Gilmor and Young became friendly
on the ride to Winchester, but they also regarded each other with mutual
respect. At one point, the frozen entourage halted to rest. Fearful that
the wily Confederate would escape, Young requested that the Scouts be
allowed to press on alone with the prisoner to Winchester. When the senior
Federal officer in charge denied his request, Young rode off in a huff with
his Scouts. Gilmor "felt my hope return, now that the lynx-eyed major
had taken his departure, and [I] was busily concocting different schemes
for my escape." Unfortunately for the Confederate partisan leader, Young
thought twice and sent back four of his Scouts, who "dashed" out of the
forest just as Gilmor was about to make his third escape attempt.[11]

Despite the Scouts' eagle-eyed presence, Gilmor made one last failed
midnight attempt at flight before the party reached Winchester and rejoined
Young at noon the next day. As they made their way toward Gilmor's ultimate destination by train to Fort Warren in Boston, Young and about half
a dozen Scouts had to guard their prisoner both from escape and from the
threatening Northern mobs that turned out to gawk at the Rebel prize.
At one point, Young, with cocked pistol in hand, faced a menacing crowd
at Harpers Ferry and whispered to Gilmor, "In case of attack, take one of
my pistols and shoot right and left, they will have to walk over my dead
body before they touch you."[12]

"From first to last he was as kind as it was possible for him to be, but
at the same time, he watched me like a hawk and was always ready to draw
his revolver," wrote Gilmor of the Yankee major. On February 10, 1865,
five days after the initial capture, Young delivered the guerrilla leader to
Fort Warren in Boston Harbor, "not losing sight of his charge until the
gates were securely closed upon him."[13]

Moorefield's treelined streets and quaint homes served as a base not only for
Gilmor but also for another Confederate partisan band known as McNeill's

Rangers—who wanted payback for the capture of Gilmor and the invasion of their town.

After the Confederate government abolished the Confederate Partisan Rangers Act in 1864, McNeill's Rangers were the only officially sanctioned partisan group other than Mosby's Rangers. Like the Thurmond brothers in West Virginia, McNeill's Rangers was a family affair. After John McNeill was mortally wounded in a raid in the fall of 1864, command passed to his son Jesse Cunningham McNeill.

In the dead of night on February 19, 1865, John B. Fay and another partisan rode all night and crossed the icy Potomac River to confirm the location of their targets, Union generals Benjamin Franklin Kelley and his superior George Crook, with a Confederate sympathizer who had spent days surveying the area. A rider then fought through a snowstorm to take the intelligence back to McNeill.

By the evening of February 20, sixty-three men from McNeill's force joined Fay. Together, they rode more than twenty miles across ice-covered mountain roads, narrow ridges, and snow-filled valleys to reach the Potomac and their destination: Cumberland, Maryland. Now in Union territory, hours before the break of dawn, McNeill, his two sergeants, and Fay approached the first set of pickets.

"Halt, who comes there?" called out a voice from the darkness still a few hundred yards away.

"Friends from New Creek," answered the Confederates.

"Dismount one, come forward, and give the countersign," responded the Union soldier.

McNeill instead spurred his horse forward as he leveled his pistol and shot at the picket's head, who was "terribly alarmed at the peculiar conduct of his alleged friends,"[14] according to Fay.

After securing all three pickets, the Confederate guerrillas tried unsuccessfully to ascertain the countersign so they could more easily slip deeper into enemy territory. A pistol to the head failed to elicit the information, but after they slipped a noose around one picket's neck and hauled him in the air, he capitulated: "Bull's Gap."[15]

The Confederates quickly captured the next group of five Union pickets they found in a shed warming themselves by a fire and playing a game of cards. Unable to take more prisoners, they gave them the chance to run for their lives, falsely warning them that a larger force followed close behind.

Concealing their gray uniforms under Union greatcoats and giving the appearance of a returning Federal unit, the raiders passed without incident through more checkpoints until they reached Revere House and Barnum House, where Crook and Kelley, respectively, slept, in the Union base of Cumberland, Maryland. Sergeant Joseph Kuykendall, whom General Kelley had previously imprisoned, led a squad of men into Barnum House and soon pushed a hastily dressed Kelley and his adjutant at gunpoint down the street.

The impressive Sergeant Vandiver, "a man of imposing size and figure, fond of dress, and full of self-assertion," led the force to capture Crook. After waking and intimidating the hotel's porter into revealing the general's location, the raiders knocked on the unsuspecting officer's bedroom door.

"Who's there?"

"A friend."[16]

"Come in." Even though it was 3 a.m., the general never imagined that he would be in jeopardy deep in Union territory, surrounded by thousands of Federal troops.

"General, I am General Rosser of Fitzhugh Lee's Division," boomed Vandiver as he stepped through the doorway. "We have captured the city, and you are my prisoner." When the general overcame his shock, he complied with "much grace and cheerfulness," later confiding to Fay, "Vandiver was such a good looking man as I supposed General Rosser to be, and I took him at his word."[17]

Crook, who had played a crucial role in shaping Blazer's Scouts and counterinsurgency warfare, would only be imprisoned for a short period. Grant recognized his talents and orchestrated a prisoner exchange, and the Ohioan was back in command within weeks.

46. SHERIDAN'S WAR

Young and Sheridan were ideally matched. The Union general hatched a plot to use a pair of double agents managed by the Rhode Island officer to spread disinformation to open his 1865 spring offensive against Jubal Early. Sheridan recalled how his scheme materialized: "A man named Lomas, who claimed to be a Marylander, offered me his services as a spy, and coming recommended from Mr. Stanton [Union secretary of war]." Sheridan determined some of Lomas' information to be useful, which Young and his men corroborated, though "there were discrepancies in his tales." Soon, Lomas brought a man who had allegedly deserted from Mosby's command and implored the general to hire him. Going by the name of Renfrew, the Mosby deserter entered Sheridan's room "completely disguised, but on discarding the various contrivances by which his identity was concealed, he proved to be a rather slender, dark-complexioned, handsome young man, of easy address and captivating manners." Sheridan later stated the handsome Renfrew bore a "strong resemblance to [John Wilkes] Booth." Sheridan shrewdly did not trust the two interlopers and had Young's men shadow the pair of Confederate spies, who concealed themselves in Strasburg, "without making the slightest effort to continue the mission," and "no doubt communicated with the enemy."[1] The two spies spun a tale of daring behind the lines, which Sheridan knew to be bogus. Instead of executing the men, he planned to use them to spread misinformation to Early.

Early's army, what remained of it, lay scattered through the valley. The general sent two infantry brigades to Staunton and ordered Tex Rosser's cavalry to their homes for lack of forage for their horses. The Confederate cavalry could be recalled in the event of fighting. A little over a month earlier, with just 300 men, Rosser had crossed steep mountains and deep snow to surprise and capture nearly 600 Union troops in Beverly, West Virginia. Early also sent John Echols' brigade to Petersburg.

After the capture of Crook, Sheridan was finally prepared to move his forces when Grant provided him with essentially discretionary orders to destroy the Virginia and Central Railroad and the James River Canal and, if practical, take Lynchburg. Afterward, Grant suggested they could move south and find and reinforce Sherman, who was short on cavalry. Sheridan had a habit of interpreting Grant's orders however he saw fit. Instead of riding hundreds of miles in search of Sherman, he planned to ignore Grant's request to travel to North Carolina and instead plead his case to reinforce Grant outside Petersburg. Two months earlier, a Union raid under Custer and Brigadier General Alfred Thomas Archimedes Torbert to destroy the Virginia and Central Railroad had proved a dismal failure. The Rebels burned bridges and fell back into substantial earthworks in a mountain gap. Their strong defense, combined with the weather, stymied the Federal advance. After the failed raid, Sheridan went all in. Instead of delegating his command to subordinates, he would lead his entire command of roughly 10,000 cavalry and artillery to Grant.

Sheridan used the Confederate double agents to cloak his troop movements by announcing "officially that a grand fox-chase would take place on the 29th of February. Knowing that Lomas and Renfrew would spread the announcement South, they were permitted to see several red foxes that had been secured, as well as a large pack of hounds which [Major] Young had collected for the sport."[2]

Sheridan's bold initiative would set up a chain of events that would change the course of the war—and the Jessie Scouts would lead the way. Jessie Scout Jim White would also furnish Rebel maps and other information needed for the journey south.[3]

Sheridan's men rode through bone-chilling weather down the Valley Pike from Winchester on February 27, 1865, and reached Woodstock by sundown. The troops encountered minimal resistance on their journey south, brushing aside occasional Confederate resistance. Mosby's Rangers were not impeding Sheridan's movement, since the bulk of the Rangers were in the Northern Neck, nearly one hundred miles to the southeast. Mud, instead of Early, became the main enemy, as one cavalryman noted: "The mud is very deep. It is impossible to take a piece of artillery out of the road. We have lost 2,500 horses through fatigue since leaving Winchester."[4] Just outside

Staunton at Mount Crawford, Virginia, at a covered bridge spanning a deep chasm where the North River flowed below, Rosser and roughly one hundred Confederate cavalrymen tried to slow the Federal advance. They torched the bridge over the North River as they dug in on the opposite side. The Union forces foiled their efforts, however. One column of cavalry charged through the flaming covered trestle while two other regiments swam the river and attacked the Confederate general's force from its flank. They succeeded in capturing the bridge, miraculously extinguishing the flames in time to save it, and dispersing Rosser's force. Had the bridge not been taken, Sheridan's wagons would have had a very challenging time marching south. Custer would later report, "The importance of our success in securing the bridge over North River cannot be overestimated. Had the enemy succeeded in destroying the bridge it would have compelled a long delay on our part, as there were no fords practicable in the vicinity."[5]

Rosser and about thirty of his men retreated to Staunton. After the Confederates evacuated the town, Sheridan destroyed anything of military value. Early then ordered Rosser and roughly 1,000 other Confederates to make a stand in nearby Waynesboro.

On March 2, Sheridan ordered Custer to finish off what was left of Early's army. Although vastly outnumbered, the Confederates dug in on the high ground of the town behind fieldworks. A Union reconnaissance revealed a gap in the left flank by the river. Custer ordered his men to dismount. With their Spencer carbines, they charged through the left flank, scattering the Confederates. Jubal Early barely escaped as his command jumped on their horses and fled. According to Sheridan, his men captured seventeen Rebel battle flags. Jessie Scout Private John Miller of Company H, 8th New York Cavalry, an immigrant from Germany, who had been in America for only five years, was a hero that day. Miller received the Medal of Honor for capturing a battle flag "with the bearer and some twenty other rebels."[6] Federal troops also recovered General Crook's battle flag. The crushing defeat at Waynesboro ended Early's career. Shortly afterward, Lee relieved him of his command.

After the battle, Sheridan moved east toward Charlottesville and commenced destruction of the Virginia and Central Railroad and the James River Canal. Even the Scouts lent a hand. While the Scouts helped remove track, a sledgehammer crushed Dominick Fannin's index and middle fingers of his left hand.[7] After destroying the track, Sheridan continued marching toward Grant.

Sheridan needed to get a message to Grant that instead of joining Sherman's army in the Carolinas, he would march south and join the Army of the Potomac outside Petersburg. He tapped his two most reliable Scouts: James Campbell, who had escaped capture and immediately went back to duty, and Arch Rowand. Starting in Columbia, Virginia, over 100 miles west of Richmond, the two Scouts made a remarkable 145-plus-mile epic journey in thirty-six hours through Confederate lines to Petersburg carrying the vital message in a tiny tinfoil capsule they were required to eat if captured.

Dressed in Confederate uniforms, the Scouts moved through enemy territory without arousing suspicion, collecting valuable intelligence and "talked to some fifty Rebels. . . . We had quite the confab with four of Gen. Lee's scouts; passed ourselves off for Gen. Reese's scouts. They, in fact, never suspected to see two Yankees right in the midst of their lines in broad daylight,"[8] wrote Rowand.

Near the Chickahominy River, the pair of Jessie Scouts met two men and a boy. Bantering back and forth, the crew warned Rowand and Campbell not to cross the river because Union troops were nearby. Almost out of earshot, the Scouts heard one of the men say, "I believe those fellows are d—d Yankees."[9] Discovered, the two men were forced to ride for their lives when the Confederates alerted a nearby Rebel cavalry patrol. "The fleetness of our horses alone saved us, as we had time to get across the river before the Rebels got to the bank," Rowand wrote to his mother. Wearing just his undershirt and putting his Rebel uniform on the pommel of his saddle, Rowand dove into the near-freezing river with his horse. "Providentially," he happened to find a small boat and rowed back to get his fellow Scout. They were forced to leave their horses behind as they sought cover in the nearby swamp. "Although we could see them coming down the road, they did not follow us any further than the bank of the river, as there is no boat, and they could not swim their horses across."[10] Giving up the chase, the Confederates fired on them from the opposite bank as the Jessie Scouts headed toward Union lines.

Avoiding Confederate patrols, the men walked the remaining ten miles toward Grant's headquarters at City Point, northeast of Petersburg, where they used all the skills they had developed over the course of the war to make their way toward Grant without being mistakenly shot as Confederates. At Harrison's Landing, the pair met a detachment of Union soldiers and convinced them to give them cast-off Federal uniforms. Even though Rowand was "so crippled in my feet, I could scarcely walk,"[11] he surprised the Union officers when the pair appeared outside Grant's headquarters.

One of Grant's staff officers recalled the scene when the weakened Scouts arrived in the second week of March 1865: "I found a man outside who was about to sink to the ground from exhaustion, and who had scarcely strength enough to reply to my questions. He had on a pair of soldier's trousers three or four inches too short, and a blouse three sizes too large; he was without a hat and his appearance was grotesque in the extreme. With him was another man in about the same condition."[12]

Grant and his staff were mystified that the Jessie Scouts had completed the journey alive, and they gave the men some whiskey. After downing the stiff drink, the men gave the message directly to Grant, three pages in length wrapped in the tiny capsule Campbell carried at times in his mouth. Grant read it aloud at a dinner party he was giving. Sheridan informed Grant he had captured artillery and destroyed many mills and factories on his march south. He planned on laying waste to the James River Canal and ripping up the track on the Central and Fredericksburg Railroad before joining the Army of the Potomac.

"The Acting Adjutant-General took us around and introduced us to Mrs. Gen. Grant and several other ladies whose names I have forgotten. They had expressed a wish to see the two men that came through the Rebel lines in open day." Grant "lionized" the Jessie Scouts and said their epic ride was "the biggest and boldest* scout trip of the war."[13] The ladies in the room peppered the men with questions, until Grant finally rose from his seat and said good-naturedly, "Well, I will never get the information I want from this scout as long as you ladies have him under cross-examination, and I think I had better take him over to my quarters."[14]

---

* Decades later, a bureaucrat in the War Department initially denied Campbell the Medal of Honor. Rowand responded in writing, "In your letter to me you state that carrying the dispatches from Columbia to Gen. Grant was not in action . . . but a man dressed in the enemy's uniform, with important dispatches, ordered to go through the rebel lines to deliver dispatches and if captured to eat them, is he not 'in extreme jeopardy of life' and does he not perform 'extraordinarily hazardous duty'? You would think so if you had stood in the shadow of the gallows, as I did when captured inside of Breckinridge's lines on the Lynchburg raid." The bureaucrats relented, after testimony from Sheridan and Rowand, and Campbell received the Medal of Honor he earned yet did not personally request.

Because of the critical importance of the message, Sheridan had not put all his eggs in Campbell and Rowand's basket. He sent two additional Scouts, Frederick Moore and Dominick Fannin, to paddle down the James River in a small boat and enter Confederate lines at Petersburg. The two Scouts passed as Confederates "deserting to Union lines," only hundreds of yards apart from Confederate lines—a remarkable feat to brave fire from both sides—"and deliver[ed] their tidings into General Grant's hands."[15] A day or two after Rowand and Campbell brought the crucial message, the second Scout team arrived at Grant's headquarters. It was not the team's first epic journey. A year earlier they and other Scouts had battled nature and the Confederates in a daring prison escape.

Sergeant William Collins, cavalryman and fellow prisoner, first met the Scouts in a tiny, cramped prison cell in Staunton, Virginia, in the last days of March 1864. Here the men plotted, bided their time, and made their escape from the county jail, as Collins would record in an affidavit after the war.

It takes a special human being to be a Jessie Scout: resourceful, intelligent, and cunning. Many of the best Scouts and Rangers also made excellent escape artists who combined all these skills and many more to break out of ostensibly impossible situations. All the men had iron constitutions that would be put to the ultimate test. "Bare-footed, bare-headed," the prisoners, after fleeing from the city, had a "brief consultation" and decided to head west into the mountains toward Union lines. One of the men had an old coat from which they made rough moccasins to cover their feet. As they trudged fourteen or fifteen miles into the mountain, snow started to "fall fast," and the men made "slow progress"[16] through drifts four to six inches deep, recalled Collins.

Crossing a valley near the town of Monterey, the escapees came across a small cabin in the middle of nowhere occupied by an old man and his wife, who showed them an oath of allegiance the man had taken to the Union. As the exhausted and cold men made their way down the mountain near Monterey, "we were halted by armed Rebels who surrounded us . . . ordered us to hold up our hands, while they searched us for arms."[17]

Jessie Scout Moore became separated from the other men and evaded capture as the Confederates brought the other Scouts and Collins into custody. The men slept in a jail cell, and the Confederates gave them cornmeal.

The next day, two "strapping young Rebs" escorted the men to their next destination. Employing their guile and wit, the Scouts were able to disarm their captors. They then proceeded to climb a steep mountain and descend "a deep ravine in the mountains where the timber was thick." Hiding out during the day and moving at night, the men stumbled upon an old house occupied by "a rank old Rebel" who would not allow the men to stay there. The Scouts and Collins traversed miles of rugged terrain and made their way to Beverly, West Virginia, where some Ohio regiments were garrisoned. Six miles before they arrived in Beverly, they met some Union people who fed the men "the first breakfast they had in many a day."[18] Eventually, the Scouts traveled up the Shenandoah Valley to Winchester and freedom.

47. The Plot to Kidnap
President Lincoln

Lewis Powell pulled the doorbell of the townhouse at 541 H Street NW, Washington, DC.[1] A resident slowly opened the door, and Powell inquired if John Surratt was at home.

After the dashing Powell sauntered into the hallway, he was greeted by the middle-aged owner of the three-story brick boarding house, Mary Surratt, who, feigning surprise, remarked, "What a great looking Baptist preacher."[2] Moving into the parlor, Powell bowed to some ladies and stated "he had been in prison in Baltimore for about a week; that he had taken the Oath of Allegiance and was now going to become a good and loyal citizen."[3] Powell then asked one of the ladies to play the piano. The Ranger turned the pages of the sheet music and started singing to the group. One of the ladies commented, "I don't think he will convert many souls!"[4]

Known as "The Nest That Hatched the Egg,"[5] the townhouse served as Powell's lodging for a few days and a meeting place for John Wilkes Booth's conspirators. With the arrival of Powell, the team's muscle, Booth's group to capture the president was complete: Samuel Arnold, Michael O'Laughlen, George Atzerodt, Dr. Samuel Mudd, David Herold, and Confederate Secret Service agent John Surratt.

Surratt, whose mother owned the home, summoned Powell to meet that evening, having contacted Powell's Secret Service handler,* David Preston Parr. Specializing in fine china and skullduggery, Parr had a shop

---

* David Parr handled or managed Powell. Parr was a member of the Confederate Secret Service, as his oath of allegiance after the war states, Confederate Signal Corps.

in the heart of Baltimore that served as a meeting place for Confederate operatives and a mail drop for messages.

Since leaving the Rangers, Powell had traveled north to Baltimore and been living in the Bransons' boarding house, which doubled as a Confederate Secret Service safe house. Powell seemed to possess a Jekyll-and-Hyde personality. While staying at the boarding house, Powell had a confrontation with an African American maid. After Powell asked to have his room cleaned, she acted with "impudence" and "called him some names." Then Powell lost control. "He struck her; threw her to the ground and stomped her body, struck her on the forehead, and said he would kill her."[6]

The badly beaten woman went to the authorities. Apparently, she knew something of Powell's clandestine activities. Instead of being arrested for assault and battery, Powell was brought in as a spy. Silver-tongued and persuasive, he talked his way out of charges despite being detained for two days. He took another oath of allegiance and was told by provost marshal detectives to "go north of Philadelphia and remain there during the war."

Rather than head north, Powell went to Parr's china shop, where a telegram awaited him: "Immediately telegraph if my friend is disengaged and can see me this evening in Washington. 541 H. Street, between 6 & 7 Sts. Harrison Surratt [an alias used by John]."[7]

At the Nest, Powell, Surratt, and the others continued to work out the details of the next steps of the operation to kidnap Lincoln. Fittingly, Reverend Payne's nom de guerre was "Mosby" for his service in the elite unit. Together, the team waited for an opportunity to capture the president.

Surratt explained the extensive nature of the operation: "After some difficulty everything was amicably arranged and we separated at 5 o'clock in the morning. Days, weeks and months passed by without an opportunity presenting itself for us to attempt the capture. We seldom saw one another owing to the many rumors afloat that a conspiracy of some kind was being concocted in Washington. We had all the arrangements perfected from Washington for the purpose. Boats were in readiness to carry us across the river." The conspirators were using as an escape route the Secret Service line that Booth had been introduced to in Montreal. Weeks of planning manifested on Friday, March 17, 1865. Surratt recalled some years later, "We received information that the President would visit the Seventh Street Hospital for the purpose of being present at an entertainment to be given for the benefit of the wounded soldiers. The report only reached us about three-quarters of an hour before the time appointed, but so perfect was our communication that we were instantly in our saddles on the way to the hospital. This was between one and two o'clock in the afternoon."[8] Surratt explained the plan: "It was our intention to seize the carriage, which was drawn by a splendid pair of horses, and to have one of our men mount the box and drive direct for southern Maryland via Benning's bridge. We felt confident that all the cavalry in the city could never overhaul us. We were all mounted on swift horses, besides having a thorough knowledge of the country, it was determined to abandon the carriage after passing the city limits. Upon the suddenness of the blow and the celerity of our movements we depended for success. By the time the alarm could have been given and horses saddled, we would have been on our way through southern Maryland towards the Potomac River."[9]

The operation proved to be a bust: "To our great disappointment, however, the President was not there but one of the government officials—Mr. [Salmon P.] Chase, if I mistake not. We did not disturb him, as we wanted a bigger *chase* than he could have afforded us. It was certainly a bitter disappointment, but yet I think a most fortunate one for us. It was our last attempt."[10] The plan to capture Lincoln's carriage at the Seventh Street Hospital having failed, the conspirators considered seizing the president in an environment Booth knew well.

Booth and Surratt hatched another plot to kidnap the president from Ford's Theater, in Washington, DC. During this time, the conspirators were also graced by the occasional presence of the Secret Service courier and spy known as the French Woman, Sarah Slater.[11] Samuel Arnold, one of the conspirators who backed out, recalled in his confession: "[We] were ushered into the presence of J. Wilkes Booth who introduced me to John Surratt, Atzerodt (alias Port Tobacco) (alias) Mosby [Powell] making in all seven persons. J. Wilkes Booth had stated to Michael O'Laughlen to bring me up in good humor (still always in the dark). Then commenced the plan. Each had his part to perform. First I was to rush in the box and seize the President whilst Atzerodt 'alias' Port Tobacco and J. Wilkes Booth were to handcuff him and lower him on the stage whilst Mosby was to catch him and hold him until we all got down. Surratt and unknown to be on the other side of Bridge to facilitate escape, afterwards changed to Mosby and Booth to catch him in box throw him down to me on stage, O'Laughlen and unknown to put gas out [kill the lights in the theater]. Surratt, Atzerodt 'alias' Port Tobacco to be on the other side of Bridge."[12]

Atzerodt, a twenty-nine-year-old naturalized citizen from Germany, owned a carriage repair business in Port Tobacco and a boat in which the conspirators hoped to transport Lincoln across the Potomac into Virginia.

Nearly a hundred miles away in the Northern Neck, four companies of Mosby's Rangers waited. Coincidentally or not, the men received orders near the end of March to go back to Mosby's Confederacy. The timing of the return of the Rangers seems to correspond with the termination of plans to abduct Lincoln. Mosby received the orders from Lee through the Confederate Secret Service Signal Corps station that ran along the tops of the Blue Ridge Mountains and Allegheny Mountains in the Shenandoah. Using semaphore flags from the peaks of mounts in telescope range, the men could transmit brief sentences of coded messages. Lee ordered Mosby, "If any of your command is in the Northern Neck, call it to you."[13] Lieutenant William H. Chapman, one of Mosby's chief battle captains, did not comply with the order until April 9, 1865. Even then, sizable numbers of Mosby's men mysteriously stayed behind in the area.[14]

During the first week of April, Powell and Booth rode a train to New York, where the men met unknown contacts. Conspirator George Atzerodt, in his later confession, provided a clue regarding the nature of the meeting and revealed the Confederate Secret Service had another operation ready to kill the president, one that involved Mosby's Rangers: "Booth said he met a party in N. York who would get the prest. [president] certain. They were going to mine the end of the pres. [president's] House near the War Dept."[15] The confession is crucial, demonstrating the Confederates' designs to blow up the White House, marking a shift in plans from abduction to assassination.

48. FIVE FORKS

Through much of March, enduring unbearable hardship, Sheridan's troopers rode through over sixteen days of rain and sleet, swollen streams, and deep mud. At Columbia, Virginia, the army halted for one day to allow the massive snaking lines of wagon trains to catch up. Rain turned the roads into a soupy morass. Wagons sank in the muck. All seemed lost for the supply train until roughly 2,000 formerly enslaved Americans came to the rescue. They had attached themselves to Sheridan's forces in their quest for freedom. Sheridan wrote, "I believe we should have been forced to abandon most of the wagons except for the invaluable help . . . they literally lifted the wagons out of the mud."[1]

Fanning out and riding deep into Southern territory, Jessie Scouts led Sheridan's Army of the Shenandoah toward White House, Virginia. Sensing an opportunity to prevent Sheridan from linking up with Grant, Lee sent troops to intercept the Federals. Jessie Scouts once again staved off disaster at the hamlet of Frederick Hall. "Young's scouts brought me word from Richmond that General Longstreet was assembling a force there to prevent my junction with Grant," wrote Sheridan. To counter the threat, he divided his forces and sent columns off to distract or "amuse"[2] the Confederates. The ploy worked, and the Union cavalry rode into White House on March 18, where supplies furnished by Grant awaited them.

The journey took a massive toll on man and beast; one soldier remembered, "The hardships of this march far exceeded those of any previous campaigns by the cavalry."[3] Many of the men lost their mounts during the journey, and most animals needed reshoeing. Horses were scarce, and Sheridan refitted his cavalry the best he could for the battle ahead.

In the darkness of the early-morning hours of March 25, General John Brown Gordon's force of picked men moved into the trenches within the Confederate works at Petersburg. Fifty men armed with sharp axes led the "Forlorn Hope," a term used for those who normally would not survive, to cut away the Union's chevaux-de-frise and other obstructions, followed by 300 trained sharpshooters. The assault forces were followed by thousands of troops coiled for the mission before them: seize Fort Stedman and destroy the Union supply depot behind it. Days later Gordon described the élan of his troops: "The indomitable spirit of my men was never more strikingly shown than in their cheerful response to this command."[4] Despite years of war, miserable conditions in the trenches, and skimpy rations, the Confederacy had a great deal of fight in it.

Against the odds, the men attacked and surprised the fort and seized it. Some Confederate troops pushed beyond the fort but were stymied by nearby Union strongpoints. The attack seemed on the verge of success, but the Union mounted a strong counterattack, forcing Gordon to ask Lee to withdraw. Union forces killed or captured thousands of irreplaceable Confederate troops during the withdrawal from Stedman. The general in chief hoped the attack on Stedman would delay Grant's attack on the vulnerable supply lines and allow the army to move south, as Gordon explained: "The purpose of the movement was not simply the capture of Fort Stedman and the breastworks flanking it. The prisoners and guns we might thus capture would not justify the peril of the undertaking. The tremendous possibility was the disintegration of the whole left wing of the Federal army, or at least the dealing of such a staggering blow upon it as would disable temporarily, enabling us to withdraw from Petersburg in safety and join Johnston in North Carolina."[5]

The nine-month siege of Petersburg lingered on.

At the beginning of the war, six railroad lines supplied Richmond. By March 1864, the Union had severed five, and only the South Side remained. At Danville, the South Side's steel rails east to west connected with the Richmond and Danville Railroad in order to access North Carolina and more of the South. Vital wagon roads also supplied Richmond and Petersburg from the west along the route of the South Side. Lee had to keep the vital arteries open in the west or his army would be trapped.

Lee realized the grave challenges his army faced, writing to Jefferson Davis in March, "I fear now it will be impossible to prevent a junction between Grant and Sherman. . . . Their two armies united would therefore exceed ours by nearly a hundred thousand."[6]

Grant knew the question was not if Lee would retreat, but when. "General Grant had been sleeping with one eye open and one foot out of bed for weeks, in the fear that Lee would thus give him the slip,"[7] remembered Brigadier General Horace Porter, a member of Grant's staff. Grant's gravest concern was that Lee's retreat might escape from the entrenchments at Petersburg and into the interior of the South, away from the Federal base of supplies, and unite with General Joseph E. Johnston's army, which had tens of thousands of men in its ranks.

After refitting his force, Sheridan arrived at Grant's headquarters on March 26. Wreathed in a plume of his "inevitable cigar"[8] smoke, Grant greeted Sheridan. Grant set those around him at ease and "always met his officers in an unceremonious way: How are You?"[9] Grant discussed Sheridan and his cavalry marching South and joining Sherman. The combined force would then march north to Petersburg and crush Lee—if the Army of Northern Virginia remained in Petersburg.

Moving south to join Sherman was an order Sheridan adamantly opposed, and he remonstrated with Grant. Sheridan believed Lee had to be attacked immediately—if Grant waited for Sherman's arrival, Lee's army would be long gone from Petersburg and difficult to bring to battle. Little Phil instinctively knew Lee would never allow his army to be cornered and massively outnumbered by two juggernauts.

Sheridan then joined Grant and President Lincoln on board a steamer and cruised up the James River. The recent attack on Fort Stedman cast a pall over the meeting. Sheridan recalled, "On the trip, the President was not very cheerful. In fact, he was dejected, giving no indication of his usual means of diversion, by (his quaint stories). . . . He spoke to me of the impending operations and asked many questions, laying stress upon the one, 'What would be the result when the army moved out to the left (moving the lines to the west), if the enemy should come down and capture City Point' [a massive Federal supply base northeast of Petersburg, on the confluence of the James and Appomattox Rivers and present-day Hopewell]."[10]

Once they reached their destination, General William Tecumseh Sherman joined them by steamboat to coordinate plans with Grant and urge Sheridan to join him in North Carolina. The meeting was held in a shanty that doubled as Grant's headquarters. Sheridan, "as soon as the opportunity afforded, dissented emphatically."[11] The next morning, Sherman pestered Sheridan one last time to convince Little Phil to march to North Carolina, but Sheridan again demurred. The Irishman knew the war would be won or lost in Virginia.

Before attacking the South Side Railroad, Sheridan received written orders from Grant. The Union commander hedged his bets and allowed Sheridan options, at least on paper: "You may return to this army" or "you may go on into North Carolina and join General Sherman." The tenor of the orders and discussion with Sherman had Sheridan worried that he would be forced to march south to North Carolina—which he felt would potentially affect the course of the war. If the Army of Northern Virginia were able to maneuver out of Petersburg, it could strike at smaller Union armies or splinter into smaller battle groups and conduct guerrilla warfare—fighting in the manner Washington's forces and Lee's father had fought over half a century earlier. But Grant mollified him. Sheridan recalled, "The portion of the instructions from which I so strongly dissented was intended as a 'blind' to cover a check [from the Confederates] the army in its general move to the left might meet with, and to prevent that element in the North which held the war could be ended only through negotiation from charging defeat."[12]

Even in the final weeks of the war, Grant was concerned a military victory could be upended by the calls of those who believed the war was unwinnable by military means and could only be won at the negotiating table. The South, in the view of its leaders, had only to survive the war, not win it. If Lee's army could have escaped from Petersburg, even if reduced, the Confederacy's options for survival would have markedly improved.

Despite four years of war, the Union only occupied small portions of the South. Remarkably, the North suffered from more than 200,000 desertions, and another 120,000 evaded conscription. Tens of thousands fled to Canada. The war was wildly unpopular. An additional yearslong insurgency of guerrilla warfare, if Lee escaped, would have further eroded already-waning political will in the North. The Union Army had been built to destroy the South's armies, not to conquer and hold the Confederacy. Fighting both guerrilla and conventional war, using a Fabian strategy of retreat and attack that Washington had used nearly a century earlier against the British, might have bought the South time for a political settlement. If the North planned to occupy the South fully, it would be costly in lives and treasure, and could potentially take years, as Mosby and the other Confederate partisans had proved.

Another terrifying prospect involved Lee breaking up his army into fragments to elude the Federals, which would have posed a massive challenge to the Union if they engaged in guerrilla warfare along the lines of operations conducted by Mosby and the other Confederate irregulars. Those had proved that diminutive forces could tie up massive numbers of Federal troops in fruitless attacks. Instead of the war being nearly over, Lee's escape could have been the start of a new bloody and violent chapter.

Sheridan's offensive against the South Side Railroad on March 29 was challenged from the start. Lee knew that if he lost the critical supply line, his army would be out of supply and trapped. He swiftly dispatched George Pickett and his 11,000-man force traveling by rail to oppose Sheridan. Pickett's forces pushed the cavalrymen back, endangering two regiments with encirclement and destruction.

Torrential rains pummeled Petersburg for days, turning the roads into quicksand; wagons descended into the muck, and horses sank to their knees in both the roads and fields. Soldiers called out, "I say, when are the gunboats coming up?" Gloom pervaded Sheridan's lines: the attack looked premature and ill-timed. Grant was quick to cut his losses and prepared to pull the plug. On March 30, he wrote to Sheridan, "The heavy rain of to-day will make it impossible for us to do much until it dries up a little, or we get roads around our rear repaired. You may, therefore, leave what cavalry you deem necessary to protect the left, and hold such positions as you deem necessary for that purpose, and send the remainder back to Humphrey's Station [on the Federal military railroad], where they can get hay and grain."[13]

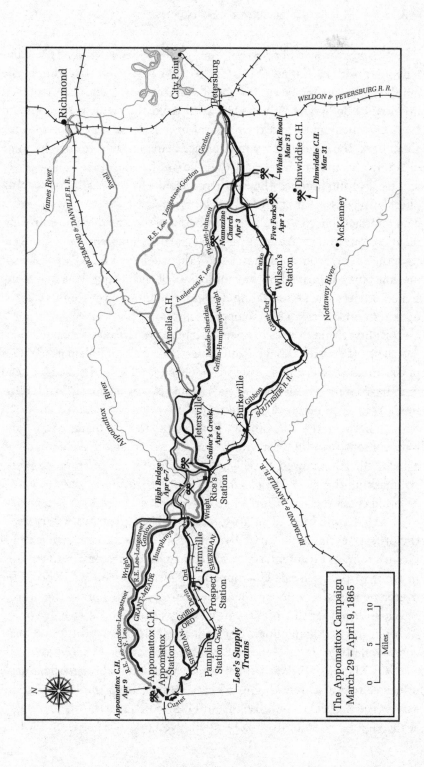

Richmond

City Point

Petersburg

WELDON & PETERSBURG R. R.

James River

RICHMOND & DANVILLE R. R.

Ewell

Gordon

R.E. Lee Longstreet-Gordon

White Oak Road
Mar 31

Dinwiddie C.H.
Dinwiddie C.H.
Mar 31

Five Forks
Apr 1

Pickett-Johnson

Namazine
Church
Apr 3

McKenney

Anderson-F. Lee

Amelia C.H.

Meade-Sheridan

Griffin-Humphreys-Wright

Parke

Wilson's
Station

Grant-Ord

Nottaway River

Appomattox River

Jetersville

Sailor's Creek
Apr 6

Burkeville

Gibbon

SOUTHSIDE R. R.

High Bridge
Apr 6–7

Wright

Rice's
Station

RICHMOND & DANVILLE R. R.

Wright

R.E. Lee-Longstreet
Gordon

GRANT-MEADE

Humphreys

Farmville

SHERIDAN

Appomattox C.H.
Apr 9
R. E. Lee-Gordon-Longstreet
R. E. Lee

Appomattox C.H.

Appomattox
Station

Custer

SHERIDAN–ORD

Griffin Devin

Ord

Prospect
Station

Crook

Pamplin
Station

Lee's Supply
Trains

N

The Appomattox Campaign
March 29 – April 9, 1865

0   5   10
Miles

Despite the lack of progress, Young's Jessie Scouts probed the Confederate positions, found the extent of their lines, and determined the number of men they faced. As Sheridan explained, "The [Confederate] infantry came by the White Oak Road from the right of the General Lee's entrenchments, and their arrival became positively known to me about dark, the confirmatory intelligence being brought in then by some of Young's Scouts who had been inside the Confederate lines."[14] The priceless tactical intelligence they gathered would prove crucial in shaping Sheridan's assessment of the battlefield. Sheridan's forces were exposed to counterattack, but so were Pickett's once out of their formidable entrenchments at Petersburg. "Young's personal gallantry and numerous conflicts with the enemy won the admiration of the whole command. . . . He kept me constantly informed of the movements of the enemy."[15] When many Union officers saw an unfolding disaster, and Grant prepared to call the operation off, Sheridan saw an opportunity.

Riding through a sea of knee-high mud, he arrived to change minds and stave off disaster. Arriving at Grant's soaked and mud-smattered tent in the middle of a cornfield, Sheridan opened the flap and poked his head in to hear Grant tell his chief of staff to suspend operations. "Well, Rawlins, I think you better take command." Sheridan sensed a difference of opinion between the staff officers. Leaving the tent, he made his case and built consensus with Grant's staff. "Pacing up and down like a hound on a leash," Sheridan vowed, "I tell you I'm ready to strike out tomorrow and go smashing things."[16] He added that if he were given an infantry corps, he could crush Pickett or force Lee to weaken his defenses at Petersburg.

"That's the kind of talk we liked to listen to at headquarters,"[17] the officers exclaimed. Shrewdly, Sheridan refused to barge back into Grant's tent, so Grant's staff "resorted to a bit of strategy"[18] to get him in front of the general. Unstoppable, Sheridan's iron will and ardor overcame any staff opposition and Grant decided to press the attack. Sheridan asked for the infantry of VI Corps, with whom he had worked so often in the Shenandoah. Instead, Sheridan received the V Corps commanded by Major General Gouverneur Kemble Warren.

On March 31, Pickett's infantry and cavalry attack brought Sheridan's offensive to a halt, but Union infantry moving from the left flank and east forced Pickett to pull back from Dinwiddie Courthouse and dig in at the vital junction of five roads called Five Forks. Lee ordered Pickett,

"Hold Five Forks at all hazards. Protect road to Ford's Depot and prevent Union forces from striking the South Side Railroad. Regret exceedingly your forced withdrawal, and your inability to hold the advantage you had gained."[19] Strategically, Five Forks at that moment was the most important real estate in North America. If the Federals could cut the railroad and wagon roads that supplied Petersburg and Richmond, the Army of Northern Virginia would be denied its supply lines and a major route of escape. Five Forks had to hold, and Lee's order called for a fight to the death, if necessary.

Random events and actions from a single individual can on occasion change the course of history. Major General Thomas "Tex" Rosser moved his division to join General Fitzhugh Lee, the nephew of Robert E. Lee, at Five Forks on March 30. He crossed the Nottoway River and noticed the waters teamed with shad making their annual migration. Rosser could not resist the temptation to fish. Borrowing a net from a local farmer, the Confederate major general, his manservant, and his staff plunged into the river, hauled in scores of the silvery green delicacy, and cooked some for dinner. The excess shad went into Rosser's headquarters' wagon.

Rosser was born in Virginia but relocated to Texas, earning his nickname of "Tex." Rosser's roommate at West Point was George Armstrong Custer. The two remained close friends despite being battlefield rivals. That rivalry would deepen in the coming days as the two faced each other at Five Forks.

In a throwback to an earlier time before the country had been torn apart by the raging war, the Southern gentleman decided to invite his fellow Confederate generals, George Pickett and Fitzhugh Lee, to a luncheon two miles to the rear of the lines. As they dined, their troops were dug in at Five Forks. Slaves served the men shad, and Madeira flowed into their glasses. The men lingered at Tex Rosser's camp for hours. Crucially, the generals failed to tell their seconds where they would be located. An attack was not expected that day, and warning signs were ignored. At 3 p.m., Rosser's pickets warned that Yankees were approaching the camp. The three generals listened for gunfire; hearing none, they returned to their lunch and drink. A natural phenomenon known as an acoustic echo canceled the thunderous sounds of battle at Five Forks.

General Pickett then requested couriers to send a dispatch to his troops at Five Forks. To their horror, the courier was captured shortly after he rode off. A second courier limped back to the camp, reporting the nearby woods to be crawling with Yankees. Pickett asked for a company of Rosser's men to serve as an escort to get back to the lines. Riding through a hail of fire, crouching and hugging the neck of his horse for cover, Pickett escaped but was too late to prevent the unfolding disaster.

Sheridan's cavalry attacked Pickett's main line in a frontal assault to pin down the Confederates while awaiting Major General Gouverneur K. Warren's V Corps to hit Pickett's left flank. The attack wavered and stalled. Warren's men did not come into position until 4 p.m. Ever the encourager, Sheridan rode his steed Winchester back and forth in front of the lines, cheering his men, "Come on, men!" he cried. "Go at 'em with a will!" Accompanied by several Scouts, Sheridan was attacking a position known as the angle where the Confederates were trying to protect their left flank. His words inspired his men to do the impossible. A bullet struck a soldier in front of the general in the jugular vein. Blood spurted everywhere. "I'm killed," the poor man cried as he fell to the ground. "You, you're not hurt a bit," argued Sheridan. "Pick up your gun, man, and move right on to the front." The "electric," irresistible charisma of his commander compelled the mortally wounded soldier to grab his weapon and march a dozen feet forward into the maelstrom "before he fell never to rise again."[20]

Sheridan charged into his floundering lines and called, "Where is my battle-flag?" Waving the standard above his head, he rallied his men, "shaking his fist, encouraging, threatening, praying, swearing, the very incarnation of battle." All around him, chaos reigned. "Bullets were humming like a swarm of bees. One pierced the battle-flag, another killed the sergeant who had carried it, another wounded Captain A. J. McGonnigle in the side, others struck two or three of the staff officers' horses."[21]

Sheridan led the crucial breakthrough, thanks to intelligence on the extent and strongpoints of the Confederate lines furnished by his Jessie Scouts. The V Corps assailed Pickett's left flank and enveloped it, capturing thousands of men as Pickett's force collapsed, and opening the path to the South Side Railroad. The railroad would soon be lost and with it all supply to Petersburg and Richmond. Five Forks would become one of the most crucial battles of the Civil War. The celebration was rapturous. "Cheers were resounding on all sides, and everybody was riotous over the victory."[22] As an additional sign of triumph, the cooks from the supply wagons kindled fires for the boilers to prepare coffee to quench the thirst of the men.

General Porter remembered Grant's first reaction to the news of Sheridan's victory at Five Forks: "As was expected, he asked his usual question: 'How many prisoners have been taken?' This was always his first inquiry when an engagement was reported. No man ever had such a fondness for taking prisoners. I think the gratification arose from the kindness of his heart, a feeling of his heart, a feeling that it was much better to win in this way than by destruction of human life."[23] Grant displayed a different sensibility from that of the August days in the valley when he ordered the execution of any of Mosby's Rangers who were captured.

Grant followed up Five Forks by ordering a massive all-corps attack on April 2 at Petersburg. Shortly after midnight, hundreds of Union guns opened up on the Confederate trenches and continued their bombardment until 4 a.m., when teams of Union pioneers hacked through obstacles followed by tens of thousands of troops. Lee immediately initiated plans to evacuate the trenches and sent a desperate telegram to Jefferson Davis, interrupting his Sunday church services and informing him that he could no longer hold Petersburg and would withdraw the army from their defenses in the city and Richmond.

On April 2, bedlam reigned in Richmond. Citizens tried to withdraw their life savings from banks. Wagons and horses choked the streets, which were filled with mobs attempting to flee the city. A train bearing the names of Confederate government departments and containing the South's treasury of gold and silver left Richmond late that evening toward Danville, the newly designated capital of the Confederate States of America. Confederates attempted to torch anything of military value. Government documents, including those of the Secret Service, were burned. "We turned to take our last look at the old city for which we fought so long and hard. . . . The whole riverfront seemed to be in flames, amid which occasional heavy explosions were heard, & the black smoke spreading & hanging over the city seemed to be full of dreadful portents,"[24] wrote one Confederate general. The city fell on April 3. Jefferson Davis nonetheless spun the loss of Richmond and found a silver lining: "We have now entered upon a new phase of a struggle, the memory of which is to endure for all ages and to shed an increasing luster upon our country. Relieved from the necessity of guarding cities and particular points, important but not vital to our defense, with an army free to move from point to point and strike in detail the detachments and garrisons of the enemy, operating on the interior of our own country, where supplies are more accessible, and where the foe will be far removed from his own base and cut off from all succor in case of reverse, nothing is now needed to render our triumph certain but the exhibition of our own unquenchable resolve. Let us but will it, and we are free; and who, in the light of the past, dare doubt your purpose in the future?"[25]

Davis called for guerrilla war, a war Mosby's Rangers and the South's irregulars had mastered.

49. THE ROAD TO APPOMATTOX

Shrouded in the darkness of April 3, multiple columns of thousands of Robert E. Lee's veteran troops, ragged and many shoeless, set out under the Virginia night sky, marching from Richmond, Petersburg, and other nearby Confederate positions. Riding among his men on his horse, Traveler, Lee had reason to be confident. After departing their trenches quickly and under the cover of darkness, the general and his veteran army had at least a twelve-hour jump on Grant and Sheridan. Every mile the men marched would be another mile from the Union supply center at City Point, straining Union supply lines, and closer to linking up with General Joseph E. Johnston's army. For years, and in countless engagements, the Confederates had outmarched their opponents.

The war had devolved into a footrace. Could Lee reach Johnston or divide his army and escape into the mountains? Throughout the Civil War, and most wars, retreating armies could flee faster than the pursuing army. The Army of Northern Virginia marched toward Amelia Court House, where supplies and precious food awaited the starving soldiers. Supply was essential and became *unum necessarium*; Lee's men only had one day's rations.

After the Battle of Five Forks, Young and his men continued to be Sheridan's eyes and ears, perilously riding deep into the columns of Lee's retreating army. On April 3, Young and six Jessie Scouts followed the army several miles from Five Forks. In the midst of the retreat, Confederate brigadier general Rufus Barringer's North Carolinians put up a desperate rear guard to allow thousands of their fellow Confederates time to escape near Namozine Church.

Sergeant McCabe yelled to Rowand, "We are going up to the next house to get something to eat. You wait here for Young." Suddenly the

Rhode Island officer appeared, and Young pointed a double-barreled shot-gun at Rowand, either in jest or mistaking him for a Confederate. Rowand then turned to his superior and said, "Why, look down at the woods!" A Confederate officer and his staff rode through the trees. Young then barked, "McCabe and the boys are in the next house getting something to eat. You go down after them and bring them back here quick and I'll go down and talk to these men."[1]

As Rowand rode to get McCabe, he came across Barringer riding a gray horse in the woods, separated from the retreating Confederate forces. "General, what command?"

"The NC Brigade. What command do you belong to?"

"Fitzhugh Lee's. We got scattered yesterday," responded Rowand.

"Any more of your men around?"

"Yes. Half a dozen."

"We better all get together," exclaimed the general.[2]

Just then Young and McCabe rode up. Rowand introduced Young as Major Grandstaff, giving him the identity of the officer who had captured Jessie Scout Thomas Cassidy at Woodstock weeks earlier. The Scouts always had a cover story and false identification.

Despite being near thousands of retreating Confederates, the ever-audacious Young cheerfully approached the dignified Southern officer with, "Good afternoon, General." The pompous Barringer responded coldly, "You have the advantage of *me*, sir."

"You're right I have, General,"[3] laughed Young as he pointed his Colt at the general's face.

Under the unwritten rules of scouting, Barringer's horse belonged to Rowand or Young. But McCabe tried to claim the horse. Rowand recalled, "McCabe and I had some words about it, and I pulled my revolver, and I told him to ride out, and we would settle it on the spot." Young intervened and declared, "The horses are Rowand's, if he wants them. All of them."[4]

Avoiding retreating Confederates, Young and his men brought their prize, the general and his staff, back to Federal lines. Angered by being duped into captivity, Barringer snapped to Colonel James W. Forsyth, Sheri-dan's chief of staff, "Scouts are spies. I would hang every one of them if I caught them." Forsyth countered, "You won't catch them during this war."[5]

That night Rowand gave the beautiful gray horse to Forsyth, and Barringer went into captivity. Barringer was the first Confederate general taken prisoner on Lee's retreat and was dined and treated respectfully by Grant's chain of command, ultimately meeting President Lincoln himself.

Young and his men were back at it the next day. This time disguised in the uniform of a Confederate colonel who had been captured, Young met another colonel from North Carolina, William H. Cheek, who informed him of Barringer's capture by the Yankees. "He, the colonel, did not exactly bewail the fate of Barringer. 'For' said he, 'I am to command; I take his place.'"

"Oh no!" Young responded. "You do not take his place; you go to the place where he is!"[6] Along with the haul came the capture of Barringer's brigade flag, which was seized by former Confederate cavalryman and now civilian Jessie Scout William Woodall.*

This would not be the last time the Scouts would capture Confederates. Young sent his Scouts to act as guides leading Confederates toward Union lines, à la Jessie Scout Jack Sterry, who had earlier tried to convince General Hood to take the wrong road to Manassas. The major's efforts proved successful; "a whole corral of Johnnies"[7] were captured whom the Scouts turned over to the advancing infantry.

The Scouts were not the only ones capturing combatants on the battlefield. General John Brown Gordon remembered his experience with two Jessie Scouts. Gordon's scout named George found two men whom he suspected were Jessie Scouts loitering near Gordon's men and had them arrested on the retreat during the night. He brought the two young men to Gordon, who personally questioned them, "finding no grounds for George's suspicions." Gordon peppered them with questions. They had plausible answers for everything and what appeared to be authentic furlough papers signed by Lee. Everything appeared in order. Gordon seemed inclined to let them go when the Confederate scout protested, "No, General, they are not all right. I saw them by the starlight counting your [men marching in] files." As the Confederates and captured Scouts marched in the darkness, they happened upon a burning log heap set by troops who passed the area earlier on the retreat. The moment the firelight touched the faces of the two young men, George shouted, "General, these are the men that captured me nearly two months ago behind General Grant's headquarters."[8]

* Woodall would receive the Medal of Honor for his actions, and the flag now resides in the North Carolina Museum of History in Raleigh.

Gordon ordered the men searched from head to toe, examining the seams of their clothing down to their boots. Initially, George found nothing. After peeling off the lining of one of the Jessie Scout's boots, he discovered an order from Grant to Major General Edward Ord instructing him to cut off Lee's retreat to Appomattox. Once the damning papers were found, the Scouts admitted they had captured George. "Well, you know your fate. Under the laws of war, you have forfeited your lives wearing this uniform, and I shall have you shot at sunrise tomorrow morning," Gordon stated. The Scouts, no more than twenty years of age, said with perfect composure, "General, we understand it all. We knew when we entered this kind of service and put on these uniforms, that we should be executed if we were captured. You have the right to have us shot; but the war can't last much longer, and it would do you no good to have us killed."[9] Gordon sent a message to Lee informing him of the capture of the Jessie Scouts and requested that their lives be spared. Lee concurred, and the captured Federals made the arduous retreat with Gordon and his men.

In the race south, Sheridan beat Lee to the punch thanks to information provided by his Scouts. "[Young] kept me constantly informed of the movements of the enemy and brought in prisoners from brigadier-generals down. The information gained through him was invaluable,"[10] wrote Sheridan. Riding with the Jessie Scouts and an escort of 200 of the 1st US Cavalry, the Union general reached the crossroads town of Jettersville, Virginia, before the Union infantry of V Corps and Lee's army. Realizing the importance of the vital crossroads, Little Phil quickly positioned his small force to hold the crossroads until the bulk of his forces arrived. Then fate interceded. Sheridan's men captured a Confederate scout riding a mule toward Burkeville. Hidden in his boot was a telegram: "The army is at Amelia Court House, short of provisions, Send 300,000 rations quickly to Burkeville Junction."[11]

Sheridan hoped to use the contents of the captured note to his advantage. "My troops were hard up for rations, for in the pursuit we could not wait for our trains, so I concluded to secure, if possible, these provisions intended for Lee. To this end, I directed Young to send four of his best scouts to Burkeville Junction. There they were to separate, two taking the railroad toward Lynchburg and two toward Danville, and as soon as a telegraph station was reached the telegram was to be transmitted as it had been written, and the provisions hurried forward."[12] Sheridan would then seize the precious food for his army and resume the pursuit of Lee. To that end, Joe McCabe and Jim White rode toward Lynchburg and two other Scouts toward Danville to deliver Lee's message to a telegraph operator and find the supply trains.

When Lee's famished and exhausted men arrived at Amelia Court House on the morning of April 4 and opened the supply train's boxcars, they contained scores of loaded caissons, hundreds of crates of ammunition, and boxes of worthless artillery harnesses, but no food. One theory holds the mistake stemmed from an administrative mix-up; another posits that Young's Scouts redirected the trains.[13] The source of the error remains a mystery to this day. Nevertheless, the lack of supplies, crucial as any in war, threatened to derail the Army of Northern Virginia's retreat and affect the course of the conflict. Starving men were expected to march for their lives and fight. Lee relayed desperate orders to send provisions and ordered his men to forage the countryside. Precious time was lost. Then Lee ordered his men to march toward Jettersville, only for his advance elements to find that Sheridan had beaten him there. Rather than fight Sheridan, he fatefully decided to move in another direction—west toward Farmville and the promise of rations for his famished army.

Sheridan also targeted Lee's horse-drawn supply wagons. On the night of April 4, Sheridan sent all his available Scouts to hunt for them. At Clemmens Bridge, the Scouts found a long line of wagons camped and ready to roll at daylight for Amelia Court House, where Lee's army bivouacked. Sheridan ordered all the Jessie Scouts and a division of cavalry to hit the wagons. With the Scouts leading the vanguard, they found the wagon train at Painesville Crossroads between Clemmens Bridge and Amelia Court House. Charging across an open field, James Campbell rode alongside wagons blazing away with his Colts. He captured a large battle flag. Battling Confederates, he seized another flag.

During the clash, twenty-two-year-old Jessie Scout Corporal William John Brewer of Company C, 2nd New York Cavalry, "captured an engineer flag."[14] Brewer enlisted at the beginning of the war and had survived a gunshot wound to the left side during the Kilpatrick-Dahlgren Raid, as Kilpatrick's orderly. According to Rowand, the Federals took "five pieces of artillery, two hundred wagons, and a large number of prisoners." After the sharp skirmish, Rowand laughingly turned to Campbell and said, "There goes your furlough now." Campbell laconically responded, "I've got no time for a furlough now."[15] Soon afterward, Sheridan tapped Campbell for a crucial mission.

Finding that Sheridan had blocked the roads at Jettersville, Lee pushed his troops westward to the limits of human endurance to avoid Union infantry and Sheridan's cavalry. The Scouts alerted Sheridan to Lee's change of direction, and he ordered troops to block the path.

General George Meade, commander of the Army of the Potomac, ill with indigestion and riding in a wagon, disagreed and believed Lee to still be at Amelia Court House, so he planned to attack the empty town the next morning. The Jessie Scouts furnished Sheridan with superior, real-time intelligence that Lee's troops were on the move to Farmville. Frustrated, Sheridan sent James Campbell to find Grant with a note: "I wish you were here yourself. I feel confident of capturing the Army of Northern Virginia if we exert ourselves, I see no escape for Lee."[16] In such a fluid battlespace, communication between the various elements of Grant's army and the Jessie Scouts played a vital and indispensable role; at great peril, they could move in and out of the retreating Confederate forces.

Suddenly, in that role a horseman in full Confederate uniform appeared at Grant's headquarters and caused a commotion. Scores of weapons were pointed at the rider as anxious Federals intercepted him. However, Grant's staff officer, Brigadier General Horace Porter, recognized a familiar face. "How do you do, Campbell?" he exclaimed, waving his men off and explaining he was "all right and was one of our own people."[17]

Grant immediately recognized Campbell, and the Scout pulled out of his mouth a gooey wad of chewing tobacco, broke it in half, and teased out of the mass a tiny ball of tinfoil. Campbell unfurled Sheridan's dispatch, then Grant read it and told the men he would join Sheridan at once, ordering Campbell to lead the way. The Jessie Scout had just delivered a crucial piece of tactical intelligence—and Grant acted on it.

Ditching his pony, named Jefferson Davis, Grant called up his big black bay horse, Cincinnati, and away they went with a handful of staff and fourteen cavalrymen into enemy territory. Riding along dark, unsecured roads through pockets of retreating Rebels, Grant took the great risk of capture or death, which seemed worth the cost considering the real chance of Lee's escape. Campbell led the cavalcade through sixteen miles of darkness to Sheridan. These actions, among others, including saving Young at

Woodstock months earlier, in time earned the Jessie Scout the Medal of Honor for extraordinary heroism.[18]

For the past several days, Sheridan's cavalry had doggedly pursued the Army of Northern Virginia, racing alongside it and hitting vulnerable retreating Rebel units. At Jettersville, Grant countermanded Meade's orders and made the decision that instead of shadowing the Confederates, Sheridan would get ahead of them to cut off their routes of escape and means of supply. Sheridan's current orders from Meade would have allowed Lee to escape. Sheridan's cavalry headed toward Deatonsville and what would become known as the Battle of Little Sailor's Creek. Sheridan planned to have a corps of infantry bring up the rear in a pincer movement intended to envelop the Army of Northern Virginia.

After bringing Grant to Sheridan, James Campbell turned in for a few hours of much-needed sleep. He slept next to Rowand, and during the night as the men slumbered, someone stole Campbell's flags and Rowand's revolvers. Finding another set of Colts, the Scouts saddled up. "Sheridan not only had the Johnnies on the jump but he had his scouts on the jump night and day."[19]

Hungry, tired, and angry, the surly Confederates were unbowed. One salty Yale-educated Southern officer recalled the mood: "Over sir? Over? Why sir, it's just begun. We are now where a good many of us have for a good while longed to be: Richmond gone, nothing to take care of, foot loose and thank God, out of those miserable lines! . . . Let them come."[20]

Come the Federals did, on April 6, at three fields of battle that would collectively become known as Little Sailor's Creek.[21] Using information from the Jessie Scouts, Sheridan effectively cut off several elements of Lee's army near the creek. While the Union infantry 2nd and VI Corps approached from the east, the infantry attacked John Brown Gordon's division as their supply trains slowly crossed bridges near the creek. The fighting was desperate and hand to hand. "By the time we had well settled into our old position we were attacked simultaneously, front and rear, by overwhelming numbers, and quicker than I can tell it the battle degenerated into a butchery and a confused melee of brutal personal conflicts. I saw numbers of men kill each other with bayonets and the butts of muskets, and even bite each other's throats and ears and noses, rolling on the ground like wild beasts,"[22] recalled one Confederate combatant. Lines crumbled. Thousands of Confederates had been killed or captured thus far. Some units broke and fled.

From his saddle, watching the carnage unfold, Lee shouted, "My God! Has the army been dissolved?"[23]

One of his officers, William Mahone, turned to him and said, "No general, here are troops ready to do their duty."[24]

Grabbing a battle flag, Lee rode out to rally his faltering men. Earlier, a handful of flag bearers had already fallen carrying the same standard. The flag flapped in the wind, bathing the general in the stars and bars as he rode toward his men.

There was immediately silence among the nearby men.

"It's General Lee."[25]

This was followed by a bellowing cry, "Where's the man who won't follow Uncle Robert!"[26] The men rallied, saving a portion of the Army of Northern Virginia and allowing it to escape after sustaining devasting losses. The Confederate defeat would become immortalized as Black Thursday.

Sheridan sensed blood and moved in for the kill, sending a Scout with a dispatch to Grant: "If the thing is pressed I think Lee will surrender." Grant passed on the message to Lincoln, who laconically responded, "Let the thing be pressed."[27]

Lee's army raced toward Farmville, a town that rested astride the swollen Appomattox River. Behind the mighty river, Lee's tattered army hoped to regroup and inhale rations that awaited the ravished troops. High Bridge spanned the river and led into the town and potential freedom. A wonder of engineering, with train tracks above and a wagon bridge below, the steel-and-wood trestle rose 126 feet over the Appomattox and spanned half a mile of the valley. The crucial choke point became an objective of both armies. On April 6, the Federals dispatched three companies of the 4th Massachusetts Cavalry under the command of Colonel Francis Washburn, a former officer with the California Battalion, along with two regiments of infantry, to torch the structure before the Confederates could cross it. To squash the threat, General Longstreet sent Major General Thomas Rosser and his cavalry division. Scouts in the area warned Washburn that

Rosser was on the way to intercept them. As Washburn approached the structure, strong earthen redoubts manned by Confederates blocked the entrance to the bridge. The cavalry officer soon heard gunfire behind him and found his infantry under attack from Rosser's Division. McCausland's and Thomas T. Munford's troopers dismounted and assailed the Federal infantrymen. Vastly outnumbered, Washburn nonetheless ordered his eighty horsemen to suicidally charge the Confederates. Cavalrymen such as mustang lieutenant Allen F. Belcher and others found themselves thrust into mortal hand-to-hand combat. Belcher received a severe saber slash across his face. A Confederate blasted Washburn in the mouth and hacked his skull with a sword.[28] The infantry fell back for a final stand. But the Confederates annihilated the force, seizing nearly 800 prisoners, six battle flags, and a brass band of musicians.

Rosser saved the bridge—for the time being—as retreating Confederate troops streamed across all day and night. Engineers assigned to the bridge's destruction did not receive orders until the last minute to destroy it. Confederate pioneers felled portions of the mighty railroad bridge but fired the wagon bridge too late, and men of the 19th Maine Infantry charged into a hail of gunfire and seized the flaming wagon bridge below the railroad trestle. Using water from canteens, tarps from tents, and anything they could get their hands on, the Federals extinguished the flames. The capture of the wagon bridge below the High Bridge would prove crucial and one of the most important small-unit actions of the Appomattox Campaign. With the bridge in Union hands, nothing stopped the Federal army from pursuing Lee's ragged, hungry, and diminished force. Both Lee and Sheridan raced for the elusive supply trains from Lynchburg.

General George Crook, recently exchanged for a Confederate prisoner, now commanded one of Sheridan's divisions, and he pounced on the retreating Confederate wagon trains. An intense battle led to the capture of one of Sheridan's cavalry commanders and nearly the destruction of one of the regiments, but with the Federals blocking the way to Danville, Lee's beleaguered army marched toward Lynchburg. At Prospect Station, Crook's and Sheridan's other divisions united. Jessie Scout James White[29] galloped up to Sheridan with dramatic news: McCabe and White had found Lee's supply trains—four trains, loaded with supplies for Lee's starving army. With the original dispatch orders in hand, the Jessie Scouts, dressed as Confederates, persuaded the conductors to move the trains east of Appomattox Station, where they could be seized. Sheridan's plan a couple of days earlier of sending two teams of Jessie Scouts down the tracks was about to contribute to ending the war. Sheridan immediately dispatched the priceless intelligence about the trains' location, and cavalry under Custer's command seized the trains and Lee's best hope of supplying his starving army.

The advancing Federals pushed Lee's army into an area that resembled a jug turned on its side: a narrow seven-mile corridor flanked by the Appomattox and James Rivers. Escape for Lee's entire army became more difficult with each hour that passed as more Federal troops arrived near the Confederates. Thanks to the Jessie Scouts' accurate intelligence, Sheridan positioned his men as the cork on the top of the jug to block Lee's path to the supply trains and Lynchburg. Faced with envelopment, Lee tasked General John Brown Gordon with an attack to break through Sheridan's position.

On Palm Sunday, April 9, a fog lingered over the fields as General Gordon assembled his men. Stretching almost a mile, Gordon's infantry and Fitzhugh Lee's cavalry attacked Sheridan's troopers, who fought from behind makeshift barricades. Gordon's attack was Lee's last hope for escape with his army intact: escape to Lynchburg or even the mountains that lay beyond. Most urgently the attack hoped to reach Lee's supply trains, though Lee couldn't have known they were already captured by Custer's cavalry. The Confederates bore down on the Federals, who peppered them with their seven-shot Spencers and other weapons. For two hours, the two sides clashed, but Gordon's men failed to break through. Sheridan appeared at the front and, satisfied with his men's positions, rode off without saying a word. But his presence alone inspired, "reinforcing the command equal to its own numbers, by the confidence the men received in him,"[30] recalled one trooper.

Frustrated by the stalwart defense, the Confederates tried to flank the center, which was held by a brigade of Sheridan's cavalry. Unable to hold against the superior numbers of enemy infantry, the troopers began to lose the field to the Confederates. Suddenly, a voice cried out, "Keep up your courage, boys; the infantry is coming right along—in two columns—black and white—side by side—a regular checkerboard."[31] Black Americans from the US Colored Troops attached to the XXIV Corps had marched all night and moved into position to check the Confederates. "How refreshing the sight of their black countenances at this time. At the spectacle, the rebel host staggered back, and their whole line wavered as if each man was terror-struck,"[32] recalled one joyous cavalryman.

A courier from Gordon brought a message: "Tell General Lee I have fought my corps to a frazzle, and I fear I can do nothing unless I am heavily supported by Longstreet's corps."[33]

A day earlier, on April 8, Grant had sent Lee a letter appealing to the Southern commander's honor to avoid further bloodshed. Lee and his officers discussed the army's options to surrender or go down fighting. Twenty-nine-year-old brigadier general Edward Porter Alexander urged Lee to disperse the army and conduct guerrilla warfare as Jefferson Davis had directed. Lee listened to Alexander's impassioned pleas. "If there is any hope for the Confederacy it is in *delay*. For if the Army of Northern Virginia surrenders every other will surrender as fast as the news reaches it. For it is the morale of this army which has supported the whole of the Confederacy."[34]

When Lee asked Alexander how many would escape, he responded, "Two-thirds of us, I think would get away. We would scatter like rabbits and partridges in the woods, and they could not scatter to catch us."[35]

Lee himself had once boasted that if the army escaped to the Blue Ridge Mountains, he could fight for twenty years. Strategically, Davis' plan for guerrilla war had merit. The stakes, as Lee considered his options near Appomattox, were enormous.

The twentieth and twenty-first centuries are replete with successful insurgencies that prevailed against occupying empires and massive armies—Afghanistan, China, the Middle East, and Vietnam, to name a few. Some conflicts shifted from irregular to conventional war. Ultimately, many insurgencies wore down the occupier. A guerrilla war in the South could have been one of the bloodiest in history and taken years to resolve. The North would have had to occupy a land mass larger than western Europe filled with mountains, swamps, and forests ideal for insurgent warfare and a population friendly to guerrillas but hostile to the occupiers. Southerners who previously had their homes burned, their industry ravaged, and hundreds of thousands of their sons slain had a rabid hatred for the North.

By 1865, despite the North's massive armies, they only occupied a small portion of the South. In any potential occupation of the South, the Federals would have tried to control the major cities while the countryside would have been hostile. There would not have been enough Union troops to hold both. Patrols leaving the cities would have been subject to attack. Smaller outposts needed to protect the population that had to be won over could potentially have been overwhelmed by Confederate forces. The grinding bloodbath would have taken years to resolve, all the bigger a challenge considering the war-weariness in the North, which could enflame the "fire in the rear" from the Copperhead movement. Arguably, paramilitary movements such as the Ku Klux Klan and Red Shirt movement could have achieved political aims and control throughout the South using terror, intimidation, and violence, as they ultimately did during the Jim Crow era. In 1865, the war could have devolved into several modes of a kinetic insurgency.

One version resembled the landscape of war-torn Missouri. Here, in the caldron that birthed the Jessie Scouts, neighbor fought against neighbor in what was known as "the war of 10,000 nasty little incidents." Determining friend from foe became difficult, sparking a cycle of violence, revenge killings, and house burnings. As in the simmering clannish feuds that existed in the eastern portion of West Virginia and gave birth to Blazer's Scouts, the Union would have needed to raise scores of similar counterinsurgency units. After four years of bloody combat, the contest seemed a forever war with no sense of closure.

Alternatively, the insurgency could also have been fought by Mosby-style unconventional warfare. The highly disciplined Confederate units could have attacked supply lines and roving patrols in the countryside and potentially been used to intimidate Union sympathizers. Multiple cells of hundreds of men spread out across the South could tie down tens of thousands, as Mosby had demonstrated: a force multiplier many times their number.

The North would not have been safe either, with industry subject to sabotage. Cities were vulnerable to arson, such as in the attempt on New York in 1864 by Confederate operatives. A divided United States was also very much in the interest of world powers. And Mexico, with its large foreign army of French troops under the control of Maximilian I, could have acted as a potential sanctuary for guerrilla fighters and a source of supply.

After Gordon's failed attempt to break through Sheridan's lines, Lee listened intently to his subordinates. "Country be damned! There is no country, general, for a year or more. You are the country to these men. They have fought for you,"[36] snapped former Virginia governor Henry Wise. Grant also recognized Lee's enormous power to determine the South's path; hence his determination to capture or destroy Lee's Army of Northern Virginia. Lee, instead, saw a future drenched in blood. Considering the possibility of ongoing guerrilla action, he raised the paramount issue of supply: "The men would be without rations and under no control of officers. . . . They would be compelled to rob and steal to live. They would become . . . bands of marauders."[37]

General Edward Porter Alexander appealed to Lee to continue the struggle. Known for priding himself on following the civilian chain of command, Lee would take the extraordinary step of shattering it. Lee responded to Alexander, "As Christian men, General Alexander, you and I have no right to think for one moment of our personal feelings or affairs. We must consider only the effect our action will have upon our country at large." Generally never a proponent of guerrilla warfare because it typically got dirty and undisciplined, Lee proclaimed, "And as for myself, you young fellows might go bushwhacking, but the only dignified course for me would be to go to General Grant and surrender myself and take the consequences of my acts. . . . I would rather die a thousand deaths."[38] "How easily I could get rid of all of this and be at rest. I have only to ride along the lines and all will be over." Tears flowed from his generals' eyes as Lee profoundly ended the discussion with a deep sigh: "But it is our duty to live. What will become of the women and children of the South, if we are not here to protect them."[39]

Refusing to act on Jefferson Davis' orders, one man, through his personal agency, would change history. Lee sent out bearers with white flags requesting a ceasefire and a meeting with Grant.

Lee and Grant met at the McLean House in the early afternoon of April 9. In 1861, the owner, Wilmer McLean, ironically had a home located in the heart of the Manassas Battlefield but moved to Appomattox to avoid the war. During the surrender negotiations, Lee brought up the issue of supplies for his starving men: "[My men] have been living for the last few days principally upon parched corn, and we are badly in need of rations and forage. I telegraphed to Lynchburg, directing several train loads of rations to be sent on rails from there, and when they arrive, I should be glad to have the present wants of my men supplied from them."[40]

"All eyes turned to Sheridan,"[41] whose Jessie Scouts had located and detained the all-important supply trains, impairing the ability of the Army of Northern Virginia to continue the fight in a conventional or unconventional manner. Nothing about Lee's retreat or surrender was preordained, and Sheridan's Jessie Scouts played a crucial* role in bringing it to a conclusion.

Grant made rations available to Lee's men. The mark of a true statesman, his terms at Appomattox were generous and farsighted. Instead of treating the Confederates like traitors and sending them into prisoner-of-war pens, he offered parole, officers could retain their swords and sidearms, and the men could keep their horses. Some would likely fight on, but Grant saw that as a risk he was willing to take. Most men went home. Pettiness and hatred put aside, the Confederates were welcomed back into the Union with honor. The reunification of America started at Appomattox.

Grant ordered a formal surrender ceremony: a grand review of the stacking of arms and relinquishing of the Confederate colors. Gordon would return the two young Jessie Scouts he had captured to Sheridan before leading the parade of Confederate divisions on the outskirts of the rolling farmland of Appomattox. He led some 28,000 members of Lee's army in a simple yet profound seven-hour ceremony. Grant placed the hero of Little Round Top at Gettysburg and Medal of Honor recipient Brigadier General Joshua Lawrence Chamberlain in charge of the ceremony. Chamberlain later described their former foes as they marched before his Federal troops: "In proud humiliation stood the embodiment of manhood . . . thin, worn, and

---

* Sheridan would later highlight Young: "I desire to make special mention of the valuable services of Major H. H. Young, Second Rhode Island Infantry, chief of my scouts, during the cavalry expedition from Winchester, Va., to the James River. His personal gallantry and numerous conflicts with the enemy won the admiration of the whole command. . . . I earnestly request that he be made a lieutenant-colonel by brevet." OR, Vol. XLVI, Pt. I, Chap. LVIII, 1113.

famished, but erect, and with eyes looking level into ours, waking memories that bound us together as no other bond."[42]

Chamberlain spontaneously ordered "carry arms" to the Union soldiers as a sign of deep respect for their vanquished foes marching before them. Gordon, "with heavy spirit," faced Chamberlain and wheeled his horse. The "rider made one motion, the horse's head swung down with a graceful bow, and General Gordon dropped his sword point to his toe in salutation,"[43] recalled the Maine officer.

Stillness and silence pervaded the field. "Honor answering honor,"[44] wrote Chamberlain.*

But the war was not over. Even after Lee surrendered, Confederate armies, consisting of more than 175,000 men under multiple commands, continued to fight throughout the Confederacy. For weeks, Davis' rickety train, holding the government of the Confederacy, rolled down the tracks from one temporary capital to another. Other elements of the Confederacy answered President Davis' call for unconventional warfare with special operations that still had the potential to change the course of history.

---

* Both Chamberlain and Gordon would fulfill their duty to live after the war. Gordon was elected US Democratic senator of Georgia and became the alleged titular leader of Georgia's Ku Klux Klan, the living embodiment of the so-called Lost Cause narrative, and Chamberlain served as governor of Maine.

50. Those Infernal Machines: Aimed at the White House

Days before Lee's surrender, clouds of black smoke billowed, stoked by a tempest of cinders that swept the streets of Richmond from burning Confederate warehouses. Shells stored inside the buildings exploded, causing the walls to collapse as Brigadier General Edward Ripley and his Union troops rode through the conflagration consuming the city. "Forward!" Ripley urged his men onward "into a sea of fire, or, rather, the crater of an active volcano."[1]

Ripley was one of the Union officers responsible for securing Richmond as the Confederates retreated and torched military supplies in their capital. Within days, President Lincoln personally visited and incredulously walked and rode through the streets of Richmond. Confederate private William H. Snyder had seen "with the greatest anxiety President Lincoln expose himself to a fearful risk of walking so carelessly unattended and unprotected through the streets filled with people whose hearts in their defeat were bitter, and it would be but human nature for someone to take the opportunity to revenge the lost cause on the person of the man who represented the triumphant cause of the Union."[2] Convinced the war was lost, Snyder felt that any additional lives taken were wanton murder, and he begged to see Ripley at his headquarters in the burned-out city. Years later, the Union brigadier general described Private Snyder's frantic pleas and warning that Lincoln was in grave danger: "A party had just been dispatched from Raines's [sic] torpedo bureau on a secret mission, which vaguely he understood was aimed at the head of the Yankee government, and he wished to put Mr. Lincoln on his guard and have impressed upon him that just at this moment he believed him to be in great danger of violence and he should take greater care of himself. He should give no names or facts, as the work of his department was secret [using proper tradecraft, the Torpedo Bureau compartmentalized its missions], and no man knew what his comrade was sent to do, that the President of the United States was in great danger."[3]

Snyder worked for General Gabriel J. Rains' Confederate Secret Service Torpedo Bureau. Knowing he was one of Rains' operatives, Ripley understood the gravity of the Confederate's story and had the operative swear under oath and recorded his deposition. Next, he asked for an audience with President Lincoln himself, who had traveled by gunboat from Washington to Richmond to witness the fall of the Southern capital. Ripley entered Admiral Porter's boat; the president sat on a long-cushioned sofa as young Tad Lincoln ran up and down the length of the couch and climbed behind his father. As Ripley later recounted, the president was "so worn, emaciated, and pallid, that he looked more like a disembodied spirit than the successful leader of a great nation in its hour of supreme triumph."[4]

"As I progressed in the explanation of my errand, Mr. Lincoln let his hands supporting his chin and clasping either cheek in an expression of the most heart-breaking weariness, his great melancholy eyes filling the cabin with the mournful light they emitted."[5]

Ripley read aloud to Lincoln Snyder's deposition and "urged upon him the reasonableness of the warning, the good faith and apparent integrity of the man." The Confederate had been waiting in a nearby room, and the Union officer begged the president to bring him in and talk to him. Lincoln slowly lifted his head and "cast upon me that face above all human faces that of a man of sorrow and acquainted with grief"[6] and said,

"No, General Ripley, it is impossible for me to adopt and follow your suggestions. I deeply appreciate the feeling which has led you to urge them on me, but I must go on as I have begun in the course marked out for me, for I cannot bring myself to believe that any human being lives who would do me any harm."[7]

Lincoln's nobility, gentle naïveté, and sense of fatefulness were on display. Ripley portentously recalled, "Snyder so honestly and prophetically warned him. I have so often thought of the web of fate I held in my important hands that morning . . . if I had been able to persuade the great President to let his friends protect him."[8]

On April 2, three days before that meeting with the president, as Richmond's defenses crumbled, one of Rains' finest operatives and an explosives expert, Frank Harney, took a train to Gordonsville. Earlier, Judah Benjamin, Confederate secretary of state, had withdrawn $1,500 in gold using the Secret Service citation for covert action. Jefferson Davis approved the draft. Since Harney was the Confederacy's agent in Richmond at the time, the money likely went to fund his operation. While it is impossible to prove Jefferson Davis' direct involvement in the assassination, "this is probably as close to the 'smoking gun' as one will ever get," according to historian and intelligence officer Brigadier General William Tidwell, who spent years tediously unearthing and analyzing the Secret Services' finances.[9] Harney carried deadly explosives, detonators, and fuses stowed in his saddlebags and rode north to Mosby's Rangers and, according to Snyder, toward Lincoln and the White House.

As word of Richmond's fall reached Mosby's Confederacy, a pall of "gloom and despondency" hovered over the men. On April 5, Mosby called a meeting at North Fork Church that drew a full attendance of Rangers. In a conversation with Ranger J. Marshall Crawford and another man, Mosby declared, "There is nothing else for me to do but to fight on." Hardcore till the end, the men responded they "would stand by him."[10]

In those final days of the war, Mosby formed a new unit, Company H, "and organized it especially for" a new officer, renowned as a scout, who had recently joined the command: George Baylor. "The foe in the Valley dreaded him as much as they did our own Chieftain, Mosby,"[11] remarked one of the men. Rangers lined up and faced Mosby. Baylor thought to himself, why "strangers select me their captain was an enigma my juvenile brain could not solve."[12] But this is how Mosby always ran "elections," and his command; he was in charge, down to the smallest details.

"Men, I nominate George Baylor, of Jefferson County, captain of this company. . . . All in favor of Baylor as captain, say aye."[13]

"[A] feeble response along the line, and much apprehension," Baylor recalled.

"George Baylor is unanimously chosen captain," Mosby announced. With the official birth of the new company, Mosby "ordered me to take it on a scout to Jefferson and baptize it" and "go out, see what I can do,"[14] recalled Baylor.

Company H had some experienced men, veteran Rangers, but mostly[15] new faces from those recently recruited into the command filled its ranks. "Fall out!" Acting according to Mosby tradition, Baylor dismissed the men for the night and ordered them to re-form in the morning at Snickersville. After they assembled on the morning of April 6, Baylor learned the Union's Loudoun Rangers camped only miles away—an opportunity to vanquish a local rival that had been a thorn in the side of Mosby's Rangers for months. Crossing the Shenandoah, Company H bore down on their prey. The fifty men first had to pass through pickets of an infantry regiment. Wearing blue overcoats and likely a sprinkling of Union blue uniforms (even though Baylor later claimed that his men in the front ranks, including himself, wore butternut or gray), they approached the Union lines.

A picket politely but nervously saluted—"Present arms."[16]

In perfect order, Baylor's fifty men passed the pickets and quietly approached the Loudoun Ranger camp's neat line of tents and horses tied up. The Unionists were engaged in various diversions and did not notice Company H until the Rangers were on top of them. Baylor reached fifty yards from the camp, outnumbered at least two to one, and ordered a charge: "We were playing a bold game, and the bold game generally wins in war as well as in cards."[17] Baylor and his men routed more than one hundred Unionists, taking sixty-five Loudoun Rangers prisoner, killing two and wounding four, taking their horses, equipment, and weapons. The raid was the final nail in the coffin for one of Mosby's nemeses. When Union general Winfield Scott Hancock received word of their demise, he heartily laughed, "Well, that is the last of Loudoun Rangers."[18]

Baylor rode to Upperville with the prisoners and was greeted by some of Mosby's men who had returned from the Northern Neck. Mosby assigned a new mission, and Frank Harney from the Torpedo Bureau was attached to the force. The one hundred men of Companies D and H "were ordered on a scout to Fairfax County,"[19] ostensibly on a mission: "to capture a train hauling wood," according to Ranger James Williamson."[20] Clearly, sending two companies of Rangers to capture a train carrying wood had zero strategic or tactical value on its face, so it is reasonable to assume the train was a cover story. The likely real mission: to create a distraction and infiltrate Harney through Union lines and deliver him into the hands of members of the Confederate Secret Service in Washington, DC. At the time, gunpowder was easy to obtain and security so lax at the White House that just about anyone could get into or out of the residence. Operatives could drive a wagon loaded with explosives up to the White House, or Harney could detonate the hidden explosives with a horological torpedo, or timebomb. Orders were compartmentalized and on a need-to-know basis, and Baylor may have had no idea of the true nature of the mission. Men under Mosby's command obeyed orders and did not question them or faced removal from command.

From Upperville, on April 8 the men rode to Salem, where the column of Rangers stopped and spent the night at Waveland, a plantation and safe house that welcomed Mosby and his men throughout the war. "Rest and refreshment were found by me at the hospitable mansion where pleasure and enjoyment could always be found with the hosts of young company usually found there," recalled Baylor. Mosby had placed his seasoned commander Captain Alfred Glasscock in command of the two companies. Still, when the Rangers assembled the next morning, to Baylor's surprise he received a note "that he [Glasscock] would be unable to accompany us on account of his wedding." Under Baylor's command, the two companies set out to Burke Station. The young officer recalled, "Having acquainted myself with the destination of our expedition and our guides, I moved off across Bull Run Mountains, not without some misgivings."[21]

The skies turned ominous, and rain came down in torrents. In the middle of the night, "one of our officers, familiar with the country and the people, informed me that a house full of young ladies was close by, and proposed that I should go with him, find shelter, and a pleasant visit." Dry shelter and women—"such a tempting solicitation could not be resisted,"[22] recalled Baylor.

Unbeknownst to Baylor, many of the Rangers had the same idea: "On reaching the house, I found quite a lot of our men had preceded me, and were in possession of the premises and the ladies, having a hilarious time." Baylor became suspicious of the party's hosts and ordered his men back to where they camped not far from Arundel's Tavern (also known as Brimstone Hill).[23] Sometime that night, Charley Dear, one of Mosby's most hardened and seasoned warriors, made out his will[24]—a seemingly odd thing to do with the possibility of the end of the war in sight. Baylor spent the "night in suspense and trepidation."[25]

At daybreak on April 10, the Rangers mounted up and started toward Burke Station. The commander of the 8th Illinois Cavalry, acting on information from "a source [he] considered reliable"[26] (likely the women in the house), took his troopers and "came upon the trail of the enemy and followed [Baylor's men] towards Burke's Station, in the neighborhood of which some shots were exchanged . . . the rebels upon being discovered beat back into the woods." At this point,[27] Baylor rode back toward Arundel's Tavern. After the head of his column passed the tavern, the 8th ambushed the two Ranger companies. To stave off defeat, two Rangers organized thirty of their fellow Rangers and charged into the Illinois men with their Colts blazing. The clash of horses and pistols initially checked the Union attack.

Baylor continued to try to rally his men—"a bold dash would save us"—as the Rangers had done in a myriad of clashes, but the "line began to waver and break, retreat was inevitable,"[28] he later recalled.

The Rangers fled toward the ford crossing the Occoquan River at Wolf Run Shoals. One Ranger dug the spurs deeply into his horse. He tried to outrun the Yankee cavalry, blindly firing over his shoulder, "recklessly but harmlessly at close intervals, till both were empty and [he] was almost dead with exhaustion."[29]

Veteran Ranger Charley Dear vainly threw himself in the melee to save his comrade, but his mount threw him into a ravine, and the horse soon followed its rider. Baylor did not fare much better as gunfire hit his horse in the nostril and foreleg, nearly unhorsing the commander of Company H.

Another Ranger tried to escape on foot as his horse was shot out from under him. Two Rangers rode up on each side of him and, "taking hold of wrists, galloped along with him until he overtook a riderless horse which he mounted, but was captured shortly afterward."[30]

The 8th Illinois also captured Frank Harney from the Torpedo Bureau on April 10. The group was headed toward Washington, DC, and according to Private Snyder, the White House. The 8th Illinois Cavalry's after-action report records among the captives "Thomas H. Harvey [Harney], Engineer Bureau, Lieutenant, Company F, 6th Missouri—brought ordnance to Colonel Mosby."[31] Harney remained silent during interrogation about the operation and the mission and was not captured with detonators or ordnance. He planned to obtain powder in Washington, where it was plentiful. The Confederate explosives expert would be released from Federal captivity at Elmira Prison months later, and after his release, he was never heard from or seen again. Years would pass before the true nature of Harney's mission would surface.

Harney's capture lent credence to his mission. Lincoln assassination coconspirator George Atzerodt later stated that John Wilkes Booth had met "a party in N. York who would get the prest [Lincoln] certain. They were going to mine the end of the pres. House near the War Depart. They knew an entrance to accomplish it through."[32] Years after the event, Ranger J. Marshall Crawford made an indirect reference to the operation, writing in his book, "Baylor lost two men killed and five or six captured, including Lieutenant Harney, whose loss was irretrievable."[33] Mosby denied any involvement in a Lincoln conspiracy. Any acknowledgment, if he were involved, would have been a death sentence to his postwar career. The Rangers most likely would have never known the full details of the mission due to the compartmentalization of the information. But the 8th Illinois Cavalry may have unwittingly stopped an attempt on the president's life. Unaware of Lee's surrender at Appomattox, Mosby and his Rangers had their last action with the 8th Illinois. Ranger John Munson later wrote, "I sometimes feel sure that, if we had known it was to be the last fight of our career, every man of us would have died rather than suffer the defeat that followed."[34] Decades would pass before the story of the mission surfaced.

However, in April 1865, Private Snyder's warning remained unheeded: "President of the United States was in great danger." Through their network, Booth may have learned of Harney's capture, which may have triggered Booth and the other conspirators to put the assassination in action and decapitate the Federal government.[35]

On April 11, the day after Harney's capture, Booth and Lewis Powell were in attendance when Lincoln spoke from the balcony of the Executive Mansion, outlining reconstruction plans. Booth implored Powell to shoot Lincoln dead with his revolver. Powell refused, and Booth replied, "That is the last speech he will ever make."[36]

51. POWELL'S MISSION

On April 14, Lewis Powell lurked in the shadows outside the "Clubhouse," the nickname Washington insiders gave Secretary of State William H. Seward's brick mansion. The Secret Service operative surveilled the home while Seward was in bed recovering from a recent carriage accident. Powell waited for an opportunity to strike and assassinate the cabinet member, which was part of an operation simultaneously targeting three men that night. Powell targeted Seward, Booth planned to assassinate President Lincoln, and George Atzerodt would strike Vice President Andrew Johnson.

The conspirators had concocted a cunning plan to kill Seward. Powell had an empty box wrapped in butcher paper that looked like a medicine delivery from Seward's doctor. David Herold, a fellow conspirator and former pharmacist's assistant, made medicine deliveries to patients and probably schooled Powell on what to say. After 10 p.m. Powell knocked on the door. Nineteen-year-old African American servant William Bell answered. Powell said he was delivering medicine for the secretary and insisted on seeing Seward in person to direct him how to take it. As Bell refused, Powell continued slowly walking up the stairs, treading heavily on each stair, and repeating the mantra "I must go up."[1]

At the top of the stairs, Frederick, Seward's oldest son, again blocked Powell. "You cannot see him," Frederick reiterated, and when the Ranger persisted, Frederick said, "If you cannot leave your message with me, you cannot leave it at all." Powell continued to insist, then finally said, "Well, if I cannot see him—" and feigned leaving but suddenly turned around and pointed his pistol at the young man. The Whitney revolver misfired, and Powell raised the pistol and repeatedly clubbed Frederick Seward over the head, breaking the weapon's ramrod, which jammed the Whitney's cylinder, making it inoperable. In the meantime, Bell ran outside the house yelling, "Murder!"[2]

Casting aside Frederick Seward, Powell then slashed Union sergeant George F. Robinson with his knife as he made his way toward the slumbering elder Seward. Seward's daughter, Fanny, who watched over her bedridden father, pleaded, "Don't murder him!"

Pinning the secretary with one hand, Powell brought the knife down with the other. He missed. The blade plunged into the mattress. In the darkness of the room, Seward squirmed. The steel cut into the old man's cheek and fractured his jaw. Repeated blows turned Seward into "an exsanguinated corpse."[3] Blood spurted everywhere and drenched the sheets. Miraculously, however, none of the wounds proved fatal.

The Union sergeant regained his senses and lunged at Powell, grabbing him in a bear hug. The would-be Confederate assassin parried and stabbed the soldier. Seward's son Gus also joined the melee, trying to wrestle Powell to the ground.

"I'm mad. I'm mad!"[4] protested the Confederate. He punched Sergeant Robinson and stabbed a State Department messenger in the back as he ran down the stairs. Fleeing the house, he mounted Booth's one-eyed horse and galloped into the maze of Washington's streets. The Ranger rode the horse hard and the exhausted animal collapsed near Lincoln Hospital, east of the capitol. For two days, Powell hid in a cemetery, until hunger forced him back to the familiar ground of the Nest, the boarding house owned by Mary Surratt.

Needing a cover and a disguise, Powell found a pickax and adopted the role of a laborer. He fashioned a hat out of the sleeve of his knit shirt. The Ranger fatefully arrived as detectives were searching the house following Lincoln's assassination for incriminating evidence from the conspirators. He knocked and rang the doorbell only to be answered by the detectives. Remarkably, after two days on the run, exhausted and hungry, Powell put together a convincing alibi and claimed he was there to dig a ditch for Surratt. Mary Surratt disavowed any knowledge of Powell: "Before God, I do not know this man; I have never seen him. I have not hired him to dig a ditch!"[5] Detectives asked a number of probing questions, which Powell answered convincingly, but when asked about where he had worked previously, he had no answers. Surratt's denial doomed both her and the Ranger. William Bell was then brought forward and very convincingly identified Seward's attacker. The Federal authorities put leg irons on Powell and threw him into the bowels of the iron-clad *Saugus*. Powell remained tight-lipped, revealing very little to Federal authorities.

52. The Last Call of Mosby's Rangers

"Sic semper tyrannis!" Booth shouted after leaping onto the stage of Ford's Theater from the presidential box, where he fired what would prove to be a fatal shot from a Derringer pistol into the head of President Abraham Lincoln. Fleeing on his broken leg through a stage door into an alley, he mounted a waiting horse and sped off into the night of April 14.

The operation to decapitate the Lincoln administration hit a snag when thirty-year-old George Atzerodt, tasked with killing Vice President Andrew Johnson, got drunk at the Kirkwood Hotel, where he lodged. Instead of carrying out the attack, Atzerodt lost his nerve and wandered the streets of Washington that night. Piecing together clues, Federal detectives arrested him six days later at his cousin's home in Germantown, Maryland.

After murdering Lincoln, Booth and fellow conspirator David Herold stealthily worked their way through the Secret Service's covert line in southern Maryland. Stopping at Surratt's tavern, they picked up a Spencer carbine, field glasses, and whiskey to numb Booth's searing pain from his broken leg. Avoiding Federal patrols, they traveled to Samuel Mudd, a member of the Confederate Doctor's Line, who set Booth's broken bone. While Booth rested, the doctor and Herold rode out and surveyed the area, which was swarming with Federal troops hunting the two men. The group fled to Confederate sympathizer Samuel Cox's home, Rich Hill, in the dead of night.

Coincidently, around the same time, "a portion of Mosby's men, under a Captain Garland Smith, just on the edge of the farms [nearby Federal farms seized by the Federal government from Confederate sympathizers]," clashed with Captain F. F. Buckley's Union cavalry. Buckley wrote on April 16, "I was overtaken by about thirty-five men of Garland Smith's command and captured one prisoner. Some very heavy skirmishing took place about 10 o'clock near Mechanicsville, [Maryland], in which I lost one man. I had to fall back in consequence of not having men enough."[1]

The purpose of the presence of Mosby's men in southern Maryland on April 16 remains a mystery. Only a few miles from Booth's escape route, were they an escort for Booth or, likely not having heard of Harney's capture, were they there to escort Harney after his mission to blow up the White House? We cannot know for sure, but their presence speaks loudly about the Confederacy's desperate last-minute attempt to destabilize the Lincoln administration.

To avoid the Union dragnet, Samuel Cox briefly harbored the fugitives and moved the conspirators into a dense pine thicket used by the Confederate Secret Service to hide agents. Thomas Jones, the chief Secret Service agent in southern Maryland, and a member of the Signal Corps,[2] brought the men food and newspapers over the next several days. Instead of branding them heroes, media in the North and even in the South condemned the conspirators' actions. Incensed by the reports, Booth wrote in his diary, "Our country owed all her troubles to him, and God simply made me the instrument of his punishment."[3]

Booth and Herold hid in the pines for days until the Union patrols diminished, and authorities believed Booth had crossed the Potomac, leading Federals to search Virginia. Sensing an opportunity for escape, Jones escorted the men three and a half miles to the Potomac in the dead of night, but currents and tides forced them back to the Maryland side of the river, as Booth recounted in his diary: "After being hunted like a dog through swamps, woods, and last night chased by gunboats till I was forced to return wet and cold and starving." Gunboats roamed the Potomac searching for the killer and, on that misty night, came very close to the two men but did not see them. Booth and Herold made landfall near Nanjemoy Creek, Maryland. Here the men approached a local farmer but received a cold reception. Booth wrote in his diary, "Tonight I try to escape these bloodhounds once more. Who, who can read this fate? I have too great a soul to die like a criminal. Oh, may He, may He spare me that and let me die bravely."[4]

At sundown on April 22, the men once again attempted to cross the river in the small boat.

Northern authorities assumed Mosby's involvement when they discovered that one of the conspirators was Ranger Lewis Powell. The War Department claimed to have evidence of Mosby's involvement in the Lincoln conspiracy and stated, "The guerrilla chief, Mosby, will not be paroled." Mosby had a price on his head. Whether the Federals considered him an outlaw or a soldier was unclear. Days earlier, General Hancock's chief of staff wrote to Mosby informing him of Lee's surrender, offering him the same conditions, and asking for a meeting with a Northern officer of equal rank to work out conditions. "It will be seen that there was considerable confusion as to Mosby's exact status," one Ranger later wrote, noting that the general "did not ask Colonel Mosby to surrender himself, but 'the forces under his command.'"[5]

Days ticked by with no response from the Gray Ghost. If he would not surrender, Hancock prepared to attack, circulating a notice throughout the area urging residents and soldiers to cooperate in the restoration of peace, but also indicating that Mosby would not be included in the terms of surrender.

Mosby finally responded. He sent a letter with four Rangers to be delivered in person to Hancock. The Rangers passed through the enemy pickets dressed in their finest uniforms, sitting high on their horses, with only a single white handkerchief on a stick as a sign of capitulation.

"What command, Major?"

"Mosby's," answered Aristides Monteiro, the Rangers' battalion surgeon.

Rather than taunting or insults, a "loud and prolonged shout" sounded along the entire line of men. One battle-seasoned Pennsylvania veteran stepped forward and extended his hand, proclaiming, "Thank God! The war is over. I know the end has come when Mosby's men surrender."[6]

The astonished Monteiro later wrote, "Our surprise was complete when those men we had fought with such savage ferocity a few days before now shed tears of joy as they greeted us once more as members of the great national family."[7]

But their celebration proved premature. Mosby's letter informed Hancock that the partisan leader had not yet received official communication regarding the surrender of Lee's army, "nor, in my opinion, has the emergency yet arisen which would justify the surrender of my Command. With no disposition, however, to cause the useless effusion of blood or to inflict on a war-worn population any unnecessary distress, I am ready to agree to a suspension of hostilities for a short time."[8]

The Federals first escorted the Rangers to Colonel Marcus Reno's accommodations. Reno offered them brandy and cigars and, at one point, asked them about a recent skirmish. "Will you be kind enough to tell me how many of your men were engaged in that fight?"[9]

Monteiro felt no hesitation, now that the war seemed to be concluding, in telling the general frankly that their force was minimal, only 128 on that occasion. "Twenty-eight thousand, you mean," replied Reno.[10] Union forces had falsely assumed Mosby had a more extensive command since, throughout the war, Mosby had successfully tied up and battled forces multiple times their number.

When the Rangers met with General Hancock, he greeted them warmly: "You have fought bravely and have nothing to be ashamed of. You have, like gallant soldiers, left your cause to the god of battles, and the arbitrament of the sword has decided against you. Let us once more kneel down at the same altar and be like brothers of the same household."[11]

After reading Mosby's letter, Hancock agreed to a truce until noon on Tuesday, April 18. On the eighteenth, Mosby arrived with approximately two dozen Rangers in Millwood, but he simply asked for an extension, having still not heard official news of Joseph Johnston's surrender in North Carolina. Hancock agreed to an extension to April 20. Grant wrote to Hancock on April 19, "If Mosby does not avail himself of the present truce end it and hunt him and his men down. Guerrillas, after beating the armies of the enemy, will not be entitled to quarter."[12]

At noon on the twentieth, Mosby and twenty Rangers arrived at the appointed brick building in Millwood, Virginia, to meet with the Federal officers. The two parties reached an impasse. The truce would not be extended. Mosby was not ready to surrender.

When the Federal commander told the partisan leader in no uncertain terms, "The truce is ended. We can have no further intercourse under its terms," both men "appreciated the serious import of the moment." Adding to the drama of the tense scene, a young Ranger, Johnny Heard, rushed in and interrupted the previously dignified meeting, exclaiming, "Colonel, the d—d Yankees have got you in a trap: there is a thousand of them hid in the woods right here."[13]

Rising to his feet, placing his hand on his revolver, and looking directly at the Federal officers, Mosby said slowly, "If the truce no longer protects us, we are at your mercy; but we shall protect ourselves," as he and his twenty men exited the room in "breathless silence."[14]

On April 21, at Salem, Virginia, Mosby ordered his Rangers to form in a field one final time. He disbanded the men but never personally surrendered. "Mosby rode along the line, looking each man in the face, it was plain that his heart was breaking,"[15] recalled Ranger John W. Munson. The Confederate leader could not bear to read the words he penned earlier at Glen Welby, so his officers read the words aloud to the men:

"Soldiers!

"I have summoned you together for the last time. The vision we have cherished of a free and independent country has vanished, and that country is now the spoil of the conqueror. I disband your organization in preference to surrendering it to our enemies. I am no longer your Commander. After an association of more than two eventful years, I part from you with a just pride in the fame of your achievements and a grateful recollection of your generous kindness to myself. And at this moment of bidding you a final adieu, accept the assurance of my unchanging confidence and regard. Farewell. John S. Mosby, Colonel."[16]

Many Rangers openly wept as they shook hands with Mosby, who stood on the side of a road near the field. He informed the men that "they could do whatever they chose."[17] Most would seek parole with General Hancock in Winchester and make an oath of allegiance to the Union.

The Rangers' former nemesis and Lewis Powell's prisoner, Richard Blazer, now provost marshal and in failing health from his months confined by the Confederacy, greeted the men after being released in a prisoner exchange. Syd Ferguson, who pursued Blazer in the long ride from the field at Kabletown and personally captured the Ohioan, embraced him. The two enemies "met and hugged each other like long lost brothers," Munson recalled.[18] Mosby and Blazer would later become friends: reconciliation and forgiveness.

Another band of Rangers, up to fifty men, stayed by Mosby, including Ranger John Munson. "Knights Errant in a new Crusade,"[19] the group headed South—toward the Confederate forces led by General Joseph Johnston—and John Wilkes Booth.

Avoiding gunboats, Booth and David Herold rowed across the Potomac in the middle of the night on April 22–23 and made landfall in Virginia. Confederate Secret Service agent Thomas Harbin arranged for a local farmer, William Bryant, to furnish the men with horses and escort them to Dr. Richard Stuart. A Confederate and enslaver, Stuart harbored agents and had spent time in a Union prison. After dark on April 23, Bryant brought the two men to Stuart's home. Herold pleaded for medical assistance, stating his brother (Booth) had a broken leg, but Stuart dismissed the plea, saying he was not a surgeon. At some point, the men exclaimed, "We are Marylanders & want to go to Mosby."[20] Their declaration could have implied they had prior arrangements with the Rangers. The men asked if they could stay in Stuart's stately summer home, Cleydael, but the doctor told them he had no room and palmed them off on his neighbor, William Lucas, a free-born Black farmer who might provide shelter and a ride to their next destination.

Lucas' dogs barked at a rap on the door, followed by "a strange voice" calling for Lucas. The farmer opened the door, terrified by the unexpected late-night visitors. Herold asked to stay the night. The men claimed to be Confederate soldiers. Lucas protested and said they could not stay. Booth pulled out a Bowie knife in a threatening manner and asked, "Old man, how do you like that?" Lucas responded, "I do not like that at all; I was always afraid of a knife."[21] The next morning, after a quick breakfast, Lucas' son drove Booth and Herold in their family wagon to Port Conway, Virginia, in the Northern Neck. Before departing, Booth penned a sarcastic note, quoting Shakespeare's *Macbeth*. Stuart's dismissive inhospitality had stuck in Booth's craw; "The sauce in meat is ceremony, meeting were bare without it."[22] Signing it "Stranger," he included $2.50 and asked Lucas to deliver it to Stuart. Lucas' son, driving a wagon pulled by two wretched-looking horses, dropped them off at a dilapidated building, the residence of an old fisherman, William Rollins, with ties to the Confederate signal service. Booth paid the boy for the ride and their hospitality.

At Port Conway, several riders crested a hill and approached Booth and Herold, who were on a landing near the Rappahannock River, waiting for Rollins to take them across the waterway and help them get to Bowling Green, Virginia. Mosby's Rangers Lieutenant Mortimer Ruggles, Private Absalom Bainbridge, and Private Willie Jett approached the two men. Ruggles was the son of a general and the second in command of Captain

Thomas Nelson Conrad's spy unit. Months earlier, Conrad had staked out the White House, carefully recording Lincoln's movements as part of the kidnapping operation. Recently, and nearby, Conrad had been arrested by Union authorities. The spymaster could not furnish Northern authorities with a good reason for being there. Ruggles gave Booth Conrad's horse, Old Whitie, to ride. Booth made an immediate impression on Ruggles, as the Ranger revealed, "He was without a doubt disappointed at the reception he met in Virginia, and said he was prepared to meet any fate. The calm courage of the man while racked by suffering, impressed me in spite of myself, for there was no braggadocio about him; simply a determination to submit to the inevitable, parleying when it should become necessary to do so."[23]

All three of Mosby's men later claimed they met Booth by mere coincidence. It is more likely the group was sent to locate the assassin. Later, newspapers around the country quoted Jett alleging Mosby's approval of Booth by supposedly stating, "By God I could take that man in my arms."[24]

There is another good reason for the Rangers' encounter with Booth. According to William Tidwell's research, Mosby had a large stay-behind group of men and a reception group to escort either Booth or Harney. Piecing together parole lists, Tidwell was able to determine that scores of Rangers remained in the area during the time of Booth's escape, so the trio encountering him may well not have been coincidental.[25] As the former intelligence officer summed it up, "Multiple coincidences, they imply the existence of some central direction in the Northern Neck dedicated to the protection of John Wilkes Booth."[26]

The Rangers agreed to accompany Booth and Herold across the river and find them a safe haven. Ruggles brought Booth and Herold to loyal Southerners, the Garretts, and fed the family a story that Booth and Herold were wounded Confederate soldiers who needed a place to rest for a few days.

With Booth ensconced at the Garretts', Jett, in a hurry to see his girlfriend, took off for Bowling Green, Virginia. En route, he stopped at a rundown tavern with a seedy reputation known fittingly as the Trap. Later, piecing together clues from various sightings, Federal detectives arrested Jett in Bowling Green and forced him to escort them back to Booth's hiding place.

On April 26, detectives and a Union cavalry troop guided by Jett approached the Garrett house. Decades later, Ruggles wrote, "I met a soldier of my command . . . who said, 'the town is full of Yankees in search of Booth.'" The Confederate officer rushed back to the house and found Booth lying on the front lawn. Booth recognized the Ranger and asked, "Well, boys, what's in the wind now?" Ruggles told him to run and hide in the ravine behind the house, as Yankees were headed his way. Booth then turned to Ruggles and said, "I'll do as you say, boys, right off. Ride on! Good-by! It will never do for you to be found in my company." Booth then turned and said, biting his lip in "desperate resolve, 'rest assured of one thing, good friend, John Wilkes Booth will never be taken alive.'"[27] Federal troops surrounded the Garretts' barn, where Booth had hidden, and set it ablaze to coax his surrender.

Disobeying orders not to open fire, Sergeant Thomas H. "Boston" Corbett, of the 16th New York Cavalry, spied Booth through a crack in the wall in the barn and allegedly fired the bullet that felled him. Accounts differ on where the gunshot originated, but Corbett came forward after the fracas and claimed he fired on Booth in self-defense. A year earlier, Corbett and his unit had been battling Mosby and he had been captured by the Rangers and sent to Andersonville, spending several miserable months in the camp before his release in an eventual prisoner exchange. Known for his bizarre behavior, the result of his being a proverbial "mad hatter" due to exposure to mercury nitrate in his prewar career as a milliner, Corbett castrated himself, before the war, with a pair of scissors to avoid sexual temptation after being propositioned by prostitutes.[28]

Detectives found on Booth's person a diary that included a bank draft he had obtained in Montreal in October. Mysteriously, many pages were ripped from the diary. The bullet severed the assassin's spinal cord. He suffered an excruciating death, fully conscious until the end, whispering, "Kill me."[29]

Only twenty-five miles away, Mosby and what was left of his command rested—and possibly waited. Mosby would have had compelling reasons to desire Booth's escape or even death. His reputation was at stake, and links to the assassination had become toxic. But word of Booth's death and of Johnston's surrender to Sherman on April 26 reached Mosby around April 27 when he received a copy of the *Richmond Whig*. With the news, Mosby disbanded the remaining men in his command. The Gray Ghost would then lie low for several months. He not only had a price on his head but was motivated not to have any connection with the conspirators as the military trial was about to commence. On June 17, with the trial nearly over and any direct links connecting Mosby and the Rangers to the assassination seemingly avoided, Mosby turned himself in to the authorities at Lynchburg. He would always fervently deny any involvement in the assassination but was never confronted with probing questions about his possible links to the abduction of the president.

After the war, Grant befriended Mosby, protecting him from potential Federal harassment and giving him an exemption from arrest. Mosby became Grant's Republican campaign manager in Virginia during the 1868 presidential election. He disavowed the Lost Cause and expressed disapproval of those who denied the role of slavery in the war, but he was not ashamed of having fought for his country. His principles generated hatred from some of his men. The former guerrilla leader received death threats, and one attempt was made to assassinate him near the train station in Warrenton.

Mosby returned to practicing law and was later appointed consul of Hong Kong, where he rooted out corruption and protected women who immigrated to the United States. His final position was US attorney for the Department of Justice. Mosby continued to influence lives while living in California. He spent time with a young George Patton Jr. on their family ranch in San Gabriel.[30] America's greatest guerrilla warfare practitioner's lightning attacks and cavalry tactics undoubtedly had an impact on the young Patton's mind as he developed his own tank and maneuver warfare tenets. Mosby remained true to his principles and would retain a mystique and gravitas—forever the Gray Ghost.

Powell and the other Lincoln assassination conspirators faced swift justice. The government opted for a military tribunal led by General "Black Dave" Hunter and other general officers, including hero of Washington, General Lew Wallace. Federal detectives and the prosecutors knew the Confederate Secret Service had played a crucial role in the conspiracy and set out to prove their case. Whether Booth and Powell received specific orders from Jefferson Davis or the Confederate Secret Service to murder the president and secretary of state or acted on their own remains a mystery to this day. Although this book does not attempt to solve that mystery, the evidence of the Secret Service's complicity seems overwhelming, especially given the other assassination attempt and the kidnapping operation staffed and funded by the service. In the days before his execution, Powell maintained he was a soldier and working for the Secret Service. Crucially, the prosecution decided to try to prove the Confederates planned to assassinate Lincoln rather than to prove the Secret Service operation to kidnap the president. The government relied heavily on two witnesses, Dr. James B. Merritt and Charles A. Dunham (a.k.a. Sanford Conover, James Watson Wallace), to testify they heard George Sanders, Jacob Thompson, and other Confederates discuss plans for assassination. Dunham mixed fact and fiction, so it was hard to discern the truth in his testimony. Both men were proven liars in court and likely double agents, and portions of their testimony were deemed false during the trial. Puppet master George Sanders of the Confederate Secret Service in Montreal likely coached Dunham to perjure himself so that the deception could be revealed in order to blow up the Federal case. They printed handbills and a statement in the *Montreal Evening Telegraph* refuting the testimony point by point.[31]

The tainted testimony destroyed the government's case against the Secret Service and Jefferson Davis and other Confederate officials. The Secret Service's plot to blow up the White House never entered the trial and would only come to light decades after the war.

Despite the tainted testimony, special judge advocate on the trial John A. Bingham summed up Davis' and the Confederate Secret Service's guilt in the operation to kill Lincoln in his final argument before the court: "What more is wanting? Surely no word further need be spoken to show that John Wilkes Booth was in this conspiracy; that John Surratt was in this conspiracy; and that Jefferson Davis and his several agents named, in Canada, were in this conspiracy. . . . Whatever may be the conviction of others, my own conviction is that Jefferson Davis is as clearly proven guilty of this conspiracy as John Wilkes Booth, by whose hand Jefferson Davis inflicted the mortal wound on Abraham Lincoln."[32] Also entered into evidence at the trial was Davis' reaction when he received a telegram, while moving from one temporary capital to another, notifying him that Lincoln had been assassinated. Davis hatefully responded, "Well, General, I don't know; if it were to be done at all, it were *better* that it were *well done*; and if the same had been done to Andy Johnson, the beast, and to Secretary Stanton, the job would then be complete."[33]

Bingham also tied Davis' guilt to an October 13, 1864, ciphered letter from the Secret Service in Canada that stated, "Their friends would be set to work as he had directed," which corresponded to Booth's arrival and meetings with the Secret Service in Canada and the beginning of Booth's mission to kidnap the president. Bingham explained, "The letter in cipher found on Booth's possession is translated here by the use of the cipher machine [also found in Booth's trunk] now in court [the machine was set to the code, "Come retribution"] which, as the testimony of [one of the witnesses] shows, he brought from the rooms of Davis' state department in Richmond." Bingham asked two simple questions: "Who gave Booth this secret cipher? Of what use was it to him if he was not in confederation with Davis?"[34]

Merritt's and Dunham's perjury did not affect the fate of the eight conspirators.

From the time of their arrest until the trial, most of the prisoners were shackled with iron balls and chains and forced to wear canvas hoods that covered their faces and heads, as ordered by Secretary of War Edwin Stanton.

Lewis Powell's guilt in attempting to murder Secretary of State Seward was almost undeniable, but his fellow conspirators' guilt was harder to prove. Powell remained tight-lipped and did not reveal much; and his lawyer claimed insanity as a defense. Interestingly, Atzerodt's attorney held up his client's well-known cowardice against the charge of attempting to kill Vice President Johnson, telling the commission that he could never have committed the crime and was unlikely to have been assigned it. Herold, the defense claimed, was a youth, impressionable "wax in the hands of a man like Booth."[35] And while Mary Surratt's boarding house was considered "the nest that hatched the egg," the prosecution still needed to prove collaboration on the innkeeper's part, not just association, with the conspirators. Multiple witnesses, however, helped bridge that gap for many of the commission members.

The seven-week-long trial by a nine-member military commission ended after the jurors' one-day deliberation. They condemned Powell, Surratt, Atzerodt, and Herold "to be hanged by the neck until he [or she] be dead"[36] and the other four conspirators to lesser sentences. Surratt would be the first woman executed by the US government, despite five of the commission members requesting that President Johnson reduce her sentence because of her sex and age.

Ominously, in the final hours before his death, Powell highlighted the role of the Secret Service, who financed and organized the operation he was a part of, cryptically stating: "You have not got the half of them."[37] The Ranger also nobly pleaded for Mary Surratt's life, claiming she did not know of the conspirators' plans. On July 7, 1865, the four convicted prisoners met their death at the gallows constructed for them in the Old Arsenal building. Powell faced death bravely, tilting his head back to accept the hangman's noose. Captain Christian Rath placed and tightened the hemp near his Adam's apple and said, "I want you to die quick, Paine [*sic*]."

"You know best, Captain," Powell said under the hood covering his head.

"Thank you; goodbye,"[38] were Powell's final words as his body dropped from the scaffold. However, he died hard, writhing in pain, jerking and convulsing for many minutes at the end of the rope. Powell's spiritual adviser watched in horror but, when reflecting on Powell's final minutes on earth, observed, "At least [he] gave to it something of dignity* by calmness, modesty and silence."[39]

From their headquarters at St. Lawrence Hall, George Sanders and the leadership of the Confederate Secret Service in Canada completed their final mission—to build a myth that Booth had nothing to do with them or they with the assassination by demonstrating the Federal star witnesses were perjurers. It can be argued that the myth continues to this day. Many believe Booth was a madman and that he and Powell acted alone and had minimal ties to the Secret Service. After successfully destroying the government's case against the Confederacy, Thompson and Sanders absconded with hundreds of thousands of dollars from the remaining Confederate Secret Service fund and fled to Europe to live in exile. The men were joined by Confederate secretary of state Judah P. Benjamin, who burned the Secret

---

* The government did not afford the same dignity to Powell. His skull was unceremoniously dumped in a wooden box, where it lay for decades. In 1991 a researcher at the Smithsonian found Powell's skull and finally returned it to his family, who laid it to rest next to his mother in Geneva Cemetery, Seminole County, Florida.

Service files before departing from Richmond. The Confederate spymaster would make his own dramatic escape. Disguised as a Frenchman trying to buy land, he traveled to Florida and secured passage on a blockade running ship bound for the Caribbean. The Union navy intercepted and boarded the ship. To avoid detection, he donned an apron, smeared himself with grease, and impersonated a cook. The ship was carrying rice and sponges, which got wet, expanded, and blew apart the hull of the ship, sinking it, but he was rescued by British lighthouse ship *Georgia*, which brought him to Bimini.[40] Fate was not finished with the elusive Confederate. The European-bound steamer he was on caught fire. After great difficultly, the crew extinguished the flames, and Benjamin eventually made it to England, where he lived out his final days as a barrister.

The full extent of Copperhead leader Clement Laird Vallandigham's seditious dealings with the Confederate Secret Service was not revealed until long after the war. In the fall of 1864, an undercover Federal agent had infiltrated the Sons of Liberty, and several ringleaders of the movement were arrested and ultimately tried by military tribunal. Testimony in the trial proved Vallandigham to be the leader of the movement. In 1866 the US Supreme Court ruled in *Ex parte Milligan* that military tribunals had no power to try civilians outside a war zone and when civilian courts were open. Vallandigham and many others would escape justice. With the war over, he jumped back into politics, ran on an anti-Reconstruction platform for the Democratic seat for Ohio in the Senate, and lost. The gifted fifty-year-old lawyer went back into private law practice. While conducting a demonstration during his defense of a client who killed a man in a barroom brawl, he accidentally shot and killed himself after drawing and firing what he thought was an unloaded pistol.

One conspirator who evaded the hangman's noose was John Surratt. Shortly before the assassination, the Confederate Secret Service agent fled first to Richmond and then to case Elmira Federal Prison, in western New York (for a possible prison break), but quickly fled to Montreal. He was accompanied by agent Sarah Slater. Federal detectives theorized Slater may have been assigned the mission to courier the orders to Surratt and Booth to assassinate the president.[41] The often-veiled spy vixen known as the French Woman disappeared and was never heard from again.[42]

Aided by Sanders and others, Surratt went into hiding first in Canada. With Federal detectives hot on his trail and a $25,000 bounty on his head, he donned glasses, dyed his hair, and fled across the Atlantic to Liverpool. Surratt stayed on the run, showing up in Italy next, where he joined the Papal Zouaves, an infantry unit dedicated to defending the papal state. Surratt assumed the alias surname of Watson. One of Surratt's acquaintances from Maryland traveled to Italy and joined the Papal Zouaves to capture him and collect the reward money. But Surratt, a former postmaster, intercepted a letter detailing the plans for his arrest. He fled again, but Italian authorities seized him and allegedly threw the spy in a prison cell perched at a height of more than 200 feet, from which he managed to escape. According to one account, Surratt executed a daring escape by jumping out the window as two men standing on a narrow ledge twenty-eight feet below "with an outstretched blanket broke the fall."[43] However, it is much more likely that Surratt escaped with the assistance of his guards by crawling through a sewer. An account of Surratt's escape appeared in a newspaper account: "He had lowered himself into the sewer and had made his way out at an opening into the neighboring rivulet. . . . As soon as the Lieutenant heard of the escape, he ordered the entire party [of guards] to be put under arrest. Still, I remember that a smile of satisfaction seemed to play around his lips, and there is no doubt in my mind that he secretly rejoiced at what had occurred."[44]

On the run, Surratt boarded a steamship headed for Alexandria and was arrested in Egypt in November 1866. US authorities detained the conspirator, still wearing his Papal Zouaves uniform, and brought him back to the United States, where he stood trial in a civilian court in 1867 and a hung jury allowed him to walk away a free man.

53. THE LAST SCOUT: MEXICO

After Lee's surrender at Appomattox, Sheridan hoped to aid in the defeat of General Joseph Johnston's Army of Tennessee before marching on to Washington, DC. He had visions of then leading his men in the Grand Review, a magnificent parade of the victorious Union Army, down the streets of Washington, DC.

It was not to be.

Johnston surrendered on April 26 outside Durham Station, North Carolina, before Sheridan and his men arrived at the battlefield. Grant seized the opportunity to send the battle-hardened general and the Jessie Scouts to prevent open war, a potentially more deadly conflict involving the Europeans.

While the American Civil War raged, the rest of the world powers had not sat by idly. With America distracted, France, Spain, and the United Kingdom collectively invaded Mexico in 1861, ostensibly to resolve unpaid debts. A year later, Spain and Britain negotiated agreements and withdrew. France remained, carrying through its true intention of conquest. In blatant disregard of the 1823 Monroe Doctrine, which stated that the United States would not tolerate colonization or puppet monarchies in the Western Hemisphere, Napoleon III sent tens of thousands of French troops and, despite an active Mexican insurgency, on April 10, 1864, he appointed Maximilian I to the throne of Mexico.

Six feet tall, blue-eyed, and sporting a forked beard, Emperor Ferdinand Maximilian Josef Maria von Habsburg-Lothringen was the younger brother of Emperor Franz Joseph I of Austria. Napoleon III's motivation for his installation in Mexico was to blunt the power and influence of the United States. Using a modern, scientific approach, French statisticians calculated that the US population would reach 512 million by 1963.[1] With so many citizens, Napoleon feared the United States would need more land and expand into Mexico and Latin America.

During the Civil War, the Europeans in Mexico gave encouragement and aid to the Confederacy. The sanctuary of friendly Mexican ports such as Bagdad, a stone's throw from Brownsville, Texas, allowed the Confederates to avoid the Union blockade. However, attacking vessels in these ports would have been an act of war on the part of the United States. Grant explained to Sheridan, "Our success in putting down secession would never be complete till the French and Austrian invaders were compelled to quit the territory of our sister republic [Mexico]."[2]

Sheridan thus received orders on May 17 to travel at once to Texas. There, he was to force the surrender of one of the last remaining Confederate armies, commanded by General Edmund Kirby Smith, and restore civil order. Due to the political sensitivity of the mission, the charges were verbal as well as written. Unlike cut-and-dried written orders, spoken directives allowed for wide-ranging interpretations, and their diplomatic fallout could lead to war with European powers. Sheridan and the Scouts would thus wage a covert proxy war against the French in Mexico. The United States struggled to come to grips with its southern border and the foreign influence on the other side. Grant looked on France's "invasion of Mexico as part of the [Southern states'] rebellion itself." However, he stressed the need to act "with great circumspection, since the Secretary of State, Mr. Seward, was much opposed to the use of our troops along the border in any active way that would likely involve us in a war with European powers."[3]

At St. Louis, Sheridan took a steamboat to New Orleans. Near Shreveport, Louisiana, Sheridan received word that Smith had surrendered under similar terms as did Johnston, but that thousands of diehard Confederates refused. "Particularly by the Texas troops . . . I was informed [Confederates] marched off to the interior of the State in several organized bodies, carrying their camp equipage, arms, and even, some artillery, with the ultimate purpose of going to Mexico."[4]

After arriving in Louisiana, one of Sheridan's men crossed paths with his old nemesis, General Jubal Early, who was fleeing toward the Caribbean with a small party of followers. Early and his men evaded capture, but two of his horses did not. According to Sheridan, Early wrote an angry missive demanding payment for the horses, claiming they were private property and adding an admonition not to bother trying to follow him, as he "expected to be on the deep blue sea."[5]

The final Confederate general surrendered nearly a month after Smith. Second chief of the Cherokee Nation, Brigadier General Stand Watie, a slave-owning division commander whose family and another owned 1,600 enslaved Americans, surrendered his command and the 1st Indian Brigade of Creek, Seminole, Cherokee, and Osage Indians to Federal authorities on June 23, 1865.

Sheridan had to contend not only with Mexico but also with Reconstruction, bringing Louisiana and Texas back into the Union. Sheridan ordered his subordinate, General Gordon Granger, "to notify the people of Texas that in accordance with existing proclamation from the Executive of the United States 'That all slaves are free.'"[6] Thereby, Granger issued General Order No. 3 on June 19, 1865, Juneteenth, proclaiming the freedom of all enslaved individuals in Texas. The Thirteenth Amendment to the US Constitution would abolish slavery forever in December that year. In command of the Southwest District and later the Military Division of the Gulf, Sheridan dealt harshly with ex-Confederate soldiers he felt obstructed Reconstruction.

Sheridan established his headquarters in Brownsville on the Rio Grande. The general deployed his "trusty Scouts"[7] to keep tabs on Early and other former Confederates and the Mexican imperial government. Mexico provided an environment ideally suited for Sheridan's covert operators. Young and a number of the best Jessie Scouts, including Arch Rowand, Jim White, and James Campbell, followed by most of the other Scouts, joined their general on the border. "From Brownsville, I dispatched all these men to important points in northern Mexico to glean information regarding the movements of the Imperial forces and also gather intelligence about the ex-confederates who had crossed the Rio Grande,"[8] Sheridan wrote.

Sheridan used the information to conduct demonstrations with his troops along the border to intimidate Maximilian and imply an invasion could occur at any time. The exercises failed to impress the emperor, who continued to consolidate power and had most of Mexico under his control. While the United States officially remained neutral, Sheridan aided the resistance, opening a public channel of communication with nationalist leader Benito Juárez and covertly funneling arms and munitions to the Mexicans resisting the occupation in one of America's first proxy wars.

Ex-Confederates poured into Mexico. "Everything on wheels. Artillery, horses, and mules have been run into Mexico. Large and small bands of Rebel soldiers, and some citizens amounting to about two thousand. . . . There is no doubt in my mind that representatives of the Imperial government along the Rio Grande have encouraged the wholesale plunder of property belonging to the United States and that will only be given up when we go and take it,"[9] wrote Sheridan. Early and other Southern leaders such as Sterling Price, Joseph Shelby, and the former Confederate governors of Tennessee and Louisiana found safe haven and founded a colony south of the border. John McCausland, who faced arson charges for torching Chambersburg, also lived in the enclave. Maximillian encouraged their emigration and solicited their assistance in quelling Juárez's insurgency. The United States tried to staunch the flow of thousands of Southern combat veterans into the neighboring country by limiting travel permits, but this had only a minimal effect on the migration.

Despite a focus on Mexico, Lincoln's assassination continued to affect Sheridan. He received numerous false reports of sightings of John Surratt. Sources also informed him Mary Surratt's older son, Isaac, had set out to avenge the death of his mother and left Monterey, Mexico, to assassinate President Andrew Johnson. "This is no humbug about the assassination, and every precaution should be taken,"[10] wrote Sheridan.

Fort Jefferson, in the Gulf of Mexico, located on the Dry Tortugas off Florida's west coast—where several of the Lincoln assassination conspirators, including Samuel Mudd, were imprisoned—also fell under Sheridan's overall control. When Secretary of War Edwin Stanton received word that the fort's commandant had assigned Mudd to surgeon duties, he fired off an angry letter to Little Phil: "This is giving honorable employment to a felon and discrediting an honorable branch of service." Stanton then ordered the practice halted. But the good doctor did not remain idle, and nearly escaped the island fortress prison by stowing away on a steamer bound for New York. Mudd was quickly recaptured and tortured. "The thumb screws applied to him, and under the pressure of pain he acknowledged that Kelly, the quartermaster, with whom he had formed an acquaintance within a few days had helped him to escape."[11] In 1869, President Johnson pardoned Mudd after the doctor helped contain a yellow fever outbreak in the fort.

As the insurgency in Mexico gained strength, Sheridan was not the only Union general running guns into the country. General Lew Wallace, the savior of Washington at Monocacy, provided military assistance to the insurgency as well. In the autumn of 1864, Wallace received secret orders from Grant to arm the Mexican resistance. One such operation involved Wallace, cavalry and volunteers from Company F, 5th Regiment California; all troops blackened their guns and brass accoutrements to avoid rays of the sun reflecting on the shiny metal, giving away their position. The men traveled about 200 miles into the desert in Mexico to Chihuahua. During the journey, unmarked US-made wagons, "the painted letters 'U.S.' had been carefully erased," arrived from somewhere loaded with long, heavy boxes of weapons. One of the men in Company F recalled the clandestine operation to arm the resistance, "The next day about noon, a squad of cavalry, thirty in number, all had their guns and accoutrements blacked, and a strange officer [Wallace], came into our camp. I appeared to take command at once." Wallace met with Mexican officers. Crates of beans and corn were substituted for the weapons. On their return to the United States, they were attacked by Apache Indians but defeated the force. After the raid, officers swore the men to secrecy, "The men must not write accounts of our maneuvers and engagements, or marches or places visited by detachments as it might give the enemy information that would damage the government."[12]

By 1865, Wallace focused much of his efforts on insurgent leader General Jose María de Jesús Carvajal to move thousands of rifles, artillery, and vast amounts of ammunition by sea. Fittingly, one of the ships bore the name *General Sheridan*. Sheridan would note the imperialists learned the difficultly of controlling a country that had long lines of communication and supply running through desert and mountains. "The Maximillian Government in Mexico is a force that holds only a few cities and towns."[13]

Carvajal hired Young and roughly fifty men, including several Jessie Scouts, to act as his bodyguards by misleading Young into believing Sheridan approved the plan. After receiving payment, raising the unit, and arriving in New Orleans, Young discovered the deception, to his and Sheridan's horror. "He said that he could not withdraw without dishonor, and with tears in his eyes, he sought me to help him," recalled Sheridan in his memoirs. "He must make good his word at all hazards; and that while

I need not approve, yet I must go far enough to consent to the departure of the men." The general relented and even loaned Young money to finish outfitting the group, but Sheridan later stated, "I have never ceased to regret my consent, for misfortune fell upon the enterprise almost from its inception."[14]

Before Young and his party arrived in Mexico, General Carvajal had been unseated by a rival Mexican general, Servando Canales, who declined the use of Young's troops. While en route to a third insurgent leader, Mariano Escobedo, they were attacked "by a party of ex-Confederates and renegade Mexican rancheros." The exact circumstances of Young's death remain a mystery to this day. Sheridan wrote of the attack, "A number of the men were drowned while swimming the river, Young himself was shot and killed, a few were captured, and those who escaped—about twenty in all—finally joined Escobedo, but in such a plight as to be of little use."[15] Young and over a dozen Jessie Scouts were likely killed by the insurgents.

Nobody knows for certain what happened to Lieutenant Colonel Henry Harrison Young or many of the Scouts. The circumstances surrounding his death was likely part of a coverup. Young and the Jessie Scouts were covert operators working in the service of the United States. Young's biographer would write, "The matter was taken up, and thorough investigation made, but without any satisfactory result." A letter from General Sheridan claimed that the report stated, "Colonel Young had been seen alive and well in Monterey, but it was never corroborated. Whether he perished in the fight at the Rio Grande, or languished within the walls of a Mexican prison, will ever be shrouded in mystery."[16]

Sheridan had an unparalleled acumen for military intelligence and wisely set up an operation to intercept Maximillian's communications with France. Information was power. After years of failed attempts and damaged cables in August 1866, the undersea Atlantic cable once again became operational, which allowed telegraphic communication between Europe and North America. On January 10, 1867, Sheridan's headquarters intercepted a coded message from France: "Do not compel the emperor to abdicate, but do not delay the departure of the troops; bring back all those who will not remain there. Most of the fleet has left."[17] According to Sheridan, the intelligence coup was accomplished by his telegraph officer and cipher clerk

Charles A. Keefer, who succeeded in "getting possession of the telegraph and managing [a] secret line."[18] As a formerly classified assessment stated, "Rare indeed is the single intelligence item that is at once so important and so unmistakable in meaning as the intercept of January 10 [1867]."[19] Prior to the intercepted communication, the US government had no way to fully verify French troop strength in Mexico or their intentions. The French troop withdrawals doomed Maximillian, who still clung to power. In an act of humanity, the United States tried to spare the emperor's life by offering to transport him out of Mexico into exile.

Sheridan would send his best, the original reluctant Jessie Scout* Jim White, on this final mission. At Brownsville, White had worn many hats: "His duties varied according to the alternate requirements of a detective, scout, guide, or dispatch bearer." On his final mission, he carried a diplomatic letter from the US State Department urging the Mexicans to spare Maximilian's life. He boarded a steamer, the *Blackbird*, to Matamoras, Mexico. From there, White navigated his way more than 1,700 miles round trip through the interior of the war-torn country, meeting with various military and government officials until he reached San Luis, where he delivered his dispatches. "The next day, he had three interviews with the heads of the Government, including President Juárez and a number of his secretaries." The officials bent over backward "to convey a favorable impression of the Liberal cause and Government through him to the United States authorities."[20] But most importantly, Mexican officials ignored the US State Department's pleas. After a trial, the emperor was executed by firing squad.

Fragments of the Jessie Scouts' story have been revealed, but their entire story has remained untold until now. Many of the men took their stories to the grave during the war or shortly after it. Scouting was hazardous and perilous duty, and at the war's end, Sheridan memorialized their extraordinary service in his own way. "To Major H.H. Young, of my staff, chief of scouts, and the thirty or forty men of his command, who took their lives in their hands, cheerfully going wherever ordered, to obtain that great

* When White found out Charles Carpenter led the group, he tried to leave the Jessie Scouts and return to his old unit.

essential of success, information. I tender my gratitude. Ten of those men were lost."²¹ More than 25 percent of the Jessie Scouts never came home during the war. Many more, perhaps up to fifteen Scouts, including Young, lost their lives in Mexico. Dead men do not tell tales or their history. After their final mission, White and the surviving Jessie Scouts faded away from conflict. Most returned to civilian life. Of the small number who survived, Arch Rowand became a successful lawyer and J. E. McCabe, a politician. Rather than going home, James Campbell went west and scouted the frontier, fighting in the Indian Wars. Most Scouts forgot about the Medals of Honor they earned and did not bother asking about receiving them until the issue was brought to their attention decades after the war. Asbe Montgomery, chronicler of Blazer's Scouts, spent the rest of his life recovering from a painful gunshot wound to the shoulder. Henry Pancake became a prominent grocer but never forgot the skills he learned during the war. When a thug "presented a pistol in his face"²² and told Pancake he should stop or be a dead man, the old Scout knocked the pistol out of his hand as the weapon discharged into the fleshy part of a horse's leg. Ohio residents elected Richard Blazer county sheriff; he would continue to protect his fellow citizens throughout the remainder of his life.

James E. Taylor would receive many more assignments in a long and successful career as a journalist and artist. His manuscript and drawings on the Shenandoah Valley would remain packed away until nearly a century after his death, when his sketchbook would finally be published. Rebecca Wright, who furnished Sheridan with crucial intelligence before the Third Battle of Winchester, received death threats from her neighbors, who viewed her as a traitor. She was forced to move to Washington, DC, where she obtained a government job with the Treasury Department. Thomas Laws faced similar threats but somehow scraped enough money together to purchase a small piece of land. Wash escaped from Mosby and survived Badger but was never heard from again. His Southern counterpart, Mosby's manservant, Aaron Burton, remained friends with the Gray Ghost, who sent money to support his old friend. The African American Ranger attended reunions, while Mosby shied away from them, attending only one.

Sheridan rose to the rank of General of the Army, but he never forgot what propelled him there. His colleagues, fellow general officers, would approach Sheridan and marvel at how he obtained his battlefield intelligence and always seemed one step ahead of his opponents. Sheridan would repeatedly respond, "My Scouts." Dumbfounded, the generals answered that they could not obtain similar intelligence from the Scouts they had, to which Sheridan would retort, "You did not have the kind of Scouts I had."[23]

The war may have faded from the headlines, but it never disappeared from the souls of the men and their families. Henry Harrison Young had a special closeness with his mother, writing many letters to her during the war. His mother pined for her son when the letters stopped. But she and his sister refused to believe he had died. "It was a sad time indeed when the letters ceased coming, and when all efforts to find him proved unavailing. . . . Although I know that no tidings of him have cheered us in thirteen years, still I cannot conscientiously say that I believe him dead." For years after, every time the daily stagecoach rumbled into her small Rhode Island town, Young's heartbroken mother would scan each new-comer, hoping against hope that Young had arrived at last.[24]

Some seventy-five years later, by 1941, Henry Young, the Scouts, the Rangers, and the Confederate Secret Service had all long passed away, but their legacy remained. Facing an existential crisis with the Axis powers on the rise, the organization that would become known as the Office of Strategic Services unearthed and looked back upon these shadow warriors for inspiration.

Epilogue

On a sunny but chilly June day in southern France in 2019, I watched parachute canopies blossom and descend as the special operators gently floated to a peaceful, verdant mountainside meadow in France's Tarn region that belied a darker past. In the summer of 1944, the area crawled with German soldiers. The men in the parachutes re-created a scene from seventy-five years earlier in which the commandos from Operational Group PAT, the direct forerunners of the US Army Special Forces—Green Berets—landed on the same mountaintop, welcomed by a covert greeting party of the French Resistance. Hastily shedding their chutes, the World War II commandos—described by one contemporary as "Ph.D.s who could win a barfight"[1]—then surprised, killed, and vanished as they employed unconventional warfare to set that area of Nazi-occupied France ablaze. Adapting tried and true techniques developed decades earlier by their American predecessors during the Civil War, they would be hunted by determined bands of the SS within hours. Hiding in safe houses by day and attacking German supply lines and organizing the resistance by night, the team, led by twenty-two-year-old captain Conrad LaGueux,* derailed vital German reinforcements hurtling toward the invasion beaches in southern France on August 15, 1944. They echoed Mosby's principles: "To destroy supply trains, to break up the means of conveying intelligence, and thus isolating an army from its base, as well as its different corps from each other, to confuse their plans by capturing dispatches are the objects of partisan war."[2] This small group of Americans would force thousands of Germans to surrender.

---

* During the Cold War, LaGueux had an extraordinary career in special operations and was one of the last Americans out of Saigon during the Vietnam War and has been compared to Oscar Schindler for his valiant efforts to evacuate many South Vietnamese families.

That day in 2019, elite commandos from the US Special Operations Command and the CIA's Ground Branch commemorated the World War II parachute drop and Operational Group PAT's extraordinary accomplishments. Each of the modern special operators had years of experience: capturing invaluable intelligence, conducting deep raids into enemy territory, and seizing high-value targets in the most hostile combat environments in recent history. The Americans following in the footsteps of their forebears may not have known the names of Henry Young, Richard Blazer, Arch Rowand, or the World War II OSS commandos, but they were carrying on their legacy. The United States has a tradition of unconventional warfare that uniquely imbues the American way of war. While the centuries may change, the shadow warriors behind these missions have not, often employing groundbreaking techniques pioneered and honed during America's first modern war—the Civil War.

Throughout American history, small groups of individuals have altered the course of events. Civil War Scouts and Rangers who forged these tactics were largely forgotten; however, their legacy remains unvanquished.

DRAMATIS PERSONAE

MAIN CHARACTERS

Archibald H. Rowand Jr.: Teen Jessie Scout who volunteered for hazardous service for nearly the entire war and would receive the Medal of Honor for his actions.

Richard Blazer: Ohioan and leader of Blazer's Independent Scouts, one of the first kill teams, and one of the first counterinsurgency units in the US Army, who hunted the South's most dangerous men.

John Singleton Mosby: "The Gray Ghost," the master spy who formed the greatest American guerrilla warfare unit in history.

Henry Harrison Young: A man born for war and leader of Sheridan's Scouts.

Major General Philip Henry Sheridan: "Little Phil," one of the Civil War's most significant generals, whose Jessie Scouts led the North to victory.

James A. Campbell: "This country will never know how much it owes to [Jessie Scout] James A. Campbell."

James White: The reluctant Jessie Scout and master escape artist.

Lewis Powell: Man of mystery, hulking Mosby's Ranger turned Confederate Secret Service assassin and Lincoln assassination conspirator.

James E. Taylor: One of the most extraordinary embedded combat artists of his generation.

Harry Gilmor: The wily Marylander and partisan chief.

Asbe Montgomery: Sergeant and chronicler of Blazer's Scouts.

James F. "Big Yankee" Ames: Traitor and deserter from the 5th New York Cavalry who became one of Mosby's officers.

THE JESSIE SCOUTS

Charles Carpenter: The original Jessie Scout who would steal anything not nailed down.

Jack Sterry: Jessie Scout who gave his last full measure of devotion.

William Woodall: Confederate soldier who became a Jessie Scout after he killed the Southern officer who insulted his sister and then deserted; also a Medal of Honor recipient.

Dominick Fannin: Jessie Scout often in the thick of the action.

Joseph E. McCabe: Scout sergeant and Medal of Honor recipient.

BLAZER'S SCOUTS

Henry Pancake: Ohio grocer and Jessie Scout in Blazer's Independent Scouts.

Thomas K. Coles: Blazer's second in command.

Joseph Frith: Sergeant and Scout "ready for anything."

Harrison Gray Otis: Initially joint commander of Blazer's Scouts and future owner and publisher of the *Los Angeles Times*.

MOSBY'S RANGERS

Adolphus "Dolly" Richards: Gentleman Ranger officer.

"Major" William Hibbs: Middle-aged local blacksmith who joined Mosby's Rangers, expert scrounger responsible for logistics who had a nose for moonshine stills.

John W. Munson: Ranger and chronicler.

James Joseph Williamson: Ranger and chronicler.

William H. Chapman: Former artillery officer, commander of Company C, and eventually Mosby's second in command.

Samuel Chapman: Fighting Ranger preacher.

Fountain "Fount" Beattie: Mosby's best friend and one of his first Rangers.

Aaron Burton: Mosby's enslaved manservant, friend, and trusted Ranger.

THE CONFEDERATE SECRET SERVICE

John Wilkes Booth: The assassin of the president.

George Nicholas Sanders: Secret Service agent always surrounded by money and beautiful women, and a proponent of the "theory of the dagger."

Jacob Thompson: Former US and Confederate senator Jefferson Davis' commissioner to Canada in command of the Confederate Secret Service in Canada.

Clement Claiborne Clay: Confederate commissioner to Canada.

Thomas Henry Hines: Member of John Hunt Morgan's cavalry, a master escape artist, and architect of the Northwest Conspiracy.

John Breckinridge Castleman: Hines' second in command and operative.

Frank Harney: Explosives expert with the Torpedo Bureau.

John Surratt: Secret Service agent, crucial mainspring within the Lincoln conspiracy, and escape artist extraordinaire.

Sarah Slater: "The French Woman," one of the South's couriers and spies trusted with the most important dispatches.

SUPPORTING WITNESSES

George Crook: Union major general instrumental to the development of Blazer's Scouts.

William Woods Averell: Union cavalry officer known for his bold raids and use of Jessie Scouts.

Bradford Smith Hoskins: British soldier of fortune who served in multiple European conflicts and volunteered for Mosby's Rangers.

Frank Stringfellow: Confederate Scout and spy who dressed as a woman to complete some of his missions.

Thomas Laws: African American hero of the Battle of Winchester.

Rebecca Wright: Schoolteacher who provided crucial information about the Third Battle of Winchester.

Lieutenant General John Brown Gordon: A natural at war and general whom the South turned to to alter the battlefield.

Lieutenant General Jubal Early: "Lee's Bad Old Man," who would wreak havoc in the Shenandoah Valley and threaten Washington, DC.

Tom Rosser: Confederate cavalry general.

John and Jessie Frémont: "The Pathfinder," politician, and Union major general; the Jessie Scouts were founded by him and named in his wife Jessie's honor, a woman renowned for her brilliance and charisma.

Lew Wallace: Major general, savior of Washington, DC, and later author of the novel *Ben-Hur.*

Clement Laird Vallandigham: Seditious Democratic congressman and leader of the Copperhead movement.

Nicholas Badger: Unscrupulous Union officer captured by Mosby.

Wash: Badger's African American manservant who barely escaped with his life.

Charles Russell Lowell: The commander of the 2nd Massachusetts Cavalry Regiment, renowned Mosby hunters. Several companies of California men formed the California Battalion within the regiment. Famed author Herman Melville rode on one of the unit's raids.

Ulric Dahlgren: Union officer and coleader of one of the most controversial raids of the war.

Ulysses S. Grant: Commanding general of the Union Army who later befriended Mosby.

Robert E. Lee: Commanding general of the Army of Northern Virginia.

Wild Bill Donovan: The director of the Office of Strategic Services and father of America's modern special operations forces.

Abraham Lincoln: The sixteenth president of the United States.

Acknowledgments

Every book is a journey. Each has found me. Two roadside signs—one marking Mosby's Grapewood Farm engagement and the other Jessie Scout Jack Sterry's hanging tree—sparked my curiosity and propelled my desire to ask questions and make connections. These previously unnoticed connections are one of the hallmarks of my books. I savor the research; it and the places and the people I have met throughout my odysseys are my favorite parts of the journey. History is my passion. I have amassed oral histories, collaborated on films and documentaries, and written books to preserve and share history for over thirty years. We must save our priceless history. Much of the story of America, sadly, is fading through either urban development or cultural shifts. Like an archaeologist, I strive to unearth shards from the past and objectively meld them together to bring to light a complete, meaningful, and often previously untold story. In this book, I let the participants tell the story in their own words through their letters, diaries, memoirs, and pension files, meshing them in a pointillistic manner to open a window into the past in order to breathe life into the Civil War and provide a new perspective on the conflict. *The Unvanquished* does not romanticize a brutal civil war but chronicles the actions of the participants objectively. Nor does it burnish the conflict with today's presentism. This war that forever changed and nearly destroyed America, like others, is full of nuance. Writing *The Unvanquished* propelled me on an astonishing journey that spanned more than six years. During that time, I spent years walking the hallowed ground where these extraordinary Americans fought and lived. I know the skirmishes, the trails, and the Ranger safe houses they hid in. I also visited their final resting spots.

One of the main characters in this book, Captain Richard Blazer, is buried in a beautiful plot in Mound Hill Cemetery overlooking the Ohio River. I visited the cemetery assuming an easily accessible registry or staff member might be available to guide me. Instead, I faced a sea of tombstones and monuments spanning over 200 years of history and stretching as far as the eye could see. I prayed. I knew I would find Richard Blazer. Within twenty minutes, I reverently stood beside his granite headstone.

The Unvanquished would not have been possible without the assistance of invaluable repositories of historical information. I want to thank the staff who helped me at the New York Public Library, the Library of Congress, the National Archives, and other historical societies and libraries. I would also like to thank the other institutions I visited that furnished essential information for *The Unvanquished,* including the U.S. Army Heritage and Education Center; Pennsylvania Historical Society; Western Reserve Historical Society; University of Texas Briscoe Center for American History, specifically Erin Harbour; and Dr. Louis Mirror from the New-York Historical Society. I'd also like to thank the excellent staff at the Rutherford B. Hayes Library and Museums for their extra effort.

Every author has friends on whom he leans for advice and early manuscript readings. I am grateful for their time and thoughtful comments. Special thanks to Micah Leydorf for all her wisdom and cogent comments that strengthened the manuscript. A special thank-you to my dear friend Ben Ibach, who always has brilliant advice on just about any topic. Ben poured over several drafts and provided key feedback. I am extremely grateful to Matthew Loewenstein for reading the early drafts and having some expert advice and encouragement. Both Matt and Ben were there for me at a moment's notice to provide great advice. I'm also thankful to historian Robert O'Neil, who took me on a personal tour of Loudoun County and the Battles of Middleburg and Upperville and encouraged me to pursue a Civil War project through our mutual contacts and friends at the American Battlefield Trust, an organization that does much to preserve America's history.

I'd like to thank my friend, the great John Batchelor at CBS Radio, whom I've known for over twenty years and who told me I needed to write this book. Ray Shearer, an exceptional historian, read the manuscript and provided powerful encouragement, as did David Mitchell. My friend Matthew Arseneault furnished important feedback. Mike Morris is methodically helping me assemble the disparate pieces needed to solve the mystery of Sergeant Joseph Frith's unmarked grave. I am thankful for the outstanding maps created by one of the best mapmakers in the business, and my friend for over twenty years, Chris Robinson. I'm grateful to fellow OSS Society board member and president Charles Pinck for his unconditional support over the years and his passion for preserving and, in some cases, reclaiming history.

Art Frith also generously provided information on his relatives who were killed in action during the war. An author's life can be a solitary one. I am deeply indebted to my beautiful fiancée, ophthalmologist Dr. Lori Snyder, for lending her brilliance to improving the manuscript with her insightful comments and eagle eye. I am eternally grateful for her and my family's support, including that of my father, who is a tough critic and loved the manuscript, and also that of Dr. Ben Lowentritt, who made an essential suggestion.

I also appreciate my agents' diligent work, specifically my literary agent, Eve Attermann, and my film and television agents, Flora Hackett and Elizabeth Wachtel, at William Morris Endeavor. I'm especially grateful to Elizabeth for encouraging me to write this book. I am profoundly grateful for the thoughtful comments and outstanding guidance provided by my exceptional editor, George Gibson, the best editor with whom I have ever had the privilege to work. His decades of experience and sage advice helped shape a complex subject into a compelling narrative. And this book would never have become a reality without the vision and support of my publisher, the legendary Morgan Entrekin.

NOTES

PREFACE

1 The quote comes from OSS, "COI Phase of SO," NARA. The friction of World War II was the catalyst that led to the meteoric rise of these remarkable groups and branches within the OSS. As with their Civil War counterparts, many elements of this dynamic organization were created almost overnight. Ideal OSS candidates included men and women: "a Ph.D. who could win a bar fight." There were genuinely avant-garde innovations and remarkable breakthroughs, such as the Maritime Unit's SCUBA and a rebreather, along with the tactics and techniques of SEAL teams. The OSS Special Activities Branch, later named the Special Operations Branch, developed: Detachment 101, which organized guerrillas and special operations in Burma; Operational Groups, precursors to the US Army Special Forces (Green Berets); and Jedburgh Teams (Jeds), three-man commando units that dropped into Northern Europe. These groups mobilized partisans behind the lines, sowed a path of destruction, and helped set Nazi-occupied Europe ablaze. The OSS, like the Scouts and Rangers, combined intelligence with special operations.

2 At that time, the organization was known as the Office of the Coordinator of Information (COI) and Donovan the coordinator of information. It would officially become the Office of Strategic Services on June 13, 1942.

3 After leaving the COI, in January 1942 Major James Roosevelt would become the executive officer of the 2nd Marine Raider Battalion, otherwise known as Carlson's Raiders.

4 Patrick K. O'Donnell, *Operatives, Spies, and Saboteurs: The Unknown Story of the Men and Women of World War II's OSS* (New York: Simon & Schuster, 2004), xvi.

5 Combined with extensive studies of the Civil War irregulars, William Donovan also drew on his travel overseas and the unfolding conflicts during the early years of World War II, which contributed to his ideas for special operations. While traveling under orders from President Franklin D. Roosevelt to conflicts in the Balkans, Greece, and Ethiopia, and while in Britain, he was introduced to British commandos in 1940. During these travels he witnessed firsthand tenets developed by irregulars during the Civil War. The draft history that was classified for decades highlights, "His studies of modern warfare had convinced him there was a place for aggressive, small mobile forces which might greatly increase the enemy's misery and weaken his will to resist." The history further explains the supreme challenges he faced in convincing the established military authorities of the importance of special operations: "Donovan's attempts to set up such forces ran a stormy course." OSS, "COI Phase of SO," draft history, unpaginated, National Archives (NARA), RG 226, Entry 99, Box 101.

PROLOGUE

1 Henry Pancake, "Narrow Escapes," *Ironton (OH) Register*, November 25, 1886.

2 Pancake, "Narrow Escapes."

3 John Scott, *Partisan Life with Col. John S. Mosby* (London: Sampson, Low, Son, and Marston, 1867), 297.

4 Pancake, "Narrow Escapes."

5 The seven Medal of Honor (MOH) recipients who performed extraordinary acts of daring and valor were Archibald Rowand Jr., Joseph McCabe, James Campbell, John Miller, John Brewer, William Woodall, and William Hart.

6 During the Civil War, the term irregular warfare meant something different from what it does today. It was often used to define special operations and guerrilla warfare (see quotes by Mosby and Jomini in this text). The modern use of the term is generally defined as a violent struggle among non-state actors and states for influence over a population. Today, the term "unconventional warfare" is broadly defined as military or quasi-military operations other than conventional (involving conventional forces such as large formations of men and modern fighting vehicles, etc.). Unconventional warfare often involves special operations, covert forces, subversion, or guerrilla warfare. US Army Special Forces define special operations as "Operations requiring unique modes of employment, tactical techniques, equipment and training often conducted in hostile, denied, or politically sensitive environments and characterized by one or more of the following: time sensitive, clandestine, low visibility, conducted with and/or through indigenous forces, requiring regional expertise, and/or a high degree of risk." ADP 3-05 Army Special Operations (Washington, DC: Army Doctrine Publication, 2019), Glossary-5. In this narrative, Civil War irregulars conducted and pioneered reconnaissance, guerrilla warfare, counterinsurgency, and raids to capture high-value targets, among many other activities associated with unconventional warfare and special operations. Formed from superb individuals, Jessie Scouts, Rangers, and the Confederate Secret Service often conducted these operations with speed, secrecy, surprise, and simplicity, allowing consistency in their results. Far more than blowing bridges and ambushing wagon trains, the Confederate Secret Service also covertly conducted political warfare to influence an election and a population.

PART I: THE JESSIE SCOUTS
VIRGINIA AND WEST VIRGINIA, 1862–1863
1. THE JESSIE SCOUTS

1 John Cussons, *Jack Sterry, the Jessie Scout: An Incident of the Second Battle of Manassas on Which Turned the Course of the Campaign and Fate of the Southern Army* ([York, PA]: Gazette Print, 1906). The dialogue and scene come from this brief nonfiction book written by John Cussons, who was head of Hood's scouts and Sterry's principal interrogator.

2 "The better man of the two" quoted from Jessie Frémont, *The letters of Jessie Benton Frémont*, ed. Pamela Herr and Mary Lee Spence (Chicago: University of Illinois Press, 1993), xviii. "General Fremont's Jessie Scouts," *Cleveland Daily Leader*, June 23, 1862, 1.

3 Beckwith West, *Experience of a Confederate States Prisoner, Being an Ephemeris Regularly Kept by an Officer of the Confederate States Army* (Richmond: West and Johnson, 1862), 32. Beckwith quotes largely from a *Philadelphia Inquirer* article on the Jessie Scouts in 1862.

4 William Gilmore Beymer, *On Hazardous Service: Scouts and Spies of the North and South* (New York: Harper and Brothers, 1912), 4.

5 "Sharp Practice of a Jessie Scout," *Star and Enterprise* (Newville, PA), March 26, 1863, 1.
6 "Sharp Practice of a Jessie Scout," 1.
7 Jessie Scout Cassidy. His story will be developed in subsequent chapters.
8 Benjamin Taylor, *In Camp and Field* (Chicago: S. C. Griggs, 1875), 218–220.
9 Mark Roth, "Secrets of a Union Spy," *Pittsburgh Post-Gazette*, May 3, 1998.
10 Numbers derived from various newspaper accounts.
11 "Romantic Adventures of Capt. Carpenter of the Jessie Scouts," *Nashville Daily*, July 11, 1862, 1.
12 "A Curious Organization," *Philadelphia Inquirer*, June 18, 1862, 1.
13 Frank Moore, *Anecdotes, Poetry, and Incidents of War: North and South* (New York: printed for subscribers, 1866), 45–47.
14 Moore, 45–47.
15 Moore, 45–47. The capture of Jessie Scout James Alexander is quoted in a letter from Sam Oliver, deputy provost marshal to Major M. Scott, provost marshal, dated, July 6, 1862, source: author collection and he is the owner of the original letter.
16 Edward Wells, *Hampton and His Cavalry in '64* (Richmond, VA: B. F. Johnson, 1899), 303.
17 Beymer, *On Hazardous Service*, 2.
18 Archibald Rowand, Civil War Service File, NARA.
19 William Gilmore Beymer, *On Hazardous Service*, 2.
20 Archibald Rowand, "Summery of Service," 1909, William G. Beymer Papers, Briscoe Center, University of Texas.
21 Beymer, *On Hazardous Service*, 3.
22 Beymer, 12, 3.
23 Beymer, 3.
24 James White, *Scout and Guide of the Union Army* (privately published, 1866), 2.
25 "Colonel Carpenter," *Daily Milwaukee News*, December 25, 1864, 4.
26 John T. Boyle, District of Indiana Judge Advocate's Office, February 27, 1865, NARA
27 "Adventures of Captain Carpenter," *Richmond Weekly Palladium*, February 13, 1863, 1.
28 Rowand, "Summery of Service."
29 Moore, *Anecdotes, Poetry, and Incidents*, 45–47.

2. THREE WINTERS AND THE RISE
OF THE IRREGULARS

1 Emancipation Proclamation, January 1, 1863.
2 Stanton's Order, in *War of the Rebellion: A Compilation of the Official Records of the Union and Confederate Armies* (Washington, DC: Government Printing Office, 1880–1901) (hereafter *OR*), Series 2, Vol. XI, 221–222.
3 *Speeches Concerning Politics and Government during the Civil War Period* (Cincinnati: Gazette, 1864), 5:1–2.
4 Thomas Goss, *The War within the Union High Command: Politics and Generalship during the Civil War* (Lawrence: University Press of Kansas, 2001), 259.
5 Alan T. Nolan, *"Rally Once Again": Selected Civil War Writings of Alan T. Nolan* (Madison: Madison House, 2000), 249.
6 "The Guerrillas in Western Virginia: A Proclamation by Col. Imboden," *Richmond Examiner*, October 26, 1862.
7 *OR*, Series 1, Vol. XXXIII, Chap. XLV, 1252.

3. "I AM MOSBY"

1 James J. Williamson, *Mosby's Rangers: A Record of the Operations of the Forty-Third Battalion of the Virginia Cavalry from Its Organization to the Surrender*, 2nd ed. (New York: Sturgis and Walton, 1909), 36. Williamson was one of Mosby's men. He includes a magazine article from Mosby in his own words on the raid from *Belford* magazine, 1892.

2 Williamson, 35.

3 Scott, *Partisan Life*, 27.

4 Williamson, *Mosby's Rangers*, 35, 37.

5 Williamson, 36.

6 Williamson, 36.

7 Williamson, 39.

8 Williamson, 39.

9 Williamson, 39–40.

10 Williamson, 42.

11 The date of the following article corresponds with a reunion of Mosby's Men. Accordingly, the *Washington Times* ran an article commemorating their exploits: "Telegrapher's Relate Tales of Early Days: Thrilling Incidents, Wherein Mosby's Men Play a Part and Cowboys Terrorize the Tenderfoot," *Washington Times*, October 10, 1906, 5.

12 Williamson, 41–42.

13 Williamson, 43.

14 John Singleton Mosby, *Mosby's War Reminiscences and Stuart's Cavalry Campaigns* (New York: Dodd, Mead, 1898), 30.

15 Scott, *Partisan Life*, 22.

16 John S. Mosby, *The Memoirs of Colonel John S. Mosby*, ed. Charles W. Russell (Boston: Little Brown, 1917), 162.

17 "Telegrapher's Relate Tales of Early Days," *Washington Times*, October 10, 1906, 5.

18 Williamson, *Mosby's Rangers*, 44.

19 Williamson, 44–45.

20 G. G. Benedict, *Vermont in the Civil War: A History of the Part Taken by the Vermont Soldiers and Sailors in the War for the Union*, Vol. II (Burlington, VT: Free Press Association, 1888), 429.

21 *OR*, Serial 52, Chap. XLII, 695.

22 Mosby, *Memoirs*, 28.

23 John Mosby to Sam Chapman, June 4, 1907, Gilder Lehrman Collection.

24 Mosby, *Memoirs*, 18.

25 John Mosby to Sam Chapman, June 4, 1907.

26 John Munson, *Reminiscences of a Mosby Guerrilla* (New York: Moffat, Yard, 1906), 17. Nearly all sources are primary sources drawn from the voices of participants such as Mosby, Munson, Williamson, and Alexander and checked with Federal sources.

27 Mosby, *Mosby's War Reminiscences*, 11.

28 Mosby, 111.

29 Mosby, *Memoirs*, 146. Confederate newspapers also recorded the incident.

30 Mosby, *Mosby's War Reminiscences*, 39.

31 Sources differ, but Mosby's memoirs reference six men. Mosby, *Memoirs*, 147–150.

32 Mosby, *Mosby's War Reminiscences*, 39.

33 Mosby, 44.

34 Mosby, 40.

35 Stuart to Jackson, July 19, 1862, *OR*, Chap. LI, Pt. 2, 594.

36 "History of the Harris Cavalry," referenced by Mosby in *Memoirs*, 128.

37 Mosby, *Memoirs*, 129.

38 Mosby, 130.

39 Mosby, 132.

40 Mosby, 132.

41 R. E. Lee to Thomas J. Jackson, August 4, 1862, Lee Family Digital Archive, https://leefamilyarchive.org/9-family-papers/602-robert-e-lee-to-stonewall-jackson-1862-august-4.

42 Mosby, *Memoirs*, 132–133.

43 Scott, *Partisan Life*, 440.

44 Mosby, *Mosby's War Reminiscences*, 41.

45 Mosby, 62.

46 Munson, *Reminiscences of a Mosby Guerrilla*, 40.

47 Mosby, *Mosby's War Reminiscences*, 45.

48 Mosby, 62.

49 Virgil Carrington Jones, *Ranger Mosby* (Chapel Hill: University of North Carolina Press, 1944), 106.

50 John Henry Alexander, *Mosby's Men* (New York: Neale, 1907), 87–88.

51 The information on Hibbs' process regarding stills is via Mosby historian Erik Buckland.

52 John Henry Alexander, *Mosby's Men*, 87–88.

53 Williamson, *Mosby's Rangers*, 29.

54 Mosby, *Mosby's War Reminiscences*, 67.

55 Eric W. Buckland, *Mosby Men* (Centreville: VA: Fateful Night, 2011), 2.

56 Mosby, *Mosby's War Reminiscences*, 67–68.

4. MISKEL FARM

1 Mosby, 99.

2 Mosby, 98.

3 Sam Chapman, "Memories of Mosby's Men: The Dranesville Raid," *Religious Herald*, January 16, 1902. Also see Horace Mewborn, ed., *From Mosby's Command: Newspaper Articles and Letters by and about John S. Mosby and His Rangers* (Baltimore: Butternut and Blue, 2005), 93.

4 Mosby, *Mosby's War Reminiscences*, 104; Munson, *Reminiscences of a Mosby Guerrilla*, 56.

5 Robert F. O'Neill, *Chasing Jeb Stuart and John Mosby: The Union Cavalry in Northern Virginia from Second Manassas to Gettysburg* (Jefferson, NC: McFarland, 2012), 74.

6 Munson, *Reminiscences of a Mosby Guerrilla*, 56.

7 Munson, 56.

8 John Henry Alexander, *Mosby's Men*, 18. Alexander was a Ranger in Company A.

9 Alexander, 17.

10 Mosby, *Mosby's War Reminiscences*, 106.

11 Munson, *Reminiscences of a Mosby Guerrilla*, 56.

12 Josiah Grout, *Memoir of William Wallace Grout and Autobiography of Josiah Grout* (Newport, VT: Bullock, 1919), 236.

13 Grout, 236.

14 Grout, 236.

15 *OR*, Series 1, Vol. XXV, Pt. I, Chap. XXXVIL, 78. Report by Jul. Stahl, major general to Major General S. P. Heintzelman.

16 Mosby, *Mosby's War Reminiscences*, 108.

17 From Hoskin's diary in Mewborn, *From Mosby's Command*, 11, 14.

18 Chapman, "Memories of Mosby's Men: The Dranesville Raid." Also see Mewborn, *From Mosby's Command*, 93.

5. THE GRAPEWOOD FARM ENGAGEMENT

1 Samuel Chapman, "Memories of Mosby's Men: The Capture of Railroad Train Near Catlett's Station," *Religious Herald*, February 6, 1902. Also see Mewborn, *From Mosby's Command*, 97.

2 Mosby, *Memoirs*, 142.

3 Munson, *Reminiscences of a Mosby Guerrilla*, 68.

4 Mosby, *Memoirs*, 147.

5 Mosby, 142–143.

6 Chapman, "Memories of Mosby's Men: The Capture of Railroad Train." Also see Mewborn, *From Mosby's Command*, 98.

7 Mosby, *Memoirs*, 144.

8 Williamson, *Mosby's Rangers*, 64–65.

9 Chapman, "Memories of Mosby's Men: The Capture of Railroad Train." Also see Mewborn, *From Mosby's Command*, 97.

10 Chapman, "Memories of Mosby's Men: The Capture of Railroad Train." Also see Mewborn, *From Mosby's Command*, 97.

11 Williamson, *Mosby's Rangers*, 65.

12 Mosby, *Memoirs*, 146.

13 Pension application of Herman Richards, NARA.

14 Mosby, *Memoirs*, 146.

15 Scott, *Partisan Life*, 67.

16 Scott, *Partisan Life*, 68.

17 Major Barker's letter 5th NYC, in Munson, *Reminiscences of a Guerrilla*, 71–72.

18 National Register of Historic Places, OMB No. 1024-0018, Auburn Battlefield Fauquier County, Virginia, 12.

19 Mosby, *Memoirs*, 149.

20 O'Neill, *Chasing Jeb Stuart*, 199.

21 Major Barker's letter 5th NYC, in Munson, *Reminiscences of a Guerrilla*, 71–72.

22 Mosby, *Memoirs*, 150.

23 Scott, *Partisan Life*, 67.

24 Mosby, *Mosby's War Reminiscences*, 151.

25 Chapman, "Memories of Mosby's Men: The Capture of Railroad Train." Also see Mewborn, *From Mosby's Command*, 98.

26 Chapman, "Memories of Mosby's Men: The Capture of Railroad Train." Also see Mewborn, *From Mosby's Command*, 98.

27 Grapewood still stands today along with a nearby decades-old, weather-beaten Virginia sign that memorializes the skirmish. After I drove by the sign multiple times and finally stopped to examine the story, this tiny thread became the inspiration for *The*

Unvanquished. Much of Mosby's Confederacy remains untouched, as it was during the Civil War, making it ideal for driving tours.

28 Chapman, "Memories of Mosby's Men: The Capture of Railroad Train." Also see Mewborn, *From Mosby's Command*, 98.

29 Williamson, *Mosby's Rangers*, 43.

30 J. Marshall Crawford, *Mosby and His Men: A Record of the Adventures of That Renowned Partisan Ranger, John S. Mosby, Col. CSA* (New York: G. W. Carlton, 1867), 79–80.

31 Crawford, 80–81.

6. BACK IN THE SADDLE

1 Mosby, *Mosby's War Reminiscences*, 157.

2 Mosby, 165–166.

3 Mosby, 167, 169.

4 Mosby, 169, 170.

5 John Henry Alexander, *Mosby's Men*, 19.

6 General Robert E. Lee to Major General J. E. B. Stuart, June 23, 1863, Lee Family Digital Archive, https://leefamilyarchive.org/9-family-papers/552-robert-e-lee-to -jeb-stuart-1863-june-23.

7 "Haymarket during the War," historical marker, Haymarket, Virginia.

8 Williamson, *Mosby's Rangers*, 48–49.

9 Williamson, 49.

10 Williamson, 51.

11 Williamson, 51.

12 Williamson, 50.

13 Scott, *Partisan Life*, 90.

14 Scott, 109.

15 The quote comes from the Rose Hill Raid historical marker, located at 6209 Rose Hill Drive, Alexandria, VA.

7. THE LEGION OF HONOR: BLAZER'S SCOUTS

1 "The Legion of Honor: A History of That Invincible Band Known as Blazer Scouts," *Ohio Soldier*, August 25, 1888, Vol. 2, No. 2, 51–52.

2 According to Blazer's service file located in the National Archives, he enrolled on July 22, 1862, and joined Captain Niday's company as first lieutenant on August 18, 1862. He was detached for special duty on September 12, 1863.

3 "Legion of Honor," 51–52.

4 "Legion of Honor," 51–52.

5 "Legion of Honor," 51–52.

6 *Architects of Our Fortunes: The Journal of Eliza A. W. Otis, 1860–1863, with Letters and Civil War Journal of Harrison Gray Otis*, 180, Recollections of the War & Santa Barbara Daily Press, Oct-Nov 1876 by Otis.

7 Order 49, dated September 5, 1863, 91st Ohio Infantry Regimental Order Book, NARA, Record Group 94.

8 "Legion of Honor," 51–52.

9 "Legion of Honor," 51–52.

10 "Legion of Honor," 51–52.

11 "Legion of Honor," 51–52.
12 "Legion of Honor," 51–52.
13 "Legion of Honor," 51–52.
14 "Legion of Honor," 51–52.

8. Deliverance: The Thurmonds

1 Recent scholarship places Confederate numbers around 20,000. Jack Dickinson, *Tattered Uniforms and Bright Bayonets: West Virginia's Confederate Soldiers* (Huntington, WV: Marshall University Library Association, 1995).
2 Enslaved individuals and owners are recorded in the 1860 US Census.
3 One of George Crooks' troopers, named Author, quoted in Jeffery C. Weaver, *Thurmond's Partisan Rangers and Swann's Battalion of Virginia Cavalry* (Lynchburg, VA: H. E. Howard, 1993), 12.
4 Weaver, *Thurmond's Partisan Rangers*, 27.
5 Russell Hastings, "The Civil War Memoir of Russell Hastings," n.d., chap. 3, Rutherford B. Hayes Presidential Library and Museums, https://www.rbhayes.org/research/chapters-1-through-3/.
6 Hastings, "Civil War Memoir," chap. 3.
7 Hastings, "Civil War Memoir," chap. 3.
8 Asbe Montgomery, *An Account of R.R. Blazer and His Scouts, Operating in West Virginia and in the Shenandoah Valley, Against William and Philip Thurmond and Moseby [sic], the Great Guerrillas* (Marietta, OH: Register's Office, 1865). The privately published manuscript is located at Ohio History Connection (OHC), formerly the Ohio Historical Society. Hereafter, the document is cited as Montgomery, *Blazer's Scouts*, 4–7.
9 Montgomery, 4.
10 Montgomery, 5.
11 Montgomery, 5–6.
12 Montgomery, 6.
13 Montgomery, 7.
14 Montgomery, 5–7.

9. Lewis Powell

1 Crawford, *Mosby and His Men*, 163.
2 Powell is listed on the Company B muster roll on October 1, 1863, NARA.
3 Lewis Payne, "Seward's Assassin," *The Times* (Philadelphia), June 3, 1882, 6.
4 Powell would later reveal Joseph Branson Sr.'s involvement in the abduction plot to Powell's spiritual adviser, Reverend Abram Dunn Gillette, before his execution.
5 Payne, "Seward's Assassin," 6.

10. "Lurk like Wild Creatures in the Darkness"

1 Theodore Lang, *Loyal West Virginia: From 1861 to 1865* (Baltimore: Deutsch, 1895), 109.
2 Frank Reader, *History of the Fifth West Virginia Cavalry, Formerly the Second Virginia Infantry, and of Battery G, First West Va. Light Artillery* (New Brighton, PA: Daily News, 1890), 207.
3 Rowand, "Summery of Service."

4 Arnold Blumberg, "Alfred Duffie: A 'Napoleon' in the Civil War," *Military Heritage*, August 2012, https://warfarehistorynetwork.com/2016/11/11/alfred-duffie-a-napoleon-in-the-civil-war/.

5 Montgomery, *Blazer's Scouts*, 5–6.

6 Taylor, *In Camp and Field*, 218–220.

7 James Ireland, diary entry for November 10, 1863, Company A, 12th Regiment, Ohio Volunteer Infantry, 1864, Morrow, Warren County, Ohio, OHC.

8 James Longstreet, *From Manassas to Appomattox: Memoirs of the Civil War in America* (New York: Da Capo, 1992), 480–483. First published in 1896 by J. B. Lippincott.

9 Abraham Lincoln to Ulysses S. Grant, November 25, 1863, *OR*, Serial 55, Chapter XLII, 25.

11. THE SALEM RAID: "LIFE IN ONE HAND AND SEEMING DISHONOR IN THE OTHER"

1 At the start of the raid, the action had strategic significance, but eventually Longstreet abandoned the siege of Knoxville as the raid unfolded. Nevertheless, the Federals pressed forward to interdict the rails and their use to supply Longstreet's forces and to distract the Confederates.

2 August 1863–March 1864, telegrams, NARA, RG 363.

3 *OR*, Serial 48, Chapter XLI, 927.

4 Rowand, "Summery of Service."

5 *OR*, Serial 48, Chap. XLI, 926.

6 *OR*, Serial 48, Chap. XLI, 927.

7 Scout Jessie Meddaugh, pension certificate 435841, and James Webb served in Milroy's Unit.

8 Taylor, *In Camp and Field*, 218–220.

9 Otis' Report, *OR*, Serial 48, Chap. XLI, 940.

10 *OR*, Serial 48, Chap. XLI, 940.

11 Otis, *Santa Barbara Weekly Press*, October 30, 1876.

12 *National Tribune* (Washington, DC), September 8, 1887, 1.

13 *National Tribune* (Washington, DC), September 8, 1887, 1.

14 *OR*, Serial 48, Chapter XLI, 942.

15 *OR*, Serial 48, Chapter XLI, 928.

16 Darrell L. Collins, *General William Averell's Salem Raid: Breaking the Knoxville Supply Line* (Shippensburg, PA: Burd Street, 1998), 79–80.

17 Collins, 90.

18 *National Tribune* (Washington, DC), September 22, 1887, 1.

19 Averell's report, *OR*, Vol. XXIX, Chap. XLL, Pt. 1, 925, 931.

20 William Davis Slease, *The 14th Pennsylvania Cavalry in the Civil War: A History of the 14th Pennsylvania Volunteer Cavalry Organization until Its Close, 1861–1865* (Pittsburgh: Art and Engraving Company, 1915), 121.

21 *Pittsburgh Gazette*, January 11, 1864, 1.

22 Edward McMahon's report to General Sam Jones, *OR*, Serial 48, Chap. XLI, 946, 6.

23 Theo Brown, "With Averell on His Raid to Salem, December 1863—Privations and Hardships," *National Tribune* (Washington, DC), July 30, 1903, 1.

24 Brown, "With Averell," 1.

25 Collins, *Averell's Salem Raid*, 120.
26 *OR*, Vol. XXIX, Pt. 1, 945.
27 General Kelly's report on Averell's raid, *OR*, Vol. XXIX, Pt. 1, 931–932.

12. Crimson Snow

1 The history of the 1st Regiment has a single mention of the action at Rectortown: "History and Roster of Maryland Volunteers," Vol. 367, 663, Maryland State Archives.
2 "Captain Albert M. Hunter's Account of the War between the States," pt. 3, transcribed by John Miller, Emmitsburg Area Historical Society, accessed July 20, 2023, https://www.emmitsburg.net/archive_list/articles/history/civil_war/hunter_account _of_coles_cavelry_p3.htm.
3 "History and Roster of Maryland Volunteers," Vol. 367, 655.
4 C. Armour Newcomer, *Cole's Cavalry; or, Three Years in the Saddle* (Baltimore: Cushing, 1895), 10.
5 Williamson, *Mosby's Rangers*, 71.
6 Crawford, *Mosby and His Men*, 141.
7 "Captain Albert M. Hunter's Account," pt. 3.
8 "Captain Albert M. Hunter's Account," pt. 3.
9 Mosby, *Memoirs*, 89.
10 John Marshall Crawford, in an extraordinary wartime article he wrote using only his initials, "Brilliant Affair in Fauquier," which appeared in the *Richmond Examiner*, claims Hunter had his horse shot out from him and he hid in the bushes.
11 "Captain Albert M. Hunter's Account," pt. 3.
12 Crawford, *Mosby and His Men*, 147.
13 "Captain Albert M. Hunter's Account," pt. 3.
14 John S. Mosby to R. T. W. Duke Jr., April 4, 1915, MSS 9521-g, University of Virginia Archives.
15 Mosby, *Memoirs*, 90.
16 Williamson, *Mosby's Rangers*, 75–76.
17 The house that served as Cole's headquarters still exists and is in private hands; a metal sign near the home marks the camp's location. See Mosby, *Memoirs*, 90.
18 Mosby, 90.
19 Williamson, *Mosby's Rangers*, 126.
20 "Captain Albert M. Hunter's Account of the War between the States," pt. 4, transcribed by John Miller, Emmitsburg Area Historical Society, accessed July 20, 2023, https://www.emmitsburg.net/archive_list/articles/history/civil_war/hunter_account _of_coles_cavelry_p4.htm.
21 "Captain Albert M. Hunter's Account," pt. 4.
22 "Captain Albert M. Hunter's Account," pt. 4.
23 Williamson, *Mosby's Rangers*, 76.
24 Williamson, 76.
25 William H. Chapman, "Death of Captain William Smith," letter, in appendix to Williamson, *Mosby's Rangers*, 486–487.
26 Mosby, *Memoirs*, 90.
27 "Captain Albert M. Hunter's Account," pt. 4.
28 Williamson, *Mosby's Rangers*, 77.

29 Mosby to Ranger Ben Palmer's father, published in the *Richmond Enquirer*, March 8, 1864. Also see Mewborn, *From Mosby's Command*, 28.
30 Williamson, *Mosby's Rangers*, 77.
31 "Captain Albert M. Hunter's Account," pt. 4.

1864

13. RIVERBOAT GAMBLERS AND GENERAL CROOK

1 *Gallipolis (OH) Journal*, February 11, 1864, 2.
2 *Gallipolis (OH) Journal*, February 11, 1864, 2.
3 "Capture of the Steamer B.C. Levi—Independent Scouts," *Point Pleasant Register*, February 11, 1864, 2. The second part of the column, on the same page, is signed "Quickstep."
4 George Crook, *General George Crook: His Autobiography*, ed. Martin F. Schmitt (Norman: University of Oklahoma Press, 1986), 12.
5 John G. Bourke, *On the Border with Crook* (New York: Charles Scribner's Sons, 1891), 112.
6 General Crook's General Order #2, February 8, 1864, NARA.
7 Montgomery, *Blazer and His Scouts*, 17.
8 Montgomery, 13.
9 Montgomery, 10.
10 Montgomery, 9, 10, 13.
11 *Norwalk Reflector*, July 26, 1864, 3.
12 Montgomery, *Blazer and His Scouts*, 13, 9.
13 Montgomery, 13, 9.
14 Montgomery, 14.
15 Montgomery, 15.
16 *Cincinnati Commercial*, May 17, 1864, 1.

14. KILL JEFFERSON DAVIS AND BURN RICHMOND: THE KILPATRICK-DAHLGREN RAID

1 J. H. Kidd, *Personal Recollections of a Cavalryman with Custer's Michigan Cavalry Brigade in the Civil War* (Ionia, MI: Sentinel Printing, 1908), 158.
2 Recent scholarship and handwriting analysis by the Smithsonian confirm that handwritten orders later found appear to be in Stanton's hand. The paper's authenticity was confirmed by historian and expert James O. Hall. The best summary of sources on the paper's authenticity is in Bruce Venter, *Kill Jeff Davis: The Union Raid on Richmond, 1864* (Norman: University of Oklahoma Press, 2016), 265–271.
3 George Meade, *The Life and Letters of George Gordon Meade* (New York: Charles Scribner and Sons, 1913), 167.
4 Shepard R. Brown, in *Stringfellow of the Fourth*, devotes a large portion of a chapter to his exploits at the party.
5 J. Marshall Favill, *The Diary of a Young Officer* (Chicago: R. R. Donnelley, 1909), 279.
6 Hamilton Howard, *Civil War Echoes: Character Sketches and State Secrets* (Washington, DC: Howard, 1907), 214.
7 Venter, *Kill Jeff Davis*, 168–169.

8 J. William Jones, ed., "The Kilpatrick-Dahlgren Raid against Richmond," in *Southern Historical Society Papers*, vol. 13, *January to December 1885* (Richmond, VA: Rev. J. William Jones, 1885), 518, 538, 521.

9 John A. Dahlgren, *A Memoir of Ulric Dahlgren by His Father* (Philadelphia: J. B. Lippincott, 1872), 216.

10 Service file of Sergeant Harrison J. Jack, M543, Roll 11, NARA via Fold3. Jack served in Company F, Maine 1st Volunteer Cavalry, and was killed in action in Richmond on March 1, 1864. Jack's first enlistment date is October 19, 1861. He battled in many clashes, and he rose from the rank of private to sergeant.

11 J. William Jones, "Kilpatrick-Dahlgren Raid," 533 (report of E. C. Fox, 5th Virginia Cavalry, mentioning five bullets).

12 *Richmond Examiner*, March 5, 1864, 1.

13 The document attributed to Custer is "Memoranda of War." Ernest Furgurson, *Ashes of Glory: Richmond at War* (New York: Knopf, 1996), 255.

PART II: THE CONFEDERATE SECRET SERVICE
15. THE DEPARTMENT OF DIRTY TRICKS

1 William A. Tidwell, *April '65: Confederate Covert Action in the American Civil War* (Kent, OH: Kent State University Press, 1995), 30–31.

2 Kenneth R. Rutherford, *America's Buried History: Landmines in the Civil War* (El Dorado Hills, CA: Savas Beatie, 2020), 45.

3 OSS would fashion similar devices in World War II.

4 Report of John Maxwell, Secret Service, Confederate States of America, Explosion at City Point, August 9, 1864, *OR*, Serial 87, Vol. XLII, Pt. 1, 954–956.

5 *New-York Tribune*, August 9, 1864.

6 Report of John Maxwell, 954–956.

16. CANADA, THE CONFEDERATE SECRET SERVICE, ELECTION INTERFERENCE, AND THE NORTHWEST CONSPIRACY

1 *OR*, Series 1, Vol. XXVII, Pt. 3, 880–881.

2 Mark A. Weitz, "Desertion, Cowardice and Punishment," Essential Civil War Curriculum, accessed January 12, 2023, https://www.essentialcivilwarcurriculum.com/desertion,-cowardice-and-punishment.html.

3 Jean Baker, *Affairs of Party: The Political Culture of Northern Democrats in the Mid-Nineteenth Century* (New York: Fordham University Press, 1983), 319.

4 Edward Pollard, *The Lost Cause: A New Southern History of the War of the Confederates* (New York: E. B. Treat, 1868), 89.

5 Jefferson Davis, *Jefferson Davis, Constitutionalist: His Letters, Papers and Speeches*, ed. Dunbar Rowland (Jackson: Mississippi Department of Archives and History, 1923), 6:236–238.

6 James D. Horan, *Confederate Agent: Discovery and History* (New York: Crown, 1954), 160.

7 William Tidwell et al., *Come Retribution*, 331, quoted in *Biographical Encyclopedia of Kentucky* (Cincinnati: J. M. Armstrong, 1878), 538–541. The biographical sketch was written by one of Sanders' close friends after the war.

8 Sanders to Davis, March 7, 1865, published in *New York Herald*, July 8, 1865, 1.
9 *Chicago Tribune*, January 15, 1863.
10 Edward Pierce, *Memoirs and Letters of Charles Sumner* (Boston: Roberts Brothers, 1877–1892), 4:114.
11 Jefferson Davis, *The Papers of Jefferson Davis*, ed. Linda Lasswell Crist (Baton Rouge: Louisiana State University Press, 1989–2004), 10:154.

17. U. S. GRANT

1 Ulysses S. Grant, *General Grant: His Life and Services* (London: Cameron and Ferguson, 1885), 38.
2 Ulysses S. Grant, *The Personal Memoirs of U.S. Grant* (New York: Charles L. Webster, 1885), vol. 1, chap. 16, https://www.gutenberg.org/files/4367/4367-h/4367-h.htm#ch16.

18. THE SCOUT TOWARD ALDIE

1 James McLean, *California Sabers: The 2nd Massachusetts Cavalry in the Civil War* (Bloomington: Indiana University Press, 2000), 18.
2 McLean, 201.
3 Williamson, *Mosby's Rangers*, 142.
4 Williamson, 143–144.
5 Munson, *Reminiscences of a Mosby Guerrilla*, 88.
6 *Fairfax Herald*, November 6, 1914, 3.
7 *Fairfax Herald*, November 6, 1914, 3.
8 *Fairfax Herald*, November 6, 1914, 3.
9 *Alexandria Gazette*, March 18, 1909.
10 Munson, *Reminiscences of a Mosby Guerrilla*, 90.
11 Herman Melville, *The Scout toward Aldie*, in *Battle-Pieces and Aspects of War* (New York: Harper and Brothers, 1866), 187–188.
12 Melville, 187.
13 Melville, 225.
14 Munson, *Reminiscences of a Mosby Guerrilla*, 141.

19. THE DUBLIN RAID

1 Ulysses Simpson Grant, *Personal Memories of U.S. Grant*, New Edition (London: Sampson Low, Marston & Company, 1895), 416
2 Montgomery, *Blazer and His Scouts*, 11.
3 E. C. Arthur, "The Dublin Raid," *Ohio Soldier*, January–April 1989, 4–5.
4 Michael Eagan, *The Flying, Gray-Haired Yank; or, The Adventures of a Volunteer* (Philadelphia: Hubbard Brothers, 1888), 169.
5 Rutherford B. Hayes, *Diary and Letters of Rutherford B. Hayes: Nineteenth President of the United States*, vol. 2, *1861–1865*, ed. Charles Richard Williams (Columbus: Ohio State Archaeological and Historical Society, 1922), 457.
6 Report of Brigadier General William Averell, May 23, 1864, *OR*, Serial 70, Chap. XLIX, 40–42.
7 Rowand, "Summery of Service."
8 Report of Brigadier General William Averell, 40–42.
9 Montgomery, *Blazer and His Scouts*, 15.

The Shenandoah Valley

20. Into the Valley: Staunton and Lexington

1 James Z. M'Chesney, "Scouting on Hunter's Raid to Lynchburg, VA," *Confederate Veteran* 28 (1920): 173.

2 M'Chesney, 173–175.

3 Montgomery, *Blazer and His Scouts*, 15.

4 Grant to Halleck, May 19, 1864, *OR*, Series 1, Vol. 37, 492.

5 "Historical Letter: Correspondence from Major-General D. Hunter (HQ Dept. of the South) to Jefferson Davis," 1863, Project Reconstruction, accessed July 20, 2023, https://projectreconstructionus.com/items/show/258.

6 Rowand, "Summery of Service."

7 Beymer, *On Hazardous Service*, 8.

8 Rowand, "Summery of Service."

9 Rowand.

10 Rowand.

11 Rowand.

12 Rowand.

13 White, *Scout and Guide*, 5–7.

14 Rowand, "Summery of Service."

15 Rowand.

16 General Averell's report, July 1, 1864, *OR*, Vol. XXXVII, Pt. 1, Chap. XLIX, 147.

17 Rowand, "Summery of Service."

18 Montgomery, *Blazer and His Scouts*, 18.

19 *Norwalk Reflector*, July 26, 1864, 3.

20 David Hunter Strother, *A Virginia Yankee in the Civil War: The Diaries of David Hunter Strother*, ed. Cecil D. Eby Jr. (Chapel Hill: University of North Carolina Press, 1961), 150–151.

21 Montgomery, *Blazer and His Scouts*, 17.

22 "General Hunter's Expedition, The Capture of Lexington," *Chicago Tribune*, July 2, 1864, 1.

23 "Narrow Escapes," *Ironton (OH) Register*, March 29, 1888.

24 Richard Duncan, *Lee's Endangered Left: The Civil War in Western Virginia* (Baton Rouge: Louisiana State University Press, 1998), 224.

25 "Recollections of Jubal Early by One Who Followed Him," *Century Magazine* 70 (May–October 1905): 311.

26 Rowand, "Summery of Service."

27 Montgomery, *Blazer and His Scouts*, 19.

28 Montgomery, 19–20.

29 Rowand, "Summery of Service."

21. Shadow War Canada: Influencing the Democracy

1 Murat Halsted, *Caucuses of 1860* (Columbus, OH: Follet, Foster, 1860), 10–11. Halsted was a reporter who provided a pithy portrait of Sanders.

2 John Castleman, *Active Service* (Louisville, KY: Courier-Journal Job Printing, 1917), 136.

3 George Sanders to Jefferson Davis, March 7, 1865, published in *New York Herald*, July 8, 1865, 1.

4 James Ford Rhodes, *History of the United States: From the Compromise of 1850 to the Final Restoration of Home Rule at the South in 1877* (New York: Macmillan, 1919), 4:517.
5 The former congressman reached out to the Secret Service first, according to Castleman.
6 Clement L. Vallandigham, *The Record of Hon. C.L. Vallandigham on Abolition, the Union, and the Civil War* (Columbus, OH: J. Walter, 1863), 177–180.
7 *Hamilton True Telegraph,* January 31, 1863.
8 Weitz, "Desertion, Cowardice and Punishment."
9 Clement Laird Vallandigham, *Speeches, Arguments, Addresses, and Letters of Clement L. Vallandigham* (New York: Walter, 1864), 181.
10 John Breckinridge Castleman, *Active Service,* 146–147.
11 *OR,* Series 1, Vol. XLIII, Pt. II, Chap. LV, 930–932.
12 George Sanders to Jefferson Davis, March 7, 1865, published in *New York Herald,* July 8, 1865.
13 Castleman, *Active Service,* 146–147.
14 Castleman, 168, 146.
15 George Sanders to Davis, Jefferson March 7, 1865, published in *New York Herald,* July 8, 1865, 1.
16 James D. Horan, *Confederate Agent: A Discovery in History* (New York: Crown, 1954), 93

22. "To Threaten Washington"

1 Jubal Anderson Early, *Autobiographical Sketch and Narrative of the War between the States,* ed. R. H. Early (Philadelphia: Lippincott, 1912), 371, 389–391.
2 *OR,* Vol. XL, Chap. XLIX, 766–767.
3 *OR,* Vol. XL, Chap. LII, 759. John Tyler, assistant adjutant general, Confederate States of America, wrote Major General Sterling Price about the proposed mission.
4 The 2nd Maryland Cavalry was also referred to as Gilmor's Partisan Rangers.
5 Gilmor, *Four Years in the Saddle,* 196.

23. Mosby's Calico Raid and Showdown at Mount Zion Church

1 John Henry Alexander, *Mosby's Men,* 78.
2 Alexander, 79.
3 Munson, *Reminiscences of a Mosby Guerrilla,* 93–94.
4 John Henry Alexander, *Mosby's Men,* 81.
5 Alexander, 83.
6 Alexander, 83.
7 James A. Ramage, *Gray Ghost: The Life of Col. John Singleton Mosby* (Louisville: University Press of Kentucky, 1999), 161.
8 Ramage, 161.
9 John Henry Alexander, *Mosby's Men,* 85.
10 Alexander, 86–87.
11 Alexander, 90.
12 Alexander, 92.
13 Alexander, 92.
14 Munson, *Reminiscences of a Mosby Guerrilla,* 96.
15 Charles A. Humphreys, *Field, Camp, Hospital, and Prison in the Civil War* (Boston: Press of Geo. H. Ellis Co., 1918), 96–97.

16 Williamson, *Mosby's Rangers*, 112.

17 Humphreys, *Field, Camp*, 96–97.

18 I am the curator of Fogg's Colt and Tyrell's saber from the battle. Artifacts that are identified as having been present at key points of history provide powerful inspiration during the writing and research process.

19 Munson, *Reminiscences of a Mosby Guerrilla*, 97.

20 Munson, 99.

21 Williamson, *Mosby's Rangers*, 112.

22 Crawford, *Mosby and His Men*, 228.

23 Munson, *Reminiscences of a Mosby Guerrilla*, 99.

24 Mosby, *Memoirs*, 92.

24: "I DON'T THINK MANY PEOPLE, NORTH OR SOUTH, REALIZE HOW CLOSE WASHINGTON CAME TO FALLING"

1 *OR*, Series 1, Vol. XXXVII, Chap. XLIX, 100.

2 Lew Wallace, *An Autobiography* (New York: Harper Brothers, 1906), 2:771.

3 *OR*, Series 1, Vol. XXXVII, Chap. XLIX, 174.

4 Early, *Autobiographical Sketch*, 389.

5 Early, 389.

6 James Johnston, "The Man Who Almost Conquered Washington," *Washington Post*, March 18, 2001.

7 John Brown Gordon, *Reminiscences of the Civil War* (New York: Charles Scribner and Sons, 1903), 314.

8 *OR*, Serial 82, Chap. LII, 175.

9 Benjamin Cooling, *Jubal Early's Raid on Washington* (Tuscaloosa: University of Alabama Press, 2007), 113.

10 John George Nicolay and John Hay, *Abraham Lincoln: A History* (New York: Century, 1890), 9:165.

11 John Hill Brinton, *Personal Memoirs of John H. Brinton, Major and Surgeon U.S.V., 1861–1865* (New York: Neale, 1914), 279.

12 Abraham Lincoln, *The Writings of Abraham Lincoln* (New York: P. F. Collier and Son, 1865), 7:178–179.

13 George Stevens, *Three Years in the Sixth Corps: A Concise Narrative of Events in the Army of the Potomac* (New York: D. Van Nostrand, 1870), 382.

14 Montgomery, *Blazer and His Scouts*, 21.

15 Brokers traded in gold bullion and gold dollar coins; two asset classes were greenbacks and gold bullion—the peak was $2.85 for $1.00 of gold on July 11, 1864. The exchange rate rose and fell based on the outcome of battles.

16 *OR*, Series 1, Vol. XLIII, Pt. II, Chap. LV, 930–932.

17 *OR*, Series 1, Vol. XLIII, Pt. II, Chap. LV, 930–932.

18 John Waugh, *Reelecting Lincoln: The Battle for the 1864 Presidency* (New York: Crown, 1997), 267.

25. THE HIGH-WATER MARK: CHAMBERSBURG BURNS

1 *OR*, Serial 70, Chap. XLIIX, 311–312.

2 Richard Miller, *Otis and His Times: The Career of Harrison Gray Otis of Los Angeles* (PhD diss., UCLA, 1964), 24.

3 Strother, *Virginia Yankee*, 280.
4 Jack Dickinson, *16th Virginia Cavalry* (Ann Arbor: University of Michigan Press, 1989), 51.
5 Rowand, "Summery of Service."
6 Harry Gilmor, *Four Years in the Saddle* (New York: Harper & Brothers, 1866), 211.
7 Gilmor, 213.

26. MOOREFIELD

1 J. J. Sutten, *History of the 2nd Regiment West Virginia Cavalry Volunteers* (Portsmouth, OH, 1892), 149. Also see Rowand, "Summery of Service."
2 Rowand, "Summery of Service."
3 Rowand.
4 Rowand.
5 J. J. Sutten, *History of the 2nd Regiment West Virginia Cavalry Volunteers* (Portsmouth, OH, 1892), 149. Also see Rowand, "Summery of Service."
6 J. J. Sutten, *History of the 2nd Regiment West Virginia Cavalry Volunteers* (Portsmouth, OH, 1892), 149. Also see Rowand, "Summery of Service."
7 Gilmor, *Four Years in the Saddle*, 233.
8 Gilmor, 234.
9 Gilmor, 234.
10 White, *Scout and Guide*, 8.
11 Rowand, "Summery of Service."
12 Gilmor, *Four Years in the Saddle*, 235.
13 *OR*, Serial 1, Vol. 90, Chap. LV, 494.
14 Jubal Early, *A Memoir of the Last Year of the War for Independence of the Confederate States of America* (Lynchburg, VA: Charles W. Button, 1867), 70.
15 Beymer, *On Hazardous Service*, 9.
16 Beymer, 9.
17 Rowand, "Summery of Service."
18 Beymer, *On Hazardous Service*, 9–10.

27. AN EMBEDDED COMBAT ARTIST, GENERAL SHERIDAN, AND MOSBY'S GREAT BERRYVILLE WAGON RAID

1 James E. Taylor, *Sketchbook* (Dayton, OH: Morningside House, 1989), 10. This extraordinary book is James Taylor's original sketches and diary from his time in the Shenandoah Valley.
2 Taylor, 7, 10, 12, 13.
3 Taylor, 34, 35.
4 Taylor, 39.
5 Taylor, 41.
6 Taylor, 41.
7 Melville, *The Scout toward Aldie*, 187–188. Melville, a civilian noncombatant, joined in scout or cavalry patrol headed by his friend and fellow poet James Russell Lowell, commander of the 2nd Massachusetts Cavalry, to find and destroy Mosby and his Rangers. The scout failed, and Melville's poem captures the terror Mosby's men evoked.
8 Munson, *Reminiscences of A Mosby Guerrilla*, 103, 15–16, 17.
9 Munson, 103.

10　John S. Mosby, "Attacked by a Very Unexpected Enemy," *The World* (New York), March 31, 1895.

11　Munson, *Reminiscences of a Mosby Guerrilla*, 103.

12　Munson, 104.

13　Munson, 105.

14　Mosby, *Memoirs*, 366–367.

15　Munson, 106.

16　Mosby, "Attacked."

17　Mosby, *Memoirs*, 145.

18　Scott, *Partisan Life*, 272.

PART III: SHERIDAN'S SCOUTS AND "COME RETRIBUTION"
28. "I HAVE 100 MEN WHO WILL TAKE THE CONTRACT TO CLEAN OUT MOSBY'S GANG"

1　*OR*, Series 1, Vol. XLIII, Pt. I, Chap. LV, 811.

2　*OR*, Series 1, Vol. XLIII, Pt. I, Chap. LV, 811.

3　*OR*, Series 1, Vol. XLIII, Pt. I, Chap. LV, 43.

4　*OR*, Series, Vol. XLIII, Pt. I, Chap. LV, 841 and 822.

5　Munson, *Reminiscences of a Mosby Guerrilla*, 147.

6　Scott, *Partisan Life*, 281.

7　Williamson, *Mosby's Rangers*, 213.

8　Scott, *Partisan Life*, 281.

9　E. A. Paul, "More about the Measure by Mosby—Rebel Treachery—Cowardly Cruelty," *New York Times*, August 21, 1864.

10　Williamson, *Mosby's Rangers*, 418.

11　Paul, "More about the Measure."

12　Montgomery, *Blazer and His Scouts*, 22.

13　*OR*, Series 1, Vol. XLIII, Pt. I, Chap. LV, 860.

14　Sheridan now led the Army of the Shenandoah. The feisty Irishman had recently received command of the reconstituted army in response to Jubal Early's march on Washington, drubbing General George Crook's command outside Winchester, Virginia, during the Second Battle of Kernstown. A recent raid by Early's forces on Chambersburg, Pennsylvania, torched a large portion of the city after officials failed to come up with the extortion money he demanded. In Petersburg, Lee's and Grant's armies stalemated and engaged in siege warfare. For three years, the war went on and appeared no closer to ending. An election loomed. The South seemed to be winning the information war, capitalizing on the slew of small victories, magnified by a press that could be unforgiving to Lincoln. The North was war-weary after hundreds of thousands of men had been killed and wounded. The Democrats offered a platform of peace and were willing to let slavery stand. Lincoln needed success on the battlefield. Mosby's latest Berryville wagon train raid, magnified by the Northern press, demanded action. Sheridan wanted Mosby's head. The Shenandoah Valley, the breadbasket of the South and route for three invasions of the North—the back door into Washington, DC—had to be shut down, and, along with it, Mosby.

15　W. A. Bartlett, "Lincoln's Seven Hits with His Rifle," *Magazine of History, with Notes and Queries*, Extra Numbers 73–76 (1921): 71–72.

16　Bartlett, 71–72.

17 Bartlett, 72.
18 President Lincoln kept the rifle, and it is now on display at the Smithsonian.
19 Several Rangers provide eyewitness testimony of the carbines, and a Scout struck one Ranger in the head with a carbine.
20 Montgomery, *Blazer's Scouts*, 22.
21 Montgomery, 23.
22 Montgomery, 23.
23 Montgomery, 23.
24 Description from the John W. Mobberly roadside marker located in Hillsboro in Loudoun County, Virginia. I recommend visiting many of the sites and locations described in this book.
25 *OR*, Serial 97, Chap. LVIII, 443–444.
26 Loudoun Ranger John W. Forsythe recorded in his memoirs that a number of skeletons were found in such condition in the mountains after the war.
27 Montgomery, *Blazer's Scouts*, 23.
28 Montgomery, 23.

29. THE MOST IMPORTANT ELECTION
IN AMERICAN HISTORY

1 Reported in *New York Daily Tribune*, September 1, 1864.
2 Congressional Union Committee, *The Chicago Copperhead Convention: The Treasonable and Revolutionary Utterances of the Men Who Composed It* (Washington, DC: Congressional Union Committee, 1864), 16.
3 Congressional Union Committee, 16.
4 Congressional Union Committee, 16.
5 *Daily Missouri Democrat*, August 30, 1864.
6 Castleman, *Active Service*, 155, 154, 160.
7 Democratic National Convention, *Official Proceedings of the Democratic National Convention, Held in 1864 at Chicago* (Chicago: Times Steam Book and Job Printing House, 1864), 26.
8 Guest book of the St. Lawrence Hotel, McCord Museum.
9 Democratic National Convention, *Official Proceedings*, 31.
10 James McPherson, *Battle Cry of Freedom* (New York: Ballantine Books, 1988), 681.
11 *OR*, Series 4, Vol. 3, 636–638.
12 Abraham Lincoln, *Collected Works*, ed. Roy P. Basler (New Brunswick, NJ: Rutgers University Press, 1953), 7:514.
13 "CONGRATULATING THE PRESIDENT; A Serenade by the Clubs, and a Speech by Mr. Lincoln," *New York Times*, November 10, 1864.
14 *New York Sunday Mercury*, March 1864 and reprinted in several newspapers in the South including the *Charlotte Western Democrat* on April 26, 1864.
15 Joseph Barrett, *Life of Abraham Lincoln* (Cincinnati, OH: Moore, Wilstach & Baldwin, 1865), 662.
16 D. F. Murphy, reporter, *Presidential Election, 1864: Proceedings of the National Union Convention Held in Baltimore, Md., June 7th and 8th, 1864* (New York: Baker and Godwin, 1864), 57.
17 Murphy, 57, 58.

30. TAKEDOWN AT MYER'S FORD

1 Montgomery, *Blazer and His Scouts*, 27.
2 Montgomery, 25.
3 Ranger accounts claim the Scouts were drunk when they attacked.
4 Montgomery, *Blazer and His Scouts*, 25.
5 Williamson, *Mosby's Rangers*, 134.
6 Montgomery, *Blazer and His Scouts*, 26.
7 Montgomery, 26.
8 Montgomery, 26.
9 Crawford, *Mosby and His Men*, 254–255.
10 Munson, *Reminiscences of a Mosby Guerrilla*, 117.
11 Williamson, *Mosby's Rangers*, 134.
12 Williamson, 134.
13 Williamson, 134.
14 Montgomery, *Blazer and His Scouts*, 26.
15 Montgomery, 26.
16 Montgomery, 26, states the force was 150 Rangers.
17 "Blazer's Report, Sept. 4, 1864 Meyer's Ford, VA," *OR*, Series 1, Vol. XLII, Pt. I, 615–616.
18 Crawford, *Mosby and His Men*, 255.

31. SHERIDAN'S SCOUTS: THE TIDE TURNS

1 Rowand, "Summery of Service."
2 Rowand, "Summery of Service."
3 Beymer, *On Hazardous Service*, 11.
4 Philip H. Sheridan, *Personal Memoirs of P.H. Sheridan, General United States Army* (New York: Charles L. Webster, 1888), 1:203–206.
5 Carl von Clausewitz, *On War*, 3 vols., trans. J. J. Graham, rev. ed., introduction and notes by F. N. Maude (London: Kegan Paul, Trench, Trubner, 1918), 1:23. Or the original quote: "War is a mere continuation of policy by other means."
6 Sheridan, *Memoirs*, 206.
7 Sheridan, 206.
8 Sheridan, 206.
9 Sheridan, 206.
10 Sheridan, 206.
11 "Famous Scout Gone," *Minneapolis Journal*, May 6, 1904, 7.
12 Thomas Laws to James E. Taylor, September 26, 1894, in Taylor, *Sketchbook*, 355.
13 Laws to Taylor, 355.
14 "A Woman's Wit Turned Defeat into Victory," *New York Times*, July 28, 1912, 43.
15 Arch Rowand to George W. Davis, September 3, 1897, NARA.
16 Sheridan, *Memoirs*, 4.
17 "Woman's Wit," 43.
18 Sheridan, *Memoirs*, 5.
19 Sheridan, *Memoirs*, 5.
20 "Woman's Wit," 43.
21 Sheridan, *Memoirs*, 9.

22 Montgomery, *Blazer and His Scouts*, 24.
23 Scott Patchan, *The Last Battle of Winchester* (El Dorado Hills, CA: Savas Beatie, 2013), 378.
24 White, *Scout and Guard*, 8.
25 W. T. Patterson Diary, OHC. Also see Patchan, *Last Battle of Winchester*, 441.
26 Taylor, *Sketchbook*, 380.
27 Ulysses S. Grant, *The Personal Memoirs of U.S. Grant* (New York: Charles L. Webster, 1886), 2:329.
28 *New York Times*, September 20, 1864.
29 *Daily National Republican*, September 28, 1864.

32. RANGER LEWIS POWELL

1 Payne, "Seward's Assassin," 6. Lewis Payne, formerly US attorney for Wyoming Territory, and the man whose identity Powell assumed, researched and wrote the article.
2 Scott, *Partisan Life*, 320.
3 Munson, *Reminiscences of a Mosby Guerrilla*, 231–232.
4 *OR*, Serial 91, Chap. LV, 273.
5 *OR*, Serial 91, Chap. LV, 340–341.
6 Munson, *Reminiscences of a Mosby Guerrilla*, 231–232.
7 Payne, "Seward's Assassin," 6.
8 Munson, *Reminiscences of a Mosby Guerrilla*, 232.
9 "The 'Big Yankee': Interesting Account of How Ames Met His Death," *Richmond Dispatch*, June 8, 1901, 8.
10 "'Big Yankee,'" 8.
11 Sheridan, *Memoirs*, 240.

33. EARLY STRIKES BACK: CEDAR CREEK

1 From pension applications and service files located in the National Archives.
2 Rowand, "Summery of Service."
3 Rowand.
4 William Jones, *Army of Northern Virginia Memorial Volume* (Richmond, VA: J. W. Randolph, 1879), 56.
5 B. F. Cobb, 10th Georgia Infantry, Battlefield Sign #2, located at Cedar Creek Battlefield.
6 Rowand, "Summery of Service."
7 George N. Carpenter, *History of the Eighth Regiment Vermont Volunteers, 1861–1865* (Boston: Deland and Barta, 1886), 215.
8 Beymer, *On Hazardous Service*, 13.
9 Gordon, *Reminiscences of the Civil War*, 341.
10 Gordon, 341.
11 Rowand, "Summery of Service."
12 Taylor, *Sketchbook*, 498.
13 Lincoln's presidential campaign slogan.
14 Rowand, "Summery of Service."
15 Kidd, *Personal Recollections*, 422.
16 Early, *Autobiographical Sketch*, 448.
17 George Pond, *The Shenandoah Valley in 1864* (New York: Scribner's Sons, 1881), 239–240.

34. THE GREENBACK RAID

1 John Henry Alexander, *Mosby's Men*, 107.
2 Mosby, *Memoirs*, 140.
3 Mosby, 140, 139, 314.
4 Scott, *Partisan Life*, 336.
5 Mosby, *Memoirs*, 140.
6 Scott, *Partisan Life*, 335.
7 Scott, 335–336.
8 Scott, 336–337.
9 Mosby, *Memoirs*, 141, 142.
10 Lewis Payne, "Lewis Powell's Exploits," *Philadelphia Weekly Times*, June 3, 1882, 1.
11 Mosby, *Memoirs*, 326.
12 *OR*, Series 1, Vol. XLIII, 390.
13 Hugh Keen and Horace Mewborn, *43rd Battalion, Virginia Cavalry, Mosby's Command*, 2nd ed. (Lynchburg, VA: H. E. Howard, 1993), 204–205.
14 Scott, *Partisan Life*, 350.
15 Scott, 338.

35. ARTIST AND RETRIBUTION

1 Taylor, *Sketchbook*, 463.
2 Benson J. Lossing, *Pictorial History of the Civil War* (Philadelphia: George Childs, 1866), 3:72.
3 Taylor, *Sketchbook*, 464.
4 Taylor, 464.
5 Taylor, 464.
6 Taylor, 464.
7 Taylor, 464.
8 Frank Rahm, *Capture and Escape from Prison, and Adventures within the Federal Lines* (Richmond, VA: Daniel Murphy, 1895), 20.
9 *OR*, Series 1, Vol XLIII, Pt. I, Chap. LV, 509.
10 John S. Mosby, "Soldiers Hung at Front Royal," *Richmond Times*, September 3, 1899.
11 Mosby.
12 Mary Elizabeth Hite, *My Rappahannock Story Book* (Richmond, VA: Dietz, 1950), 194.
13 Rahm, *Capture and Escape*, 20.
14 *OR*, Series 1, Vol. XLIII, Pt. II, Chap. LV, 910.
15 *OR*, Series 1, Vol. XLIII, Pt. II, Chap. LV, 910.
16 Much of the ground where the action in the book takes place remains untouched, as it was during the Civil War. I traveled to all the sites in this book, including the field where these men drew their straws, which is located outside Rectortown. The old train depot used to jail the men is also nearby.
17 *OR*, Series 1, Vol. XLIII, Pt. II, Chap. LV, 566.
18 *OR*, Series 1, Vol. XLIII, Pt. II, Chap. LV, 920.

36. DOPPELGANGERS

1 Gilmor, *Four Years in the Saddle*, 272.
2 Gilmor, 273.

3 Gilmor, 273.

4 Rowand Summary,

5 *New York Times*, October 29, 1864.

6 Edward McPherson, *The Political History of the United States and the Great Rebellion* (Washington, DC: James J. Chapman, 1882), 633.

7 Hines to Seddon, June 1, 1864, Hines Papers, quoted in Tidwell, Hall, and Gaddy, *Come Retribution*, 236–237.

8 *OR*, Series 1, Vol. XLIII, Pt. II, Chap. LV, 930–932.

9 Frank Flower, *Edwin McMasters Stanton: The Autocrat of Rebellion, Emancipation and Reconstruction* (Boston: George M. Smith, 1905), 250.

10 *OR*, Series 1, Vol. XLIII, Pt. II, Chap. LV, 930–932.

11 Edward McPherson, *Political History*, 633.

12 Waugh, *Reelecting Lincoln*, 354.

13 Butler to Wendell Phillips, December 20, 1864, *OR*, Series 3, Vol. 4, Pt. 4, 1001.

14 John A. Bingham, *Trial of the Conspirators for the Assassination of President Lincoln, Argument of John A. Bingham, Special Judge Advocate, Delivered June 27, and 28 before the Military Commission, Washington, D.C.* (Washington, DC: Government Printing Office, 1865), 60–61.

37. JOHN WILKES BOOTH AND SPECIAL OPERATIONS THAT "WOULD MAKE THE WORLD SHUDDER"

1 Guest book of the St. Lawrence Hotel, McCord Museum.

2 Asia Booth Clarke, *John Wilkes Booth: A Sister's Memoir*, ed. Terry Alford (Jackson: University Press of Mississippi, 1996), 83.

3 Benn Pitman, ed., *The Assassination of President Lincoln and the Trial of the Conspirators* (New York: Moore, Wilstach, and Baldwin, 1865), 39. Official records of the trial.

4 Barry Sheehy, *City of Secrets* (Montreal: Baraka Books, 2017), 200.

5 George Atzerodt's confession has a description of Slater and also links her to multiple trips to Surratt's boarding house. He claims she was a widow. The confession was lost until the 1970s when it was found in papers that belonged to Atzerodt's attorney. James O. Hall Papers, George Atzerodt's confession.

6 J. Harrison Surratt to Mr. Brooks, March 26, 1865, James O. Hall Papers, JOHRC.

7 "Thoughts from an Assassin: The Journal of John Wilkes Booth," National Park Service, June 27, 2021, https://www.nps.gov/foth/learn/historyculture/thoughts-from-an-assassin-the-journal-of-john-wilkes-booth.htm. Booth's diary was recovered on his body upon his capture. Many pages of the diary are missing, causing a great deal of speculation on who removed them. Additionally, the government failed to produce them as evidence in the original court case.

8 Thomas Conrad, *Rebel Scout: A Thrilling History of Scouting Life in the Southern Army* (Washington, DC: National Publishing, 1904), 119.

9 Tidwell, *April '65*, 75. Tidwell followed the money and analyzed the transactions of the Confederate Secret Service.

10 Thomas Conrad, *Confederate Spy* (New York: J. S. Ogilvie, 1892), 72.

11 Tidwell, Hall, and Gaddy, *Come Retribution*, 308. Captain Jacob Manning went to Mosby's headquarters, and Lieutenant James Carey was assigned to the Northern Neck.

12 William Edwards and Edward Steers Jr., eds., *The Lincoln Assassination: The Evidence* (Champaign: University of Illinois Press, 2009), 435. The book reproduces the original

evidence gathered for the trial and housed in the National Archives; most of the material had not been unearthed by historians until the 1980s.

13   Terry Alford, *Fortune's Fool: The Life of John Wilkes Booth* (Oxford: Oxford University Press, 2015), 188.

14   Sanders told George Augustus Sala the quoted sentence, but he was never asked to testify or submit a deposition to Federal authorities. The statement was reported in the *New York Times* on May 6, 1865.

15   Edwards and Steers, *Lincoln Assassination*, 340–341.

38. BLAZER STRIKES AGAIN: BATTLE IN THE VINEYARD

1   Mosby, *Mosby's War Reminiscences*, 150.

2   "From Sheridan's Army; the Late Attack upon a Detachment of the Seventieth Pennsylvania Cav.," *New York Times*, November 21, 1864.

3   Crawford, *Mosby and His Men*, 297.

4   "From Sheridan's Army."

5   The bridge now spans the river, and Harry Bird Highway crosses over the structure.

6   The estate still exists and is located on Clay Hill Road in Boyce, Virginia.

7   Pancake, "Narrow Escapes."

8   Scott, *Partisan Life*, 292.

9   C. W. Coleman, "The Homes of Some Southern Authors," *The Chautauquan*, March 1888, 343.

10   Bulletin Board: In Their Own Words, Gordon Silleck, relative of Grogan, in Buckland, *Mosby Men*, 81.

11   Buckland, *Mosby Men*, 81.

12   Burwell's Island is located near the bridge where Route 50 crosses the Shenandoah River.

13   L.M.L. [pseud.], "Col. Edward Bridill's Fate," *Confederate Veteran* 2, no. 10 (1894): 311.

14   L.M.L., 311.

15   Scott, *Partisan Life*, 292.

16   L.M.L., "Col. Edward Bridill's Fate," 311.

17   L.M.L., 311.

39. SHOOTOUT AT KABLETOWN

1   Williamson, *Mosby's Rangers*, 302.

2   Munson, *Reminiscences of a Mosby Guerrilla*, 118.

3   Munson, 118.

4   John Henry Alexander, *Mosby's Men*, 119.

5   Alexander, 119.

6   Keen and Mewborn, *43rd Battalion*, 218.

7   Williamson, *Mosby's Rangers*, 180.

8   Munson, *Reminiscences of a Mosby Guerrilla*, 122.

9   Munson, 122.

10   Scott, *Partisan Life*, 295.

11   Pancake, "Narrow Escapes."

12   Williamson, *Mosby's Rangers*, 178.

13   Scott, *Partisan Life*, 295.

14 John Henry Alexander, *Mosby's Men*, 122–123.
15 Pancake, "Narrow Escapes."
16 Pancake.
17 Pancake.
18 Williamson, *Mosby's Rangers*, 178.
19 Williamson, 179.
20 Pancake, "Narrow Escapes."
21 Scott, *Partisan Life*, 296.
22 John Henry Alexander, *Mosby's Men*, 123–124.
23 Munson, *Reminiscences of a Mosby Guerrilla*, 123.
24 John Henry Alexander, *Mosby's Men*, 126.
25 Alexander, 125–126.
26 Williamson, *Mosby's Rangers*, 179.
27 John Henry Alexander, *Mosby's Men*, 125.
28 Alexander, 126.
29 Alexander, 126.
30 Pancake, "Narrow Escapes."
31 Scott, *Partisan Life*, 297.
32 Pancake, "Narrow Escapes."
33 Pancake.
34 Munson, *Reminiscences of a Mosby Guerrilla*, 121.
35 Crawford, *Mosby and His Men*, 301.
36 Pancake, "Narrow Escapes."
37 Pancake; John Opie, *A Rebel Cavalryman with Lee Stuart, and Jackson* (Chicago: W.B. Conkey Company, 1899), 278.

40. The Road South and Rising from the Ashes

1 *Gallipolis Journal*, March 16, 1865.
2 A. H. Windsor, Winchester, to Brig. Gen. W. H. Steward, Washington, DC, in Edwards and Steers, *Lincoln Assassination*, 1362–1363. In the press, Powell was often referred to as Payne shortly after his capture.
3 *Gallipolis Journal*, March 16, 1865.
4 *Gallipolis Journal*, March 16, 1865.
5 Joseph A. Brown, "Fighting Them Over: What Veterans Have to Say about Their Campaigns: Captured by Mosby," *National Tribune* (Washington, DC), October 31, 1889.
6 Brown.
7 Brown.
8 Nicolas Badger, "My Capture and Escape from Mosby," *United States Service Magazine*, June 1865, 549–560.
9 Badger, 549–560.
10 Badger, 549–560.
11 *Richmond Dispatch*, December 23, 1902.
12 Badger, "My Capture and Escape," 549–560.
13 Munson, *Reminiscences of a Mosby Guerrilla*, 233.
14 Badger, "My Capture and Escape," 549–560.
15 Badger, 549–560.
16 Badger, 549–560.

17 Badger, 549–560.
18 Badger, 549–560.
19 Badger, 549–560.
20 Badger, 549–560.
21 Badger, 549–560.
22 Badger, 549–560.
23 Badger, 549–560.
24 Joseph A. Brown, "Fighting Them Over."
25 Brown.
26 Badger, "My Capture and Escape," 549–560.
27 Joseph A. Brown, "Fighting Them Over."
28 Brown.
29 Brown.
30 Brown.
31 Brown.
32 Badger, "My Capture and Escape," 549–560.
33 Badger, 549–560.
34 Badger, 549–560.
35 Badger, 549–560.

41. Henry Harrison Young: A Man Born for War

1 Oliver Edwards, "War Memories: Sheridan's Chief of Scouts, Col. Henry Young's Daring Career," *Springfield Daily Republican*, February 7, 1887, 1.
2 Beymer, *On Hazardous Service*, 83.
3 Beymer, 85.
4 Oliver Edwards, "War Memories," 1.
5 Edwards, 1.
6 Edwards, 1.
7 Edwards, 1.
8 Beymer, *On Hazardous Service*, 85.
9 Jacob H. Martin, *Campaign Life of Lt. Col. Henry Harrison Young: Aide-de-Camp to General Sheridan and His Scouts* (Providence, RI: S. S. Rider, 1882).
10 William A. Spicer, *Colonel Henry H. Young in the Civil War, Sheridan's Chief of Scouts* (Providence, RI: E. A. Johnson, 1910), 40.
11 William Gilmore Beymer, "Young," *Harper's Monthly*, December 1909, 33.
12 Spicer, *Colonel Henry H. Young in the Civil War*, 19.
13 "How Sergeant J. E. McCabe Became One of General Sheridan's Scouts," in *History of the Seventeenth Regiment Pennsylvania Volunteer Cavalry*, by H. P. Moyer (Lebanon, PA: Sowers), 219.
14 "How Sergeant J. E. McCabe," 220.
15 "How Sergeant J. E. McCabe," 222.
16 Arch Rowand to Major George W. Davis, War Department, Subject: Medal of Honor, October 22, 1897, found in the National Archives after extensive research by the author.
17 Beymer, "Young," 30–35.
18 Beymer, 29.
19 Sheridan, *Memoirs*, 2:104.

42. "THE DEVIL TAKES CARE OF HIS OWN"

1 *Gallipolis (OH) Journal*, March 23, 1865, 2.
2 Dolly Blazer pension number 325591, 41, 19, NARA.
3 *Gallipolis (OH) Journal*, March 23, 1865, 2.
4 *OR*, Series 1, Vol. XLIII, Pt. II, Chap. LV, 672.
5 Mosby, *Memoirs*, 338.
6 Mosby, 339, 340, 341.
7 Mosby, 341.
8 Mosby, 345, 342, 352.
9 Munson, *Reminiscences of a Mosby Guerrilla*, 7.
10 Taylor, *Sketchbook*, 589.
11 Taylor, 589.

43. "A CHANGED MAN"

1 *Philadelphia Times*, June 3, 1882, 2.
2 *Philadelphia Times*, June 3, 1882, 2.
3 "The Last Days of Payne," *New York World*, April 3, 1892. Powell told a spiritual adviser, Daniel Gillette, days before his death. "He was a soldier and for month previous, while in the Secret Service," journeyed back and forth to and from Richmond.
4 "They Knew Payne," *Richmond Dispatch*, December 11, 1902, 8.
5 "Testimony of Lucy Ann Grant," in *The Conspiracy Trial for the Murder of the President*, by Ben Poore (Boston: J. E. Tilton, 1866), 503. Also see testimony of Margaret Kaighn, June 2, 1865, in Pitman, *Assassination of President Lincoln*, 166.

1865

44. YOUNG'S SCOUTS AND THE JOURNEY

1 Entry by J. W. Forsyth, Sheridan's chief of staff, January 21, 1865, *OR*, Series 1, Vol. XLVI, Pt. II, 199.
2 Rowand, "Summery of Service."
3 Archibald Rowand, letter of recommendation for James Campbell, September 3, 1897, NARA.
4 Rowand, letter of recommendation .
5 Rowand.
6 Rowand.
7 Rowand.
8 Rowand.
9 Horace Porter, letter of recommendation for James Campbell for a Medal of Honor, NARA.
10 Archibald Rowand to General Horace Porter, April 21, 1897, NARA.
11 Archibald Rowand to William Beymer, October 14, 1909, Beymer Papers.
12 Rowand, "Summery of Service."
13 Rowand.
14 Rowand.
15 Rowand.
16 Rowand.

17 Rowand.

18 Multipage document titled "Sheridan's Scouts," written by one of the Jessie Scouts, perhaps McCabe, Beymer Papers.

45. TO CATCH A PARTISAN CHIEF

1 Rowand, "Summery of Service."

2 Sheridan, *Memoirs*, 106.

3 Rowand, "Summery of Service."

4 Gilmor, *Four Years in the Saddle*, 278.

5 Gilmor, 278, 279.

6 G. D. Mullihan, "The Capture of Maj. Gilmor and Capt. George Stump," in Moyer, *History of the Seventeenth Regiment*, 226.

7 William E. Hart MOH, NARA.

8 Mullihan, "Capture of Maj. Gilmor," 226, 224–227.

9 Mullihan, 227.

10 Mullihan, 227.

11 Martin, *Campaign Life*, 21–26.

12 Gilmor, *Four Years in the Saddle*, 285.

13 Gilmor, 285.

14 James W. Thomas and T. J. C. Williams, *History of Allegany County Maryland: Including Its Aboriginal History, the Colonel and Revolutionary Period and Subsequent Growth* (New York: L. R. Titsworth, 1924), 389–396.

15 Thomas and Williams, 389–396.

16 Thomas and Williams, 389–396.

17 Thomas and Williams, 389–396.

46. SHERIDAN'S WAR

1 Sheridan, *Memoirs*, 109–111.

2 Sheridan, 111.

3 White, *Scout and Guide*, 8.

4 James McClean, *California Sabers*, 223.

5 *OR*, Series 1, Vol. XLVI, Pt. I, 502.

6 Quote from an undated Civil War newspaper clipping included in the MOH file on John Miller, NARA.

7 Dominick Fannin's Pension application, NARA, of note some wartime documents list his name as "Fannon" but his application is labeled and signed "Fannin."

8 Archibald Rowand to his mother, March 13, 1865; NARA, Rowand, "Summery of Service."

9 Horace Porter, *Campaigning with Grant* (New York: Century, 1897), 398.

10 Rowand to his mother, March 13, 1865; Rowand, "Summery of Service."

11 Rowand to his mother, March 13, 1865; Rowand, "Summery of Service."

12 Porter, *Campaigning with Grant*, 396.

13 Rowand to his mother, March 13, 1865; Rowand, "Summery of Service."

14 Horace Porter, *Campaigning with Grant* (New York: Century, 1897), 397–398.

15 Sheridan, *Memoirs*, 120–121.

16 Statement from William Collins, in pension application of Dominick Fannin, NARA.

17 Statement from Collins.
18 Statement from Collins.

47. THE PLOT TO KIDNAP PRESIDENT LINCOLN

1 The townhouse still stands on H Street and is currently a Chinese restaurant.
2 Louis J. Weichmann, *A True History of the Assassination of Abraham Lincoln and of the Conspiracy of 1865*, ed. Floyd Risvold (New York: Alfred A. Knopf, 1975), 97.
3 Testimony of Louis J. Weichmann, in Pitman, *Assassination of President Lincoln*, 115.
4 Weichmann, *True History*, 97.
5 A phrase coined by President Andrew Johnson.
6 Testimony of Margaret Kaighn, June 2, 1865, in Pitman, *Assassination of President Lincoln*, 161.
7 Preston Parr interrogation, NARA; Parr folder, JOHRC.
8 John Surratt, speech, Rockville, MD, December 6, 1870, Surratt folder, JOHRC. Surratt gave a speech for an hour and a fee was charged to those who attended.
9 Surratt, speech.
10 Surratt, speech.
11 Confession of George Atzerodt, 1865, Atzerodt file, James O. Hall Papers, JOHRC.
12 Confession of Samuel Arnold, April 18, 1865, Arnold file, James O. Hall Papers, JOHRC.
13 *OR*, Serial I, Vol. XLVI, Pt. 3, 1359.
14 Tidwell, Hall, and Gaddy, *Come Retribution*, 482–487. The authors extensively studied the paroles of Mosby's men and found a sizable number in the Northern Neck.
15 Confession of George Atzerodt.

48. FIVE FORKS

1 Sheridan, *Memoirs*, 122.
2 Sheridan, 122.
3 Sheridan, 123.
4 Gordon, *Reminiscences of the Civil War*, 421.
5 Gordon, 403.
6 Robert E. Lee, *The Wartime Papers of Robert E. Lee*, ed. Clifford Dowdey and Louis Manarin (repr., Boston: Da Capo, 1987), 917.
7 Horace Porter, "Five Forks and the Pursuit of Lee," in *Battles and Leaders of the Civil War*, ed. Robert Underwood Johnson and Clarence Clough Buel (New York: Century, 1888), 4:708.
8 Porter, 708.
9 Sheridan, *Memoirs*, 126.
10 Sheridan, 126.
11 Sheridan, 132.
12 Sheridan, 129.
13 Porter, "Five Forks," 709–710.
14 Sheridan, *Memoirs*, 149.
15 *OR*, Series 1, Vol. XLVI, Pt. I, Chap LVIIL, 1113.
16 Porter, "Five Forks," 710.
17 Porter, 710.
18 Porter, 710.

19 LaSalle Corbell Pickett [Mrs. G. E. Pickett], *Pickett and His Men* (Atlanta: Foote and Davies, 1899), 386.
20 Porter, "Five Forks," 713.
21 Porter, 715.
22 Porter, 715.
23 Porter, 715.
24 Edward Porter Alexander, *Fighting for the Confederacy: The Personal Recollections of General Edward Porter Alexander*, ed. Gary Gallagher (Chapel Hill: University of North Carolina Press, 1989), 519.
25 Jefferson Davis, "Address, Danville, Va., April 4, 1865," in *A Compilation of the Messages and Papers of the Confederacy*, ed. James D. Richardson (Nashville: United States Publishing, 1905), 1:568–570.

49. THE ROAD TO APPOMATTOX

1 Rowand, "Summery of Service."
2 Rowand.
3 Beymer, *On Hazardous Service*, 126.
4 Archibald Rowand to William G. Beymer, March 27, 1909, Beymer Papers.
5 Rowand to Beymer, March 27, 1909.
6 Beymer, *On Hazardous Service*, 127.
7 Martin, *Campaign Life*, 59.
8 Gordon, 425–428.
9 Gordon, 425–428.
10 Sheridan's reports, *OR*, Series 1, Vol. XLVI, Pt. 1, 1101–1110, 1113.
11 Sheridan, *Memoirs*, 176.
12 Sheridan, 176.
13 John Bakeless, "The Mystery of Appomattox," *Civil War Times*, June 1970, 18–32.
14 William J. Brewer service record and MOH, NARA.
15 Rowand to Davis, wartime activities related to the Medal of Honor for Scouts, September 3, 1897, NARA.
16 *Harper's New Monthly Magazine*, "Monthly Record of Current Events," vol. XXXI (New York: Harper & Brothers, 1865), 122.
17 Porter, "Five Forks," 719–720.
18 James Campbell, MOH citation, NARA, cites that he captured two Confederate battle flags at Amelia Court House and the incident at Woodstock.
19 Rowand to Davis, Medal of Honor, September 3, 1897.
20 Robert Stiles, *Four Years under Marse Robert* (New York: Neale, 1904), 318.
21 Historian Chris Calkins examined in detail the origins of the various titles and spellings of the battlefield; see Chris Calkins, *The Appomattox Campaign* (Boston: Da Capo, 1997), 118, for a full accounting.
22 Stiles, *Four Years Under Robert*, 333.
23 Douglas Southhall Freeman, *Lee's Lieutenants: A Study in Command*, vol. 3, *Gettysburg to Appomattox* (New York: Charles Scribner's Sons, 1935), 711.
24 Freeman, 711.
25 Douglas Southhall Freeman, *Robert E. Lee: A Biography*, 3:86.
26 Freeman, *Robert E. Lee*, 86.
27 Sheridan, *Memoirs*, 176.

28 Civil War service file of Allen Belcher, NARA; D. H. L. Gleason, *A History of the First Regiment of the Massachusetts Cavalry Volunteers* (New York: Houghton Mifflin, 1891), 277. I am the custodian of Lieutenant Belcher's Civil War uniform.
29 White, *Scout and Guide*, 10.
30 Edward P. Tobie, *History of the First Maine Cavalry: 1861–1865* (Boston: Emery and Hughes, 1887), 425.
31 Tobie, 425.
32 Henry Edwin Tremain, *The Last Hours of Sheridan's Cavalry: A Reprint of War Memoranda* (New York: Bonnell, Silver, and Bowers, 1904), 427.
33 Gordon, *Reminiscences of the Civil War*, 438.
34 Edward Porter Alexander, *Fighting for the Confederacy*, 531–532.
35 Alexander, 531–532.
36 John Sergeant Wise, *The End of an Era* (New York: Houghton, Mifflin, 1901), 434.
37 Edward Porter Alexander, *Fighting for the Confederacy*, 532.
38 Alexander, 532.
39 Emily V. Mason, *Popular Life of Gen. Robert Edward Lee* (Baltimore: John Murphy & Co., 1872), 314.
40 Porter, *Campaigning with Grant*, 482.
41 Porter, 482.
42 Joshua L. Chamberlain, *The Passing of the Armies* (New York: G. P. Putnam's Sons, 1915), 260.
43 Chamberlain, 261.
44 Chamberlain, 261.

50. THOSE INFERNAL MACHINES: AIMED AT THE WHITE HOUSE

1 Edward Ripley, *The Capture and Occupation of Richmond, April 3, 1865* (New York: G. P. Putnam's Sons, 1907), 24.
2 Ripley, 24.
3 Ripley, 24.
4 Ripley, 24.
5 Ripley, 24–25.
6 Ripley, 25.
7 Ripley, 25.
8 Ripley, 25.
9 Tidwell, *April '65*, 162–164. Tidwell spent months following the money: financial records are some of the only records to survive of the Confederate Secret Service files, which were nearly all burned by the Confederates at the end of the war.
10 Crawford, *Mosby and His Men*, 356, 353.
11 Crawford, 354, 353.
12 George Baylor, *Bull Run to Bull Run* (Richmond: R. F. Johnson Publishing Co., 1900), 311.
13 Baylor, 311.
14 Baylor, 311, 312.
15 Munson, *Reminiscences of a Mosby Guerrilla*, 256.
16 Baylor, *Bull Run to Bull Run*, 312.
17 Baylor, 312.

18 James William Head, *History and Comprehensive Description of Loudoun County Virginia* ([Washington, DC]: Park View, 1908), 153.

19 Baylor, *Bull Run to Bull Run*, 322.

20 Williamson, *Mosby's Rangers*, 211.

21 Baylor, *Bull Run to Bull Run*, 322, 323.

22 Baylor, 323.

23 Brimstone still exists and is located in Fairfax Station on the corner of Ox Road and Burke Lake Road.

24 Munson, *Reminiscences of a Mosby Guerrilla*, 258.

25 Brimstone still exists and is in Fairfax Station on the corner of Ox Road and Burke Lake Road.

26 Charles Albright's report, *OR*, Series 1, Vol. XLVI, Pt. 3, Chap. LVIII, 1310. See also Baylor, *Bull Run to Bull Run*.

27 Baylor stated, "As we approached Burke's Station, we found the mule teams, the object of our raid, gone, our scheme and enterprise frustrated, and the enemy preparing for us a warm reception." Baylor, *Bull Run to Bull Run*, 322.

28 Baylor, 324.

29 Munson, *Reminiscences of a Mosby Guerrilla*, 258.

30 Munson, 257.

31 Charles Albright's report, *OR*, Series 1, Vol. XLVI, Pt. 3, Chap. LVIII, 1310. See also Baylor, *Bull Run to Bull Run*.

32 Tidwell, *April '65*, 175.

33 Crawford, *Mosby and His Men*, 359.

34 Munson, *Reminiscences of a Mosby Guerrilla*, 263.

35 Ripley, *Capture and Occupation*, 24.

36 Testimony of Thomas T. Eckert, in Judiciary Committee of the House of Representatives, *The Impeachment Investigation: Testimony Taken before the Judiciary Committee of the House of Representatives in the Investigation of the Charges against Andrew Johnson* (Washington, DC: Government Printing Office, 1867), 674. Eckert interviewed Powell in prison to obtain the statement.

51. POWELL'S MISSION

1 Pitman, *Assassination of President Lincoln*, 154.

2 Pitman, 154.

3 T. S. Verdi, "The Assassination of the Sewards," *Republic: A Monthly Magazine*, July 1873, 291. Verdi was the doctor on the scene.

4 Pitman, *Assassination of President Lincoln*, 157.

5 John Surratt, *Trial of John H. Surratt in Criminal Court*, vol. 1 (Washington, DC: French and Richardson, 1876), 333.

52. THE LAST CALL OF MOSBY'S RANGERS

1 *OR*, Series 1, Vol. XLVI, Pt. 3, Chap. LVIII, 801.

2 Jones' book details his work in the Signal Corps as an agent: Thomas A. Jones, *John Wilkes Booth: An Account of His Sojourn Through Southern Maryland* (Chicago: Laird & Lee, 1893).

3 "Thoughts from an Assassin."

4 "Thoughts from an Assassin."
5 Munson, *Reminiscences of a Mosby Guerrilla*, 264, 265.
6 Aristides Monteiro, *War Reminiscences by the Surgeon of Mosby's Command* (Richmond, VA, 1890), 154.
7 Monteiro, 155.
8 Munson, *Reminiscences of a Mosby Guerrilla*, 265.
9 Monteiro, *War Reminiscences*, 156.
10 Monteiro, *Mosby Guerrilla*, 156.
11 Williamson, *Mosby's Rangers*, 379.
12 *OR*, Series 1, Vol. XLVI, Pt. 3, 839.
13 Munson, *Reminiscences of a Mosby Guerrilla*, 267.
14 Munson, 268.
15 Munson, 270.
16 Munson, 270. An original copy of Mosby's address was also consulted via Heritage Auctions, February 2023.
17 Munson, *Reminiscences of a Mosby Guerrilla*, 270.
18 Munson, 270.
19 Munson, 271.
20 Statement of Dr. Richard Stuart, NARA, RG 153, M599, 6, 205–211.
21 "Statement of William Lucas (Colored)," May 6, 1865, in Edwards and Steers, *Lincoln Assassination*, 823–825.
22 Testimony of Eckert, in Judiciary Committee of the House of Representatives, *Impeachment Investigation*, 677.
23 "Pursuit and Death of John Wilkes Booth: Major Ruggles' Narrative," *Century Illustrated*, January 1890, 446.
24 One such paper, the *Memphis Argus*, printed what appeared to be a national story that ran in multiple newspapers around the country. The story ran in the *Argus* on May 10, 1865, 1, with no author: "Booth the Hunt of the Detectives for the President's Assassins." The quote is not included in Jett's formal testimony to authorities.
25 Tidwell, Hall, and Gaddy, *Come Retribution*, 480–487.
26 Tidwell, *April '65*, 192.
27 "Pursuit and Death," 445.
28 W. C. Jamison, *John Wilkes Booth: Beyond the Grave* (Boulder, CO: Taylor Trade, 2013), 128.
29 *The Great Conspiracy: Biographical Sketches of J. B. Booth and John Wilkes* (Philadelphia: Barclay, 1866), 178–179.
30 Ladislas Farago, *Patton: Ordeal and Triumph* (New York: Dell, 1963), 54–55.
31 Tidwell, *April '65*, 152–154.
32 John A. Bingham, *Trial of the Conspirators for the Assassination of President Lincoln, Argument of John A. Bingham, Special Judge Advocate, Delivered June 27, and 28 before the Military Commission, Washington, D.C.* (Washington, DC: Government Printing Office, 1865), 68–71.
33 Ben Perley Poore, ed., *The Conspiracy Trial for the Murder of the President, and the Attempt to Overthrow the Government by the Assassination of Its Principal Officers* (Boston: J. E. Tilton, 1865), 2:443.
34 Poore, 443.
35 Pitman, *Assassination of President Lincoln*, 274.

36 Pitman, 248.

37 Testimony of Eckert, in Judiciary Committee of the House of Representatives, *Impeachment Investigation*, 673–75.

38 "The Assassins Executed," *Boston Daily Advertiser*, July 8, 1865.

39 "Last Days of Payne," *New York World*, April 3, 1892.

40 Rodney Kite-Powell II, "The Escape of Judah P. Benjamin," *Sunland Tribune* 22 (2018): article 9, https://digitalcommons.usf.edu/sunlandtribune/vol22/iss1/9/.

41 After the war, Union authorities became very interested in arresting Slater because they suspected she carried the orders to assassinate the president. She was never found to confirm the theory. James O. Hall, "The Saga of Sarah Slater," draft, 22, Sarah Slater Folder 1, James O. Hall Papers, JOHRC.

42 James O. Hall, "The Saga of Sarah Slater," pt. 1, *Surratt Society News*, January 1982; pt. 2, February 1982.

43 John H. Surratt, *Life and Extraordinary Adventures of John H. Surratt* (Philadelphia: Barclay, 1867), 39.

44 Frederick Hatch, *John Surratt: Rebel, Lincoln Conspirator, Fugitive* (Jefferson, NC: McFarland, 2016), 3126–3132. The newspaper account is from an American, Henry Lipman, who also joined the guard.

53. THE LAST SCOUT: MEXICO

1 Edward Shawcross, *The Last Emperor of Mexico: The Dramatic Story of the Habsburg Archduke Who Created a Kingdom in the New World* (New York: Basic Books, 2021), 26.

2 Sheridan, *Memoirs*, 210.

3 Sheridan, 210.

4 Sheridan, 211.

5 Sheridan, 212.

6 General Correspondence, June 1–15, 1865, image 25, Philip Henry Sheridan Papers, Library of Congress (LOC).

7 Field Dispatches and Telegrams, Vol. 2, August 1865, image 303, Sheridan Papers, LOC.

8 Sheridan, *Memoirs*, 214.

9 Field Dispatches and Telegrams, Vol. 2, June 1865, image 320, Sheridan Papers, LOC.

10 Field Dispatches and Telegrams, Vol. 2, image 366, Sheridan Papers, LOC.

11 Field Dispatches and Telegrams, Vol. 2, images 325–328, Sheridan Papers, LOC.

12 A. W. Barber, *The Benevolent Raid of General Lew Wallace, How Mexico Was Saved in 1864, The Monroe Doctrine in Action, Testimony of a Survivor Private Justus Brooks* (Washington, DC: R. Beresford, 1914), 7 and 14.

13 Field Dispatches and Telegrams, Vol. 2, images 346–348, Sheridan Papers, LOC.

14 Sheridan, *Memoirs*, 221, 222.

15 Sheridan, 222–223.

16 Martin, *Campaign Life*.

17 Field Dispatches and Telegrams, Vol. 2, images 454–455, Sheridan Papers, LOC.

18 Edwin Fischel, "A Cable from Napoleon," Langley, VA, CIA Historical Review Program, December 22, 1993, 12.

19 "A Cable from Napoleon," 15.

20 White, *Scout and Guide*, 10, 13.

21 Sheridan's Final Report, Winchester to Petersburg, February 1865 to March 27, *OR*, Series 1, Vol. XLVI, 481.
22 "A Shooting Affair," *Cincinnati Enquirer*, October 9, 1878.
23 Rowand to Beymer, April 17, 1909, Beymer Papers.
24 Beymer, *On Hazardous Service*, 131.

EPILOGUE

1 The words were spoken by legendary operator, Major General Victor Hugo, 2009, Donovan Awards.
2 Mosby, *Mosby's War Reminiscences*, 44.

INDEX

Note: Figures and notes are indicated by *f* or *n* following the page number.

Blazer's Independent Scouts vs.,
181–185, 193–198, 218, 219–220,
237–255
burning homes and crops of, 179–180,
262
Calico Raid by, 150–154
capture of, 90, 220–224
Cole's Cavalry vs., 85–90
Confederate Secret Service and, 108,
232–233, 291, 321–322, 324, 328–329,
331–335
criticism of, 48
deaths of, 40, 45–46, 89–90, 119, 175,
196, 204, 206–207, 220–223, 233,
237–238, 252
description and role of, 21–26, 34–36
disbanding of, 331, 334
escape from, 250–255
Fairfax raid by, 21–26
Forbes' forces vs., 154–156
at Grapewood Farm, 44–46,
366–367n27
Greenback Raid by, 214–218
growth of, 66–67, 121
Jessie Scouts vs., 54, 184, 206–207, 214
at Kabletown, 239–245
leader of, 26–31 (*see also* Mosby, John
Singleton)
legacy of, 351–352
Lincoln assassination role of, 291, 324,
328–329, 331–335
Lincoln kidnapping role of, 232–233,
263–264
Loudon Rangers vs., 151–154, 321
manhunt for, 181–185
at Miskel Farm, 37–41
at Myer's Ford, 193–196
northern invasion screened by, 48–54
number of, 22, 29, 47–48, 173, 330,
380n16
officers of, 48, 320
origins of, 27–29
poems on, 119–121, 173, 377n7
Powell and, 66–67, 153, 204–206, 216,
224, 244, 246, 266–267, 329, 385n2
prisoners of, 24–25, 28, 40–41, 49, 53,
86, 119, 156, 175, 181, 185, 216–217,
223–224, 232, 243–255, 321
railroad attacks by, 42–44, 53, 140,
150–154, 205–207, 214–217

recruitment and volunteers for, 35, 66–67
retribution toward/by, 220–224
safe houses for, 34, 47, 151n., 173,
262–263, 322
2nd Massachusetts and 16th New York
Cavalry vs., 117–121
in Shenandoah Valley, 140, 179–185,
214–218, 223–224, 236–246
Sheridan vs., 173–176, 179–185, 197–198,
204–207, 214–218, 224, 262–264, 282,
378n14
truce with, 330–331
at Valley Pike, 214–218, 224
weapons of, 39, 42, 44–45, 151–153, 155,
379n19
Mount Zion Church, engagement at,
155–156
Mudd, Samuel, 234, 288, 327, 344
Mullihan, G. D., 276–278
Munford, Thomas T., 311
Munson, John
in Berryville Wagon Train Raid,
174–175
burning of homes response by, 180
in Calico Raid, 152
on Company D, 121
description of, 354
Forbes' forces vs., 156
at Kabletown, 239, 243
on last mission, 324
on Mosby, 27, 35, 174, 249, 331
railroad attacks by, 206
2nd Massachusetts and 16th New York
Cavalry vs., 118–119
Myer's Ford, 193–196

Napoleon III, 341–342
Native Americans. *See* Indians
Nelson, Joseph N., 194–195
Nest That Hatched the Egg, The,
288–289, 326–327, 337
New Market, Battle of, 133
New River Bridge, 125
New York City, burning of, 235, 314
9th West Virginia Infantry, 63, 75, 96
19th Maine Infantry, 311
91st Ohio Infantry, 55, 56, 75, 77
North River bridge, 283
Northwest Conspiracy, 112–114, 141–142,
144–145, 227